TABLE OF CONTENTS

I will be myself. I will speak my own name.

–MAYA ANGELOU, 2003
on "Life Mosaic" desktop cards by Hallmark

PROLOGUE

This book has had a long gestation period. Originally conceived when I was still the Executive Director of Rape Response Services (RRS) in Bangor, Maine, the project would not let me rest during the early years of my retirement. I actually wrote in my journal on November 15, 2004, eighteen months before I retired, that I was "excited about compiling RRS history, either before I leave or in retirement."

When RRS became a subsidiary of Penquis CAP in 2008, I felt a renewed sense of urgency to write the history of a well-known center that no longer existed in a free-standing form as it had from its earliest days. Begun by women and maintained through the efforts of many women over the first 30 years, RRS has a story to tell of the early years of feminism, a story that deserves to be preserved by those of us who were involved.

I was still procrastinating, too busy with other projects and hesitant about tackling this one. In April 2010 (Sexual Assault Awareness Month, fittingly), my husband and I rented a condominium on the pier in Eastport, Maine. I took my laptop and the box of RRS scrapbooks, determined to begin writing the history.

Fate intervened to provide me with another incentive for this project. Across Water Street from our condominium in Eastport was Bank Square Pizza where we picked up takeout meals. On one particularly pleasant day, the woman who owned the pizza shop was standing outside the door, and we exchanged greetings. Later when I went into the shop, she was behind the counter and asked, "How do I know you?"

I had experienced the same question because she looked familiar. When I mentioned being from Bangor, she immediately said: "Rape Response Services!" Marilu Scott was a hotline volunteer who had completed the required training in 2000 and filled many hotline shifts before moving to Georgia. Scott had nothing but good things to say about her RRS experience and how what she learned had helped her be a better high school teacher when she moved to Eastport.

Incredible people like Scott have been involved in RRS from its earliest years. I want to be sure that their names and contributions are not forgotten. Preserving our history is not something that women typically do because we are often too busy living our lives. Getting through each day is believed to be more important than thinking about how our activities will be viewed by future generations. As I have told others about this book, my comment has been: "we women must tell our stories."

For 12 years, RRS consumed my life, and I was incredibly proud to be part of an organization that was continuing to do so much good for so many people. Being sure that documents were preserved, and scrapbooks were maintained became part of my self-assigned tasks as Executive Director. I also kept a detailed datebook and wrote daily entries in my journals. All of my organizing skills have served me well while writing the following pages.

What I have written, however, is not about me as much as it is about all of us and about being part of the ongoing movement to end sexual violence. The more things change, the more they stay the same is unfortunately true when rape is the subject. This crime continues to occur with frightening frequency in Maine and around the world.

Just as I did not shy away from using the word "rape" during my RRS years, I believe that this word is a vital part of the history that must be told. People who have been involved with RRS, me included, have always worked hard to overcome our own myths about rape so we could be present for the hotline caller or the person at the hospital emergency room. These myths persist. This history, therefore, becomes a book without an ending, a living document that celebrates where we have been and acknowledges how far we still have to go before rape is eradicated.

Following an introduction, I have organized the material into a chapter for each year beginning in 1989 and continuing through 2006. A chapter titled "The Early Years" at the front of the book depicts just that, the period from 1976 through 1988 when RRS began, was closed for a few years, and eventually reopened. Finding that some documents throughout the entire period of this book had been destroyed and were no longer available was disheartening. RRS scrapbooks and files, plus my personal scrapbooks, journals, datebooks, and interviews have, however, provided a wealth of materials for me to use. I was motivated to keep writing before more papers were destroyed and memories had faded.

This book is my small attempt to preserve the contribution of each person named in these pages. History is found in the details, the minutiae of each day. Details abound in this book, especially for the final two decades. Articles, journal entries, and reports have all been quoted in full (with original punctuation) rather than lose their essence by trying to condense them. Allowing other women's words to shine through these pages gives many women the recognition they deserve for their devotion to RRS.

—Kathy White Walker
January 2014

INTRODUCTION

The earliest rape crisis centers in the United States were established around 1972 as a grass roots effort by rape survivors within the larger feminist struggle for women's liberation from a patriarchal society. With the focus on rape victims, a typical center might not have had an office building, a board of directors, or outside funding. Decisions were made by consensus in a non-hierarchical format. Broader social change was a goal of some of the early efforts, including clarity in the legal definitions of consent and rape. Perhaps the early founders of rape crisis centers like RRS thought there would no longer be a need for such places after a few years. What has changed in more than three decades and what has remained the same?

The subtitles of two books published in 2013 suggest that very little has changed. *Up Against a Wall: Rape Reform and the Failure of Success* by Rose Corrigan (New York University Press, 2013) and *Rape is Rape: How Denial, Distortion, and Victim Blaming are Fueling a Hidden Acquaintance Rape Crisis* by Jody Raphael, JD, (Chicago Review Press, 2013) describe both a societal backlash against women who report crimes of sexual violence and a refusal to believe that rape occurs. Even a recent editorial in the *Bangor Daily News* (BDN) (1/12-13/2013) titled "Build a Case Against Rape," stressed the need for improvement in the handling of rape cases in Maine. Actually taking a rape case to court and obtaining a conviction are as difficult now as when the author (hereinafter referred to as Walker) retired from RRS in 2006.

What has also not changed is the variety of terms used to denote sexual crimes. RRS made a conscious decision to use the word "rape" in the early years and upheld that decision while similar centers adopted the term "sexual assault" in an effort to be more inclusive of all forms of sexual violence, including incest and harassment. The belief through the years at RRS was that "rape" is an in-your-face kind of word, and everyone knows what it means. Naming it makes rape real.

Renee Ordway, columnist for the BDN addressed this issue on April 7, 2006, when she wrote about Walker's pending retirement from RRS:

> *Sometimes rape is just that. Rape. I know it's not always called that today. You hear a lot more about sexual assault than you do rape. In fact, I think legislators have taken the word "rape" completely out of the statutory language.*
>
> *But I think rape better describes the true horror and pain of a "sexual assault." A child who is a victim of "unlawful sexual contact," for example, has in my opinion been raped. But like with lots of other things these days, the language surrounding sex crimes has become all fuzzy and benign.*
>
> *As a state, and as media, we are sooner to describe the development of our land as the "rape" of our forest than we are the rape of a woman, a child, or even a man. Despite the politically correct language with which we all live today, rape still is just that. Rape. And that word should not be retired.*

Changes have occurred, however, in media attention to rape. During the 2012 national elections, two men running for office were, thankfully, defeated, partly or wholly due to their rape-related comments that received national attention. Richard Mourdock, running for a U.S. Senate seat in Indiana, suggested that when children were conceived as a result of a rape, this conception was "something God intended." U.S. Representative Todd Akin, Missouri, was expected to unseat the U.S. Senator from Missouri until Akin stated that women have natural ways of preventing pregnancy resulting from rape, "legitimate rape" in his terms. That both men even thought of making such comments in 2012 demonstrated that there was still a long way to go before rape crisis centers were no longer needed, but the public anger expressed against the two men would not have occurred 30 or even 20 years ago.

No longer does media attention about rape come solely from newspapers and television. Instant messaging via all forms of social media has changed the way that the public hears not only outrageous comments such as these but also reports of rape. Two high school football players in Ohio, for example, were arrested in March 2013 for raping a girl; two girls were later charged with online harassment of the victim. In addition, Congressional committee hearings to investigate sexual violence in the military are broadcast live and become news immediately.

Another major change occurred in January 2012 when the Federal Bureau of Investigation (FBI) announced a long-awaited revision of the definition of forcible rape. On the books for 83 years, the previous definition referred only to women and to penile-vaginal penetration. The new wording more accurately defined rape: "the penetration, no matter how slight, of the vagina or anus with any body part or object; or oral penetration by a sex organ of another person without the consent of the victim." Several years will probably now elapse before this change is reflected in the annual Uniform Crime Report (UCR) data. The change may prompt more victims to report, and when fully implemented, can present a more realistic picture of how pervasive rape and other forms of sexual violence continue to be.

Since the early days of rape crisis centers, various pieces of legislation at both the federal and state levels have been passed to partially fund victims' services. Maine's entire Congressional delegation, for example, voted with the majority in February 2013 to pass the much-delayed and overdue renewal of the Violence Against Women Act (VAWA). (Note: Glossary of Abbreviations appears at end of book.) First passed in 1994 and championed by then-Senator, now Vice President Joe Biden, VAWA provided funds that have figured prominently in the history of RRS. Reauthorized every four years since 1994, the newly-passed VAWA was signed into law by President Barack Obama in March 2013. Statistics released with the signing reported that one in five women and one in seven men have been raped in their lifetimes. Acknowledging that rape remains one of the most underreported violent crimes in this country, VAWA will continue to provide grant funding to states for victim services. A key provision of the law requires college campuses to provide students with information about sexual violence and the number of these crimes that occur on or near campus. Stopping violence before it starts is also a focus of the law, with funding for prevention work in schools and youth organizations.

In support of VAWA, Maine Senator Susan Collins was quoted in the BDN on March 1, 2013: "The Violence Against Women Act has made a significant difference in combating domestic violence, sexual assault and stalking, through grants to state and local governments and nonprofit organizations. Since its inception in 1994, the programs authorized under this law have provided state and local partners with more than $4.7 billion in assistance. This assistance helps to ensure the victims of violence get the help they need to recover, and has prevented incalculable suffering by stopping violent crimes before they happen." The same article quoted Maine's Second District Congressional Representative Mike Michaud: "I've long supported strengthening and updating these critical programs, and I'm pleased this bipartisan bill passed the House today. It streamlines current programs and will lead to smarter polices that will help combat violence in even more effective ways."

Noting that more than 16,000,000 people in this country had experienced domestic or sexual violence since the VAWA funding expired in 2011, Maine Senator Angus King stated in the BDN on February 13, 2013: "While the passage of today's legislation [*the Senate reauthorization*] will not entirely end these heinous crimes, it will restore critical support resources and strengthen successful programs that strive to not only combat, but when possible, prevent domestic violence, dating violence, sexual assault and stalking."

The more things change, the more they stay the same is certainly true when the subject is rape. That rape victims' services are still needed is evidenced by the statistics about the prevalence of sexual violence, statistics that have changed very little through the years. The following pages of RRS history are, therefore, a microcosm of what has occurred throughout the United States since the seventies. While rape prevention may be the ultimate goal of RRS and similar centers, providing quality services to the individuals who experience sexual violence in any form will continue to be the daily reality.

THE EARLY YEARS (1976-1988):
ORIGINAL RAPE CRISIS CENTER IN BANGOR

Not much is known about the earliest years of the first rape crisis center that predated RRS in Bangor or about the reason for its demise. Any paper records were apparently destroyed. What does exist is a copy of the *Maine Freewoman's Herald* (Nov/Dec 1976) published in Portland. This issue of the *Herald* was billed on the first page as "a comprehensive issue on rape." Diane Elze and Kate McQueen were listed as staff of the paper (Note: after a person's full name is first used, all later references to that individual use last names only for brevity).

An article in the *Herald* written by Elze told about a newly formed Rape Crisis Center (RCC) in Bangor. Elze was later mentioned in an undated excerpt by Linda Monko in *Maine Times* that stated: "During the 1970s, Diane Elze established a reputation for aggressive, people-centered political action and effective coalition building. When we first met in 1975 we founded the Bangor Rape Crisis Center together." Monko was Coordinator of Women's Programs and Services at the University of Maine from 1974 to 1976, and was also Assistant Director of Emergency Services in charge of Dial HELP at the Bangor Counseling Center (now Community Health and Counseling).

Elze wrote in the *Herald* article: "…a group of concerned individuals in the Bangor area began last spring [*1976*] to organize a free 24-hour counseling and referral service for victims of rape and sexual molestation. The idea originated when the Orono Women's Center was first organized at the University of Maine in November 1975; at that time, a number of women expressed an interest in establishing a rape crisis center to service the needs of the greater Bangor area. In February 1976, the first meeting was held to discuss the project. Approximately thirty campus and community women shared personal experiences and discussed the social and political roots and implications of rape. Throughout March and April, the objectives of the center were outlined and the decision was made to function in joint proprietorship with the Bangor Counseling Center. This joint effort was initiated due to the issuance of a federal mandate requiring all community mental health centers to have services for rape victims."

Working with the Orono Women's Center was the Bangor Chapter of the National Organization for Women (NOW) of which Janet Beaulieu was the Chapter President. A February 20, 1976, issue of the Bangor NOW Newsletter contained a paragraph about this effort: "The Bangor Chapter of NOW's Rape Crises [*sic*] Task Force has had two meetings with the Women's Resource Center at UMO [*University of Maine at Orono*]. It looks like progress is being made in establishing a co-ordinated Crises [*sic*] Center involving these two groups and the [*Bangor*] Counseling Center. It is hoped that an all day meeting will be scheduled for sometime in March to help further this effort."

Another mention was made in the April 23, 1976, issue of the Bangor NOW newsletter: "There is a training session at the Women's Resource Center, Orono, Saturday 4/24, 10 A.M. to 4 P.M. This session is the beginning of the training for anyone interested in working for the Rape Crises [*sic*] Center. The training is being handled by people from the [*Bangor*] Counseling Center and people with counseling backgrounds who are connected with the Women's Resource Center." These training sessions, according to the *Herald* article, began in April and continued throughout the summer. In an attempt to establish a cooperative relationship with medical, law enforcement, and judicial personnel, Elze noted in the *Herald* that training sessions included "meetings with Assistant District Attorney (DA) Paul Chaiken, Lt. Fred Clark of the Bangor Police Department, and Dr. Cressey Brazier of Eastern Maine Medical Center's emergency room staff."

Beaulieu wrote a letter dated May 20, 1976, to the NOW National Task Force on Rape and requested the addition of her name to the mailing list. She noted: "You will be interested to know that we are working on a joint project with the Women's Resource Center at the University of Maine at Orono, the Counseling Center, and members of the medical, law enforcement and legal communities to attempt to set up a Rape

Crisis Center for the Greater Bangor Area. Although it's a little early in the planning stages to predict how things are going to go, the outlook is definitely promising."

The RCC received funding through the University Student Government as part of the Women's Center budget. The *Herald* article continued: "The Greater Bangor Rape Crisis Center, which officially 'opened' September 1 [*1976*], provides: 1) 24-hour counseling and emotional support to victims of rape or sexual molestation, and to family and friends of the victim; 2) information on the medical services available to and needed by the victim; and 3) information on procedures involved in reporting and prosecuting the crime. If the victim so desires, a counselor will accompany her to the hospital, the police, and to court if she decides to prosecute. In an attempt to combat the myths and misconceptions about rape that continue to exist, and to educate the community about the crime, the Center also provides speakers to interested community organizations."

Meeting the medical, emotional, and legal needs of a person who had been raped was a top priority of the RCC. Individual counseling and support groups ("rap groups" in the *Herald* article) were offered. Groups were seen as a way to provide both support and an outlet. Elze wrote: "According to rape crisis counselor McQueen, 'By sharing with one another our experiences of rape, we have a means to ventilate and direct our anger.'"

Renata Cirri, another counselor, was quoted in the *Herald*: "For a woman to get in touch with us, she should call the Dial HELP number (947-6143) and the phone worker will immediately contact the rape crisis counselor who is on call for that day. Within ten minutes, the victim will be called back by the rape crisis counselor. We're hoping that the police and the DA will refer rape victims to us for counseling, and that the emotional support we provide will enable more women to report and prosecute the crime."

Dial HELP was the 24-hour crisis phone line of the Bangor Counseling Center. Answered by "trained telephone counselors," according to a Dial HELP brochure, the hotline served the entire state with a toll-free number, with primary responsibility in Hancock, Penobscot, Piscataquis, and Waldo counties. "Phone workers work with a diversity of people experiencing a range of difficulties from mild discomfort to intense suicidal thoughts and feelings," the brochure continued. "In short, where there is a problem, Dial HELP is there to offer support, assistance, referral, information, and effective crisis intervention."

"A unique feature of the Bangor Rape Crisis Center," Elze noted in the *Herald*, "is the presence of a male staff member. Michael Mulligan became involved in the project after two close friends who had been raped came to him for support." Mulligan was quoted in the article: "I believe I can be especially helpful in counseling husbands, lovers, and male friends of rape victims and in helping men gain an understanding of the relationship between male power, sexuality and rape in our society."

By the time the *Herald* was published in November, six trained counselors were available at the Bangor RCC, and 11 more were expected to complete the training. Contact information for the RCC was the University Women's Center located in Fernald Hall, Orono. A tri-fold flyer inserted in the *Herald* advertised the "GREATER BANGOR RAPE CRISIS CENTER" sponsored by Bangor Counseling Center's Dial HELP and the Orono Women's Center, Fernald Hall, UMO, Orono, Maine 04473. The Dial HELP number (947-6143) was provided as the "crisis phone." [emphasis in original]

In addition to some paragraphs about rape myths and facts, the flyer encouraged readers to call the Dial HELP number and "ask for Rape Crisis Center." Suggestions about keeping safe at home ("keep curtains or blinds closed") and on the street ("always look confident") were listed, as well as what to do "if you are raped." Inside the flyer was a list of what "The Rape Crisis Center Provides:

- Trained volunteers who offer 24-hour counseling and support for the rape victim, her family and friends.
- Information on medical services available to and needed by the victim.
- Information on procedures involved in reporting and prosecuting the crime of rape or sexual molestation.
- A counselor who will accompany the victim to the police, hospital and court, if she should desire it.
- A public education service and speakers to interested schools and organizations."

An early 1977 issue of the Maine NOW statewide newsletter contained a paragraph about the Greater Bangor RCC: "Since September 1976, the Greater Bangor Rape Crisis Center has been providing 24-hour counseling and support services for victims of rape and sexual molestation. They have worked in close cooperation with personnel at Eastern Maine Medical Center's emergency room, the Penobscot County District Attorney's Office, the State Police, and area police departments. Upon a most favorable recommendation from [*Penobscot*] District Attorney David Cox, the Somerset County District Attorney's Office has requested our assistance in establishing counseling services for rape victims in Somerset and Kennebec counties. Overall, we have been very pleased with the efforts being made in Penobscot County to deal with the problem of rape. The Rape Crisis Center welcomes the opportunity to speak with organizations, and strongly feels that meaningful dialogue about the problem of rape, and an informed, concerned community, can help demystify and discourage the crime." Elze was listed as the contact person in care of the Orono Women's Center at the University; the Dial HELP number was also provided.

Jan Oblinger of the BDN staff mentioned in an article on July 7, 1977, a special meeting of Bangor NOW. Billed in a news release prior to the meeting as a program that would "feature an overview of the problem of rape—the crime, the prosecution of the rapist, the social stereotypes surrounding both the crime and the victim and recommended actions," part of the meeting would consist of a "values clarification workshop" that would "help participants become aware of their own attitudes and reactions to the crime." Headlined "Court rape decision gets local support," Oblinger's article referred to a United States Supreme Court decision banning the death penalty for the crime of rape:

> *Diane Elze and Mary Anne Turowski of the* [rape crisis] *center said there are "few enough convictions as is" because judges and juries are hesitant to convict rapists because of severe penalties. The decision may also mean more convictions of middle and upper middle class men, the group least likely to be handed a death penalty. "These men do rape," Ms. Elze said, meaning that rape is not a low class crime although convictions would seem to indicate otherwise. Lengthy prison sentences aren't the answer either, they said. "The*

prison system is just not the answer," Ms. Turowski said. "A man goes in a rapist and comes out a rapist. The prison system is not set up to reform, rehabilitate or re-educate. What is needed is a good rehabilitation program for rapists in prisons."

Organized in September 1976, the Bangor [rape crisis] *center so far has received close to 40 calls. Much less are actually reported to police. Asked how many rapes go unreported in the Bangor area, Ms. Elze said no figure is available but it would probably be very close to the FBI report for the entire country which says that only 10 percent are reported. Many of their calls are from women who were raped several years ago but who have finally decided to talk to somebody about it. Interestingly enough, the center volunteers added, they had had several male clients. One male caller said he felt mentally coerced into the act and afterwards felt humiliated and degraded. "Most people, men and women, have been raped in some way," the speakers said and not just physically as defined under the law. There can be "psychological manipulation," the two counselors said. Latest figures cited by them was* [sic] *from 1975 during which 25 rapes were reported to police. The rape counselors estimated that only about five cases were prosecuted.*

Additional community support for the Bangor RCC was evident in several subsequent BDN articles. One published on December 7, 1977, by Nancy Remsen of the BDN staff was titled "Kiwanians help rape crisis center":

Every woman in the greater Bangor area should know the telephone number 942-7442 as well as they know their own telephone number, said an area service club member. The number is for the Greater Bangor Rape Crisis Center, an organization of volunteer counselors who will help a woman with information and emotional support if she has experienced sexual abuse. The phone number is new and is courtesy of the Bangor Kiwanis Club. The club has taken on the task of helping the rape crisis center become more well known as its way of fulfilling the goal of the National Kiwanis aim of "reaching out" into the community.

Several members of the local Kiwanis club and representatives of the rape crisis center held a news conference to explain how they are working together. Rape is a community problem, said Linda Monko, president of the rape crisis center. And it is a problem in this community, she added. During one year of operation, the rape crisis counselor received about 70 calls from the Bangor area.

Capt. Jim Hughes of the Bangor Police Department agreed that rape and sexual assault is [sic] a problem in the area, but reporting of attacks has been low, he said. Even the establishment of a rape crisis center a year ago wasn't reaching as many women as it could have because the counselors had no telephone line of their own, Harold Newman of the Kiwanis Club said. Calls went into Dial Help, leading to some confusion for persons seeking help. With the grant from the Kiwanis Club, the rape crisis center now has its own line still answered by Dial Help workers, but answered with the words, "Rape Crisis Center." As before, Dial Help workers contact the rape crisis counselor on call when a woman calls in seeking help, Monko said. Counselors usually get back to the troubled person within five minutes. Rape crisis counselors will provide information about medical services, how to report the incident to the police and help in facing the emotional problems that result from rape, Monko said.

Lack of reporting by women who have been sexually assaulted is "usually a result of social attitudes," Monko said. "But we really feel that this is changing in Penobscot County," she said. The main reason is that more police are going through special training to help in questioning a rape victim and investigating the case. Hughes said Bangor police have a special team to deal with rape cases.

Kiwanis support has also made possible a widespread publicity campaign on behalf of the rape crisis center. Billboards, posters, public service radio and television announcements have all been donated through the efforts of Kiwanians. And the Kiwanis Club is spreading the word about rape crisis counseling to the nine clubs in Penobscot and Piscataquis Counties and part of Hancock. The key to crime prevention is community education and involvement, one Kiwanian said. That is what the club is trying to foster.

A follow up to Remsen's article about Kiwanian support was

written six months later by Oblinger. She reported in the BDN (6/1/78) that "Rape help calls have doubled":

> *Having completed the legwork in its Rape Crisis Center Awareness Campaign, the Bangor Kiwanis Club reported on its success Wednesday noon and thanked members of the area's news media for their support. Calls to the center, previously reached through Dial Help at the Counseling Center, have doubled since the campaign began last December, according to Harold Newman, chairman of the club's Major Emphasis Committee. The club is making it possible for the agency to have its own direct line telephone service for two years.*
>
> *Tony Sivik, chairman of Major Emphasis Projects for the clubs in District 25, explained that the club has completed its legwork in making people aware of the center and its new phone number, 942-7442. It was printed on 5,000 pressure sensitive stickers distributed in the area's junior highs, high schools and colleges as well as the general public. The campaign also included billboards, large place cards, informational pamphlets and decals, an Awareness Day at area shopping centers, and public service announcements. As a result of the exposure, speaking engagements by the center's staff have increased substantially, Newman reported.*
>
> *Sivik noted that the club's involvement with the center is not over. It will continue to finance the telephone. Newman cited "the tremendous response by all news media" in the Bangor area to the campaign which was kicked off by a news conference at the Bangor Police Department last Dec. 6. Certificates of appreciation were presented by Newman at the luncheon to 12 media representatives with a special tribute to Dick Bronson, whose company served as the volunteer advertising agency for the project. The club's speaker said the man donated 100 hours of work on the campaign. Newman said the campaign, a joint venture of the center, made it possible for the center to get off the ground by helping to make it as an easy-to-reach agency.*

The new hotline number experienced many calls over the next few years. A series of rapes in the Bangor area in 1979 was covered extensively in the BDN, including an article by Oblinger in the weekend edition (November 3ʳᵈ/4ᵗʰ) about two incidents in mid-October on a well-lit street: "The Oct. 17 incident disputes the long-held stereotype that rape occurs in a dark alley, points out Mary Anne Turowski of the Rape Crisis Center in Bangor. Although not directly involved in either case, the volunteer said it proves that even here in Maine rape can occur anywhere, even in a well-lit, heavily-trafficked area. Neither Sgt. [*David*] MacDonald [*investigator*] nor Ms. Turowski wants to create panic in the community. The incidents do serve, however, to remind women not to walk alone at night in areas they feel uncomfortable in [*sic*]." Turowski was quoted later in the article: "…such acts should not be viewed as sexual offenses but as violent acts of humiliation. It has nothing to do with sex, it's a violent, humiliating attempt with the sex organ used as a weapon."

When Michael Commeau was indicted by a Penobscot County Grand Jury in December 1979 on three counts of rape and three counts of gross sexual misconduct, this brought to an end "the climate of rising fear among women in the area," according to an article by Arthur Layton Jr. of the BDN staff on December 15ᵗʰ. At the same time David St. Louis was indicted for rape and burglary, and police believed that he "was the person calling the Rape Crisis Center during the height of the rape scare in the Bangor area and in a feminine voice claiming to be a rape victim."

Commeau's rape trial in 1980 generated extensive coverage and commentary in the BDN. Beverly Shumaker, a hotline volunteer, wrote a letter to the editor that was published on July 29ᵗʰ. The words "Greater Bangor Rape Crisis Center" followed her name at the end of the letter. Shumaker noted:

> *After reading the recent editorial and your commentary on the Commeau rape trial, I feel compelled to write to you and air my feelings. I think the NEWS did a fairly decent job of covering the trial. Some of the articles were very confusing to me, but I'm sure the situation within the courtroom was very confusing and the reporter was just doing his job. I felt a lot of anger through the whole trial, because of the way I could see it being botched up.*
>
> *Rape itself is a very emotional subject. And emotions really soar during a rape trial, especially because justice has not always*

prevailed in these situations. After being with the Bangor Rape Crisis Center since it began, I have seen many angry and frustrated women who have been raped and never saw any real justice. I have also seen what reports of rape do to other women in the community, and the feelings are highly emotional. Rape is an ugly act of aggression, one that women have too long been a victim of.

Please continue your coverage of rapes and rape trials because it is very important, and do it in a mature, objective, detached, unemotional fashion. But do not expect women in the community to act the same way.

Sharon Barker was interviewed by Walker in August 2004, and provided additional information about the early years of rape crisis services in Bangor. She stated that the RCC was incorporated in 1979, when increased publicity about rape in the greater Bangor community was occurring. Jade Lee was hired as the executive director (ED). Barker was invited to be a board member in 1982 or 1983 when the board was being set up, as required by the state before the first money for rape crisis services, allocated by the Legislature in 1984 from the Maine General Fund, could be released. These funds were administered by the Maine Department of Human Services (DHS) which required accountability from the rape crisis centers, including contracts and statistical reports.

The first RCC in Bangor was involved in what was probably its last public event, a Take Back the Night (TBN) rally and march on June 1, 1984. Begun in the late seventies, TBN symbolized the reality that women did not feel safe on the street at night. TBN events became a nationwide trademark of the anti-rape movement and usually included speakers, candles, and a walk or march along a planned route, all occurring after dark. The TBN Coalition that organized the Bangor event was broad-based with as many as 35 women and two men as members. Greater Bangor NOW facilitated the weekly planning meetings beginning in late April, wrote extensive meeting minutes, and issued press releases. A publicity flyer listed RCC (942-7442) as a contact for further information. Almost 200 women marched through downtown Bangor in what was hoped to be an annual event.

THE EARLY YEARS (1976-1988):
THE END OF THE FIRST
BANGOR RAPE CRISIS CENTER

This first RCC in Bangor was eventually shut down by the state when DHS ended the contract in 1985, primarily because no reports had been filed for over a year, very few volunteers were left, and all Board members had resigned. Two EDs of other centers in Maine, Janine Winn (from the Farmington center) and Marty McIntyre (from the Lewiston center) remembered in conversations with Walker during 2005 that DHS tried to help by visiting the Bangor RCC and by being lenient about reporting requirements to the state. Barker noted in her 2004 interview with Walker that from the beginning there was a split between board and staff over setting policy, with the staff unwilling to take guidance from the board. The board members were not raising money. An issue arose about the role of men in the center, with the board having serious issues about men answering the hotline.

The Bangor center shutdown and subsequent reopening a few years later were similar to other rape crisis organizations throughout the country which began at the grass roots level and then had to adjust to the requirements of funding entities like DHS. Acceptance of additional money from the state was good but always had strings attached, including sanctions for non-compliance.

Despite the internal problems, the RCC was filling a need in the Bangor area. According to a BDN article by Jeanne Curran (4/13/88): "During the last month of its operation [*1985*], the center received 342 calls, with 56 crisis calls." When the hotline ceased operations, no one was keeping statistics on the incidents of rape in Bangor. The article continued: "People who live three hours away are trying to find help for victims in Bangor and are not necessarily familiar with services in Bangor. There's no face-to-face help, no advocacy." Curran quoted Barker who mentioned "internal management problems" at the center and "not enough state resources to support it."

A short paper found in the RRS files corroborated Barker's assessment of the reasons for the demise of the first Bangor center. This two-page document, "History of Rape Response Services," apparently was written in early 1991 as part of a draft plan of work. "It took some digging and interviewing of those connected with the old center to uncover some of the 'real' reasons it failed to survive," noted the unnamed author. "Aside from the very real financial difficulties experienced by the agency, their effectiveness was seriously undermined when the Dial HELP hotline was discontinued and the agency had no means to operate a hotline independent of Dial HELP. Either of these would be reason enough to cripple almost any organization, but the center suffered additionally from an increasing credibility problem within the legal and professional communities as well as internal organizational problems."

DHS continued to allocate an annual sum of $28,000 for a Bangor RCC which no longer existed. Other centers in Presque Isle, Brunswick, and Waterville that were providing services to Bangor-area residents billed DHS against that allocation. An additional $9000 was available to a Bangor center through the Victims of Crime Act (VOCA), federal funds which were also administered by DHS and had to be matched by the local community. Available beginning in 1985, VOCA funds came from fines, penalties, and bond forfeiture for federal crimes, all of which totaled millions of dollars each year.

THE EARLY YEARS (1976-1988): "BANGOR NEEDS A RAPE CRISIS CENTER"

A t the same time that the Bangor RCC was undergoing changes, the decade of the 1980s was significant for the rape crisis movement across the country. Universities began anti-rape programs and funded academic research around the issue of rape. Myths about rape were discussed in many forums. Special exam rooms in hospitals were encouraged, as well as training for police officers. Fragmentation occurred, however, as centers became less grass roots, more professional, and more politically-centered instead of victim-centered to secure support and funding. Former supporters like NOW moved on to other issues, including the Equal Rights Amendment.

For several years in the mid- to late-eighties, there were no services in the Bangor area for victims of sexual assault except for what they could locate on their own. Medical examinations following a rape were provided at St. Joseph Hospital in Bangor, where staff in the emergency room (ER) offered both emotional support and referrals to private counselors. Hotline numbers for the Presque Isle and Waterville RCCs were also given.

An unsigned "Preliminary Plan for Community Based Rape Crisis Services" from this time period stated that what was needed included a 24-hour hotline, medical services, legal information and advocacy, community education, and program administration. The Plan assumed that more than one institution or center would collaborate to offer the identified services. A possibility was that St. Joseph Hospital could develop a rape crisis service for the Bangor catchment area (defined as the geographical area served by an institution), which then included Penobscot, Piscataquis, Washington, Waldo, and Hancock counties.

Spruce Run (SR), the domestic violence project in Penobscot County, was willing to provide a 24-hour hotline, according to the Preliminary Plan, for emotional support, crisis counseling, legal information, and referrals. Reimbursement for a portion of the telephone costs could be made to SR as a subcontract with St. Joseph.

Medical attention, according to the "Preliminary Plan," would be provided by St. Joseph Hospital or by personnel trained at St. Joseph. This plan assumed that a rape crisis services coordinator would be identified at the hospital and would provide community education. SR would be part of the hiring process if St. Joseph decided to hire a coordinator. Funds for the position were available from DHS. Training volunteers to be available at the hospital would be the responsibility of St. Joseph, which was already cooperating with the victim/witness advocates employed by the DA's office. Under the plan these individuals would provide legal advocacy. Domestic violence projects like SR in the other counties could assist where needed, and the Maine Coalition on Rape (MCR) might provide speakers and organize activities. MCR had been organized in the early eighties by the EDs of the rape crisis centers that were in existence at that time in Maine. The Plan was "a community response to a pressing need for at least the interim period, which at this point appears to be an undeterminable length of time."

Another area group, however, became involved around this time. The Eastern Regional Commission for Women was established in the fall of 1987 as one of three regional branches of the Maine Commission for Women. Governor John McKernan founded the Maine Commission earlier in the year to promote full equality for all Maine citizens. Maine's First Congressional District Representative Olympia Snowe welcomed attendees at the first annual meeting of the Maine Commission with these words: "…you're on the proverbial front line when it comes to addressing so many of the issues that are critical to women here in the state of Maine…" Regional Commissions were seen as an opportunity for advocacy on behalf of women and their families at the local level.

A public meeting of the Eastern Regional Commission was held in October 1987 at the Community Center on the Davis Road in Bangor. The purpose of the meeting was to hear from local women about their greatest needs. Approximately 50 women from most demographic categories attended. Surveys completed at the meeting indicated that the loss of sexual assault counseling services was the issue that concerned everyone. "We wanted to determine what project the public felt we ought to work on," stated Barker in a later BDN article by Ardeana Hamlin Knowles (4/30-5/1/1988). "Reopening a rape crisis center was given a high priority."

The Eastern Regional Commission responded to the need by forming a Rape Crisis Center Committee (RCCC), chaired by Barker, to do the primary research necessary for getting a new rape crisis center established. Martha Wildman, Patti Lissey, and Barbara Bowler were the other members of the RCCC. For several months, they collected information about available funding, assessed community support, and interviewed several volunteers from the previous center. The Committee members also inventoried materials left from that center and checked with MCR to determine what services would be available for a new center. Several meetings were spent analyzing what went wrong with the previous center.

A second public meeting was scheduled by RCCC on April 28, 1988, at the Isaac Farrar Mansion in Bangor. The notice for this meeting stated that it was "being called to explore community interest/resources in re-establishing a Rape Crisis Center for the Greater Bangor Area." Barker authored this notice on Maine Commission for Women letterhead. "Currently, victims of sexual assault in this area are calling rape crisis hotlines as far away as the Aroostook County and Lewiston areas," she stated.

"Bangor Needs a Rape Crisis Center," headlined another flyer. "Bring your ideas and enthusiasm to a public meeting." Child care was available. Two notices of the meeting appeared in the BDN, on April 13th and April 27th. Judy Brann, identified as an ER nurse at St. Joseph Hospital, was quoted in the April 13th article: "A key point is that it has to come from people out there, members of the community itself. It has to be a community effort because we failed before." Barker stated: "What we want from this meeting is a spirit of cooperation from the community and recognition [that] the community has a responsibility for this," noting "optimistic signs we could get something going."

About 30 people attended this second meeting, and others submitted written comments of support. Dr. Robert Dana wrote: "It is truly inconceivable that a city the size of Bangor does not have a resource as critical as a Rape Crisis Center. The time is right! You have my support." Dana continued: "As Coordinator of the University Substance Abuse Services and as a Bangor resident I am exposed to much discussion around this issue. All of it calls for the development of a program to serve the immediate and critical needs of sexual assault victims."

Many at the meeting agreed with Dana's assessment. "A lot of people are going without help," stated Brann in the BDN article quoted above. She added: "There's a fear of what rape is and what's expected of a center. It's a don't-talk type of issue."

About 12 attendees came forward and agreed to form a core group to move ahead with plans for a Bangor center. After two initial planning sessions, three of the four members of the RCCC stepped aside, as was originally intended, and left further organizational tasks to the new group, called a Rape Crisis Advisory Committee (RCAC). The state had continued to allocate funds each year for a Bangor center. What was left of the 1988 allocation, after other centers were reimbursed for Bangor-area hotline calls, could be used to hire a coordinator in Bangor. Sue Harlor from DHS was quoted in the BDN (4/30-5/01/1988) after the April 28th meeting: "The Rape Crisis Center would be state-supported, but it will not be a 'state' program. It is intended to be a cooperative effort." Before the Eastern Regional Commission became involved, the plan at DHS was to have St. Joseph, SR, and MCR cooperate to re-establish rape crisis services in Bangor.

THE EARLY YEARS (1976-1988):
RAPE CRISIS ADVISORY COMMITTEE

The first meeting of this newly-formed RCAC was held on June 8, 1988. In attendance at this meeting were some of the 12 individuals who stepped forward at the forum and who stayed with the process until a new center was incorporated, including Laurie Eddy, Denise Perkins, Bill England, Terry Burgess, and Jane Siegler. Others at the meeting were Janet Redfield, Donna Tumosa, and Barker. Barker mentioned that she was stepping down from the RCAC but would be available for phone consultation because of her "overriding interest in the project."

Determining the sources and amounts of available funds was seen as an immediate need. A space for the meetings, guidance in organizing, and recruitment of additional individuals were also identified as needs. Subcommittees formed included Organizational Development (Eddy, Burgess), Community Outreach (Perkins), Fundraising (Siegler), Publicity (Redfield, Tumosa), and Volunteer Recruitment. A determination was made to contact all individuals who had expressed an interest in the center by sending copies of minutes from the RCAC meetings and asking the individuals to serve on a subcommittee.

In the undated two-page "History of Rape Response Services," early goals of this group were identified. "Get organized and incorporated to qualify for 'our' money from the Department of Human Services," was the primary goal. Other goals included:

- "to seek and obtain the services of a qualified business manager who would help administer the funds most efficiently" and

- "to set high standards of professionalism for the Board and paid and volunteer staff."

England volunteered the use of the Penobscot Valley Health Association building on Broadway in Bangor for meeting space. Potential sources of funds were identified as Lions Club, Junior League, Rotary, fraternities, local physicians, and the Maine Community Foundation. The offer from Aroostook County Rape Crisis Center to funnel state funds through to Bangor was also discussed at the first meeting.

Prior to the next RCAC meeting, a proposed agenda was developed by the Organizational Development subcommittee that wanted the "meeting to be as focused and efficient as possible." Time was allotted to discuss each item: choose facilitator and review agenda (10 min), Augusta news (5 min), incorporation (5 min), center location news (5 min), hiring staff person (25 min), summary of findings from MCR (10 min), RCAC role, function, group process (15 min), firm up subcommittees (5 min), choose next meeting date and facilitator (5 min), and evaluate meeting (5 min). The subcommittee noted "a packed and exciting agenda" which was flexible depending on whether the RCAC wanted to spend more time on hiring concerns or on the role of the RCAC. The statement "We may decide, for example, to leave lots of the hiring concerns to a hiring committee…," was noted in a paragraph at the top of the agenda.

By the date of this next meeting in mid-July, several actions had occurred. Some members of the Committee had attended a meeting of MCR in Augusta, reporting that individuals at other RCCs were very supportive and would do what they could to help. Advice was given to postpone hiring a staff person in the near future but to focus on the processes of accessing DHS funds and incorporation. Two additional subcommittees were formed at this meeting: Budget and Personnel. For financial reasons, it was determined that no further minutes after this meeting would be mailed to those individuals not willing to volunteer their time to the RCAC.

Community involvement was a key recommendation to establish credibility within the greater Bangor area. The minutes of the July meeting indicated this "might be a possible problem with the new center because of the poor record of the last rape crisis center." By the time that DHS pulled the Bangor center's contract in 1985, credibility of the center within the law enforcement and medical communities had suffered. Services to victims continued to be offered at the expense of any community education or outreach.

By the mid-August meeting, members of the Budget and Personnel subcommittees had met several times. A tentative budget and a job description for an ED were discussed. Income in the proposed budget included $23,000 from the DHS Bureau of Social Services (BSS) and $9000 from VOCA, less than what had been available the previous fiscal year (FY). Both of these amounts were to be included in the new center's allotment from the state.

Although all the meeting minutes referred to an ED, the draft job description was for a Coordinator who reported to the Board of Directors and whose supervisor was the Board President. The job summary read: "Initially the coordinator will primarily spend time developing a program, nurturing community support for the program, and securing funding. Later s/he will implement the program, which will include a 24 hour hotline; services to accompany rape victims to rape protocol exams, police interviews and court hearings; public speaking; and other components as determined by staff and Board."

Duties and responsibilities of the Coordinator were spelled out in detail under five separate headings.

> *1. Community organization and education:*
> > a. *Provide or coordinate community education to the public and other agencies about rape and related issues.*
> > b. *Educate community about Rape Crisis Services [RCS].*
> > c. *Develop a coordinated response between RCS, hospitals, police and courts.*
> > d. *Network with relevant individuals, agencies, and organizations.*
> > e. *Supply educational and informational materials for community clients, volunteers, and agencies.*
> > f. *Assure media coverage of RCS activities and programs.*
>
> *2. Direct service:*
> > a. *Develop and oversee a 24-hour hotline to provide crisis counseling services to victims, their families and*

significant others.

b. *Develop a program to accompany victims to rape protocol* [forensic collection of evidence] *exams, police interviews and court hearings.*

c. *Develop and implement volunteer training programs.*

d. *Recruit, supervise, and support volunteers.*

e. *Insure that quality services are provided to clients.*

3. Financial responsibilities:

a. *Prepare and oversee program budget and insure compliance with all State and Federal regulations. This responsibility is shared with the Board Treasurer.*

b. *Solicit funds and grants; insure proper and timely preparation of grants, contracts and reports.*

c. *Order materials and equipment, approve and pay for bills up to an amount specified by the Board; proposed expenses over the Board-determined maximum cost must be approved by the Board.*

4. Administrative duties:

a. *Serve as a liaison between RCS and Board.*

b. *Attend all regular Board meetings and special meetings as requested by the Board.*

c. *Prepare oral and written reports, including a financial report, for all regular Board meetings.*

d. *Create yearly management plan/time line for program, to be approved by Board.*

e. *Insure proper and accurate maintenance of all program records, files and data.*

f. *Represent RCS at monthly meetings of MCR.*

g. *Supervise any future staff.*

h. *Perform other duties as needed.*

5. Finally, the Coordinator will:

a. *Serve as a role model in demonstrating compassion, sensitivity and understanding of rape and rape-related issues.*

> b. *Provide leadership characterized by team-building, flexibility and interpersonal skills for RCS programs and activities.*
>
> c. *Possess car and valid driver's license.*

The job description was discussed at length. Somewhere in the process, not recorded in the minutes, a determination was made that the new center would operate under a hierarchical management model rather than a consensus model. Periodic performance reviews of the coordinator were preferred over a probationary period, with the first review to be held six months after the date of hire. A month's annual vacation was seen as a way to compensate for the low stipend. Twelve holidays plus one personal day per year would be part of the package, as was one day per month of sick time, forfeited if not used.

At the end of the meeting, members were encouraged to suggest a name for the center, which had been referred to as RCS despite the words, "try to avoid the phrase 'Rape Crisis'—it has negative connotations," included in the unsigned meeting minutes. Attorney Clarissa Edelston had offered to complete the incorporation process without charge except for a small filing fee of $10 to $20. She had all the information needed except the center name. Although the admonition to avoid "rape crisis" was noted in the minutes, the official name for the new center selected at the August 25, 1988, meeting of the RCAC was "Rape Crisis Services of Bangor, Inc." Present at the meeting were Nancy Rampe, Maureen Guerin, Siegler, Eddy, Bowler, England, and Tumosa.

A mission statement from another rape crisis center was used with minor revisions to create one for RCS:

> *Our mission is, quite simply, to offer hope, support, understanding and education to victims, significant others and the community. Victims of sexual assault are our primary focus, with services geared toward helping them to recover both mental and physical health; to let them know we care about them as fellow human beings, that they are worthy of our care and that their status as sentient beings has been in no way diminished by the brutal, dehumanizing treatment they have received at the hands of their assailants; to help them understand not only what has happened but also their reactions to it; to help the victims' friends and loved*

ones cope with and understand this shattering experience; to help
the community to understand the significance and ramifications
of sexual assault so that it is dealt with in a humane, intelligent
manner that helps the victim and offers appropriate punishment for
the perpetrators—no matter what their positions; and finally, to help
the community to re-educate itself as to the true nature of sexual
assault and to create a climate in which the message is delivered in
unequivocal terms: sexual assault is a crime of violence that will not
be tolerated against any person, from any quarter.

The center would be a membership organization with dues, similar
to how other RCCs were set up at the time. Membership dues would be
$15 per year for active status, and $25 per year for supporting members.
Businesses and professionals could become members for $50 per year.
What benefits were available for the various levels of membership were
not specified in the minutes. Board members were to be elected by the
membership, with officers chosen by the board members. A consensus
of board members would determine policy. Each board member would
serve three years, with another three-year term optional, then one year
off after two consecutive terms.

The timeline adopted at this meeting specified that a staff person
would be hired by January 1, 1989. Prior to this date, office space would
be obtained, and a full board of ten members recruited. An interim
treasurer was to be in place by October 1, 1988, so that state funds could
be obtained. In an attempt to recruit board members, a decision was
made to send postcards to community organizations.

At the next meeting on September 8th, the incorporation application
was still pending because some questions on the form had not been
discussed. The members present decided to use temporary information
and change it once a full board was selected to vote on the unanswered
questions. Application for tax exempt status could not be completed
until the center was incorporated. Obtaining a logo and stationery was
discussed, including the possibility that these might be obtained at low or
no cost from individuals or businesses. Bumper stickers were suggested
as a way to create awareness; someone agreed to check on prices.

RCAC meetings in September and later were held at St. Joseph
Hospital in the Willette Conference Room. The directors of two RCCs,

Jeanne Lamond (from the Waterville center) and Margaret Rowland (from the Presque Isle center) were guests at the September meeting, and provided information about volunteer training and screening, hotline call procedures, director's responsibilities, and office costs. The announcement was made that office space in South Brewer was available for $1800 per year. Maria Kreilkamp was willing to serve as treasurer.

The minutes of the September 22nd meeting outlined an agenda for the meeting on October 13th. No minutes for this October meeting were located. According to the agenda, the incorporation process was to be finalized. Visitors from the Lewiston and Augusta RCCs would be present. Walker later confirmed that Marty McIntyre and Laura Fortman were the visiting directors from the Lewiston and Augusta centers, respectively.

An article by Curran in the October 10th BDN encouraged public attendance at the October meeting: "Rape and sexual assault victims in Penobscot and Piscataquis counties soon may get the support and help they need from a newly formed service organization. The region had a rape-crisis hotline for several years, but it ran into financial and political problems and disbanded. Since then, regional victims calling the toll-free rape crisis number in the telephone book have found themselves speaking to counselors in Farmington or Aroostook County. Those counselors have had difficulty referring victims to services in Penobscot and Piscataquis counties."

Eddy, identified in the article as the "acting chairwoman," stressed the need for "lots of different hands," including board members and hotline volunteers. She noted: "Everyone is getting calls for this, and they have nowhere to refer. It's very frustrating. A lot of health-care people will be delighted." The article continued with the statement: "The Board would like to see the community become more involved in fundraising." Eddy stressed in the article: "The center will serve any sexual-assault victims, female or male." The hotline was expected to be operational by spring or summer, 1989. "Referrals, crisis counseling, and court and hospital advocacy" would also be available.

Articles of Incorporation were apparently adopted at the October 13th meeting because the document was filed by the Secretary of State on October 18th. The $20 filing fee was acknowledged on November 9, 1998, the official incorporation date. The name of the corporation was

"Rape Crisis Services of Bangor." Eddy was the registered agent; the minimum number of directors was six, maximum 35. Stated purposes for the corporation were:

1. "to provide support for rape crisis victims including a 24-hour hotline, services to accompany rape victims to rape protocol exams, police interviews and court hearings;
2. to provide community education about rape and related issues"

A section within the Articles described members: "Membership of the corporation shall be unlimited. The initial members shall be elected by the incorporators at the first meeting. Thereafter the membership may elect new members at any time. The members shall elect the Board of Directors at each annual meeting of the corporation. Any member wishing to withdraw from membership may do so at any time by delivering written notice to the clerk." Incorporators who signed the Articles were Perkins, Eddy, Tumosa, Guerin, and Bowler.

The first set of signed minutes of the RCAC was from the November 1st meeting. Maureen Guerin's signature appeared at the end of the report. Others in attendance included Sue Estler, Alexa Wiley, Dawn Mace, Dr. Jim Westhoven, Eddy, Rampe, England, and Bowler. Guerin agreed to meet with Dr. Richard Sagall regarding concerns about the space he was offering at 451 South Main Street in Brewer. These concerns included the inability to counsel clients in the director's office, the notice needed for canceling the lease, and the too-expensive fee of ten cents per copy.

Rampe noted that the coordinator's position would be advertised by the middle of the month, with a deadline for applications of December 1st. Rampe, Guerin, and Estler volunteered to interview the applicants and make a recommendation to the board for approval. The two inch square ad appeared in the BDN as follows:

RAPE CRISES [sic]
COORDINATOR
Knowledge, sensitivity and/or experience
with rape issues. Strong interpersonal, orga-
nizational, leadership and financial manage-
ment/grant writing skills. Minimum
requirement BA or equivalent experience.
Salary is $16,400. Full-time, job sharing a
possibility. EOE. Application deadline:
Dec. 1, 1988. Send resume and references to:
Rape Crisis Services of Bangor, Inc.
P.O. Box 1162
Bangor, ME 04401

At the next meeting of the RCAC in mid-November, the announcement was made that the coordinator's position had been advertised in the *Portland Sunday Telegram* and the BDN. Nancy Plouffee would replace Estler on the hiring committee. Other members of the committee were Rampe, Guerin, and Wiley. The minutes noted that a consistent set of structured questions was needed for the interviews, with role playing included. Follow-up phone calls would be made to the people who provided written references.

According to the November minutes, the Zonta Club donated $400 to the center, marking the beginning of many years of support from this local branch of an international women's organization. Because no state funds were expected for five to six weeks, a member of RCAC agreed to loan the center $1000. Eddy and Guerin could sign checks for expenses. Bonding, liability insurance, and workers compensation insurance still had to be determined.

An agreement had been reached and was approved at the November meeting to sign a lease for office space with Dr. Sagall in Brewer for $150 per month. He would charge the center only five cents per page for use of his office copier, with paper to be provided by the center. Clients could be seen in the director's office as long as there was not an excessive number. England donated a desk, file cabinet, and three chairs to the center.

A set of By-Laws for RCS of Bangor was also adopted at the meeting. "The purposes of this corporation shall be to provide counseling and other related services to rape victims, including community education, and to do such other things as may be permitted by non-profit corporations under Maine law." Administration was vested in a Board of Directors, not less than three members or more than 12. The calling of meetings, what constituted a quorum, and filling of vacancies were all covered in Article II.

A Chair, a Secretary, and a Treasurer were the officers that Article III specified in the first section, but in Section 3 the chair was referred to as "President," and was also the "Chief Executive Officer." Officers were elected by the Board which could fill vacancies at any time. The duties of each officer were spelled out, with the stipulation: "The Treasurer shall segregate from general corporate funds all gifts, grants and contributions received by the corporation which are subject to specific restrictions."

Committees could be appointed by the Board and were limited in Article IV to "members of the Board of Directors of said corporation and their designees." Article V specified that an annual meeting of the members would be held, but "failure to hold an Annual Meeting shall not in any way invalidate the actions of the Directors or officers." A special meeting of the members could be called by the President by vote of the Directors or upon request of any two Directors. Indemnification was outlined in Article VI, as was the stipulation that insurance could be purchased and maintained on behalf of all persons indemnified. Amendments to the By-Laws, according to Article VIII could be made by a majority of the Board at any meeting, following written notice.

The final meeting of the RCAC before it evolved into the board of directors for the new center was held early in December. In attendance were Rampe, Eddy, Kreilkamp, Wiley, and Plouffe, plus Karliese Greiner, Alisa Harris, M.J. Watkins, and Kathy Bodkin. New subcommittees were formed or reorganized at this meeting: grant management (Eddy, England); fiscal, payroll, time card (Kreilkamp); clinical/training (Susan Polyot, Rampe, Bodkin); public relations/fundraising (Watkins, Greiner, Bowler); public education (Guerin, Harris); personnel policies (Rampe, Wiley); and Administrative (Eddy).

Benefits for the coordinator were finalized and included health insurance, workers compensation, bonding, malpractice insurance, and 12 sick days per year. Travel would be reimbursed at 22 cents per mile. The draft job description reviewed at an earlier meeting was approved.

Members of the hiring committee stated that telephone calls would be made to let candidates know their applications were being reviewed. The two top choices would be reviewed by the committee, unless there was a "glowing choice." In that case, a review would not be needed. An informal evaluation of the coordinator would be made after three months. Questions still to be resolved included backup for the coordinator during vacation and sick leave, and whether one person from the committee/board should be a point of contact for the coordinator.

Following this meeting, it appeared that the new center continued to have problems accessing the funds from BSS. A letter in the files was signed by Patricia (Patti) Bourgoin, chair of the Maine Commission for Women in Augusta, and addressed to Peter Walsh, director of BSS. Dated December 15, 1988, the letter stated:

> *Thank you very much for being willing to look into the first payment for the new organization in Bangor which will provide much needed services to sexual assault victims. The Bangor area has not had any services for rape victims for quite some time and the initial funding needed to hire an Executive Director and pay for costs already incurred is urgent. Anything you are able to do to expedite the process so that the Rape Crisis Center is able to receive their initial payment by the first of January is truly appreciated. The Maine Commission for Women knows that Commissioner Ives and your Department are very concerned about sexual abuse in Maine and your continued support in funding services to help the victims of these crimes is extremely important.*

Similar to the seventies when rape crisis services were initiated by concerned women, the effort in the late eighties to re-establish a center in Bangor owed its success to a dedicated group of women (and a few men) who came together, volunteered their time and talents, and worked hard for six months. By the end of 1988, the rebirth of the Bangor RCC, with a slightly different name, was imminent.

1989: REBIRTH OF A RAPE CRISIS CENTER IN BANGOR

As planned, the first ED of a reopened Rape Crisis Services of Bangor, Inc. began paid employment during the first week in January 1989, although the center was not scheduled to officially open until July. Lennie (Lenore) Mullen-Giles was paid a salary of $15,640, according to the W-2 filed for the agency in 1989. One of her first responsibilities was to locate new office space because Dr. Sagall sold his Brewer office building in February and wanted RCS to vacate as soon as possible. In a letter to Rick Jones, DHS Contract Specialist, dated February 24th, Mullen-Giles stated that she had "located new office space at 157 Park Street in Bangor. The new rent is $300.00 a month plus electricity (est. $20.00 per month). Heat and maintenance are included in the rent. The new landlord is [State] Representative Jack Cashman of Old Town. We will move into the new office on March 10th, and the first rent payment will commence on April 1st." The rent was double what had been paid to Dr. Sagall.

Although Greiner, a Board member, suggested that changing the name to Rape Response Services would allow the agency to distance itself from the poor publicity surrounding the previous RCC, this action did not occur until later in the year. Both names were used during the interim months. Greiner also designed the logo for the new center, choosing teal and gray as the coordinating colors because they were soft yet eye-catching. Teal later became the nationally-recognized color for sexual assault when wearing colored ribbons to support a cause was popular. The logo was a rectangle with a darkened square on top. In the square appeared the phrase "A sexual act committed without consent" above a large font "RAPE." Two lines outside the square and under the word "RAPE" had "RESPONSE" and "SERVICES" printed in justified type. First appearing on stationery which was obtained on June 1st, the logo was to stay with the agency throughout its first 20 years.

Some provocative questions were delineated in what was called a long-range plan developed by the RCS Board at this time: "Where do we see the agency going? What should we be doing in five years, ten years? Are we always going to be renters? Do we want to consider free-standing space owned by the corporation? Would our services and security be better served if we sought some sort of confederation with other agencies? Spruce Run, Family Planning and Mabel Wadsworth Women's Health Center come immediately to mind as being most closely allied to us in spirit. Could shared space and services strengthen each agency and offer financial security? How do we treat volunteers? As unpaid staff, subject to the same rules and regulations, including dismissal? How do we 'reward' them—in lieu of money? How do we keep them motivated?"

Goals for the five years from 1989 through 1994 were part of this long-range plan and included listings under finance, personnel, public relations/recruiting, fundraising, nominating, and training. Establishing sound business practices and an endowment plan topped the list. Recruiting both public relations and fundraising committees for the Board meant that non-Board members could be included. An annual membership drive would be held. The list also included the development of personnel policies for both paid and volunteer staff, and the performance of annual staff reviews.

The long-range plan concluded with the following paragraph: "This, like any other long-range plan, is a starting point, ideas to consider. Neither this nor the finished plan will be cast in stone. A good plan retains flexibility. We cannot foresee the future. This plan is, at best, a roadmap into that future—or at least five years ahead—that is simply meant as a guide with some suggested points of interest and importance. What IS important is that we have cared enough to spend the time to make this plan—the best one we can—and have the will and energy to carry it out as best we can." [emphasis in original]

A document titled "Articles of Amendment" to the Articles of Incorporation was adopted by the Board on August 23rd and filed with the Secretary of State on September 20th, becoming official with a five dollar filing fee on October 6th. The stated nature of the change read:

"This is a formal request to change the name Rape Crisis Services of Bangor to Rape Response Services, Inc. The amendment to implement this change reads: Barb Bowler moved, and Karliese Greiner seconded, 'the name of Rape Crisis Services of Bangor be officially changed to Rape Response Services, Inc., effective immediately and the Executive Director contact the Secretary of State's office and request the official paperwork to complete this change.' Motion passed unanimously."

The second section of the amendment document required checking a box to indicate that the change was adopted "by majority vote of the board of directors." In parentheses before this option were the words "if no members, or none titled to vote thereon." Eddy signed the amendment as president and Mace as secretary. Mace also signed an adjacent box titled "must be completed for vote of members" and certified that she had "custody of the minutes showing the above action by the members." No one in the Secretary of State's office apparently ever questioned that there were no members, only a board of directors at RRS.

A Community Presence

A "Dear Friend" letter from Mullen-Giles was sent early in July to professionals (counselors, medical and legal personnel, law enforcement departments) in the greater Bangor community. The letter began: "Rape Response Services (RRS) is pleased to announce the opening of our 24-hour sexual assault crisis hotline (**989-5678**). The service became effective on Monday, July 24, at 8:00 A.M. We want EVERYONE to know we are in business and we mean business. The hotline is the first crucial step in our goal of helping victims of sexual assault—whether it happened an hour or twenty years ago." [emphasis in original]

Posters were included with the letter for recipients to put up in their offices. These white cardstock posters with teal and gray lettering introduced the new hotline number for RRS. The letter-size posters included a small pad of tear-off sheets on which was printed the hotline number.

A flyer announcing the opening of the hotline invited the public to a press conference:

Because of your Support—
Personally, Emotionally and as Legislators—
We Are Able to Announce
the Sexual Assault Crisis Hotline
which serves Penobscot and Piscataquis Counties
will Open Officially on
Monday, July 24, 1989.

In Token of our Appreciation
You are Invited to Share the Event
with Us by Attending a Press Conference
Monday, July 24
at 10:00 A.M.
in the Lecture Room
of the Bangor Public Library
145 Harlow Street

R.S.V.P. by Friday, July 21, Ph. 945-5597

The July 25th edition of the BDN featured the RRS opening in an article by Margaret Warner titled: "New rape-crisis hotline ready to offer aid and counseling." Warner noted that many organizations, "including Penquis CAP *[Community Action Program]*, Penobscot Health Care, the district attorney's office for Penobscot and Piscataquis counties, and St. Joseph Hospital emergency room, are represented on the RRS board of directors." Warner wrote that collect calls to the hotline were accepted. Mullen-Giles observed in the article that about 50 calls had been directed to the new office of RRS since January, "long before the new hotline opened." She emphasized: "We are not professional, long-term counselors," but can make referrals for counseling.

An undated mailing to prospective members was headlined: "RAPE CRISIS CENTER READIES FOR OPENING. After nearly a year of hard work by a group of concerned women and men, we have entered into the final phase of our plans to open Rape Response Services, Inc. These services have not been available in the Bangor area for the past several years."

The letter continued: "We have set ambitious goals, but with the help of the entire community, we can realize all of them. You can help by becoming a member of Rape Response Services." The attached enrollment sheet offered several annual membership levels: active ($15), supporting ($25), business and professional ($50). No indication was given as to what benefits accrued to the three membership categories. It was also possible to volunteer by checking spaces for "hotline counseling," "board member," or "one-time committee work." The form was to be returned to Rape Response Services Inc. at Post Office Box (POB) 2516 in Bangor.

At the conclusion of the membership invitation letter, Mullen-Giles noted: "In short, we need your money, we need your time, in order for rape crisis services to be available on a continuing basis in our area. Statistics show that **one in three women will become a victim of rape**. That means that you, your daughter, your mother, sister, aunt, grandmother, niece—**every female you know** is at risk. The person you help could be you or someone you love!" [emphasis in original]

In addition to hotline services for victims of rape, Mullen-Giles presented outreach and educational programs. The October 18th edition of *The Maine Campus* provided coverage of a "lecture on rape" attended by about 50 people during Rape Awareness Week. The event was presented by the University of Maine Rape Awareness Program Committee. Mullen-Giles provided facts and figures about rape, and delineated "three myths held by victims of sexual assault crimes." These included the beliefs that victims would no longer be desirable to men, that they were "ruined forever," and that they should have stopped the assault. "To help a victim of rape, it is important to listen and not judge," she was quoted as saying. "Be available and encourage the victim to call a hotline or get counseling." Mullen-Giles concluded her remarks by advising attendees to allow rape victims to "make their own choices."

Hotline Volunteers

Although 40 names were listed on a document titled "Volunteers for Advocate Training," the final list of those who completed the training in May had 17 names. (Note: The words "advocate" and "volunteer" are used interchangeably throughout this book and in rape crisis work to denote a person trained to provide unpaid services to, and to advocate for, anyone who has experienced sexual violence.) Besides Mullen-Giles, the list included Anne Tobias, Debra Hammond, Janet Badger, Leesa Cook, Becky Israel, Judy Botelho, Kathy Cummings, Betty Ann

O'Connell, Vyvyenne Richie, Mace, Bowler, Greiner, Wiley, Rampe, Plouffe, and Polyot. Another training was held in September. Forty to fifty advocate training manuals were available from the former Bangor center. Mullen-Giles interviewed each of the prospective volunteers and assisted other directors from MCR with the training sessions.

A computer printout from Page Answering Service [later Com-Nav] in Brewer, dated December 30th had more advocate names and telephone numbers listed. Some of the names listed above remained, including Badger, Bowler, Cook, Cummings, Mace, and Rampe. Nancy Bailey, Mary Ellen Bryner, Jenny Burkhart, Stephanie Cote, Judy Holt-Spencer, Dawn Levasseur, Sarah Lowden, Dorothy Mitchell, Katie Moirs, Shannon Morency, Wendy Norko, Shelly O'Bar, Susan Pinnette, Tracey Taylor, and Rose Walker had been added to the call list, on which Mullen-Giles was also listed.

The instructions on the printout for telephone operators at the answering service were as follows:

1. *Hello, this is the rape crisis hotline operator.*
2. *Are you in a safe place now? (If yes see 3.) If no, may we contact the police? (If caller does not wish to involve police, put on hold and connect with the advocate.)*
3. *Take first name (may be fictitious), phone number, I will have the rape crisis advocate return your call ASAP.*
4. *Thank you. I will page the advocate immediately. If they do not respond within thirty minutes, please call me back and I will call another advocate.*

To contact the advocate, instructions were clear:

1. *See schedule for on call person, page to answering service or try requested number.*
2. *If no response in ten minutes or if advocate is already on a call, page backup beeper.*
3. *If no response to backup try Executive Director.*
4. *Try anyone on the list.*

The advocate call list on the printout included the residence and work numbers for the more than 20 advocates. Some numbers had been entered into speed dial, including the pager numbers. It was expected that advocates on call would check in with the answering service at the beginning of their shift, letting the operator know whether to reach them by telephone or pager. No male advocates were listed in this first group.

Money Matters

The first fundraiser undertaken by RRS, at the suggestion of Mullen-Giles, was a Stay-at-Home Ball, an occasion that became a signature RRS event for more than 15 years. Instead of hosting an actual dance or ball, the Board of Directors chose this relatively easy way of raising money. The only expenses were printing and mailing ($800 for both) the 500 invitations. As stated on the invitation:

Rape Response Services
cordially requests the honor of your absence
at their
1ˢᵗ Annual Stay-At-Home Ball
to be graciously held in the comfort of your own home
on Saturday, October 28, 1989
from twilight to midnight
Dancing to your own choice of melodies
Dining on your lovingly prepared gourmet treats
Dressed in your favorite attire

The invitation further read:

We are not…
inviting you to a fancy ball…
taking you away from your family for the evening…
asking you to socialize with people you don't know…
Instead, consider contributing to the Rape Response Services,
the local non-profit agency serving victims of rape, incest,
and all other forms of sexual assault and abuse
in Penobscot and Piscataquis counties.
Dance and party away in the comfort of your own living room!

Tax-deductible contributions could be returned to RRS with the

RSVP card and unstamped envelope that were enclosed in the mailing. Suggested donations included $10.00 that might have otherwise been spent for gasoline and parking at a real ball, to $25.00 for flowers, up to the maximum suggestion of $195.00 for "The whole incredible evening!" A donor chart for 1989 listed the names of 83 individuals who gave a total of $2305. The amounts ranged from a low of two dollars to a high of $195 for the Ball. Several donations were made at the $15 active membership level.

Mullen-Giles prepared the DHS contract with RRS for fiscal year 1990 (FY'90) which began on October 1st and ended on September 30th of the following year. Eddy signed the document as Board President; Kreilkamp was listed on the authorization page as Financial Director. Required before any funds could be released to the rape crisis centers, these DHS contracts were large, consisting of 40 or more pages in Riders A ("Specifications of Work to be Performed, Compliance and Program Requirements") and B ("Payment and Other Provisions"). These documents were often amended and/or revised during the contract period. A final approved copy of the contract and of each revised or amended version was mailed back to the center, even after 2005 when the initial contracts could be submitted online.

Most of the pages in Rider A had to be completed by RRS. These included general agency information and an extensive overview of the program and all services that would be provided during the contract period. The projected numbers of individuals served on the hotline and in support groups had to be included, along with the estimated cost per client hour. Rider A also contained a prohibition against lobbying and a certification that RRS was a drug-free workplace.

Rider B contained the name of the contract specialist, the contract period, and generic information which did not change from year to year, including non-discrimination and mandated reporting requirements, an indemnification statement, civil rights assurances, and a termination clause. The list of reports and the dates when they were due, plus the expected dates when equal monthly payments would be mailed to RRS, and all budget pages completed by RRS, made up the remainder of Rider B.

In Rider A of the proposed contract, Mullen-Giles estimated that during the fiscal year, 20 additional hotline volunteers would take the forty-hour training, joining with those already taking hotline shifts.

Two fifteen-week support groups, one for rape survivors and one for incest, were planned, to be facilitated by two volunteer advocates who had received 16 hours of additional training sponsored by the Augusta Area Rape Crisis Center. Ten presentations on date rape were to be made in area schools, as well as ten community education programs and two eight-hour trainings for professionals.

In addition to goals and objectives in Rider A which were related to the hotline, support groups and community education, one objective that was not achieved for several years was "to promote and support the implementation of a rape protocol exam site in Piscataquis County." Described in detail in the contract was the need for this service: "Presently, sexual assault victims in Piscataquis County who desire a rape protocol exam must travel to St. Joseph Hospital in Penobscot County to receive the service. This measures into a two hour, 85-mile drive from Greenville, the farthermost town in Piscataquis County, or a one hour, 45-mile drive from Dover-Foxcroft, the largest city [*sic*] in Piscataquis County. Complicating the time and drive factors are winter hazardous driving and/or seasonal traffic traveling to the Moosehead Lake recreational area."

The development of a Sexual Assault Awareness Speakers Bureau was also described as an objective in Rider A. "Presently RRS has one paid staff person. RRS will develop a Speakers Bureau utilizing the RRS Director, trained RRS Board members and volunteer advocates with specialized training. As we increase our visibility, outreach, and media presence, the requests increase for additional information and workshop presentations. To meet this need, RRS will have in place by the spring of 1990 a minimum of six identified and trained public presenters, i.e. a trained individual to present an appropriate presentation for K-6th grade, junior high school, high school, and higher education and training re: rape, incest dynamics, acquaintance rape and sexual harassment. Trainers will be able to provide information on dynamics of the problem, where to go for help and prevention precautions."

In addition to presentations at the school level, it was also deemed necessary to offer educational opportunities for professionals in the community. Three-hour workshop presentations would be offered after December 31st to staff at hospital ERs, police and sheriff departments, and the DA's office. A Public Service Announcement (PSA) was also planned: "RRS Director and Board members are presently attempting to identify an area group, agency or corporation willing to produce a PSA promoting the availability of sexual assault crisis services through accessing the Hotline number. Bangor, in Penobscot County, has three television stations which broadcast to northern and central Maine and cover a six county geographic area. Additionally, the PSA will advertise a brochure outlining the available services sexual assault centers can provide. The brochure will be available free of charge by calling the hotline."

Budget pages in Rider B of the proposed contract noted that a total of $34,500 in BSS reimbursable expenses was available, including $30,000 from State Funds for Purchased Social Services (SFPSS) and the remainder from VOCA. An estimated 883 individuals would be served by these funds and 1056 by the total program. Other program revenue was $9500 from fundraising. In-kind personnel revenue totaled $6760, donated by a University intern ($1612), hotline advocates ($1476), and Board members ($3672).

Expenses equal to income ($44,000) that were budgeted in Rider B included:

- *Salaries and wages ($24,000)*
- *Telephone ($4500) ($40 per month to the hotline answering service and reimbursement to advocates for long-distance calls)*
- *Staff travel ($1000)*
- *Other travel ($200) (advocates and Board members)*
- *Rent ($3600)*
- *Meal allowance ($520) (staff plus snacks for training)*
- *Office supplies and equipment ($3030)*
- *Liability insurance and bonding ($800)*
- *Conferences ($2000)*
- *Support groups ($2000)*
- *Advertising ($450)*
- *Posters/brochures ($1000)*
- *Coalition dues ($400)*
- *Emergency fund for victim assistance, etc. ($500)*

By the end of 1989, Mullen-Giles and the RRS Board of Directors could take pride in what had been accomplished in 12 months. Not only was a local hotline operating again with a large number of dedicated volunteers, but the center was also becoming known in the Bangor community and at the University of Maine through fundraisers, editorials, and newspaper coverage. As evidenced in the proposed DHS contract, however, much more work remained.

1990: BACK IN BUSINESS

A t the beginning of the year, Mullen-Giles was probably excited to report to DHS the first statistics from the "new" rape crisis center in Bangor. From July 24, 1989, the first day of operation to January 30, 1990, RRS recorded a total of 167 hotline calls, of which 92 were first-time, 32 follow-up, and 43 informational. Hours provided by volunteers on the hotline were 182. Non-hotline clients who participated in groups or dropped by the office numbered 45. Of the callers, acquaintance rapes totaled 73; 12 stranger rapes, 29 cases of incest, plus gang rape, marital rape, attempted rape, and "unknown" were also recorded. What was not included in the statistics was an indication of how recently any of the sexual assaults occurred.

One of the tasks required by DHS was a monthly compilation of statistics, including the number, types and duration of calls to the hotline, number of persons participating in support groups, and an estimate of the number of people attending community education events, including school presentations. The hotline statistics were totaled by staff from the reporting forms that advocates completed after each call and mailed to the RRS office. Advocates were given copies of the form on the last night of training, and self-addressed stamped envelopes in which to return the forms were also provided. The form included lines for basic information: phone number, date and time of call, name of caller and location (if known), and advocate's name. Present age of the victim and age at the time of the assault, plus the date of the assault and the gender of the victim, could be provided if known. A column of choices to identify the perpetrator listed acquaintance, stranger, family member, gang, marital, live-in partner, and unknown.

There was also a space on the form to check if this was the caller's first contact or a follow-up with RRS, or if this was an informational call. The advocate was then asked on the form if any collateral contacts were made on behalf of the caller to police, hospital, another agency or advocate, or to an RRS staff person. Finally the amount of time spent with the caller and with any collateral contacts was recorded. Data from these forms was then used to compile monthly and annual statistics for DHS, which provided mail-in forms on which all these statistics were to be recorded. DHS forms remained consistent through the years in how they were formatted and in the type of data requested. The total number of rapes reported in hotline calls was always higher than in reports to local law enforcement agencies, because many people chose not to tell anyone, or only the RRS advocate.

The statistical report for the period ending January 30, 1990, also recorded that 41 people had taken the advocate training in either May/ June or October/November. Only a portion of these individuals became hotline volunteers. Six attended the MCR Volunteer Conference in June, and Mullen-Giles went in July to the National Coalition Against Sexual Assault annual conference in Philadelphia. Group facilitator training had been taken by five people, and four participated in a session at St. Joseph Hospital on "Caring for the Sexual Assault Victim."

The weekend edition, February 3rd/4th of the BDN, featured an article by Renee Ordway titled: "Rape Response Services marks first year in Bangor." Mullen-Giles was quoted: "In one year volunteers at RRS handled about 200 rape-crisis calls…it has become increasingly clear that there are a large number of rape victims in Penobscot and Piscataquis counties." The majority, she stated, "are unreported to police."

The 23 volunteers on the RRS hotline were an example, Mullen-Giles stated, of the "great support" in the community. "Volunteers at RRS handle each call differently, but are trained to help the victim find the kind of individual help she needs. During the summer, three women were raped by strangers in the Bangor area. These rapes were similar and involved women whose cars had broken down. One case was reported, but the rapist was never found. The other two women did not report the incidents." While noting that strangers in these three cases were the apparent rapists, Mullen-Giles commented: "Acquaintance rape is more common in the Bangor area."

An undated BDN article announced: "Beginning Monday, Sept.

30, Rape Response Services will hold its first support group for women survivors of incest." The group was scheduled to meet for 12 weeks, 90 minutes each Monday evening, free of charge. Facilitators would be two unnamed advocates who had "received additional training in working with incest survivors and group dynamics." By this time, RRS had already held three twelve-week support groups for survivors of rape, beginning in February, and a fourth was scheduled to begin on October 2nd. The medical advisor for both of the groups, according to the article, was Dr. Joan Settin, a clinical psychologist from Bangor. Mullen-Giles stated in the article that interested people should call RRS and schedule an interview with the group facilitators "[b]ecause compatibility is so important to the success of the groups." She announced that calls could be made to the "center's toll-free number, 1-800-310-0000 anytime."

A Community Presence

The final portion of statistics was titled "Community Education and Awareness" and listed several locations where Mullen-Giles had made presentations:

- *Tuesday Forum, Bangor;*
- *Bangor High School Health Fair;*
- *University of Maine (six classes);*
- *Womancare, Dover-Foxcroft;*
- *Catholic Youth Group, Orono;*
- *YWCA, Bangor;*
- *Kiwanis Club, Hermon;*
- *Six freshman classes at Brewer High School;*
- *Foxcroft Academy Peer Helper Program;*
- *Veazie Junior High School;*
- *AFL-CIO training, Bangor;*
- *Training for Residence Hall Directors and Assistants, University of Maine.*

Late in September, RRS sponsored "Caring for Victims of Sexual Assault: A Program for Health Care and Social Service Delivery System Providers." This full-day event was held at the Ramada Inn in Bangor. The registration fee of $65.00 included lunch and materials. Intended audience members were "nurses, counselors, social workers, physicians, emergency room personnel, EMTs, and police." It was noted in a later report that 37 participants attended the event.

Attendees were welcomed at 8:00 A.M. by Jim Mitchell, identified in the brochure as a member of the RRS Board of Directors and a partner in Mitchell & Mitchell, a marketing firm. Laura Fortman, Director of the Augusta Area RCC, delivered the opening segment, "Rape Trauma Syndrome: Effects of Sexual Assault on the Victim." The nurse's role in the rape protocol exam at St. Joseph Hospital was discussed by Guerin, the ER Nurse Manager at St. Joseph and a member of the RCAC. Dr. Westhoven, medical advisor for RRS and an ER physician at St. Joseph, talked about medical management of the rape protocol exam. Closing out the morning's session was Alison Phelps from the Maine State Police Crime Lab who spoke about forensic evidence collection.

After a "poolside" lunch, Christopher Almy, DA for Penobscot and Piscataquis counties, and Michael Roberts, Assistant DA, presented remarks titled, "Effective Investigation and Prosecution of the Sexual Assault Perpetrator." Mullen-Giles closed the day's program by speaking about the "Role of the Rape Crisis Center." A good relationship with the DA's office and local law enforcement agencies in the two counties was established early by RRS and maintained through the years, allowing RRS to be more assertive when speaking up for the best interests of victims.

Money Matters

The second annual Stay-at-Home Ball was co-hosted for the first time by a radio station, WPBC-FM, Brite 93, on December 1st. Music for dancing was provided on the radio from 8 to 11 P.M. Recipients of the invitations were encouraged to donate to RRS the money they might have spent by attending a ball. These contributions would support the continuation of the services provided: crisis intervention, advocacy and referral, and community education. "RRS serves both male and female victims of rape, incest and all other forms of sexual assault and abuse. Our catchment area is over 7,000 square miles. It's a big job—but we can do it with your help," concluded the invitation.

Another contract with DHS was prepared by Mullen-Giles prior to October 1st for a two-year period, until September 30, 1992. A letter from Mullen-Giles to Jones at DHS reported that Bowler had been elected Board President in February, replacing Eddy who planned to remain active as a Board member. Kreilkamp would continue to serve as Board treasurer. Donations to RRS in 1990 totaled $1749 from 68 individuals. The total budget for the fiscal year ending September 30, 1990, was $39,000. Copies of the W-2 and W-3 forms submitted for the year 1990 showed Mullen-Giles as the only employee with a salary of $20,635. With her enthusiasm and initiative, Mullen-Giles capably got the word out that a rape crisis center in Bangor was back in business.

1991: "A HIGH STANDARD OF PROFESSIONALISM"

In its second full year of existence, the "new" RRS was achieving the purposes stated in the Articles of Incorporation: support for rape victims and community education about rape. Early successes, however, did not mean that either Mullen-Giles or the RRS Board of Directors would think their work was done.

In January, Mullen-Giles submitted a document to Rampe and the RRS Personnel Committee titled "RRS Goals and Objectives Progress." Identified as "projected goals and objectives for the period of October 1, 1990 – September 30, 1992," this document provided many details about the work focus for RRS in 1991.

Goal One: Victim Services

1. *Continued operation of the 24-hour hotline, which was operating "on a regular and consistent basis."*
2. *Expand victim services by offering two support groups, one for rape survivors and one for survivors of incest.*
3. *Recruit and train approximately twenty additional volunteer advocates to be available for the Hotline and community education.* Because many of the advocates were University of Maine students who were graduating, another training would be needed in the fall of 1991.
4. *Promote and support the implementation of a rape protocol exam site in Piscataquis County.* The need for this service reflected the visionary focus of Mullen-Giles and RRS Board members, but further development of such a site would not begin until the late 1990s.

Goal Two: Community Outreach

1. *Develop and promote a Sexual Assault Awareness Speakers Bureau.* Mullen-Giles noted that four members of the RRS Board (Burkhart, Cook, Bowler, and Settin), two volunteer advocates (Sue Vertigan and Mace), and two student interns (Carol McMahan and Bryner) were either available for or had completed public speaking engagements.

2. *Promote and coordinate victim services among hospitals, the DA's office, and law enforcement departments.* At the time the "RRS Goals and Objectives Progress" document was written, the ERs at St. Joseph Hospital and Eastern Maine Medical Center (EMMC), plus Cutler Health Center at the University of Maine, all had a policy in place to call the RRS hotline when a victim of sexual assault presented at their facilities. A volunteer advocate would then go to the facility. To further implement this sub-goal, a second "Caring for Victims of Sexual Assault" workshop would be held in September 1991. A memorandum of understanding (MOU), being drawn up between RRS and the University of Maine Public Safety office, would require officers to call the RRS hotline when rape victims reported to them.

3. *Develop a public service announcement (PSA) and accompanying brochure to promote "the availability of our services for victims and/or their significant others."* Several at-risk groups (elderly persons, persons with physical and mental disabilities, non-readers) were identified for outreach.

4. *Promote Rape Awareness Week in September 1991 at local colleges and universities.* Mullen-Giles noted her intention to represent RRS at the meetings of the University of Maine Rape Awareness Committee; the two student interns mentioned earlier, McMahan and Bryner, were also members of the committee, with Bryner representing the Bangor campus. Work with Husson College in Bangor

was just beginning; nothing was being done at Beal College or at Eastern Maine Technical College, the two other colleges in Bangor.

Goal Three: Data Collection and Monitoring

1. *Catch up with reports due to the State, with financial reports expected to be completed by the end of January and statistics by early February.*
2. *Write annual evaluations of each volunteer advocate by June 1991.* Mullen-Giles was in regular contact with all advocates and was on backup for hotline shifts or to process calls with advocates. She evaluated the student interns in writing and with on-site visits.

A Community Presence

At the end of this "RRS Goals and Objectives Progress" document, Mullen-Giles wrote that about 20% of her time was devoted to fundraising activities, including events, grant-writing, and attendance at county or city budget meetings. Walker remembered Mullen-Giles in attendance at a meeting of the Penobscot County Commissioners. She wore a button, "What part of NO don't you understand?" which elicited comments from at least one Commissioner, who referred to Mullen-Giles as the "rape lady." Despite the joking, the Penobscot County Commissioners provided long-time financial support for RRS with an annual gift of $1250, maintained despite the County's cuts to other social service agencies.

Mullen-Giles also noted that she attended monthly meetings of MCR in Augusta, and represented MCR each month at the Women's Legislative Agenda Coalition (WLAC). She and the directors of the other nine rape crisis centers were expected to meet with their area legislators before June and discuss WLAC's requests for legislation. Mullen-Giles noted that her "office participated actively in contacting individuals and groups to write letters to the BDN editor as one opportunity to do some community education around the serious consequences of date rape."

A tri-fold brochure, printed in black on blue paper and reprinted at least once, marked the fulfillment in fall 1991 of one portion of Goal

Two, and was modeled after a similar document from a sexual assault center in Pennsylvania. The brochure could be mailed: a center back section contained a return address for RRS and provided space for address labels to be attached. Prominent at the top of the brochure's front section were the RRS logo and hotline numbers. The toll-free number (1-800-310-0000) was provided. Other "**free** confidential services" that were listed inside the brochure included:

- *A 24 hour crisis hotline*
- *Information on medical & court procedures*
- *Support for victims & their families*
- *Community education*
- *Support groups for survivors of rape & incest*
- *Volunteers who can accompany a victim to the hospital or through the court process if the victim chooses either of these options*
- *Information and referrals to other area services*

Inside also were several sub-sections that defined rape, acquaintance rape, child sexual abuse, and incest.

> *Rape is: an act of VIOLENCE, not overwhelming passion; usually PREMEDITATED, not spontaneous; often committed by people KNOWN to the victim; committed against women and men, girls and boys of ALL DESCRIPTIONS; committed mostly by HETEROSEXUAL people who are NOT mentally ill.*
>
> *Acquaintance rape is: unwanted sexual contact by someone KNOWN to the victim; as TRAUMATIC as rape by a stranger; called DATE RAPE when the rapist is someone with whom the victim consented to be; a crime in MARITAL relationships as well as unmarried relationships.*
>
> *Child sexual abuse is: a misuse of one's POWER and AUTHORITY over a child; ANY physical contact of a sexual nature; visual intrusions of privacy and bodily exposure intended to shock or entice a child; committed most often by someone KNOWN to the child; the cause of EMOTIONAL PAIN long after the abuse occurs; usually not violent—victims are tricked or*

enticed by people who offer them love, affection or other rewards.

Incest is: child sexual abuse by someone RELATED to the victim; has reached EPIDEMIC proportions in Maine; has long lasting psychological effects including intense feelings of betrayal.

Following these definitions, the third inside panel was titled "Self-Protection: There is no perfect way to protect yourself against sexual assault, but the following have worked for many people:

- *Trust your feelings. If you feel you are being pressured into unwanted sex, you're right.*
- *Know you have the right to set limits. You may have different limits with different people. Your limits may change. It's a good idea to know what you want or don't want before you end up in the back seat of a car.*
- *Pay attention to behavior that doesn't seem right. Someone sitting or standing too close who enjoys your discomfort. Power stares—looking through you or down at you. Someone who blocks your way. Someone speaking in a way or acting as if he/she knows you more intimately than he/she does. Someone who grabs or pushes you to get his/her own way. Someone who doesn't listen or disregards what you are saying, like "NO."*
- *Be assertive. Get angry when someone does something to you that you don't want. Act immediately with some kind of negative response such as talking, yelling, leaving, pushing away. Stand up for yourself; it's okay to be rude to someone who is sexually pressuring you, even if it hurts their feelings; after all, they're not paying attention to your feelings.*

A back section of the brochure listed ways to help a friend:

- *Let your friend know you want to listen. It doesn't matter so much what you say, but more how you listen. Understand that talking about sexual assault is not easy.*
- *Believe your friend. Stories are rarely made up about a sexual assault.*

- *Keep the confidentiality among your peers. DO NOT tell other friends.*
- *Let your friend know the sexual assault was not her/his fault. Blaming questions such as "Why didn't you scream?" or "Why were you hitchhiking?" are not helpful. Instead you might say, "It's difficult to scream when you're frightened" or "Hitchhiking is risky, but you were asking for a ride, not a rape."*
- *Take care of yourself too.* [emphasis in original]

Program Plans

A comprehensive Plan of Work for RRS, developed by the Board of Directors in May and labeled "draft," set the tone for the center in the years to come. The opening paragraph of the Executive Summary suggested the triumphs and stresses of the beginning years: "Starting a social service agency from scratch is exciting and frightening. Exciting because your group is going to fulfill an expressed community need, mend a hole in the societal fabric and help many people who have not fit into any of the existing niches. Frightening because, at the outset, sources of financial support are minimal: state or federal funds, a grant, etc. To expand that financial base, the agency relies heavily upon the community goodwill it is able to generate, the willingness/expertise of the Board to fundraise, and careful and creative planning."

Under a section titled "Services," the twenty-four hour hotline was listed as "our most important goal and the most prominent phrase in our mission statement." Maintaining this service was paramount. "The lifeblood of our agency is continued recruitment of hotline volunteers." A minimum of 28 advocates was desirable at all times, so that the schedule of two twelve-hour daily shifts gave each advocate four shifts per month: two on call and two on backup. Shifts began at eight o'clock in the morning and eight o'clock in the evening. The document listed some alternatives to this schedule, including paid staff, volunteers in the office during daytime hours, and shorter shifts. A necessity to both "schedule in-service trainings on various subjects," and to "recognize our outstanding volunteer(s) in some way" was noted.

"While there are no educational requirements beyond the basics, we need advocates with average intelligence, common sense and the ability to work with a wide variety of people—from victims/survivors to law enforcement and medical personnel. Advocates need to be compassionate enough to comfort a hysterical victim and tough enough to tell a family member, doctor, nurse or police officer that their behavior is inappropriate. And we ask them to do this for FREE, at all hours of the day and night, weekends and holidays, for at least twelve months!"

The draft Plan of Work noted that a classified advertisement for advocates was placed once a year each in the BDN and *The Maine Campus* at the University of Maine. The only other recruitment was by word of mouth. "Each applicant [*for advocate*] is interviewed and those deemed unsuitable are rejected. It would be in our future best interests, perhaps, to develop places within the agency for some of those deemed not suitable as crisis intervention advocates. They have, after all, indicated an interest in the organization and might be useful in another capacity." Advocates were asked to work at least one shift per week for 12 months if possible. Exit interviews with advocates who left RRS were scheduled with Mullen-Giles.

Information about support groups, "our next most important service" after the hotline, was contained in the draft Plan of Work. Each group cost the agency an estimated $1000 because of stipends paid to a professional counselor and to two "volunteers." The professional was available when the group or an individual group member needed special attention, or when the direction of the group was "not what the facilitators had originally planned." Facilitators were paid "a modest stipend—$25 each per week—because of the time (and additional stress) planning for and running the group takes. Because of our grant limitations we can recoup none of this from group members and indeed, would be reluctant to do so because most of them indicate that even a modest sum would present a financial hardship." Offering the service for free was seen in the plan as "an additional inducement to survivors." Concurrent groups were not run. Incest and rape survivor groups were offered separately because "incest tends to involve much more family feelings and interaction on a level quite different" from rape.

In addition to recruitment of advocates, the draft Plan of Work mentioned the need for more Board members. By January 1, 1992, the goals of revamping the Board recruitment policies and filling all Board slots would be realized, according to the Plan. Packets would be sent to prospective Board members, and biographical forms would be returned and evaluated by the Nominating Committee. The evaluation would include reference checks and one-on-one interviews. Training of Board members would be an orientation session, three hours in length, to include a video and discussion of rape and sexual assault issues, and a review of RRS programs, policies, goals, and objectives. Board meetings would provide training pieces.

A section on Promotion in the draft Plan of Work noted that RRS was "a highly visible 'business,'" and it was "relatively easy to place an article in or obtain interviews with the BDN." The three local commercial television stations were also viewed as being "very supportive and willing to cover events." A goal was to have at least once-a-month media coverage from letters, articles, press releases, and interviews.

Money Matters

Finances continued to be a concern in the draft Plan of Work. A letter of interest was sent in May to become a United Way agency, both for the financial benefit and for credibility within the business community. A fundraising calendar had been developed, and several ideas were listed in the Plan: self-defense class for women, "Model Mugging," the Stay-at-Home Ball (not held in 1991), letters targeted to doctors and to lawyers, a direct mail appeal, and foundation grants. RRS earned $400 from items donated by Board members and volunteers and sold at the World's Largest Garage Sale sponsored by WLBZ-TV Channel 2.

The need to hire both a Volunteer Coordinator and a Community Outreach Coordinator was mentioned in the draft Plan of Work. No funds were then available for either position. A part-time employee position had been budgeted for fiscal year 1990 but was not filled. A review by MCR of staffing structure in the nine centers (Waterville was not included), dated July 17, 1991, showed RRS with a total budget of $43,355, the lowest except for the Presque Isle and Ellsworth centers. Each center except Portland and Presque Isle received the same state allocation of $35,225. All centers had more paid staff than RRS. The number of monthly contacts to the hotlines depicted on the MCR staffing chart varied widely, from a high of 250 in Presque Isle to a low of 15 in Ellsworth. RRS had reported 28.

The Executive Summary of the draft Plan of Work concluded with the following paragraph: "The goal we would really like to attain is to be no longer needed, but we realize that is impossible, given the structure of today's society. What we <u>can</u> do, and do very well, is to provide crisis counseling for victims of rape, incest and sexual assault. What we <u>need</u> to do is improve our delivery of community education services throughout Penobscot and Piscataquis counties. The linchpins of that goal are better, more effective promotion and fundraising. The rest is easy." [emphasis in original]

School-Based Education

At the time the draft Plan of Work was written, community education programs were limited. A suggestion was made in the Plan of Work to make a presentation at every high school and middle school in the RRS "primary" area (Bangor and vicinity) every year, and in as many schools as possible in the "secondary" area (northern Penobscot county and Piscataquis county) every other year. Surveying the schools, especially those with "sex ed" programs, could help RRS determine if a pamphlet about date rape would be useful.

Whether or not the survey was done, RRS did create and distribute to high school teachers before schools opened in the fall of 1991, a tri-fold brochure titled: "It's Time We Started Thinking About The Unthinkable Crime…DATE RAPE!" Additional information on the front of the brochure included: "Over 30% of first sexual experiences are the result of acquaintance rape," and noted that this is less likely to be reported and to be viewed as a crime. "Acquaintance rape happens every day. Innocent dates turn into nightmares." On the back panel, Mullen-Giles was listed as the ED, and DHS as a partial funder. No hotline number was provided on the brochure. Services provided by RRS were "crisis counseling, referral, support groups, victim advocacy and community education."

Inside the brochure were more hard-hitting statements that could almost be construed as victim-blaming. Under one panel labeled "Why?" the words were:

> *In the mind of our entire society—women most of all—"date" implies a good time, a pleasant interaction between two people.* ***Because of this perception, women are totally unprepared for aggressive sexual behavior from their "dates."*** *Young men are*

taught, from the cradle, that to be a man is to be "macho," to compete, to win, to overcome obstacles. **For some young men, when a woman says "No," her resistance becomes an obstacle to overcome.** Males who are potential rapists do give early warning signals:

1. **If he won't listen to what you say** during a conversation, he may hear "beg me a little" when you say "No."
2. **Terms such as "bimbo," "stupid bitch,"** or the like indicate hostility and anger toward women.
3. **If he thinks only of himself,** makes all the decisions about where to go on the date, he probably has one ultimate destination in mind.
4. **If he calls you "uptight" when you object to sexual advances.**
5. **If he has unrealistic ideas about women,** such as "A woman's place is to serve her man," he's probably not going to listen to your objections about sex.

A center section had the label "An Ounce of Prevention..." and listed five steps to take to avoid [*sic*] date rape:

1. **Don't date a stranger**—*even if he's your best friend's brother! If there's no way to gracefully avoid a date, make it a double date or other group activity.*
2. *If a double date or group activity isn't possible,* **meet in a public place** *and provide your own transportation. Being alone in a room with a closed door puts you at a disadvantage from the start.*
3. **Always have a** [*sic*] **change for a phone call;** *decide in advance who to call.*
4. **If you start to feel uneasy, RESPOND TO THOSE FEELINGS!** *Make that phone call. Above all,* **DO NOT REMAIN IN A SITUATION THAT PUTS YOU AT RISK. DO NOT FEAR HURT FEELINGS ON YOUR DATE'S PART—HE CERTAINLY ISN'T WORRIED ABOUT YOURS!**
5. *If all else fails,* **SCREAM FOR HELP!**

"A Pound of Cure" was the final section: "If, despite exercising normal care and caution, you do become a victim of acquaintance rape, for your own protection, here's what to do:

1. *Get to a* **SAFE PLACE.**
2. **Call someone**—*a crisis hotline, your parents or a close friend.*
3. **DO NOT WASH YOUR HANDS OR FACE OR TAKE A SHOWER, DO NOT CHANGE YOUR CLOTHES.** *Your skin and clothes contain valuable evidence needed for prosecution of this crime. As much of the evidence as possible must be preserved.*
4. **Seek counseling** *through Rape Response Services and a group support or work with a private counselor.* **YOU ARE NOT ALONE!**
5. *Remember—***YOU** *are the* **VICTIM. YOU DID NOTHING TO CAUSE THE RAPE.** [emphasis in original]

Personnel Changes

The annual evaluation of Mullen-Giles was completed by the RRS Board in January. She had met regularly with the Board President, and monthly with Rampe, who represented the Clinical/Training Committee of the Board. After her evaluation, Mullen-Giles was praised in a document dated May 13th: "She is energetic, hard working and enthusiastic, and has earned a reputation among professionals as being concerned, reliable and cooperative." The document further noted that Mullen-Giles had set a high standard of professionalism which everyone connected with RRS was expected to equal, and had daily demonstrated that she understood very well why the center was needed.

Statistical reports filed with DHS for the last month of 1991 clearly showed the utilization of the RRS hotline and support groups, stressing again the strides made by the center under the leadership of Mullen-Giles. Seventy clients had called the hotline or participated in a support group in December. Over 75 volunteer hours had been provided.

Documents filed with the Internal Revenue Service for 1991 again showed Mullen-Giles as the only paid employee with a total wage of

$21,965, a small increase from the previous year. Despite the glowing evaluation and continued progress at RRS, Mullen-Giles resigned from her position as ED on November 20th. Her letter of resignation, sent to each Board member, stated:

> *I notified the RRS Board President on Tuesday, November 19th that I am hereby submitting my resignation to RRS. I have been offered the position of Executive Director with the Maine Democratic Party. The opportunity to serve in a statewide position is too good for me to turn down. It is with sadness I leave this agency. This position provided me with an opportunity to fine tune my skills and to develop new skills. I thank you for that opportunity. I have enjoyed working with each of you and will miss you very much.*
>
> *I am prepared to work out a four weeks notice effective November 19th. The focus of this time will be spent on preparing for an orderly administration transfer. Before leaving this position, I will complete all necessary paperwork according to our grant contract with DHS, develop a calendar of upcoming RRS commitments and what needs to be done when, additionally, I will connect with the volunteer Advocates and work with them to insure a smooth transition and mail out the December Hotline schedule. I can complete this work sooner than four weeks and if it is at all possible, I would like to be released from my contract on December 13, 1991. I will abide by the decision of the Board of Directors. I thank you for the opportunity to serve this agency, and again, I will miss you all.*

Mullen-Giles had capably served for two years as the first ED of RRS, fulfilling the detailed duties and responsibilities delineated in the job description for a Coordinator, the advertised position for which she had been hired. Many volunteers were trained, and a hotline was again serving callers from the greater Bangor area. Education, community awareness, and fundraising events were occurring. DHS contract funds were once again being utilized by a local rape crisis center in Bangor.

1992: TURMOIL

T he resignation of Mullen-Giles was the beginning of several tumultuous and unsettled years for RRS. When she left, student interns, Judy Holt Spencer and Sarah Lowden, served without pay as part-time volunteer coordinators and incest support group facilitators during the school year. No volunteer trainings were scheduled. Bowler, Board president, assumed responsibility for attending the MCR Board meetings in January and February 1992 until a replacement for Mullen-Giles was hired.

Faced with the lack of an ED and without any additional staff, the RRS Board worked hard to be sure basic services, especially the hotline, were maintained. At the same time, an extensive document titled "Final Reorganization Plan" was developed and approved by the Board in January. Including everything from Board meeting frequency to Board size (12 to 20 members) and composition, the Plan appeared to describe how the Board could better manage a transition process from one ED to another.

The relationship between the ED and the Board was viewed in Part 2 of the Plan as "a partnership in which the ED and Board members raise concerns and suggestions." An expectation was that the ED would "guide and motivate the Board." After noting: "The State's rule is that none of the ED's salary which comes from money they give us is to go towards fundraising," the Plan concluded that a lot of fundraising needed to be done. "Each Board member is expected to donate money to RRS in an amount s/he believes s/he can afford." Board members could be asked to resign if they did not take responsibility for fundraising.

Parts 5 ("Job Descriptions") and 6 ("Committees Needed") of this Reorganization Plan dealt with the structure of the Board. A statement in Part 5 noted: "Clear job descriptions are needed for the whole Board, each Board officer, and each Committee." The Standing Committees were delineated in Part 6 as Fundraising, Finance, Public Relations, Personnel, Administrative, Advisory, and Nominating. The Plan suggested that the Organization/Structural Committee in the By-Laws had "never functioned" and should be replaced by the Administrative Committee, also in the By-Laws. The purposes of the Administrative Committee were to "draft for Board approval the job descriptions of the Board and each Board officer, to monitor and advise the ED about the overall functioning of the agency, to make recommendations to the Board to improve Board and/or agency structure and functioning, and to provide guidance as needed between Board meetings." Members of this Committee were to include someone with grant expertise because "knowledge of the State grant requirements and process is complicated and integral to our current existence." The Board Treasurer and representatives from both the Personnel and the Clinical/Training Committees were named as members of the Administrative Committee.

Expressing the value of RRS advocates, a new Committee, Advocate Support, was recommended in the Reorganization Plan to "address advocate needs which are initiated either by the Board, an advocate(s), or the Executive Director." An example of responsibilities included advocate recognition activities. The Board was charged with clarifying the budget for volunteer recognition "since volunteers are the backbone of RRS," and Mullen-Giles "wanted to make sure we showed volunteers sufficient appreciation."

In Part 8 of the Plan titled "Committee Composition," the recommendation was made that one or more advocates be asked to serve on each Committee, including Advocate Support, and on the RRS Board. The chairperson of each Committee was to be a Board member. Only Board members could serve on the Administrative Committee. Members of the public who were neither Board members nor advocates could join any of the other Committees.

The Board was expected to arrive at decisions by consensus. Ideally, the entire Board and staff would be "in agreement of all decisions. If the staff is not comfortable with the Board's decision, continued discussion is encouraged until a total consensus is achieved; in the meantime, the Board's decision holds because ultimately the Board is responsible for RRS."

Part 4 of the Plan ("Delegation and Follow Thru System") delineated the parts of a standard Board meeting structure and the need for Board member facilitators "who are skilled at both following this meeting structure and promoting Board members' participation in discussions." Each Committee was to choose a chairperson who would call meetings, insure minutes were taken, and provide a report at Board meetings. The Board President was "an ex officio member of each Committee, responsible for keeping track of Committees' goals and following through if deadlines are missed." Part of the President's job description, not included in the Plan and still to be developed, was to "keep abreast of the overall picture of RRS."

Personnel Changes

The RRS Board hired Co-Directors, Burkhart and Ries Wichers, on March 2, 1992. Burkhart was a member of the Board and a hotline volunteer at the time that Mullen-Giles resigned. Her clinical skills were balanced by the administrative experience of Wichers, who responded to the job advertisement. An abbreviated timeline in the files from this period noted that the Board "spent a lot of time agonizing over [*the*] decision." Burkhart was given the title of Co-Director for Clinical Services; Wichers' title was Co-Director for Administration and External Relations. These two positions appeared to split the duties and responsibilities that Mullen-Giles performed as ED. The job descriptions for both positions, dated April 1992, began with the statement that each co-director was "responsible to the RRS Board of Directors with an assigned advisor to provide support, guidance and to serve as a procedural resource."

The specific duties and responsibilities of these new co-director roles are outlined in the chart on the following pages:

Role	Co-Director Clinical	Co-Director Administrative
Primary focus	Provide leadership and administrative coordination to the RRS hotline and associated services	Nurture community support for RRS programs, oversee budget and planning, serve as Board liaison in fundraising efforts, seek and coordinate writing of grants, prepare appropriate reports
Direct service	1. Coordinate a 24-hour hotline to provide crisis counseling services to victims, their families and significant others	1. Not applicable
	2. Coordinate a program to accompany victims to rape protocol exams, police interviews and court hearings	2. Not applicable
	3. Develop and implement volunteer training programs	3. Not applicable
	4. Recruit, supervise and support volunteers	4. Not applicable
	5. Insure that quality services are provided to clients	5. Not applicable
Community organization, education	1. Provide or coordinate community education to the public schools, colleges, organizations and agencies about sexual assault and related issues	1. Provide or coordinate community education to the public schools, colleges, organizations and agencies about RRS and its role in the community
	2. Supply educational and informational materials for clients, volunteers, community, schools, colleges, agencies, organizations	2. Not applicable
	3. Assure media coverage of RRS activities, programs	3. Same
Financial duties and responsibilities	1. Not applicable	1. Prepare and oversee program budget and insure compliance with all State and Federal regulations. Share this responsibility with Board Treasurer.
	2. Not applicable	2. Solicit grants; insure proper and timely preparation of grants, contracts, reports
	3. Not applicable	3. Routine financial management: order materials, services and equipment as necessary; approve and pay bills within specified budget guidelines; seek Board approval for extraordinary expenses
	4. Not applicable	4. Liaison for Board fundraising efforts

Administrative responsibilities	1. Serve as liaison between RRS personnel and Board	1. Same
	2. Attend all regular Board meetings and special Board meetings as requested	2. Same
	3. Prepare oral and written reports regarding clinical services for all regular Board meetings	3. Prepare oral and written reports, including a financial report, for all regular Board meetings
	4. Create yearly management plan/timeline for clinical program, to be approved by the Board	4. Create yearly management plan/timeline for program, to be approved by the Board
	5. Cooperate with Co-Director for Administration to insure proper and accurate maintenance of all program records, files and data	5. Insure proper and accurate maintenance of all program records, files and data
	6. With Co-Director, represent RRS at monthly meetings of Maine Coalition on Rape	6. Same
	7. Supervise volunteers	7. Not applicable
	8. Perform other duties as needed	8. Same
General duties and responsibilities	1. Serve as a role model in demonstrating compassion, sensitivity and understanding of sexual assault and related issues	1. Same
	2. Provide leadership characterized by team-building, flexibility and interpersonal skills for RRS programs and activities	2. Same
Qualifications	1. Understanding of clinical, legal and/or political issues related to sexual assault	1. Same
	2. Administrative skills	2. Same
	3. Strong interpersonal skills: teambuilding, supervision, consultation, public relations, public speaking	3. Same
	4. Agreement with philosophy and purpose of RRS	4. Same
	5. Ability to be flexible regarding scheduling and other job-related contingencies	5. Same
	6. Counseling, management and/or grant-writing experience	6. Same
	7. Contact information for three references who can speak to job qualifications	7. Same

A Community Presence

Outreach, a quarterly newsletter from RRS, was launched in the winter of 1992. Burkhart was the editor, Scarlett Davis the publisher, and Wendy Norko and Bowler were listed as "Contributors." The two-sided black and white publication, with a few illustrations, was printed on letter-size paper. Board members at the time the newsletter was printed included Bowler as President, Moirs, Secretary, and Jane Veeder, Treasurer. Others were Leesa Easton (formerly Cook), Carolyn Forget, Clare Hudson Payne, England, Estler, Rampe, and Sockbeson. The staff listed were Burkhart, Clinical Director, and Wichers, Administrative Director.

Articles in the newsletter included a meditation on finding peace within oneself and information about rape in the military. The new Mabel Wadsworth Women's Health Center located in Bangor was profiled. Readers were encouraged to set aside items for the World's Largest Garage Sale to be held in June, sponsored again by WLBZ-TV Channel 2. Pickup by RRS of all donated items except clothing could be arranged after the first of the year.

A director's column in the newsletter included information about the fall training class which "graduated" 19 advocates in November. Twelve-week support groups, one for rape survivors and one for incest survivors, were to begin in January. Both the hotline number and the administrative office number were provided on the second page. The column also noted that RRS participated in Rape Awareness Week activities at the University of Maine and Husson College.

In large capital letters at the bottom of the first page of *Outreach* were the words: "Volunteers are not paid, not because they are worthless but because they are priceless!!!" Half a column on the first page of the newsletter was devoted to one of these volunteer advocates in an "Advocate Profile." The first advocate to be highlighted in this first edition of the newsletter was Janet Badger. The following was her profile:

> *My name is Janet* [Badger]. *I am a native of Maine and a graduate of Bangor High School. I have worked with children and adults with mental retardation and/or mental illness since 1985. In 1990 I became a full-time assistant teacher at a day program here in Bangor. I very much enjoy working with these people at the*

center. I became involved with Rape Response Services in 1989 and have worked many long and hard hours with this center. I became interested after going through my own experience of child sexual abuse and healing. As a survivor, I feel I have assisted clients in their healing process, whether the assault was many years ago or just last night. On our hotline I have talked to hundreds of people who were in crisis, or wanted information or just wanted to talk. I have enjoyed working with past clients and intend on helping many more.

Community outreach was also achieved during the year by offering trainings for businesses. The Maine Legislature in their 1991 session had passed a requirement for sexual harassment education in all workplaces with 15 or more employees. Employers also had to have strategies in place for dealing with sexual harassment complaints. RRS and other sexual assault centers in Maine organized trainings in 1992 to help businesses comply with this new law. In late September, RRS sponsored a half-day "Sexual Harassment Education and Training Seminar" at the Bangor Hilton. The brochure for the event was titled: "HAS YOUR ORGANIZATION COMPLIED WITH MAINE'S NEW SEXUAL HARASSMENT EDUCATION LAW? TIME IS RUNNING OUT... AND LIABILITY CAN BE COSTLY." Employees were encouraged to attend the seminar from 8:30 to 10:15 A.M. for a fee of $30.00, and would learn about their "rights and responsibilities in maintaining a work environment free of sexual harassment." [emphasis in original]

Supervisors and managers, for a fee of $60.00, could attend the employee session as well as two additional hours, until 12:30 P.M. The format of the seminar was described in the brochure: "The first part of the seminar will combine both employees and supervisors/managers for an overview of what constitutes sexual harassment in the workplace, its effects, the reasons for its prohibition, employees' rights, and Maine's new law. The second part of the seminar will continue with just supervisors and managers, focusing on risks and responsibilities associated with sexual harassment and effective management strategies related to the issue."

A sample sexual harassment policy and poster would be provided, as well as "strategies and procedures for dealing with sexual harassment complaints." Dr. Suzanne Estler, Director of Equal Opportunity at the

University of Maine and a Board member at RRS was the presenter, described in the brochure as having "over twenty years of experience in organizational management and equal opportunity work. She is known for her intelligent, informative, and clear presentation style." Videotaped case studies would be shown. Advance registration was required, one week before the date of the seminar.

Sexual Assault Awareness Week

In a letter to the editor of the BDN on April 18th, Wichers identified herself as the "Administrative director" of RRS and noted that a statewide observance of National Sexual Assault Awareness Week was occurring the following week. She mentioned TBN marches in Augusta and in Bangor on April 24th and 25th, respectively. A request had been made to all churches for a statewide bell-ringing at noon on Sunday, the 26th, to acknowledge this special week. Wichers then presented a questionnaire which she invited readers to answer. Questions asked about rape statistics and definitions. Responses could be sent to RRS, where the results would be compiled for publication one month later in the BDN. No records exist to indicate that survey results were compiled or published in the newspaper. The letter concluded with a description of what RRS provided with the help of volunteers. Although the RRS address was provided at the end of the letter for return of the questionnaire, neither the hotline number nor the office number was printed.

An article about the march and speak-out that Wichers had noted in her letter to the editor was written by Darlene Henderson of the BDN on April 22nd. The purpose of the event was "to heighten awareness of child sexual abuse and incest in Maine," and the organizer was "a newly formed People Against Child Sexual Abuse in Maine [PACSAM]." Burkhart, identified as "clinical director of Rape Response Services, Bangor" was one of six speakers. Five students in a community organization course at the University of Maine organized the event and co-founded PACSAM. One of the students, Jenny Johnson Winship, was quoted in the article: "It was realized that a stop-sexual-abuse campaign, organized with the same determination as that of Mothers Against Driving Drunk, was needed."

Long-term goals of PACSAM were listed: "coordination of information about support services available in the state; modification of legislation to provide a more just and protected environment for children; increased training and education in schools; the development of quality and affordable treatment facilities for survivors and perpetrators; and the continued effort to raise public awareness." Jim Green, another student organizer, "said that national statistics indicated 'one in every three to four girls will have been sexually abused by the age of 18; one in every six to 10 boys will have been sexually abused by that age; and 90 percent of the perpetrators are known to the child victim—often a parent, relative or other care-provider. Child sexual abuse occurs in all social, ethnic, religious and socio-economic groups.'" The second planned event of PACSAM was an organizational meeting in mid-May at the RRS office; no record exists about this or future meetings of PACSAM.

The September 12th/13th weekend section of the BDN contained an extensive description of many activities that were to occur at the University of Maine during the "annual Rape and Sexual Assault Awareness Week" that was held on campus at the beginning of each school year. According to the article, the week would begin with the "creation and dedication of a 'memorial' to anyone who has been victimized or affected by the crime of rape." The "memorial" was built as people tied red ribbons on a rope that was strung among trees near Fogler Library at the end of the Mall, a large grassy area in the center of campus. Participants could tie a ribbon on the "memorial" for every person they knew who had been raped or sexually assaulted or whose life had been affected by sexual crimes. Ribbons would be available throughout the week at a table on the Mall. "The purpose of the 'memorial,'" the article continued, "is to show support by recognizing and talking about the crimes of rape and sexual assault." Burkhart was to lead a discussion, "Understanding Rape Trauma Syndrome," during the week.

Money Matters

The Stay-at-Home Ball was again offered as a fundraiser on a Saturday at the end of June with music provided by WPBC-FM, Brite 93. The response card offered the option of being billed monthly, semi-annually, quarterly, or annually for any donations. One-time gifts were also accepted. The same levels of giving as in earlier invitations were listed. Those who could not contribute were encouraged to return the card if they were "interested in learning more about [*the*] organization."

Incongruous with the late-June date of the event was the invitation's new cover drawing of a blazing fire in a fireplace. Another report indicated that the net proceeds from the event were $775 plus. The garage sale earlier in June earned $454 for RRS.

A copier was donated to RRS by Vascular Associates in Bangor. Non-profit mailing status was approved in September 1992. Wichers negotiated an annual $1500 contract with Husson College for on-campus services similar to those provided at the University of Maine

The final financial report for the period ending September 30, 1992, the end of the two-year contract which Mullen-Giles had written, was signed by Wichers. Expenses exceeded income by $6743 because only $9256 was received from donations and fundraising instead of the budgeted $16,260. Personnel expenses were also higher with two employees serving as co-directors.

A new contract for the fiscal year that began on October 1, 1992 was also prepared by Wichers. The funding sources in the contract with DHS included SFPSS at $29,061; Preventative Health & Health Services Block Grant (PHHSGB), a new federal fund at $1644; and VOCA, now renamed Crime Victims Assistance Program (CVAP) at $9500. The value of in-kind volunteer advocate hours was estimated to be $87,600 (five dollars per hour for two on call each day). Program goals and objectives in the contract were focused on the hotline with the intent to provide 220 direct service hours and individual advocacy to at least 200 victims. The need to "provide services to victims in the outlying regions of catchment area" was again mentioned. Four support groups with ten incest survivors in each would be initiated, and 40 new volunteer advocates were to be recruited and trained. Continuing education for all staff and volunteers was listed as a way to "increase effectiveness of services."

Community education plans outlined in the contract were listed:

- *Six workshops for professionals, three hours each*
- *Forty contact hours with clergy and one eight-hour conference*
- *Twenty classroom presentations, 90 minutes each*
- *Ten civic/professional presentations, ninety minutes each*
- *Ten TV, radio, newspaper interviews and three marches/ speak outs*

- *Three workshops at Husson College, two hours each*
- *Six workshops at University of Maine, two hours each*

Hotline Volunteers

By the end of the calendar year, statistics showed that the RRS Board's desire to maintain basic hotline services during the transition to co-directors had been achieved. As an example, statistical forms prepared by Burkhart for five months recorded 74 advocacy hours provided in March for 52 clients and 18.5 hours in May for 17 clients. The hour and client numbers in March included support groups. Hotline hours were provided by a large number of volunteers, with 16 attending the early September advocates' meeting.

A PSA in the BDN on August 20, 1992, was titled "Training sessions for hotline workers":

> *Rape Response Services is accepting applications for hotline counselors* [sic], *Jennifer Burkhart, clinical director for the agency, has announced. Qualifications are minimal: you must be at least 18 years old, but there is no upper limit. "The things I look for are compassion and patience," said Burkhart. "We need people who can understand our callers' pain, and who can be patient with someone who often can only cry for the first few minutes they have you on the phone. Sometimes it's hard for a victim to talk about an assault, especially if it's just happened."*
>
> *The thirty-hour training session covers in detail the differences between rape, sexual assault and incest. Advocates learn the dynamics of rape—what kinds of people commit this violent crime, what causes them to rape, and how to deal with its aftermath. Also included are visits to a hospital emergency room and District Attorney's office. In addition, volunteers are briefed on the legal ramifications of sexual assault.*

Responding to the PSA, 21 potential advocates participated in the fall training; 19 completed all the sessions and volunteered on the hotline. Whether or not they learned what caused people to rape, as stated in the PSA, could not be determined. No pre-test or post-test was ever administered to the RRS trainees.

As they joined the 16 advocates already taking shifts on the hotline, this large group of new volunteers helped RRS usher in the next year on a positive note. What no one could foresee was the additional turmoil that the agency would experience in 1993.

1993: OPTIMISTIC ABOUT THE FUTURE

D espite optimism about the volunteers, RRS continued to experience growing pains in the fifth year of its existence as a new entity. Many changes in Board leadership and membership, as well as more personnel turnover, created uncertainty about the future direction of the agency.

Personnel Changes

Wichers left RRS in June, and Burkhart became the sole ED. At the same time, Wendy Norko volunteered as a hotline advocate and represented the advocates on the Board. She was hired as the Administrative Assistant to Burkhart early in August for 15 hours per week.

Outreach (Newsletter)

Volume 1 Number 2 of *Outreach* was published in the spring. Board members, Forget and Hudson Paine, were profiled. Staff members, newsletter staff, and Board members (except Cook) remained the same as in the first issue, printed the previous year. A new Board President, Moirs, replaced Bowler, and Hudson Paine had taken Moirs' place as Board Secretary.

Latona Torrey, an advocate, was profiled. She wrote:

> *I am a feminist woman, a mother and a student at the University of Maine in Orono. I am a social work major, and am in the process of doing my senior field practicum placement at RRS. I immensely enjoy my work at this organization and the people I work with. I am a mother of a 24 year old daughter and a 20 year old son. Other work I have done has included being a stay-at-home mom*

for fifteen years, working in a private school as a teacher's aid [sic]*, working for a small Maine country inn as a bookkeeper, hostess and waitress. One of my most interesting jobs was working as a ranger at Baxter State Park after my divorce. I enjoy spending time with friends...cooking, eating, and conversing with them. But my favorite social love is hiking, especially long distance hiking. My greatest hiking experience (to date) is that I am one of the 350 women who have ever hiked the entire Appalachian Trail (2,144+ miles).*

A short article titled "New Life for Violence Against Women Act" presaged Federal legislation that was to figure prominently in RRS history over the next 15 years: "The Senate Judiciary Committee has given top priority to the Violence Against Women Act, according to Sen. Joseph Biden, committee chair. The legislation, which addresses sexual assault and domestic violence would make gender-based violence a federal 'hate crime.' The bill was approved by the Senate Judiciary Committee and the House Judiciary Subcommittee on Crime and Criminal Justice in 1991, and appears certain of a hearing soon after the 103rd Congress convenes." Maine Senator William Cohen was credited in the newsletter as a co-sponsor of a federal law which made stalking a criminal act. The legislation would address "the lack of effective state laws protecting innocent people from stalkers" by holding hearings to develop a model anti-stalking law for states.

The weekend edition of the BDN on April 17th/18th described an upcoming march and rally on April 30th: "Speakers will be Chris Almy, Penobscot County District Attorney; Sharon Barker, director of the Women's Resource Center at UMaine; Katie Moirs, president of the RRS Board of Directors; and Don Carrigan, district representative for Sen. William S. Cohen. The event was planned to call attention to a rapid increase in violent crimes against women. Jennifer Burkhart, clinical director for RRS, said that 78 sexual assaults happen each hour in the United States—one every 46 seconds, 24 hours a day. Almy will explain steps law enforcement officials must take before prosecution. Carrigan will speak on the Violence Against Women Act and the stalking bill, both cosponsored by Sen. Cohen in Congress." A photo by Bob DeLong, printed two weeks later in the BDN, showed many women carrying signs and marching through downtown Bangor, "calling attention to Sexual Abuse [sic] Awareness Month." One prominent sign asked "What Part of

NO Don't You Understand?"

The next issue of *Outreach* in Summer 1993, a "Community Education Project of Rape Response Services," contained a column "From the Director's Desk" which highlighted the march and speak-out on the last day of Sexual Assault Awareness Month: "Approximately 50 people marched through downtown Bangor carrying signs that read 'Kids Don't Lie,' 'Friends Don't Force Friends,' and 'No Means No.' The march proceeded to West Market Square where additional people gathered for the speak-out."

The ED's column in *Outreach* continued: "In April, RRS hosted its annual Advocate Appreciation Night. We enjoyed an evening of bowling, pizza and fun. RRS welcomes the opportunity to thank advocates and to formally recognize our advocates for their service and dedication." Several local organizations were listed and thanked for their donations of goods or services to the Advocate Appreciation Night, including Doug's Shop 'n Save, The Grasshopper Shop, Johnson Florist, Miller's Restaurant, Plus Video, Regis Hairstyle, and Family Fun Lanes.

Two co-facilitated support groups for survivors of incest had been held during the spring, according to the newsletter. A total of 12 participants "learned they were not alone in dealing with incest. Both groups did excellent work dealing with personal growth issues as well as dealing with subjects such as anger, guilt, confronting family members, and how to manage memories of their abuse."

A tear off portion of *Outreach* could be returned with a donation "to help RRS continue its work!" Burkhart's title was ED, the only staff listed, along with Board members Moirs (President), Veeder (Treasurer), Holly Stover, Bowler, England, Estler, Forget, Rampe, and Sockbeson. Rampe was profiled:

> *I've been on the Board of RRS since its infancy, when we were setting initial goals and looking forward to the day we could hire our first director. My main jobs have been with the Personnel and Clinical Committees; I also helped with the first Advocate Training and have served as the staff's advisor. Throughout my involvement I've been impressed with both the commitment all RRS folks have shown to providing quality services and the genuine caring people have shown toward each other.*

The Winter 1993 issue of *Outreach* included a lead article: "4 [*sic*] Bangor Women Victims of Attacks." Three women in the Bangor area had been raped and one beaten as of the first day of November. While some similarities existed, "there does not seem to be a definite pattern tying all four assaults together." Females were urged by police to take "normal precautions." An adjacent article offered a "Sport PAAL personal alarm" as a possible holiday gift for "your widowed Auntie Em who lives alone." This "cheerful yellow" device could be obtained from RRS for $36.00. Complete with a belt clip and sensor attachment, the PAAL, with batteries included, "slips neatly into door jamb or window frame and emits a brain-frying sound if anyone attempts to break in." The proposed 1993-94 budget included $150 revenue from the sale of PAALs.

Stover, who had been a member of the Board of Directors for six months, was recognized for her service as she left the area to take a new position. Area legislators Sean Faircloth, Mary Cathcart, and Deborah Plowman, were also recognized "for their continued support." No Advocate profile was included in this issue of the newsletter. Reaching out to a friend when in crisis was the focus of the meditation, with a friend being "even a voice on the other end of the phone line."

Two telephone numbers for the administrative office were listed in the newsletter: 945-5597 and 941-2980. A change-over to the latter number might have occurred at this time, when RRS was also contemplating a move into a larger suite at 157 Park Street.

Money Matters

The "Fifth Anniversary Stay-at-Home Ball" was held on a Saturday in late July. Another radio station, WSHZ 92.9 "Soft Hits," provided the music for dancing from 8 to 11 P.M. Although the call letters later changed to WEZQ, this station (92.9) would continue to sponsor the Ball during the remaining 14 years of its existence. Later reports indicated that the 1993 Ball had gross receipts of $1545 and expenses of $92.77. The "fifth anniversary" apparently referred to the five years in which RRS had been in existence instead of the fifth annual ball, as there are no records of this event in 1991.

Burkhart prepared the DHS contract for the fiscal year beginning October 1st. SFPSS funding had decreased to $25,773, CVAP remained at $9500, and PHHSBG increased to $3402, for a total in DHS funds of $38,675. For the first time the budget income summary in the contract listed $1300 to be received from county and towns, plus $2800 from the University of Maine and $1500 from Husson College. In-kind income from hotline volunteers remained the same at $87,600. At a meeting of the Board on August 25th, Burkhart was authorized to execute contracts in the name of RRS, and both Burkhart and Veeder were authorized to submit requests for payments. This Board action was attested by Moirs' signature as Board President.

The DHS contract funds were divided into 12 equal payments and mailed to RRS at the beginning of each month. Spelled out in Rider B of the contract were the dates on which each of the financial and program reports had to be mailed to DHS. Neither the payment schedule nor the reporting requirements changed during the ensuing years; sometimes both checks and reports arrived late.

Program Plans

A program overview was prepared by Burkhart and appeared in the DHS contract: "RRS operates and supervises a 24 hour per day sexual assault crisis hotline. Thirty volunteer advocates assist victims and/or significant others to access (within our catchment area) counseling and support services appropriate to their needs. During the grant period 1993-1994, RRS will train approximately 30 volunteers to serve as hotline advocates and assist the program in community education. [*The volunteer training was described elsewhere as thirty hours of classes plus approximately fifteen hours of outside reading.*] RRS will organize and supervise four support groups for survivors of sexual assault." The number of individuals to be served on the hotline was 355, with an additional 40 to participate in the support groups.

As stated in the contract overview: "RRS has a strong wish to increase its visibility, especially in the more rural areas of Penobscot County and in all of Piscataquis County. If at all financially possible, RRS will disperse more information and present more community education programs in those areas."

Several statements were provided in a program overview titled "Education" in this contract:

- *Much attention is given to information/prevention programs about date rape in all schools, public and private, high schools as well as elementary schools.*
- *Colleges and Universities are central in the focus of RRS. Once again RRS will be closely involved with the Rape Awareness Committees at the University of Maine and Husson College. We sponsor Rape Awareness Weeks in addition to participating in ongoing educational programming.*
- *Education via posters and written materials (in so far as monies allow) put in central places, particularly in remote areas in Penobscot and Piscataquis counties.*
- *Upon request we hold workshops or seminars for any group that invites us.*
- *Radio and television presentations are frequent occasions for education to a larger audience.*
- *We are developing a relationship with* [Penobscot] *Job Corps and will be assisting in a Rape Awareness Week* [there].

Specific objectives to achieve the above community education goals were listed:

- *Direct contacts with local TV and radio stations; the PR* [Public Relations] *committee* [of the Board] *will address this need.*
- *Participating in health fairs sponsored by local schools.*
- *Providing presentations to schools; we plan to send a packet of information and brochures to each middle school, Jr. high and Sr. high in Penobscot and Piscataquis counties; also included will be descriptions of programs we are offering.*
- *Preparing a quarterly newsletter to be distributed to all financial contributors, schools, social service agencies, legislators, etc.*
- *Offering volunteer training programs to train volunteers to participate in speaking engagements and community education programs.*
- *To continue negotiation of policies and procedures in various*

systems, including criminal justice, mental health, medical and social services. We plan to continue being involved with trainings to professionals (physicians, E.R. staff, police officers, staff of other social service agencies). We also plan to work with local, statewide and national sexual assault committees. Locally, we serve on three rape awareness committees (U. Maine, Husson College, and Job Corps), and serve as consultants to other agencies. Statewide, we are members of the Maine Coalition Against Rape [MCAR, formerly MCR] and serve on various committees through that organization.

- *To provide consultations with third parties about sexual assault issues. This may include partners, family members, friends, law enforcement officials, medical personnel, therapists, etc.*
- *To provide technical assistance to students. We currently are supervising two senior practicum students and two junior interns. We also respond to numerous requests for information from students throughout the year.*
- *To provide assistance in a court watch program.*

Annual Report and End-of-Year Fundraising Letter

The 1993 Annual Report, a first for RRS, addressed the personnel changes in a section titled "1993—Looking Backward" by Burkhart. "This was a year of change," were the opening words. "Mid-year I became Executive Director, and in August, Wendy Norko came on board as Administrative Assistant." After describing hotline training, student interns, and programs at Husson College and the University of Maine, Burkhart noted: "In 1993, we became a designation agency of United Way of Penobscot Valley. That means we only receive money that is specifically designated as ours by donors. For first-timers we really did rather well—almost $7000."

Burkhart's section concluded: "In evaluating our successes and accomplishments, as well as the failures, we can honestly say that at the end of 1993 we are a better, more cohesive, better functioning agency than at its beginning." The total number of advocates was 30, including one male. Seven hundred twenty-four contacts were made to RRS in

1993. New clients numbered 247; on-going, 257. Twenty-six trips to the hospital were made with "victims." Six professional trainings were held with 106 participants. Over 1400 people participated in over 50 hours of community education.

Another section of the Annual Report, "1994—Looking Forward," by Burkhart mentioned: "We hope to accomplish a great deal. We have set our fundraising goals higher than last year and are planning to make a number of grant applications, at least one of which will be for capital improvement. We also hope to be able to do some meaningful work on outreach in 1994, as well as begin building at least one program which will be income-producing."

Board members listed on the Annual Report included Moirs as President, with an asterisk noting that she had resigned. Under Moirs' name, Estler and Rampe appeared as "Co-President." Noted in other documents were the dates of November 30, 1993, for Moirs' resignation, and January 26, 1994, for election of the "Interim Co-Presidents." Other names on the Board of Directors list were Eileen Gervais, Patti Woolley, Deb Mitchell, England, Forget, Sockbeson, Bowler, Polyot, and Veeder.

Another logo for RRS was developed sometime during 1993. The line drawing of a woman weeping in the foreground appears in a box above the script, "Rape Response Services." Two heads in the background suggest comfort for the woman. The new logo figured prominently on the cover of a fundraising letter signed by Burkhart at the end of 1993. "The most wonderful time of the year!" was printed on a fold over section, with "wonderful" crossed out and replaced by "dangerous." The letter was printed inside:

> *Somewhere, someone sits <u>weeping</u>, dreading the holidays with its reminders of a <u>sexual assault</u> that took place at <u>this season</u> last year, five years ago, decades ago. Every year, the season you and I eagerly welcome means sadness and fear to countless women—and men, too. Their <u>enjoyment</u> of this festive time is tainted because sexual assault and harassment do not go away for the holidays. Instead, the numbers and kinds of <u>social events</u> with an endless supply of <u>alcoholic beverages</u> offer almost unlimited <u>opportunities</u> to those who <u>prey</u> on the vulnerable. The increased volume of sexual assaults turns this joyous season into the <u>most dangerous time of the year</u>!*

Recipients of the letter were encouraged to send a year-end donation to RRS. "Your <u>investment</u> in RRS is an investment in a <u>better, safer community</u> for you, your children, wife, sister, brother, husband, father or mother." The tax-deductible financial donations would support hotline improvement, recruitment of advocates, and initiation of more support groups.

The 1994 priorities listed at the end of the fundraising letter included:

- *<u>sexual harassment training</u> in the schools*
- *<u>more community outreach</u> education programs*
- *<u>increased work</u> with physically and mentally disabled survivors*
- *<u>more intensive recruiting</u> for hotline volunteers*
- *<u>more innovative training</u> opportunities*
- *<u>increased liaison</u> with the <u>law enforcement</u> community*
  [emphasis in original]

A postscript to the letter suggested: "If you know a survivor of sexual assault a gift to RRS would be a thoughtful way to express your support and concern." Both the United Way logo and the "new" RRS logo were printed on the back of the fundraising document. The Board member listing was the same as in the 1993 Annual Report, with no officers so designated.

Burkhart's statements in the DHS contract and at the end of the year were optimistic about the future of RRS. Many activities were planned. The center could take pride in a large number of hotline volunteers who continued to provide services, despite staff and Board upheaval.

1994: VOLUNTEERING AT RRS

Walker's involvement in RRS began as a financial donor and expanded to participation at the hotline training sessions in the fall of 1994. No one at that time, especially Walker, predicted what the future would hold based on these simple actions.

An Inside Look at Hotline Volunteering

The RRS Mission Statement had been condensed during April and would remain the same throughout the next several years, appearing on many publications. The final revised version of this statement read: "To offer hope, understanding, support, and advocacy to victims of sexual assault and their significant others, and to educate the communities of Penobscot and Piscataquis counties about all aspects of this violent crime."

Offering "hope, understanding, support, and advocacy to victims" was the responsibility of the RRS hotline volunteers. For several years, Walker had considered volunteering on the RRS hotline but had not taken the initiative until early September 1994 when she responded to a notice in *The Weekly* on August 27th: "Rape Response Services is looking for volunteers to answer calls to its Bangor hotline from people who have been sexually assaulted. The agency is interviewing prospective advocates. A training class will begin Oct. 4. Training takes about 35 hours." A graduate student in social work at the time, Walker called the RRS office and requested a Volunteer Application form. In response to the telephone call, a form letter was received from Burkhart/LeClair (formerly Burkhart), ED:

Thank you for your interest in volunteering for Rape Response Services. RRS has a wonderful group of volunteers who work shifts on our 24-hour hotline. We need people like you to continue to provide crisis counseling, support and education to victims of sexual assault.

Enclosed is a volunteer application for our 1994 Fall training. Please fill it out and return it to RRS as soon as possible. When I receive your completed application, I will contact you for an interview and provide you with complete details on the training schedule and hotline procedures. The first training session will be held on Tuesday, October 4, 1994 at 6:00 P.M.

Thank you for your interest. It is the spirit and dedication of individuals such as you that makes Rape Response Services possible in the community. I am looking forward to meeting you.

Walker's reason for completing the application was: "I wish to volunteer where my services and training are needed." Two things she could offer the program were: "I am a good listener who does not panic in a crisis, and who is comfortable with telephone contact. I also have some experience with crisis intervention via the telephone in previous employment."

The application asked if anyone Walker knew (or she personally) had ever been a victim of sexual assault or another violent crime, or had she ever witnessed a violent crime. She answered "No" to both these questions. She also did not expect to have any difficulties dealing with a long list of prospective clients ("minority women, prostitutes, drunk or high women [*sic*], welfare mothers, incest victims, lesbians, and children") because "I have had experience working with all these groups in volunteer or employed situations, and have acquired additional skills through my graduate school education."

When answering a question about being especially comfortable or well-qualified to deal with a particular client, Walker stated: "I have worked and studied extensively in the area of PTSD [*post traumatic stress disorder*]." The question pertaining to prior training/experience in advocacy, counseling and/or sexual victimization prompted this response: "I interned and then worked full-time at the Bangor Vet Center, where I counseled, one-on-one and in groups, both Vietnam veterans and/or their significant others, many of whom were victims of sexual abuse."

"Being able to help people" was what Walker expected to find most rewarding; "avoiding burnout" was seen as most difficult. She was willing to make a one-year commitment to RRS and had never been convicted of a felony or misdemeanor.

A few days after mailing back the application, a telephone call from Penny Day, graduate student intern at RRS, set up an interview on Tuesday morning, September 20th at the RRS office. The building at 157 Park Street where RRS was located was owned by Pro Realty (David Giroux and Jack Cashman). Carol Pomroy, the long-time housekeeper for this building and others owned by Pro Realty, became a good friend to RRS and to Walker personally. None of the suites at 157 Park Street had its own restroom facilities. Communal restrooms were available on the second and third floors of the building.

By the end of March in 1994, RRS had moved from Suite One at the bottom of the front stairs to the much larger Suite Six, also below ground level, where it would remain until July 2008. The outer door opened into a space which became the welcoming area where future Volunteer Coordinators had a desk. This led into a much bigger room which was used for volunteer trainings, support groups, and all meetings. The doors to three separate offices opened off this room. One was larger than the others, the ED's office. A large kitchen area with a shelf on two walls and a sink was located behind the reception/welcoming area. This room had one of the two windows in the suite, both at ground level and sometimes completely blocked by snow. A long narrow room that one passed through to get to the kitchen housed the copier and a bookcase that contained office supplies.

Walker knew Day somewhat because they were both in the Social Work program at the University of Maine. She was the person who corrected Walker's misconception that hotline calls were taken at a central location/office where advocates went to wait for the telephone to ring. This was and continued to be a common misunderstanding of the hotline procedure. That every advocate was provided with a pager to use when on call was something Walker and other prospective volunteers had not considered.

The interview must have gone well, and the references checked out, because Walker began the volunteer training on October 4th from 6 to 9 P.M. Her journal entry for this date noted: "Training at RRS with a mixed bag of women from college age to older than me." The large group of 17 at the beginning included Kristan Rancourt who was to remain a volunteer throughout Walker's tenure at RRS, Karen Grotton, and new employee, Delina Rowe, who had been hired at the end of September for 15 hours per week as Volunteer Coordinator.

Hotline training sessions were taught by Cecilia Adams, another social work intern, and Burkhart/LeClair. The "Advocate Training Manual" that was used had been created by MCR in 1987/88 as a collection of handouts and other materials from the centers' own volunteer trainings. Completely revised and professionally printed by MCR within the next five years, with another revision being developed in 1993, the manual that was given to Walker was the pre-1993 edition. A lighted candle in front of an outline of the state on the cover page depicted the MCR's motto: "lighting the way to understanding sexual assault and violence." RRS provided the red loose leaf binders that contained copies of the comprehensive manual that was initially funded by MCR and given to all advocates.

(Note: By this time, the Maine Coalition on Rape [MCR] had changed its name twice, first to the Maine Coalition Against Rape [MCAR] as noted in 1993 and finally to the Maine Coalition Against Sexual Assault [MECASA]. The latter change had been proposed in May 1994 and became official in October. MECASA was comprised of ten sexual assault or rape crisis centers which were partially funded by DHS throughout the state. In addition to RRS, other centers were located in Augusta, Brunswick, Ellsworth, Farmington, Lewiston, Norway, Portland, Presque Isle, and Waterville.)

Printed tabs delineated the separate sections of the original manual and separated the more than 200 pages into topics that were covered at the training sessions. These included rape or sexual assault, special populations that could be victimized (elderly, male, adolescent, disabled, adolescent, homosexual), child sexual abuse, ritualistic abuse, sexual harassment, medical and legal protocols, mental health concerns, and crisis intervention.

What was stressed most clearly throughout the training was that advocates were not counselors, and were not to meet in person with any callers except at the hospital, police station, or in court. The role of the advocate was to provide crisis intervention on the telephone, answering questions, offering resources, and listening for as long as necessary to get the caller through the crisis that precipitated picking up the telephone.

Guest speakers at the training sessions included a law enforcement officer, a representative from the DA's office, a therapist, and staff members from local social service agencies including domestic violence projects, the Eastern Maine AIDS office, and the Mabel Wadsworth Women's Health Center. Advocates were expected to read relevant sections of the manual before each training session.

The most useful parts of the manual were the boxes scattered throughout each section and labeled "Considerations for Advocates." In the first section on rape, for example, the box noted that advocates needed to: "Understand that you are asking a lot when you ask a victim to trust you. It may be very difficult for that person to trust anyone at that time. You can help by telling them exactly what you can do for them and then following though as promised."

At the end of the manual were two pages of possible ways to begin open-ended questions that would elicit more than a one-word answer from the caller. "I'm glad you called" and "What would you like to see happen?" were two examples. "Why" questions were to be avoided because of their victim-blaming tendencies. Saying "I understand" was also not acceptable; no two situations would ever be completely alike. Trainees were also advised to not tell a caller what to do, even when asked directly. The best response was to provide options and always leave the final decision up to the caller.

Two sections at the end of the manual, "Resources" and "Policies and Procedures," were provided at the last training session. An extensive listing of area therapists who had been surveyed and were available for referrals was invaluable for advocates. Contact information for these 20 or more individuals, and their particular areas of expertise, could be offered to callers who requested such services. A survey to update this list was sent to therapists every two or three years, and new pages were printed for the manuals.

After the first week, three-hour training sessions were held mostly on Tuesdays and sometimes on Thursday nights. For the November 15th session, the group met at St. Joseph Hospital where the rape protocol exam was described by an RN who performed the exams.

The final training session in mid-November consisted of role playing which Walker had also done in a social work class earlier in the day. As noted in her journal for that date: "Role plays in class, at RRS, left me feeling unsure." New advocates were given copies of policies in effect at that time, including how to block both call waiting and caller identification on home phones before taking hotline calls. The answering service could patch calls through to the caller if blocking could not be done. Later that week, Walker officially completed the training by taking a practice call. Her journal entry noted that "the practice RRS call was affirming."

Advocates were also advised about the RRS policy to always use a secure telephone line when calling a client or when making any calls about a client, to ensure confidentiality. The preferred telephone was a corded landline phone, and advocates were reminded to return all hotline calls in a physical location that was free of distractions and private, even if this meant telling the answering service to have backup take the call.

All 12 women who completed the training signed release forms authorizing RRS "to obtain information about me from the State Bureau of Identification (SBI) and DHS. I understand that any information obtained will only be used to determine my eligibility to be a Rape Crisis Volunteer Advocate." The forms sent to SBI in the Department of Public Safety, a division of Maine State Police, requested all conviction data on file for each individual who signed a form. A date of birth was required. DHS required a list of trainees, not separate forms, with other names and date of birth for each person. The report from DHS listed any cases of child abuse or neglect attributed to the prospective volunteer. These background checks were required by DHS; reports of convictions or abuse could result in dismissal of RRS staff members and advocates. Copies of the results of the background checks were retained in the personnel or advocates' files.

Trainees also signed copies of the Policy of Disclosure and Confidentiality:

> When a RRS Advocate knows or has reasonable cause to suspect that any person who is less than eighteen years of age has received or is likely to receive a threat to such person's health or welfare by physical or mental injury or impairment, sexual abuse or exploitation, a

deprivation of essential needs, or lack of protection from any of these, by another who is responsible for the person under eighteen years of age, then such Advocate shall immediately report same to the Department of Human Services, or cause a report of same to be made through the RRS Program Coordinator [sic]. If the Advocate reports directly to DHS, she must also report to the Coordinator.

No written records of any communication with or about a client shall be made by any RRS Advocate except as required by the forms provided to the Advocates by RRS for that purpose. The written records of all communications between any agent or employee of RRS and any client shall be maintained in a file in the office of RRS and shall not be removed therefrom [sic] or disclosed without the express approval of the Director of RRS. Such files shall be locked whenever unattended by a RRS Advocate or employee.

Confidentiality was covered in Part 2 of the policy:

All information about clients or their family members that comes to RRS Advocates through their association with RRS is confidential. This information may come from a victim of actual or attempted sexual assault or harassment, or it may come from any person involved with such a victim, including other Advocates. The information may come over the Hotline, through face-to-face contact with a victim, or through the process of in-house case review. Occasionally, individuals reveal rape trauma as a result of social contact with an Advocate.

No information is to be disclosed to family members or friends of the client, to community agencies' staff, to police officers, doctors, lawyers or others without the expressed consent of the client. No information is to be revealed to friends or family members of the Advocate without the client's consent. Advocates should seek support from the Program Director [sic] or other members of the RRS Hotline staff, when needed. Support is also available through the case review process at the monthly Advocates' meeting. When discussing this information with other RRS personnel, caution must be exercised to protect the privacy of the client. An Advocate's association with RRS may be terminated if confidentiality is broken.

A second document which was signed on the last night of training was titled "RRS Volunteer Guidelines":

> In order to assure the safety of our Hotline Advocates, the following guidelines have been adopted by RRS.
>
> 1. Hotline Advocates will identify themselves by their first names only.
> 2. Hotline Advocates will not give out their home or work phone numbers.
> 3. Hotline Advocates will meet victims only for the initial referral at the Emergency Department of the hospital. Advocates are not to go to a victim's home, or meet him/her in out-of-the-way places. Follow up meetings must take place in public areas such as restaurants, etc.
> 4. Hotline Advocates will not transport victims at any time.
> 5. Hotline Advocates will not take a victim to their own home for any reason.
> 6. While on call, Hotline Advocates will remain substance free.
> 7. Confidentiality will be strictly adhered to unless:
>   a. Report must be made to CPS [Child Protective Services] as mandated by law.
>   b. Hotline Advocate is subpoenaed to court.
>   c. Hotline Advocate believes that someone's life is in danger.
> 8. Hotline Advocates must agree to attend one staff meeting per month. When a volunteer staff person's presence is required and they are unable to attend, they must call the RRS office in order to obtain information distributed or discussed at the meeting.
> 9. Advocates will fill out reporting forms after handling each call, and will submit them promptly to the RRS office. A copy of any written report submitted to CPS must be sent to the RRS office.
>
> As a volunteer Advocate for RRS, I agree to abide by these guidelines, and release RRS from any liability if I do not adhere to this agreement. Non-adherence to the guidelines may lead to dismissal.

The monthly advocates' meeting in December was a holiday party at Rowe's home in Brewer. New advocates were given certificates which marked the completion of training, a practice that was continued through the years. Because of the move into a larger suite at Park Street, spring hotline training had not been held, and the 12 new advocates were warmly welcomed.

It was at this meeting where advocates learned from Burkhart/ LeClair that she was leaving RRS. Staff changes continued to plague the agency. Despite having her working hours increased from 15 to 20 per week at the beginning of the year, Norko had left in mid-September, replaced by Bonnie Bates as the Administrative Assistant early in October for eight hours per week. Federal wage and tax statements filed in 1994 showed total paid wages of $30,693, including a full year for Burkhart and partial years for Norko, Rowe, and Bates.

Money Matters

Grant writing and fundraising efforts continued throughout the year. Bowler sent a letter in June to the Agnes Lindsay Trust in New Hampshire, requesting a grant of $7641 to purchase new office equipment. She identified herself as chair of the RRS Development Committee. The items that would be purchased were an Apple-Macintosh Quadra 650 for $2159, a color display monitor with a 14" Trinitron tube at $456, an extended keyboard for $150, a Ricoh FT4415 photocopier and Brother 980 Fax at $3995 and $879, respectively. Early in August a letter and $5000 check were received from Robert L. Chiesa, managing trustee. As mentioned in her letter of request, Bowler's belief was that "assistance from the Agnes M. Lindsay Trust would make an enormous difference in our capability to serve our clients, as well as expand our community education efforts."

Another Stay-at-Home Ball was held on Saturday, July 30th in collaboration with WEZQ 92.9. A second fundraising event was "The First Annual Pizza Tasting Extravaganza" on Sunday, September 11th from noon to 3 P.M. at the Brewer Auditorium. For a $5.00 fee ($3.00 for children under 12), guests could enjoy pizza from fifteen different booths. Vendors who contributed pizzas for this event included Pat's Pizza, Orono and Hampden; Pizza Hut, Napoli Pizza, Pizza Palace, Cosmo's Pizza, Fairmount Market, Domino's Pizza, Spanky's, Tommy's, and Seguino's, all in Bangor; Pizza Dome and Pizza Villa, Old Town; Papa Gambino's, Brewer and Bangor; and Mike's Pizza, East Holden. Beverages were available from Coca-Cola Bottling Company of Bangor. A total of $750 was made at this event.

A Community Presence

The Penobscot County Legal Secretaries Association conducted a seminar on rape as "a continuing legal education opportunity and more importantly as a community service," according to a bright pink flyer. Held on a Saturday afternoon in January, the "Rape: Personal Safety and Awareness" event was going to "cover investigation and medical treatment, the victim's advocate, assertiveness, prosecution, the police officer's role, legislative acts, and how the Rape Crisis Center can help. We are inviting the concerned public, especially those at high risk to attend this seminar. Our mission is to educate the public so that they will be better prepared to avoid compromising situations [*sic*]." The minimal registration fee of $10.00 per person was kept low to attract "high school and college students, their friends, families, educators, in an effort to educate them on how important it is to be alert to their surroundings and what to do if a rape does occur."

Community and school presentations, the education component of the revised mission statement, were promoted by RRS in 1994. Two single-fold brochures were printed and distributed during the year to advertise available programs. Local and toll-free hotline numbers were boldly printed on the backs of both brochures. "No More 'Hostile Hallways'" was the title of one document, with the subheading: "A commonsense approach to ending sexual harassment in our schools." The brochure's title referred to an American Association of University Women (AAUW) study of sexual harassment by the same name. RRS offered "a simple comprehensive program which explains:

- how sexual harassment differs from normal banter and/or flirting
- how it hurts others
- how to combat sexism wherever you are
- how to react to someone who is sexually harassing you
- what to do if you are sexually harassed"

School personnel who received this brochure and were interested in making arrangements for this program were asked to call the RRS office. Quotes from the AAUW study were included on the brochure. Apparently as a result of the brochure, presentations on sexual harassment were made during the year by Burkhart/LeClair at 41 schools in the catchment area.

The second brochure, sent to community organizations, was titled "Candles in the Dark: Shedding Light on Sexual Assault." Offered as "a community education program," the "candles" program had three goals:

- "to explain what sexual assault is—legally and actually
- to teach commonsense avoidance skills
- to acquaint you with our services if you, a friend, relative or significant other becomes a victim of sexual assault"

Workshops could be tailored to fit the participants' schedules, and fees were negotiable. At the bottom of this brochure was printed: "Remember—No One Ever Asks Or Deserves To Be Raped."

Flyers advertising support groups "for women only" were distributed around the community and to therapists' offices during the early part of the year. Separate groups for incest survivors and for rape survivors would be focused on "information, education and support" and would run for ten or twelve weeks respectively. These single-sheet photocopied flyers advertised each group as "confidential" and "free of charge," and provided both the RRS office number and the toll-free number "for additional information." Each evening session ran from 6:30 to 8:00 P.M.

As the year ended, Walker looked forward to becoming more involved on the hotline. What the new year would hold for RRS in terms of personnel was anyone's guess, but there was a consensus among Board members and advocates that services to hotline callers would not suffer during the transition.

1995: PERSONNEL CHANGES...AGAIN

Similar to the previous years, what seemed to be a revolving door at RRS saw employees leave and be replaced by others throughout this new year. Volunteers like Walker were peripherally aware of the staff turmoil but were not informed directly until new staff was hired. Board members attempted to make sure that the hotline continued to function well, that support groups for survivors of rape or incest were ongoing, and that RRS stayed true to the original vision of rape crisis services in Bangor.

By the time Burkhart/LeClair left RRS early in the year, the Board had hired Sarah (Sally) P. Strout as ED. Strout then hired Janeen Teal to replace Rowe who also left. Teal responded to the following advertisement in the BDN dated February 9th:

VOLUNTEER COORDINATOR
15 hours per week. Rape Response Services is looking for a highly motivated individual to supervise volunteers. Bachelor's degree preferred, plus two years related experience. Strong communication and public speaking skills necessary. Competitive pay and benefits. Send resume by Feb. 24 to: PO Box 2516, Bangor, ME 04402-2516.

Hotline Volunteers

Because of Walker's graduate school schedule, she was unable to sign up for any hotline shifts until early January when she was on call from 11 P.M. until 8 A.M. the following day. The next Monday she extended this shift to one that ended at 11 P.M. on Tuesday. This was to continue to be "her shift" on the hotline throughout the year until November. A few additional shifts were picked up here and there. Instead of the original two daily twelve-hour shifts, advocates could choose from three shifts in each twenty-four-hour period: 8 A.M. to 5 P.M, 5 P.M. to 11 P.M, 11 P.M. to 8 A.M.

When Walker first took shifts, she completed the paper reporting form which she either mailed or delivered in person to the office for statistical purposes. As the years went by, with Volunteer Coordinators more consistently in place at RRS, the advocates called the office to report hotline activity, and the paper forms were completed by staff with this information. Stamped envelopes were no longer provided by RRS.

In late February, a snow day for the University of Maine when Walker was at home, her journal entry read: "pager for RRS kept me busy for a change." She would have been taking her usual twenty-four-hour shift during this time. Later on April 11th, during the same full-day shift, she "passed up a rape protocol at EMMC; I knew I couldn't handle it emotionally when I am stretched so thin right now. Luckily found someone else." The "someone else" would have been the backup person, usually staff but sometimes an advocate, who was available on every shift. It was the responsibility of the on call advocate to tell the answering service to page the backup person when a call could not be taken. Advocates did not directly call backup unless there was a need to process or talk about a call that was difficult.

At the end of March, Strout sent a memo to the advocates, commenting on meeting with them in February, and noting that she "was especially impressed with the fact that an entire month's scheduling was completed in a matter of a few minutes. I have worked with volunteer hotlines for more than thirty years and, I must confess, have never observed such an exceptional phenomenon. So, pat yourselves on the back and congratulate yourselves for a job well done."

During this time, the advocates met only every other month, despite what was written in the Guidelines. One of the agenda items for each advocates' meeting was to process difficult calls with others who may have heard from the same people. Two so-called chronic hotline callers were discussed at the June meeting, along with ideas about how to end such calls. Helping the caller to make a plan for what to do after hanging up the phone was a crucial part of the process. Usually a member of the RRS Clinical Committee, a trained therapist, was present at the meetings to help with this processing. In later years, Carol Veits, a long-time member of the RRS Clinical Committee and a licensed clinical social worker (LCSW), not only attended advocates' meetings but also was willing to be called at home or at her office by an advocate or staff member who wanted to talk about a difficult call.

The guest speaker at the October advocates' meeting, Detective Tim Jameson of Penobscot County Sheriff's Department (CSD), became a familiar name to RRS and to Walker over the next decade. Outreach to law enforcement agencies in the two counties was a vital part of the RRS mission to help victims because police officers were often the first responders to the crime of rape. Detective Jameson spoke about the three separate crime scenes when a rape occured—the victim's body, the perpetrator's body, and the physical space. The location of the rape was where it should be reported to law enforcement. Jameson mentioned that the most common defense by the perpetrator was that the sex was consensual, and cautioned advocates that the system moved slowly. "Do not lie to the victim," he said, by telling her or him that charges would be filed after a rape. Prosecuting the crime of rape or filing charges was the sole purview of the DA. Anonymous reports when the victim did not want to provide names or details were discouraged by Jameson.

The first hotline call Walker took that resulted in accompanying someone to the hospital did not occur until mid-November. Her journal entry noted: "an unexpected twist to my last shift on call—got called to ER for five hours, home at 1 A.M. Not as bad as could have been, as she had two supportive friends there, Dr. was great." Walker was glad to have a bag of clothing for the victim in her car. For many years, RRS collected new and gently used sweatshirts, sweatpants, and socks in small, medium, and large sizes, and kept a supply of them at the office for hospital calls. Advocates could take bags of these items in each size to keep in their cars and have clothing to provide to a victim who had to leave what was worn at the time of the rape for evidence. Local churches, the United Way, and other civic groups publicized the need for this clothing, and generous donations of the items were received.

Support Groups

In mid-August, Teal signed a memo to the Clinical Committee regarding support groups: "I am very concerned that as we go into the autumn we have no plans for a support group for either rape or incest survivors. As of now, we have a waiting list of eight people for the incest group and nine for the rape group. Many of these people called as early as March of this year. I am sure that if we advertised we would have sufficient numbers to run both groups. We have several advocates who are interested in becoming facilitators and are waiting to hear about training." The memo then proposed a meeting at the end of August "to discuss how to proceed with plans for facilitator training and the possibility of someone from the committee running a group this fall." Members of the committee were Laura Zegel, Terri Clarke, Rampe, and Veits.

Another memo dated early in September was sent by Teal to the Clinical Committee: "After looking in the files for information that I could pass on to you about the history of the Clinical Committee I called Nancy Rampe (because there is nothing in the files!). Nancy said that the history basically consists of this: the committee did the first advocate training in 1989, has consulted on problem situations (the cult calls), has helped out with advocate training and has acted as staff support on a minimal basis."

The memo continued: "What I am asking of you is this: to utilize what materials we have from the Coalition and pull together a two day training session for prospective group facilitators, two people to do the training (Laura Zegel has said she will be one); help out as a supervisor to groups when they begin; help out as needed during advocate training; be available to advocates to process troublesome calls. Someone needs to take on the role of chair. It sounds like a lot but in actuality I don't think it will take a great deal of time, once we have groups up and running. The primary concern is to get at least one group going this fall." Support groups were required as part of the DHS contract which did not allow RRS to charge group participants.

Money Matters

Woolley, new Board President, signed two letters dated April 5th thanking the Strouts, and Bindy and Tom Palmer, for their computer donations to RRS. The total value of the gifts was $2350. An IBM 386 and 286 were each accompanied by a 14" color monitor and a dot matrix printer, one an Epson and the other a Panasonic. A secretary's chair was also donated by the Strouts.

By the end of June, Strout had prepared and submitted the DHS contract for the fiscal year beginning October 1, 1995. The reimbursable amount from the state would remain at $38,675, with $25,773 from SFPSS, $9500 from CVAP and $3402 from PHHSBG. Woolley signed the certificate of authorization on June 23rd, attesting that Strout and Veeder were authorized at a February 22nd Board meeting to execute contracts on behalf of RRS. The program overview and goals and objectives were the same as those described in the FY'94 contract, completed two years earlier by Burkhart.

Revisions of this FY'94 contract were submitted by Woolley and Strout. A memo from Woolley to Nancy Holcomb, DHS Contract Specialist (Holcomb had replaced Jones in June) on July 6th, stated:

> *In its 1994-95 State contract, RRS committed to fundraising $15,000. As of this date, it appears that our organization may not be able to honor that obligation. Since last October, RRS has experienced a complete staff turnover. This unfortunate occurrence has required the Board members to focus their attention towards interviewing, hiring and re-aligning staff job descriptions. In addition, a number of the members rotated off the Board, as required in our by-laws. This left many tasks to be performed by few experienced Board members. RRS is currently in the process of recruiting and adding to its Board membership.*
>
> *In 1994/95, through no fault of the organization, one of the planned fundraising activities proved to be an ill-fated endeavor. A Baseball card collection,* [donated to RRS and] *valued at $8500 on November 20, 1994, was expected to add to our efforts to raise funds. Because of the nationwide* [baseball] *strike, the collection's value decreased significantly. The Board members have decided to wait until the collection increases in its value.* [Note: The collection never was sold for its assessed value.]
>
> *Recently, we launched our annual fundraising letter. We are expecting to receive a substantial response. Between now and the end of our contract year, we will also be raising funds through a pizza tasting party for University of Maine freshmen and families. The RRS Board anticipates fundraising at least $9000 before the end of this contract year. The organization and its Board members assure*

you that this year's changes have <u>not affected</u> units of service or the overall viability of the program. [emphasis in original]

Strout's memo of July 24th to Holcomb provided more details about the revisions:

> *The revised budget indicates a reduction in income and expenses from the original $59,925 to the current $51,183. The changes reflected in income are lower private funding ($9700 including United Way and other fundraising activity versus the projected $15,000) and lower program income ($1000 versus expected $2500). These two items account for an income reduction of $7800.*
>
> *The reduced expense was derived through lower personnel expenses ($34,183 versus $38,620) and generalized reductions in all other expenses. The personnel budget sheet clearly indicates the staff changes that have occurred this past year. The Executive Director was replaced in January, at a slightly reduced salary (down by 2%). The original budget was established with an anticipated 5% salary increase. The total impact reduces the Executive Director's salary by 7%.*
>
> *The Volunteer Coordinator's position was vacated in the second quarter, and the Administrative Assistant's position was vacated in the third quarter. The Volunteer Coordinator has been replaced, at the same salary but a month's service (and associated salary) was lost. The Administrative Assistant has not yet been replaced. The work is being assumed by the Executive Director. These changes have resulted in a favorable effect on personnel expenses. There were various reductions in the "all other expense" category, which was reduced from $21,305 to $17,630.*

Strout and Woolley co-signed a "Dear Friend of RRS" fundraising letter sent in July to all previous supporters whose names and addresses were on a mailing list. The letter began:

> *Since Rape Response Services' inception in October of 1987* [sic], *our advocates and professional staff have made many trips to local emergency rooms to comfort victims of sexual assault.*

> *Whether the client was male or female, adult, teenager, or child, we have found them in pain. Some ached from physical injuries inflicted by their attacker; ALL suffered from an emotional trauma far more devastating. A shot or pill will ease physical discomforts; but the passage of time, plus <u>support and empathy are the only medicines</u> for wounds of the spirit. Often, just being able to hear someone say, "It's not your fault. You are not alone," is enough to begin the long process of healing psychological and emotional wounds.*

The four-page letter continued by describing the services provided by RRS. **"It is vital that we continue to be a voice to those in crisis. With your help we will."**

Included with the letter was a list of "a week's worth of simple, affirmative steps you can take…beginning right now! Please post it where you and others can refer to it frequently." The steps were:

1. *Speak out against sexual violence.*
2. *Ask your school to host an educator from Rape Response Services.*
3. *Talk openly and honestly to your children about sex.*
4. *Teach your children to set limits.*
5. *Teach your children to respect the rights of others.*
6. *Teach your children strong moral values.*
7. *Invest in your children's future.*

The concluding paragraphs of the letter asked for "continuing financial support of RRS. **A $50 gift to Rape Response Services will make possible 2 school-based educational programs, pay for 1 survivors' support group meeting, defray the cost of training one crisis intervention advocate. A $100 contribution will purchase printed materials used in school and community education programs, pay half of the hotline telephone bill for one month, enable us to buy a new video tape to be used for advocate training and community education programs.**" [emphasis in original]

Two fundraisers during Rape Awareness Week in September at the University of Maine were scheduled to benefit RRS. "Women With Wings," a grass roots choral group from the greater Bangor area presented a concert with a suggested donation of $2.00. The second (and last) RRS Pizza Tasting Party was held at the Memorial Union on campus during the lunch hour on Saturday. A donation of $5.00 for adults or $3.00 for children under 12 enabled attendees to try pizzas from a variety of area restaurants. Donating pizzas and beverages were Pat's Pizza, L&A Market, both in Orono; Broadway Pizza Hut, Bangor Mall Pizza Hut, Harlow Street Pizza Hut, Fairmount Market, Tesoro Pizzeria, Cologero Pizza, Leadbetter's Super Stop, all in Bangor; Angelos and Governor's Restaurant, both in Old Town, and Coca-Cola Bottling Company, Bangor. Baked goods were also available for purchase, made by Board members, staff, and advocates.

Walker attended the concert and worked at the pizza party. A letter dated early in October, signed by Board member Nancy Harrison, thanked Walker for generously "supporting our 2nd Annual Pizza Tasting Extravaganza held at the University on September 23, 1995. With the help from area pizza vendors, volunteers and other business donations we were able to raise over $600 that Saturday afternoon. The funds raised will help Rape Response Services to continue to aid persons in need of support through our advocacy programs, the 24 hour hotline, incest survivors support groups, educational programs and community outreach programs. We look forward to next year's event to be even a greater success! Thank you again for your participation and continued support of Rape Response Services."

Personnel Changes Continue

Shortly after cosigning the fundraising letter in mid-summer, Strout left the agency, and Teal became the Interim Director. By the first of September, Teal was named the ED by the Board, continuing a pattern at RRS of promoting from within. Part of the reason for this practice was because staff members were required to take the volunteer training in the early weeks of their employment at RRS. Someone hired from another position within the agency would have already completed training and could hit the ground running.

The weekend edition of the BDN on September 9th/10th contained an advertisement for the position of "Administrative Coordinator" at RRS. Advocates had heard about this part-time, newly-created job prior to the official announcement. As ED, Teal wanted to continue her responsibilities as Volunteer Coordinator and did not want to be involved in financial matters. The advertisement read:

> *The person hired will report to the Director and will manage all day to day administrative aspects encompassing a wide range of duties, including the maintenance of office logistics under leadership of the Director, bookkeeping and financial management, preparation of reports to Board and funding agencies and providing support for solicitation of grants. Will occasionally represent the agency in the community. The successful candidate will have a demonstrated understanding of sexual assault and related issues. Strong organizational, interpersonal, written and oral skills necessary; grant writing experience a plus. Ability to travel to meetings statewide. 25 hours per week. $10 per hour. Send letter of application and resume by September 25th to Rape Response Services.*

Walker's recent completion of the Master's of Social Work (MSW) program inspired her to submit her resume for this position. The opening paragraph of the detailed job description which Teal sent to Walker upon receipt of her resume stated: "The Administrative Coordinator is responsible (along with the Board Treasurer) for the timely preparation and filing of all state budget reports and contracts, maintaining RRS financial records, seeking and writing grants and maintaining daily, weekly and monthly office support procedures."

Additional and specific responsibilities for this newly created position included:

- *Maintain the RRS checking and savings accounts*
- *Pay all agency bills*
- *Function as liaison with and support for Board Fundraising Committee*
- *Maintain mailing list*
- *Attend all regular Board meetings*
- *Prepare written and oral reports and ensure the preparation of a monthly financial report to be given to the Board*
- *Work with the Director to create yearly management plan for income and expenditures to be approved by the Board*

- *Responsible for coordinating clerical tasks of organization and office procedures, i.e. picking up mail, doing mailings, maintaining and organizing materials, ordering office supplies and maintaining office equipment, maintaining resource library*
- *Assist with supplying and developing educational and informational materials for clients, volunteers, communities, schools, colleges, agencies and other organizations*
- *Represent RRS at public functions and educational opportunities when necessary*
- *Represent RRS at MECASA meetings when necessary*
- *Take crisis calls on occasion*

Qualifications for the position were listed on the job description as:

- *Ability to work in a collaborative atmosphere*
- *An understanding of clinical, legal and/or political issues related to sexual assault*
- *Agreement with the philosophy and purposes of RRS*
- *Strong interpersonal skills, the ability to communicate effectively in the public arena*
- *Strong administrative skills, including budget and finance*
- *Strong writing skills*
- *Ability to be flexible regarding scheduling and other job-related contingencies*
- *Grant writing experience, or willingness to learn*
- *Contact information for three references who can speak to job qualifications*
- *Ability to travel for meetings and presentations; car and valid driver's license desirable*
- *Educational background appropriate to the responsibilities of the position*

Walker's interview was conducted by Teal and Joan Roberts, a Board member, at the RRS office near the end of September. What she remembered most about the interview was the requirement that she go into a separate room and compose and print a letter requesting funding from Penobscot County. She could thankfully close the door while Teal and Roberts waited in the larger training room. Although Walker had just completed a graduate program, she did it without the benefit of a computer, which were not widely available at the time. She used a word processor at her home and was really not familiar with computers, including those at RRS that had been donated earlier in the year. The MS-DOS program on the computer that confronted her for completion of this interview requirement was totally foreign, and Walker was either too proud or too stubborn to admit this might be a problem. After taking much longer than was necessary to create and print the requested letter, she finally rejoined Teal and Roberts.

Walker's journal early in October noted: "Accepted a paid job today in the midst of lots of volunteer activities. Feel good about it, compared to the other positions I have considered, primarily due to volunteering there and liking Janeen." Two days later Walker wrote: "Affirmed at the RRS Board meeting tonight, and wholeheartedly endorsed for position. What a good feeling I have going into this job!" A later October entry was: "What a welcoming first day on the job! A plant delivered from the Board and Janeen, and a desire from everyone to help me get settled in as smoothly as possible." Walker moved into the office with a window where she had been interviewed for the advocate training just over one year earlier.

After more than a month on the job, Walker mentioned in her journal a "longer day at office than planned, but check-writing went well, just lots to do." She was responsible for accounts receivable and accounts payable, including paychecks. A program had been set up on the computer, identical to the one which the Board Treasurer Veeder used. All checks required two signatures. Walker could sign after filing a signature card at Bangor Savings Bank, and it was her responsibility to track down either Veeder or Harrison for the second signature. Both individuals as well as the Board President were authorized to sign checks, but Woolley worked in Waterville and was not easily reached.

Two of the first financial tasks Walker faced as Administrative Coordinator were the completion of final reports to DHS for the contract year ending September 30, 1995, and a significant revision of the FY'96 contract that became effective on the first day of October. An additional $19,000 was allocated to RRS for Piscataquis County outreach in FY'96, increasing the amount of SFPSS funds to $44,773 and necessitating Walker's first attempt at a contract revision. Holcomb, DHS contract specialist, came to the RRS office in mid-November to outline the necessary steps, knowing that Walker was new to the process. Total in-kind income of $75,517 included volunteer advocates, clinical advisors, plus auditing, bookkeeping and legal services. Non-allowable expenses which had to be paid with RRS funds were coalition dues (now up to $1500) and any costs associated with fundraising ($600) such as printing and postage.

A Community Presence

A Rape Awareness Week at the University of Maine was held in mid-September with a full slate of activities. Sponsors of the events were the Rape Awareness Committee (RRS was a member), the Health Impact Group, Student Health and Prevention Services, and the Division of Student Affairs. The week began with the dedication of a "memorial" (ropes strung between trees) on the University Mall, similar to what had been done in 1992. Those attending were invited to tie a red ribbon on the "memorial" to "remember a survivor of sexual assault."

The keynote address was given by Jackson Katz, founder of Real Men, a nationally-recognized group. A presentation was made on personal safety by Deb Mitchell, a Rape Aggression Defense (RAD) instructor, former RRS Board member, and the Crime Prevention Officer in the University Department of Public Safety. Athletes for Sexual Responsibility at the University offered a video and discussion. A brown-bag session co-sponsored by RRS and the Socialist and Marxist Studies Luncheon Series was titled "Rape and the Theory of Interlocking Oppressions."

A letter to the editor from Teal was published in the BDN in early December following an article about inappropriate comments made by a naval officer and reported in an earlier November BDN edition. Teal took Admiral Macke to task for suggesting that the three Navy servicemen charged with the rape of a twelve-year-old girl in Okinawa could have visited a prostitute instead. Reminding readers that rape is not sex, Teal commented on the pervasive rape culture of which prostitution can be seen as a product. She was glad that Macke was forced to resign and hoped that the military forces would be educated about the criminal act of rape.

End-of-Year Fundraising Letter

"A Special Announcement from the Board of Directors of Rape Response Services" was mailed to RRS supporters at the end of 1995. Board members listed were Vikki Justus, Barbara Lehmann, Estler, Grotton, Harrison, Roberts, Veeder, and Woolley. The letter stated:

> We are happy to announce the hiring of Janeen Teal as Director and Kathy Walker as Administrative Coordinator of Rape Response Services. Janeen was the Volunteer Coordinator at this agency, and comes to us with many years of experience in grass roots organizing and project management. Kathy is a former municipal official and county administrator, and has been a hotline advocate for the past year. Rape Response Services welcomes these two talented and energetic women.
>
> The primary focus of the agency continues to be the provision of a 24-hour crisis counseling hotline. Fifteen new volunteer advocates have received training in the past year. [Only 13 were active on the hotline at this time.] Education of the community about sexual assault is ongoing, with outreach into schools and civic groups, and collaboration with other agencies.
>
> Members of the Board of Directors thank you for your previous support of Rape Response Services. The problem of sexual assault, unfortunately, does not go away, and the need for our services continues to increase. We hope that you will consider a generous year-end gift to this agency. Together we can work to make the new year a safe one for each of us.

A postscript at the end of the letter reminded readers to "Save the date of February 10, 1996 for our annual Stay-at-Home Ball. Details will follow." The office telephone number was provided on this letter. Enclosed with the letter were a teal-on-white response card, a return envelope, and a separate teal card which offered recipients a "Holiday Gift Opportunity: The contribution you make to Rape Response Services may be designated as a gift to honor a special person. To do so, please return this completed card and the response card in the enclosed envelope. An announcement of your gift will be sent to the person(s) you choose to honor, if you wish."

New names and faces were evident in paid positions at RRS by the end of 1995. What remained consistent throughout the year, however, was the number of dedicated hotline volunteers who continued to provide exceptional service to anyone who called to talk or to request hospital accompaniment.

1996: A PRESENCE IN PISCATAQUIS COUNTY

L ong a goal of RRS, providing services in Piscataquis County was elusive. An early decision had been made by the Board to become firmly established in the Bangor area before branching out into the rural areas. Subsequent personnel changes at RRS meant that the rural outreach had not occurred five years after first being discussed. This new year would be different.

An additional $175,000 in CVAP funds for sexual assault centers had been received by the state in the fiscal year that began on October 1, 1995. Rather than divide up this total equally among the ten centers, MECASA voted to give RRS an additional $19,000 in the DHS contract for outreach into Piscataquis and northern Penobscot counties. This funding provided the impetus for moving forward with the original RRS goal, and prompted a meeting in mid-January with Julie Plummer, ED of Womancare, the domestic violence project in Dover-Foxcroft. The purpose of this meeting, attended by Wendy O'Brien, Teal, and Walker, was to discuss ways to collaborate and make the best use of the extra dollars. O'Brien was a social work intern at RRS.

A decision was made to recruit volunteers in Piscataquis County to specifically accompany sexual assault victims to the hospitals and to court in that area. Sherri Richards was employed part-time at Womancare and, at Plummer's recommendation, she accepted an additional 15 hours a week to be the part-time Volunteer Coordinator for RRS in the Dover area. Office space for Richards was available at Womancare, which received a small monthly fee from RRS for the space, office supplies and use of office equipment.

A separate telephone line for the Dover-Foxcroft office was installed (564-8924), and POB 673 was rented in Dover-Foxcroft. Richards would complete the spring hotline training at the Bangor office. An order of the blue RRS brochures developed a few years earlier was printed with the Dover-Foxcroft address and telephone number so they could be mailed from that office. The content of the brochure did not need to be changed at that time.

Personnel Changes and Responsibilities

During the first few months of the year, Teal experienced health problems that required an extended period away from RRS. The Board made Walker the acting director in Teal's absence, and agreed with Walker's recommendation that O'Brien, who was still a student, be paid for ten hours a week to assist with volunteer coordination and training. O'Brien was co-facilitating an incest survivors' support group at the same time.

Early in April, Walker met with Dr. Patty Coleman, social work professor, and her graduate assistant, Cecilia Adams, for O'Brien's final field experience evaluation. Having recently completed the MSW program, Walker was able to assume responsibility for O'Brien's supervision at RRS, and was also familiar with the expectations. O'Brien not only met but exceeded all requirements despite the upheaval at the agency during most of her internship.

Teal left RRS in early May, leading to Walker's hiring as ED. A promotion from within once again made decisions easier for the RRS Board. Woolley sent a letter later in May to each of the advocates informing them of the changes at RRS. "Janeen Teal, the Director, has resigned effective immediately," the letter began. "Members of the Board of Directors appreciate the many contributions Janeen made to the agency, especially in the area of increasing our visibility within the community. I am pleased to tell you that Kathy Walker has been hired as Executive Director of RRS. Kathy is a hotline advocate, and has been employed as Administrative Coordinator at the agency since October. She has a Master's degree in social work, and was a counselor of Vietnam veterans and their family members at the Bangor Vet Center. Kathy held administrative positions in the town of Hampden and in Penobscot County, and is active as a volunteer in several local and state organizations. The services provided by RRS will continue uninterrupted during this transition in leadership."

An undated article from *The Weekly* was mounted in the RRS scrapbook: "Kathy Walker of Hampden has been named executive director of Rape Response Services. She is a former chairwoman of the Hampden Town Council and was most recently Penobscot County clerk. Wendy O'Brien of Bangor and Sherri Richards of Guilford are volunteer coordinators at Rape Response Services. O'Brien works in the Bangor office and Richards in Dover-Foxcroft."

Walker never did move into what had been the office used by previous EDs at RRS. That room did not have a window. Although her office was smaller, the window and other amenities convinced her to stay there throughout her tenure at RRS. At some point, the couches from the training room were moved into the former directors' office, which housed the lending library of professional resources, and became a cozy and welcoming place for interviews of volunteers and staff members.

The RRS Board agreed that Walker could continue to perform the bookkeeping jobs of cutting paychecks and paying bills that she had enjoyed since becoming Administrative Coordinator, and would be paid for thirty-five hours per week. In hindsight, this was probably not the best use of Walker's time during the ensuing years, but on the fifteenth and thirtieth day of each month, or dates closest to them, she arranged her schedule to be at the office in her role as the bookkeeper. Getting accustomed periodically to new financial software programs that were identical to those the Board treasurer used was part of the challenge.

The position of part-time Volunteer Coordinator in Bangor had been vacant since Teal became ED. O'Brien submitted her application for this job and was interviewed by Roberts and Walker early in June. The personnel committee and the full Board approved hiring O'Brien, and she began paid employment later in the month. Both Walker and O'Brien were enthusiastic about their new positions.

One of O'Brien's student responsibilities at RRS had been to preserve in scrapbooks newspaper clippings related to sexual violence. These archives became invaluable resources in future years when information gleaned from them was used in classroom and community presentations. This practice continued throughout Walker's years at RRS, with various staff members taking on the task of putting the articles in binders. Walker also began what was called the "read and initial file" where printed information (newsletters, magazine and journal articles, letters) relevant to sexual violence was placed. The expectation was that staff members would read these resources in a timely fashion.

The oversight for what staff did or did not do was the responsibility of the ED. Walker scheduled weekly supervision meetings with each staff member and student intern while at RRS, trying to meet staff in their outlying offices as much as possible. The word "supervision" came from social work education, as it is a vital part of being a licensed social worker. For many feminists, however, the word had connotations of a hierarchical structure that did not belong in a grass roots organization. Walker modeled the supervision sessions after her own experience as a social work intern. Providing an opportunity for give-and-take was her goal as the week was reviewed, plans were made, and excitement or frustration was shared.

These meetings occurred in addition to the bi-weekly staff meetings which were also scheduled occasionally in the outlying offices. Such scheduling added to the mileage reimbursement expenses for RRS, but Walker felt that this was an important commitment, and the Board agreed. To this end, Walker spent a lot of time on the road, as the Dover-Foxcroft office was about one hour away from Bangor. RRS had not had satellite offices in the past, but being a local presence, not just Bangor-based, was a goal that the agency worked hard to fulfill.

Annual evaluations of each staff member were also instituted. A form was developed to be completed separately by the staff person and by Walker. This one-page document included a space for listing three strengths, three areas for improvement, and three goals for the next year. Walker then met one-on-one with each employee to discuss the separate lists and to agree on a final evaluation which was signed by the staff person and included in her personnel file. The Board evaluated Walker annually.

Sexual Assault Awareness Month

The contract with DHS required each agency to hold an annual meeting, something that had not been done at RRS for several years. With input from the Board, plans were made to hold a dinner meeting at Pilot's Grill restaurant in Bangor early in April, the beginning of Sexual Assault Awareness Month. The invitation, which was computer-generated and photocopied, was sent to individuals who had responded to earlier fundraising appeals.

"Advocates are honored guests at the dinner and will be recognized for years of service to the agency" was typed on the invitation. Some of the guests paid $15.00 for their own dinner and an additional $15.00 for an advocate's meal. Others who could not attend sent in $15.00. Justus' husband, Dale, was a jeweler who offered to create gifts for the advocates. He crafted a two-inch pin out of silver-plate in the shape of a teardrop from the RRS logo. Charging the agency only for materials, Justus made enough pins to distribute to Board members, staff, and advocates.

What became an annual event in April was the H.O.P.E. (Help Organize Peace Earthwide) Festival sponsored by the Peace and Justice Center of Eastern Maine. Held at the Brewer Auditorium on a Saturday close to Earth Day, the room was full of tables with information from a large number of area social service agencies. Table space could be rented for a nominal fee. Volunteers assisted O'Brien and Walker at the RRS table, handing out brochures and selling coffee mugs, buttons, and bumper stickers, all leftovers at the office from previous sales attempts.

Another Sexual Assault Awareness Month event, which Teal had begun to organize, was a vigil and march against sexual assault on the last Friday of April in the evening. A notice in the April 20th edition of *The Weekly* invited people to "bring a candle and take a stand against sexual assault." The event began in the parking lot behind 157 Park Street, from which participants walked to the corner of Union and Main Streets. The steeple of the historic Unitarian Church at this corner had been lit all month to bring attention to sexual assault. A large banner in front of the church explained the reason for the lighting and included the RRS hotline number.

Roxanne Moore Saucier provided extensive coverage of the event in the BDN on April 27th. Accompanied by a photo taken by Bob DeLong, the article began:

> *She came to the vigil, to the march, because she herself had been raped—and no one had listened. So on Friday evening, she joined a couple of dozen women, men and children, and spoke out against sexual assault.*
>
> *The rape happened a few years ago, when she was home on break after her first semester of college. The boy who assaulted her was someone she had been dating. "I told someone I thought I*

could trust immediately," she said before the vigil, *"but that person didn't really believe me. I clamped up. It was very important to have someone to go to who would listen...I doubted myself. I felt like it was my fault."*

Healing is a longtime process, she said. *"It starts with being a victim, and moving on to being a survivor. There's a stage beyond— that's living."* Moving through the stages requires *"taking the shame away and placing it where it belongs,"* she said, *"with the perpetrator."*

Now she's an advocate, making sure there's someone there to reach out a hand or be on the other end of the phone when a victim of sexual assault needs to tell. Now she can come forward *"to show support for many of the women, children and some men who don't have the strength to be out in public"* because they were raped, she said.

The vigil meant a lot to her. *"I didn't see things like this when I needed them,"* she told the group, a lone tear rolling down her cheek. *"When I needed to talk, I didn't know who would listen."*

In Bangor, several people took turns sharing readings on the subject, from poetry to excerpts of an article in *Newsweek*. A middle-aged woman related statistics supporting the concept that teen pregnancy is often a form of child abuse. According to a survey in California, babies born to 11- and 12-year old mothers were fathered by men in their 20s. In other studies, more than half of teen mothers were raped or molested before they became pregnant.

After each reading or testimony, the group responded, *"Healing through unity. You are not alone."* Soon it was time for the march. The candles wouldn't light because of the wind, so walkers shared the few battery-powered candles. But they also carried the wax candles of various shapes and colors, prompting Rape Response Services staffer Kathy Walker to comment that the tapers were *"as different as the stories of the victims and survivors who were being remembered."*

The Bangor vigil was sponsored by Rape Response Services, which has its office at 157 Park Street. The agency's free, confidential services include information on medical and court procedures, volunteers to accompany victims to the hospital or through the court process, and support groups for survivors. The 24-hour hot line is available by calling 989-5678 or 1-800-310-0000.

A journal entry mentioned that Walker was "nervous about what press coverage of tonight's event will be. Wind blew out our candles, and the crowd was small, but we followed through on [*Teal's*] idea."

Hotline Volunteers

New training manuals were finally printed by MECASA, with the help of a $13,000 grant from the Maine State Troopers Association, and were available for spring training in 1996. Both the manual and the basic training outline, supplemented by additional printed materials and guest speakers, were used throughout the years Walker spent at the agency. MECASA discontinued printing the manuals after a few years, and photocopies were made by RRS and the other centers.

Most of the interviews of prospective volunteers who would take the spring training in Bangor had been completed by Teal. O'Brien and Walker co-facilitated the sessions throughout April. A journal entry that Walker made near the end of April noted: "training continues to go well, despite my fears that I'm not prepared enough. I surprise myself at my ability to be spontaneous about hotline issues, and value my ongoing experience there." Walker had been picking up hotline shifts again to fill open slots on the schedule. She also wanted to know what issues the volunteers were experiencing on the hotline and didn't want her hotline skills to become rusty.

In addition to Richards, three of the six people who completed the spring training were to become an integral part of RRS: Ann Hartman, Larry Lussier, and Darlene Bean. It was at this time that exit interviews were implemented by Walker with anyone who completed the training. After she was no longer a trainer, Walker continued to meet, usually on the last night of training, with each new volunteer to discuss how the training sessions were for them, hear suggestions for improvement, listen to any concerns they might have about being on the hotline, and welcome them to the agency.

When O'Brien became Volunteer Coordinator, she assumed responsibility for the Bangor advocates' meetings and for being sure the hotline shifts were filled. The newly-trained advocates were ready and willing to sign up for shifts on the hotline. This was accomplished at each advocates' meeting by passing around a blank schedule with the dates and hours of the three daily shifts. Those present filled in their names for the shifts that fit their schedules. If blanks remained, it was the responsibility of the Volunteer Coordinator to call missing advocates and sign them up. Staff members took shifts that could not be filled by advocates.

Deciding to hold the advocates' meetings every month instead of bi-monthly, O'Brien's first meeting in July had a full agenda. A celebration occurred of the 3431 hours donated by advocates on the hotline and at other activities for six months from January through June 30th. In alphabetical order, the 16 advocates were Badger (third highest at 405 hours), Angelica Baeza, Jan Blake, Bean (131 hours since end of April training), Dawn Bouchard, Amy Eyles, Marianne Fricke, Grotton, Hartman, Lussier, Deanna Partridge (highest at 474.5 hours), Rancourt (second highest at 470 hours), Amanda Ross, Alicia Sinclair, Sally Wolever, and Kellie Holmes.

Several of these individuals (Grotton, Holmes, Blake) attended group facilitator training in the spring and were anxious to lead a support group. Some had participated in the vigil and march. Partridge had given more hours than anyone (23.5) in the "other" category by making presentations at the University of Maine, Husson College, Maine State Hair Academy, Hermon and Newport Junior High Schools, and Stearns High School in Millinocket for which RRS was given a $100 donation.

The August advocates' meeting featured a discussion of topics the group would like to explore with guest speakers. Parental consent, how to handle mandated reporting, cult abuse, perpetrators, teen issues, and sexually transmitted diseases were all ideas for future meetings. The decision was made to have an in-service training every other month. Advocates were recruited to participate in role plays at the upcoming fall training and also suggested ideas for role play scenarios. What was stressed at all trainings and advocates' meetings during Walker's tenure at RRS was that volunteers could not provide counseling on the hotline or at the hospital. The center was not licensed as a counseling agency, and Walker's eventual social work license did not permit her to be a counselor. Only crisis intervention could be offered to callers.

In addition to maintaining the hotline schedule and communicating with the volunteers, O'Brien was responsible for organizing and overseeing the fall training in Bangor. Lanphere-Ames (formerly Richards) took on this task in Dover-Foxcroft. Joni Averill, who put together a column called "The Standpipe" every day in the BDN, mentioned the new Dover-Foxcroft office on August 26th when she wrote about RRS training:

Volunteers are being sought for Rape Response Services, a 24-hour crisis hot line with offices in Bangor and Dover-Foxcroft. Training is provided to these volunteers, who assist not only people who have been sexually assaulted, but also their significant others. If you have good listening skills and can help, you have two training opportunities. For the first time, separate five-week courses are being offered in Piscataquis and Penobscot counties. The Piscataquis County training, from 6 to 9 P.M. Mondays and Wednesdays, will be conducted in Dover-Foxcroft. That first training date is Sept. 9th.

Training for Penobscot County, also 6 to 9 P.M, will be Tuesdays and Thursdays in Bangor beginning Sept 10th. Once trained, hot line advocates agree to a minimum of one eight-hour hot line shift per week. Pagers are provided to allow flexibility for those on duty. For more information, call RRS Executive Director, 941-2980, or the staff at the Dover-Foxcroft office, 564-8924.

The September/October 1996 issue of the Peace and Justice Center of Eastern Maine newsletter also mentioned the two offices and the upcoming training. "Sexual assault is a problem that will be with us for a long time," began the notice. "Rape Response Services is providing support and counseling for those affected by this situation and community education to reduce and prevent such occurances [*sic*]. RRS now has a Dover-Foxcroft office (564-8924 or POB 673, D-F 04426). Both offices will hold volunteer crisis hotline training sessions."

Interviews of prospective advocates in Bangor had been completed by O'Brien and Walker together during the last two weeks of August. Walker would be supervising the social work interns from the University of Maine, something she continued to do throughout her years as ED. Once they completed the training and began taking hotline shifts, the social work interns met with Walker weekly, either on campus or at the RRS office. Total hours they were on call counted toward the hours needed for the Bachelor's of Social Work (BSW) internship. One of the students was a male, the second to complete the training. RRS developed a protocol with the answering service that a caller would be told upfront that a male was the first responder. If talking to him was uncomfortable for the caller, the person on backup would be paged to take the call.

Several volunteers joined O'Brien, Lanphere-Ames, and Walker to attend a MECASA-sponsored Volunteer Conference at the University of Maine at Augusta in mid-October. This all-day event provided networking and educational opportunities for the RRS volunteers and was well-attended by all ten centers. Workshop topics included men as victims, advocacy with parents of abused children, suicide intervention, victims who have a mental illness, and new ideas for support groups.

The concluding paragraph of a September memo from Walker to the Clinical Committee related the good news that "training is underway [*in Bangor*] with nine prospective advocates, including three social work students, a senior and two juniors." Walker mentioned that members of the Clinical Committee would be contacted about doing practice calls in mid-October. Despite publicity and plans, no training was held in Dover-Foxcroft.

The November advocates' meeting included a reminder that the victim needed to request RRS accompaniment to the hospital or the police station before an advocate responded. Some law enforcement officers and hospital personnel were calling the hotline directly to request an advocate's presence without checking first on the victim's preference.

Support Groups

Required as part of the DHS contract, support groups continued to be an issue in 1996. Scheduling groups and finding co-facilitators was as challenging as it had been the previous year when Teal met with the Clinical Committee. Members of the Committee were therapists (Clarke, Rampe, Veits, and Zegel) who advised RRS staff and Board members about clinical or therapeutic issues and policies. Walker signed "Notes of Clinical Committee Meeting" in early May 1996 as the "note-taker." A support group for survivors of incest, with six names on the waiting list, was slated to begin in June, with Rampe and Grotton as co-facilitators. The notes indicated that Rampe called the following day to say that she could not facilitate until fall. Walker agreed to call the people on the list to see if they could wait.

A discussion of mandated reporting at the May Clinical Committee meeting generated more questions than answers. The consensus was that RRS needed to develop a policy that was more detailed than the existing Policy of Disclosure and Confidentiality. "We know we must report if children are involved or if perpetrator continues to have contact with children" was written in the notes. Questions asked included whether a report was required if only the first name and phone number were known, or if the location of the perpetrator was unknown. "What about the confidentiality of our hotline services?" was also asked.

On another issue, the consensus of the Clinical Committee members, according to the May notes, was: "group members need to be hooked up with a counselor during group because of the intensity of the issue, and because of the history of RRS re: inexperienced group facilitators. It was suggested that an 'open relationship with a therapist' would be sufficient, someone who could be called on but not necessarily meeting in weekly sessions. It was also suggested that the following could be added to the disclaimer that was signed by group members: 'I understand that I have to be in contact with a therapist during the course of the group sessions.'" Committee members agreed that written group policies were needed for screening, absenteeism, dropping out, and therapist availability. The suggestion was made that both co-facilitators needed to do each screening if possible.

Another meeting of the Clinical Committee was held on the last day of May with all members present. Walker requested that the Committee members consider a policy regarding follow-up calls from advocates to callers after a hospital visit or an immediate trauma. Advocates were concerned that callers not feel abandoned after spending a lot of time on the phone or in person at the hospital with an advocate. RRS did not want to suggest, however, that this was the beginning of a therapeutic relationship with the caller.

The Clinical Committee was unable to meet again until late August; this was to be the last time the Committee formally met. A memo from Walker to the Committee included proposed final wording of two policies, based on previous discussions, to be presented to the Board of Directors for approval after the Committee members agreed. The mandated reporting policy was subsequently adopted by the RRS Board in September:

> Any incidents of the present abuse of a child (a person under the age of 18) must be reported by RRS even when the name and whereabouts of the perpetrator are unknown. If the RRS advocate or

any other representative of RRS is told that a perpetrator of past abuse currently has contact with children, such information should also be reported, even if the name and whereabouts of the perpetrator are unknown to the agency. The person providing the information may also be encouraged to report to DHS. Reporting requirements consist of (1) a telephone call to DHS, made by the advocate or the representative of RRS who obtained the information, and (2) a written account of the date, time, and reason for the call provided to the Executive Director of RRS. The contact with DHS and the written report are to be completed as soon as possible after the information is obtained.

A proposed policy on follow-up calls was: "The hotline advocate will provide the caller-victim with a choice regarding a follow-up call. If such a call is desired, arrangements will be made by the advocate for time of call, procedures to follow if the victim is not there, and how many attempts to make. No follow-up calls will be made without the victim's consent." This policy was also approved by the Clinical Committee and by the Board and guided RRS for the next several years.

The August memo from Walker to the Clinical Committee included a survey "which has been mailed to over 100 mental health practitioners in the two-county catchment area. We have already received a good response," Walker noted in the memo. "I hope you will take a few minutes to complete the survey so we will have updated information from each of you. We can spend some time at the meeting reviewing the responses, especially from those who have indicated an interest in doing groups." The purpose of the survey was to update the therapist pages in the training manuals.

A final memo was sent to the Clinical Committee in mid-September to report on the August meeting. Walker was pleased to note that a group would be underway at the end of September for 11 weeks with Rampe and Grotton as co-facilitators and Veits providing supervision. The group would meet weekly at the RRS office. The memo continued: "We have not publicized this group because there appeared to be enough names on the waiting list, and there was a short amount of time in which both Grotton and Rampe could be available for screening. It looks as if there will be six to eight participants." Copies of support group guidelines, the disclaimer that this was not a therapy group, and a release of information form were included with the memo. The latter two forms were to be signed by support group participants during the screening interviews. Walker expressed appreciation to the three women for "volunteering this time to the agency!"

Three male victims had expressed an interest during the year in a men's group, and a request for a "partners of survivors" group had also been received. No one on the committee had found a male therapist who was available to co-facilitate a male survivors' group, and RRS was never able to offer one. The best the agency could do was offer books from the lending library.

A Community Presence

As ED, Walker was increasingly in the public eye. Maine's Second District Congressman John Baldacci created an advisory committee on juvenile crime, drug abuse, domestic violence, and hate crimes during the year. In late June, Walker was part of a panel which was invited to discuss these issues at a public meeting. Other participants were Mary Cathcart, U.S. Commission on Child and Family Welfare; Norris Nickerson, principal, Bangor High School; Colonel Alfred Skolfield, Maine Public Safety; DA Almy; and Kristen Gwinn, a University of Maine student. Baldacci opened the afternoon with welcoming remarks.

A letter dated July 1st was addressed to Walker at RRS from the Congressman: "Thank you for offering testimony at the Juvenile Crime & Drug Abuse, Domestic Violence, and Hate Crimes Advisory Committee Public Meeting held recently in Bangor. As you know, I asked this committee to gather comprehensive information about crime-related problems experienced in Maine, and to report to me with what they have learned by December 1, 1996. Your sharing of your first-hand experience with these issues will enable the committee to realize this objective. Thank you again."

The BDN published a letter from Walker on July 11th in which she referred to the panel:

> *Kudos to Rep. John Baldacci and the members of his Anti-Crime and Violence Advisory Committee and also to the BDN editorial board for highlighting the issue of violence against women. By whatever name—domestic violence, sexual assault, date rape,*

battering, acquaintance rape, marital rape—violence based on gender should be as unacceptable as any other hate crime. Increased collaboration among agencies is essential for spreading the word that we as a community and a state have zero tolerance for all violent acts perpetrated against women.

Television was a venue in which Walker surprised herself by being more at ease with live interviews than expected. During her early months as ED, Walker began a working relationship with Alan Grover, a reporter for WABI-TV Channel 5; the rapport between these two individuals greatly benefitted RRS through the years. The agency was fortunate to be the only sexual assault center in close proximity to three local television stations, and Walker was frequently called for interviews on all of them, either at the studios or with reporters coming to the office. Before the advent of social media, newspapers and television were the primary venues in which the public received news. Letters to the editor of the BDN and television interviews disseminated information about RRS and sexual assault to a wide audience in both Penobscot and Piscataquis counties.

Walker's first interview with Grover was in mid-August, live on the studio set at 6:15 A.M. He usually called when the state and federal crime statistics were released to get an "official" take on the increases or decreases in reported rapes. These interviews provided Walker with an opportunity to educate the viewing audience about how difficult it was for someone to report being raped, and about how much in denial our society was about the frequency of rape.

Walker also believed that RRS needed to be a part of as many community-based groups as possible in the two counties. The crimes of sexual violence impacted everyone despite the widespread denial that such violence occurred. She did not hesitate to use the word "rape" and to describe the agency's services whenever she introduced herself at a meeting.

Resource Exchange in Dover-Foxcroft was one group that RRS joined early in Walker's tenure as ED. Representatives of a wide variety of agencies in Piscataquis County met monthly in the early morning to share news about the activities in which each was engaged. Mayo Regional Hospital, the Area Agency on Aging, Womancare, Cooperative

Extension Service, the YMCA, the local Chamber of Commerce, and others were well-represented at each meeting. Because RRS was a new presence in the area, the invitation to join the organization for nominal annual dues was welcomed.

For the same reason, the newness of RRS to the area, Walker was pleased to become part of the Katahdin Area Response Effort for Non-Violence (K.A.R.E.) in Millinocket. This group was truly grass roots, begun by individuals who were concerned about interpersonal violence in northern Penobscot County. Walker had the privilege of connecting with two of these individuals, Sally Danforth and Jane McGillicuddy, in November 1995, when Teal and Walker attended a forum on domestic violence sponsored by Congressman Baldacci in Bangor. A year later in November, RRS was invited to a K.A.R.E. meeting at Kathy Klein's office in East Millinocket. Walker had met two weeks earlier with Danforth at her Millinocket home to discuss how the two organizations could work together to address issues of violence against women in this part of the RRS catchment area. These contacts were the beginning of a collaborative effort and of friendships that extended throughout Walker's tenure at RRS.

RRS was a member of several committees and task forces in the greater Bangor area. The Rape Awareness Committee on the Orono campus of the University of Maine met monthly throughout the summer, primarily charged with organizing sexual assault awareness week activities when the students returned in early September. The week's events included a kick-off rally on the first day at noon, and a march on the last night. Despite a busy week, Walker "had to speak at beginning of march on campus in evening," according to her journal, and was "surprised at interest of students and their willingness to talk."

An area Domestic Violence Task Force met occasionally at the Bangor Police Department, providing good networking opportunities with local law enforcement officers, media personnel, and representatives from SR. Sexual assault was sometimes part of domestic violence, and the presence of RRS at these meetings provided another voice for victims.

Increased exposure for RRS in the community meant that requests for educational presentations were becoming more common. This was to precipitate big changes in the next few years, but at the time, O'Brien and Walker were meeting the requests as they came in, mostly from area colleges. Walker wrote in early October about "a good experience for me to be at Husson College from 9 to 12 last night and watch a date rape movie with a floor of first year girls. A nice group, and important for me to see another side of college students, or young people in general." She had provided the opening remarks to kick off Rape Awareness Week on campus earlier in the school year.

A Rape Awareness Week was held in mid-November at University College (UC) in Bangor, part of the University of Maine at Augusta (UMA). The kickoff event at the entrance to Eastport Hall on campus included remarks by Dr. Owen Cargol, President, UMA; Dr. Charles MacRoy and Dr. Tracy Gran, Dean and Associate Dean at UC; Curtis Marsh, UC Student Government President; and Walker. A video on acquaintance rape and a discussion facilitated by Walker immediately followed the kickoff.

The next day Walker facilitated a panel "What We Need to Know" on the UC campus. Panelists were Sharon Elaine Closson, Victim-Witness Advocate in the DA's office; Meredith Bruskin RN, Coordinator of the Evidence Collection Protocol at Eastern Maine Medical Center (EMMC); Detective Robert Gould, Bangor Police Department; DA Almy; and Detective Jameson, Penobscot CSD. The panel encouraged the reporting of the crime of sexual assault and described the procedures which would occur after a report was made.

A TBN march concluded the week, with participants meeting at Eastport Hall and being bussed to downtown Bangor for the march. Co-sponsors of the event included the UC Women's Resource Center, Bangor NOW, RRS, Peace and Justice Center of Eastern Maine, and the Penobscot County Chapter of Maine Won't Discriminate. Such extensive collaboration did not often occur, and Walker was pleased to be part of it despite, as noted in her journal, "walking miles in sub-zero temperatures." Credit for pulling the week's events together went to Yvonne Thibodeau, student intern coordinator of the UC Women's Resource Center. Walker met with her on campus and put her in touch with some of the speakers, but the idea was hers, and she came through with what might have been the only such event on the UC campus.

Money Matters

The first fundraiser which bore Walker's stamp was the revamped Stay-at-Home Ball held in February for the first time. She designed the invitations with a Valentine's Day theme of a teal heart on white cardstock. Bangor Letter Shop printed the four pieces (inner and outer envelopes, invitation, and response card), 900 of each. The interior was similar to the invitations to earlier Balls. New this year, after consultation with Dave Russell at WEZQ 92.9, was the opportunity for listeners to call in to the RRS office during the hours of the Ball with monetary donations. Walker stayed at the office from 8 to 10:30 P.M., listened to the Ball and did not receive any calls for donations. The hotline number was also provided on the radio throughout the evening, but no calls were made to that line either.

The United Way of Eastern Maine (UWEM) logo, as well as the logos for RRS and WEZQ 92.9 were printed on the back of the invitation. Walker had high hopes for the financial success of this fundraiser, and had hand-addressed all the envelopes. RRS had not renewed the bulk mailing permit, so the invitations were sent first-class. A good reason for mailing them this way was the opportunity to update addresses on those pieces that were returned.

One of the responsibilities of the ED was the contract with DHS, the source of the overwhelming majority of RRS funds. The state fiscal year ended on the last day of September, and proposed contracts for the next year were due in Augusta in late July or early August. A training session on writing outcome- or performance-based contracts, a change from earlier years, was held in Augusta, facilitated by DHS, in May. The Program Goals and Objectives pages of the contracts were to be replaced with performance-based pages. Reports of these performance-based activities could be submitted semi-annually instead of quarterly. The completed, typed, and signed (by Woolley and Walker) contract proposal was delivered by Walker to Steve Greenlaw in Augusta by mid-August. Greenlaw had replaced Holcomb as Contract Specialist.

Before the end of September, the previous year's contract had to be revised to reflect a change in income and expenses that was not projected in the original document submitted by Strout. Any contract in which the budgeted amount of income from sources other than DHS funds was less than actual by more than ten percent required a revision. A line item for interest had been omitted from the contract budget; Walker's revision pages added the estimated amount of $300 to both the income and expense pages. This was her first experience with the cumulative impact of a simple revision on one page of a contract necessitating changes in many other pages.

At a MECASA meeting in September, Greenlaw encouraged the centers to set up a separate checking account for deposits of fundraising proceeds, separating these dollars out from the DHS funds. Named a "Board Account for Cash-Flow Purposes," the separation was to be reflected in the Board minutes by a motion at the end of the fiscal year to "restrict excess fundraising dollars to a separate Board account." Cost-sharing enumerated in the final financial reports to DHS created the potential for the state to claim a percentage of excess fundraising dollars.

Early in November, the RRS Board held a day-long planning retreat, facilitated by Ilze Petersons of the Peace and Justice Center, at the Town Café restaurant in Hampden, primarily to discuss fundraising. Four Board members, five advocates, and the three staff persons attended what "turned out to be a productive and affirming day, with what looks like a solid fundraising plan." One of the ideas proposed by Harrison was to hold an auction in 1997. Little did RRS know that this suggestion would start an annual trend for the agency, and would be copied by many other area social service agencies throughout the ensuing years.

The retreat began with introductions, how participants became involved in RRS, and a sharing of expectations and fears about the day. Walker had identified some short-term goals for FY'97, and in groups of two, attendees rated these with happy faces or red flags. Goals receiving a higher number of happy faces were:

- *the establishment of relationship with a contact person in each middle and high school in two counties to continue and expand the school programs*
- *the facilitation of fundraising events and efforts*
- *getting men involved in both of these goals* [added by the male advocate who was present].

Other goals receiving support were:

- *the continuation of the current level of services on the hotline*
- *the publication of a newsletter and annual report*
- *offering support groups and collaborative events with Womancare and/or SR.*

Long-range planning issues that arose from the group included:

1. *expansion of staff hours*
2. *adult community education*
3. *school-based education*
4. *legislative advocacy and education*
5. *education of professionals*
6. *state-based initiative for education of preschoolers*
7. *court watch*
8. *men against rape*

Barriers to fundraising were also listed, especially the need for more Board members to share the load. The medical, legal, law enforcement, mental health, University, and ministerial communities all needed to be represented on the Board. Petersons led a brainstorming session about future fundraising. There was less consensus around these ideas, with the most (four) in favor of a phonathon, and two each for a sports-related fundraiser and an art show and auction of survivors' artwork. At the end of the day, note-taker Lanphere-Ames commented: "it was a wonderful opportunity for Board, Staff and Advocates to get together and work on important agency issues."

A vital part of not only fundraising but also community awareness for RRS was the financial support of Penobscot County and a few municipalities in the County. In late November, Walker appeared before the Penobscot County Budget Committee to successfully request a continuation of the $1250 gift that RRS had been receiving annually since 1989. The following years found her appearing at these meetings as well as before the Hermon and Millinocket Town Councils, expressing appreciation for past support and requesting inclusion in the new budget. She did not provide specific rape statistics for each town because of the confidentiality of the services, but was able to say that the hotline had served callers from each. RRS also received an annual donation from the City of Brewer without needing to appear at a Council meeting. Despite the inclusion of the agency in each of these budgets, a letter requesting the funds had to be sent to the municipality or county each year. A copy of the Annual Report was included with each letter.

Good news about finances was often received unexpectedly and without solicitation. A long-time donor gave RRS a gift of 55 shares of stock, worth over $1000. The Board made the decision to sell the shares and deposit the proceeds in the agency's account.

RRS was still a designation agency of UWEM, meaning that the only money received was specified for RRS by the donor. Following the kickoff of the 1996-97 campaign in September, each agency was expected to select a representative who could make short presentations to area businesses about the importance of UWEM funds. The hope was to inspire employees at the business to be as generous as possible in their payroll deductions or outright gifts. Training for the agency speakers was mandatory, held at the UWEM office in late August.

In this role as agency speaker, Walker was asked to tell a true story, without breaking confidentiality, about someone who received RRS assistance. Her introductory words could specify the name of the agency and the services provided, but she could not ask directly for designated gifts to RRS. Usually she provided a composite snapshot of someone who called the hotline, and always thanked the employees for their generosity in the past campaigns. The time allotted to this segment was five minutes or less, as UWEM staff presentations and sometime a video were part of the short employee meeting. The weeks of the campaign saw Walker making presentations in a wide variety of settings throughout Penobscot County. From banks to paper mills (Millinocket and Old Town), department stores to insurance agencies, hospitals and car repair shops, she tried to be as available as her schedule would allow until the campaign finale in early December. This pattern would continue throughout Walker's years as ED while RRS remained a UWEM agency.

Annual Report and End-of-Year Fundraising Letter

For the first time in several years, RRS published an Annual Report 1995-96 (FY'96) that was distributed throughout the service area. The tri-fold, two-sided report was designed and written by Walker and printed at Bangor Letter Shop in teal on off-white paper. This report and each subsequent one were compiled and printed after the RRS auditor's report became available. The Board of Directors at the time the annual report was published consisted of Woolley, President, Veeder, Treasurer, and Harrison, Secretary. Other members of the Board were Karen Greaney, Estler, Grotton, Justus, Partridge, and Roberts.

Statistics for Penobscot and Piscataquis Counties in the fiscal year ending September 30th included 174 hours of service provided to a total of 175 clients. Fifty-three sexual assaults had occurred that year and had been reported to the hotline. RRS had provided 137 hours of community education, reaching 2042 participants of all ages. Volunteer hours on the hotline totaled 8784. A statement at the end of the statistics column read: "Rape Response Services could not fulfill the mission without hours of time generously donated by hotline advocates, therapists, an auditor, an attorney, and an accountant. The value of these in-kind services was conservatively estimated to be $60,977." The Annual Report also noted: "eleven new hotline advocates received 35 hours of training; twenty-one advocates available to take hotline shifts."

The income statement in the Annual Report showed total income of $70,990, including DHS funds of $57,675, and expenses of $68,856. A surplus was not allowed under the state contract, necessitating a note: "Additional funding for Piscataquis County Outreach was not expended in its entirety due to personnel changes and the unavailability of state funds until February 1996." Salaries and benefits comprised almost half of the expenses, at $43,577. Rent of Suite Six and the office at Womancare was $10,680. Telephone costs of $3572 included the answering service, phone lines in both offices, and pagers.

A copy of the Annual Report was included in each year-end fundraising letter dated November 1996 and sent to "Dear Friends of Rape Response Services." Signed by Woolley and Walker, the letter began:

Thank you for your loyal support of this agency through the seven years since its incorporation. Rape Response Services continues to be a strong, community-based voice for victims and survivors of sexual assault in Penobscot and Piscataquis counties.

We are pleased to provide you with the enclosed copy of our Annual Report for the fiscal year ending September 30, 1996. As we enter FY '97, the Board members, volunteers, and staff are working together toward the following new goals:

- *To expand our services in the Millinocket area;*
- *To offer at least one support group every quarter;*
- *To edit and mail a quarterly newsletter to our supporters;*
- *To sponsor a collaborative training event with other social service agencies;*
- *To establish an ongoing relationship with school and hospital personnel throughout the catchment area*

In addition, we will maintain the current high-quality services on our hotline, always seeking and training new volunteers. Your financial support is crucial to Rape Response Services. A donor card is enclosed for your convenience in returning your year-end gift. We invite you to use the reverse side of the card if you wish to honor someone with a special holiday gift.

If you have designated a gift to Rape Response Services through the United Way, we sincerely thank you for that support. Your donations to this agency are gratefully appreciated. Together we are working to ensure safety for everyone in the new year.

Taking shifts on the hotline, or providing week-long backup, was something Walker continued to do as ED, and the year ended on an especially poignant note because of this decision. Christmas Eve found Walker at EMMC with a caller. Her journal entry brought that experience back: "I found Christmas at the hospital this afternoon, despite the rain and 48° temperature which washed away our little bit of snow. A victim was in need of my help to find a safe place to stay tonight, and doing so helped me see that Christmas is not about who's home or not at my house, but about giving the love of this day to others."

Walker was a member of Grace United Methodist Church (UMC) in Bangor and wrote of this experience for the church newsletter in January 1997:

On Christmas Eve afternoon, I was called to Eastern Maine Medical Center to be with a victim of rape. Although such hospital calls, tragically, are not uncommon, something about being there on Christmas Eve made this one especially poignant. It was quickly determined by the detective from the Sheriff's Department, and by me, that this victim could not return to the place where she had been staying because the rape had occurred there. All her clothing and personal possessions were at that place, from which she had walked over a mile to the nearest residence for help on Christmas Eve morning.

A part of the medical/legal procedures involved in the rape protocol exam requires that the clothing worn by the victim at the time of the crime be retained at the hospital for evidence. This is turned over to the law enforcement agent on the scene, along with the other evidence, and sent to the crime lab in Augusta. Clothing is eventually returned.

Finding clothing for the person at the hospital was easy, thanks to the generosity of Grace Church. At the end of the recent rummage sale, many outfits were donated to RRS for the express purpose of making it possible for the agency to supply victims with suitable clothing to replace those taken for evidence. I was able to return to my office and get a pair of sneakers, a sweatshirt and pants, all from the rummage sale. The clothing turned out to be a perfect fit and a favorite color.

More difficult was finding a safe place, not only for Christmas Eve but for Christmas Day and night as well. The usual shelters were full or unwilling to provide a bed. It suddenly occurred to me that RRS was supposed to have an account at an area hotel for such emergency situations. Never having faced the need for this service before, I made a phone call and was told that a room was available for the two nights, and basic toiletry items were provided.

As the rain poured out of what was now a pitch-black sky, the victim and I were offered a ride by hospital security personnel to the hotel. I completed the paperwork, making arrangements for the bill to be sent to RRS. When the victim saw the lighted Christmas tree in the lobby, and learned that a free breakfast was available on

Christmas morning, a smile lit up her face. And that smile was one of the nicest Christmas gifts I have ever received.

Only on Christmas morning did the reality of my Christmas Eve experience register fully with me: the victim's name, I remembered, was Mary, and I had found her a room at the Riverside Inn.

A crazy year at RRS was at an end, and this one incident told Walker that every stress-filled moment had been worth it. To help Mary and others like her was the reason why RRS existed and why the agency worked so hard to provide services.

1997: FIRST ANNUAL AUCTION AND AWARDS NIGHT

T he new year began an exciting decade for RRS and for rape crisis centers in Maine. Innovative programs and increased funding not only benefitted the clients served on the RRS hotline but also built both infrastructure and community support throughout the two counties. In a letter to support the application for Walker to become a Licensed Master Social Worker (LMSW) in March, Woolley wrote: "A piece of the strategic plan involved expanding RRS collaborative relationships in Piscataquis and northern Penobscot counties. Kathy has successfully begun bridging the gap between Bangor and the rural parts of our catchment area, growing partnerships with agencies and individuals that will allow for the comprehensive delivery of services." This essentially summed up Walker's leadership style that had been evident the previous year and continued throughout her remaining years at RRS.

Money Matters

As a part of community outreach, the summer of 1997 saw the resurrection of the RRS newsletter with a new name, *The Rape Response Reporter*, last published in 1993. Printed by Bangor Letter Shop on teal paper, this four-page single-fold document contained an insert about the upcoming "Fall Festival Auction on September 4th," an event first proposed by Harrison at the previous year's retreat. A decision was made at the time the auction was scheduled to hold this event in September and thereby avoid any overlap with domestic violence awareness month in October.

A letter from Walker appeared on the first page of the newsletter: "Board members volunteer their time to establish policies and to do fundraising activities for the agency. You are invited to support the Board's efforts by attending our Fall Festival Auction and Awards Night on Thursday, September 4th. Please see the enclosed registration form for additional information, and for a preview of the exciting items available at the auction. On the fourth we will also be recognizing the volunteers who provide invaluable services in Penobscot and Piscataquis counties for victims and survivors of sexual assault. Thank you for your continued support of Rape Response Services." Board members who were putting the auction together were also listed on the first page: Woolley, President; Veeder, Treasurer; Harrison, Secretary; Leanne Harvey, Greaney, Estler, Grotton, and Justus.

During the summer, the RRS Board voted to establish the Janet Badger Volunteer Award which would be presented annually at the auction. In describing the award, the newsletter stated: "Janet Badger became a hotline advocate for RRS while she was still in high school, and continued to volunteer faithfully for the next eight years, sometimes taking more than four shifts a week." This annual Award, which was presented to Badger at the 1997 auction, would "honor someone who displays the same level of caring commitment [*as Badger*] to the clients of Rape Response Services."

Woolley and Walker chose a small four-inch square wooden paperweight at Atlantic Awards to present to the award recipient. The brass plate attached to the wood was inscribed with the RRS logo and underneath were engraved the award name and year. A wooden wall plaque with the name of each awardee and the year engraved on a separate plate was hung at the RRS office. The logo and "Janet Badger Volunteer Award" were engraved on a plate at the top of the wall plaque.

Others recognized with appreciation awards at the Fall Festival Auction included Joe Baldacci and Com-Nav. "Joe has been providing pro bono legal services for five years," the newsletter noted, "the value of which can never be repaid. Com-Nav in Brewer, specifically Matt and Art Tilley, provides quality paging services 'round the clock at a fraction of the cost that other sexual assault centers are paying elsewhere." Bangor Letter Shop donated the printing of tickets for the auction. A "big thank you" in *The Rape Response Reporter* went out to "The Attic and Cosmic Changes, both of Bangor, for their generous donations to our clothing drive. Your contributions will be given to victims of sexual assault whose clothing must be taken as evidence upon arrival at the hospital. This is one way that we can help restore dignity to a victim. Others who wish to donate used clothing (sweatsuits and sneakers are best) may contact the office."

An absentee bidding form for the silent auction was included in the newsletter. Items ranged from gift certificates to a watch, from a savings bond to a red ball gown. One of the auction attendees modeled the gown during the event. A last-minute addition to the live auction was an autographed side panel from the Pepsi 400 race car driven by Maine native, Ricky Craven. Stephen King donated an autographed copy of one of his novels. A poster from the movie "Phenomenon" was signed and donated by John Travolta. Handmade items in the live auction included a quilt and matching stained glass wall hanging, a christening gown, a "wearable art" vest, and a baby afghan.

Joni Averill's "Standpipe" column in the August 21st BDN was headlined: "Popular items to highlight fundraising auction. Board members for Rape Response Services in Bangor have worked hard to secure some terrific items for their first Fall Festival Auction and Awards Night beginning at 5 P.M. Thursday, Sept. 4th, at Jeff's Catering in Brewer. Executive Director Kathy Walker said board members were able to secure items from some favorite celebrities that she hopes will make this event a huge success. 'We need the money,' she said simply."

Averill also mentioned: "A board member who favors the work of sculptor Forest 'Toby' Hart requested—and he agreed—to donate a small bronze sculpture of a black bear. The early interest stems from the fact that people on the RRS newsletter mailing list already have the information you are reading today. Included in that information is something a bit unusual for a fundraiser such as this—forms for absentee bids. 'We've received quite a few bids for the Craven panel already,' Walker said."

Averill's article continued: "The $10 admission fee includes the auction and awards presentation, entertainment by Sharon Pyne on the Irish flute and Julia Lane playing the Celtic harp, hors d'oeuvres and a cash bar. If you would like to view the auction items in advance or purchase advance tickets, call 941-2980. Absentee bids will be accepted on most items. Tickets also will be available at the door. Walker said 200 tickets are available and she hopes all will be sold." A similar article about the auction also appeared in the *Piscataquis Observer,* a newspaper published in Dover-Foxcroft.

Maine Times, a statewide weekly newspaper, reported on the auction under the heading "When We Were Kings" in the August 28th issue: "A recent press release for a benefit auction in Bangor elevated local giant Stephen King to top man in the list of donors. King's donation, an autographed novel, ranked above a sculpture by Forest Hart and autographed items from Ricky Craven, John Travolta and Rosie O'Donnell."

Follow-up to the press releases was a positive report in Averill's column on September 11th: "The news from the first Fall Festival Auction and Awards Night, sponsored earlier this month by Rape Response Services in Bangor, was that it was a tremendous success. 'We grossed more than $4,500,' reported RRS Executive Director Kathy Walker. 'The response from the business community and 22 individuals—including some celebrities—was really overwhelming. More than 41 separate businesses made wonderful donations, and the people who came to our fund-raiser commented on the quality of those donations.'

"Walker considered the results 'a really good effort for a first-time event' and said there was a great deal of interest expressed in having it become an annual RRS fundraiser. 'Not only was this event a show of support for the agency, but the bottom line is that it was a show of support for victims and survivors,' Walker said while expressing her gratitude to those who made the donations and those who bid on them. 'We just want to be sure all the businesses and individuals know how much we appreciated their help,' she said."

A time-consuming procedure remained in place for this event and for all future fundraisers: the manual charge card "swiper." Not only did credit card charges have to be entered by hand, but each individual transaction also had to be called in separately to a toll-free number after the event. Enabling donors to charge their gifts not only increased sales, but also added more tasks to be completed as soon as possible after the auction. On one or two occasions the card number was rejected, and the donor had to be tracked down to obtain a different number or method of payment.

Another RRS signature fundraiser, the Stay-at-Home Ball, was held on Valentine's Day. One thousand invitations, similar to the previous year, had been mailed in mid-January. Walker spent the three hours for this scheduled event at the RRS office again, listening to the Ball on the radio with one advocate present, but no telephone calls with donations came in during the Ball.

At the invitation of Jeff Wahlstrom, the ED of UWEM, Walker submitted an application in February to start the process for RRS to become an allocation agency of UWEM, beginning with the fall campaign. This change from a designation agency was later granted by the UWEM Board of Directors for the express purpose of increasing the prevention programs in the public schools. An initial amount of $5000 was provided. Any designated gifts made to RRS by UWEM donors would also be available, in addition to the allocated amount. RRS was recognized at the UWEM finale in December when Board members, staff, and volunteers were present to receive the plaque for Outstanding United Way Agency Campaign. The employees at RRS had pledged more than $400 to the annual campaign.

Additional financial resources also became available during the year. MECASA and the Maine Department of Mental Health, Mental Retardation and Substance Abuse Services (DMHMRSAS) had entered into a six-month agreement in July to provide what were called "enhanced hotline services." This new "Trauma Survivor Support Line" was offered as part of each center's hotline services, specifically for sexual assault survivors with trauma-related emotional disorders who were at risk of becoming (or already were) clients of the mental health system. RRS received an additional $7629.20 from MECASA who had a sole source contract with the Department. Dr. Ann Jennings, the Director of the Office of Trauma Services at DMHMRSAS, was the initiator of this collaborative effort.

The grant provided the same amount of money to each center, and was specifically earmarked for a coordinator's stipend and fringe benefits, clinical support, paid advocates, telephone, teletypewriter (TTY), insurance, supplies, and administration. Monthly invoices detailing the amount spent in each of these categories were submitted to MECASA before reimbursement checks were paid. (Note: The TTY component of the grant did not become accessible until January 15, 1999, when the Lewiston Sexual Assault Crisis Center (SACC) agreed to house the necessary equipment, take the statewide calls, and notify the local centers only if a face-to-face interaction with the caller was necessary. In an earlier year, MECASA had established a statewide toll-free number from which calls were automatically routed to the center in the area from which the call originated.)

A welcome delivery of new Gateway computers arrived at RRS in September. Congress had passed the first Violence Against Women Act (VAWA) three years earlier. The Justice Assistance Council (JAC), which administered VAWA grants in Maine, decided earlier in the year that $180,000, or the second year of this funding, would be spent on a computer upgrade for each of the ten sexual assault centers and ten domestic violence projects. An assessment by MECASA determined what was currently in each center and set some minimum standards. RRS received $7116 worth of two Gateway desktops, one laptop, and two HP printers. Microsoft Office software had already been installed by Gateway. The front-office desk of the Volunteer Coordinator received one desktop and printer, and the second set went to the Dover-Foxcroft office. Walker used the laptop throughout her tenure at RRS, even after receiving a new desktop a few years later.

A letter received at RRS early in November, signed by Deborah Kelley Rafnell from the State of Maine Department of Public Safety, informed RRS that the grant proposal to create a "Web Page for Rape Awareness" had been "reviewed by the JAC and recommended for funding in the amount of $2,487." This grant of VAWA funds gave RRS the opportunity to be the first sexual assault center in Maine with its own Web page.

Early in December, Walker met with Carey Nason, a hotline volunteer, to discuss her interest in designing the Web page. She was a college student at the time; college students were the targeted audience for the Web page. A software program specifically for Web page design was purchased with grant funds. Nason was paid a stipend and worked for the next three months on the page, choosing a sunflower as the focal point. This sunflower choice was to be incorporated into a new RRS logo in subsequent years. The four sections of the Web page developed by Nason, in addition to "Home," were "Information," "Food 4 Thought," "Safety Tips," and "Resources."

Small fundraisers were held during the year, including a phonathon which yielded camaraderie but little money. Board members, staff, and volunteers met on a Saturday morning at one Board member's office where many phones were available for calling previous donors and asking for financial pledges. Raffles of Beanie Babies which had been donated by Board members and were extremely popular at the time, generated excitement and some funds in December 1997 and 1998.

Outreach into Northern Penobscot County

Walker had written an application in late June for over $16,000 in VAWA funding to do outreach into the Millinocket area. That amount had been rejected by the JAC, but after asking Kelley Rafnell directly for reconsideration, Walker was informed that RRS would receive $8419 for a "Community Based Training Model." Arguing forcefully for the VAWA grant to serve the Katahdin region was a reflection of Walker's passion for taking much-needed services to the people where they lived. "Good news about VAWA grants," Walker wrote in her journal. "I got not only half of Millinocket approved but full Web page application as well. Wow!"

Walker met with Danforth and McGillicuddy in Millinocket in November to talk about implementation of the grant funds. Movers and shakers in K.A.R.E., these two women had provided information for the grant application process, shared Walker's disappointment when the grant was initially not funded, and were now excited to move forward.

An article in the November 25th edition of *The Katahdin Times* described this effort under the headline, "Sexual assault victims to be helped":

> *The Katahdin Region has received over $8,000 in federal funds by* [sic] *the Maine Justice Assistance Council through the Violence Against Women Grant. The goal of the grant is to improve local medical, legal and support services for victims of sexual assault through education and training of local law enforcement and health care personnel.*
>
> *The grant money is the result of a collaborative effort between Rape Response Services of Bangor (RRS) and Katahdin Area Response Effort for Non-Violence (KARE). RRS Executive Director Kathy Walker authored the winning grant. Walker highlighted the fact that legal, medical and support services for victims of sexual assault and their families are lacking in northern Penobscot County. She added that most victims must travel over an hour to receive those needed services.*

The educational and training opportunities will take place throughout 1998, with dates and times to be announced. The grant was bolstered by letters of support from local municipal and health care officials as well as the district attorney's office.

This community based collaborative project will fund four separate training events in underserved, rural areas of Northern Penobscot County. Millinocket Regional Hospital personnel will be trained to administer the rape protocol exam. In addition, training of volunteer advocates who can accompany victims of sexual assault to the hospital will be provided. Also, support group facilitators will be trained. The grant also provides for important in-service training for local law enforcement personnel concerning working with victims. Publicity, including public service announcements, will be funded through the program.

Walker, in her grant presentation, noted that victims of sexual assault in Northern Penobscot County are an underserved population because medical, legal, and support services are located more than an hour away in Bangor. This project, she said, will increase the level of services available in this area of Maine.

Walker noted that the 24-hour crisis hot line operated by Rape Response Services throughout Penobscot and Piscataquis Counties, accepted more than 45 calls from Northern Penobscot County in 1996. "Given the facts that RRS has no visible presence in this area, and that victims are reluctant to report a sexual assault," she declared, "the number of calls indicates a clear need for the victims' services proposed in this project." Katahdin Area Response Effort (KARE), a grass roots effort, has been working since 1989 to address the needs of area victims and to educate the public about assault. KARE and RRS will work collaboratively to implement this project.

A Community Presence

Fundraisers were one way to increase both community awareness about sexual violence and community support for RRS. Another mechanism which Walker put to good use throughout the next decade was the submission of guest editorials and letters to the editor in the BDN. On January 14th, the letter was titled "Frank talk on abuse":

Kudos to hockey player Sheldon Kennedy and to Gary Thorne for speaking out about sexual abuse. It takes a lot of courage for a victim, male or female, to tell anyone that he or she has been sexually abused or assaulted. Sexual assault is the crime that no one wants to believe or accept. Only when we stop blaming the victims and start listening to their stories, all too often similar to Kennedy's, will this crime be stopped.

Resources are already available throughout the state of Maine for victims of sexual assault and abuse. Whether they be athletes, college students, children, adults, high school students, male or female, help is available through the 10 sexual assault centers in Maine. Rape Response Services, for example, operates a 24-hour crisis counseling hotline (1-800-310-0000) for victims and survivors of rape, incest, abuse, harassment—all forms of sexual assault. Both female and male volunteers are trained to take calls and to provide immediate support, as well as referrals. Kennedy's courage in speaking out will let others know that no one is alone in facing the aftermath of sexual abuse.

Another letter from Walker was published in the BDN a month later when she responded to a brief article in the February 3rd edition about a drop in the reported rapes and sexual assaults for 1995 as compiled by the U.S. Department of Justice. What was not factored into these statistics were the increasing numbers of women serving in the United States military who reported being sexually assaulted during their service years. Walker wrote:

The same issue of the Bangor Daily News which reported that the number of sexual assaults nationwide is the lowest since 1989, also contained news of two reported rapes in the Bangor area. Is it possible that this crime is increasing in our area but not elsewhere?

First, it is important to note that what has declined is the number of rapes reported to law enforcement agencies, a number which is usually very different from the number of rapes which actually occur. The primary reason for this discrepancy is that rape continues to be the one crime where the victim is made to feel as if she is to blame for what happened to her, either because of what she was wearing or drinking, or because of where she went. A victim of rape feels that she will not be believed if she tells anyone, especially a law enforcement officer who is usually a male.

Disclosures in the military and year-end statistics at Rape Response Services tell a different story than the numbers from the Justice Department. Fifty-six sexual assaults reportedly occurred in Penobscot and Piscataquis counties during 1996. This number reflects only a small percentage of the total calls which came into the hotline at Rape Response Services, and does not include all the rapes which are alleged to have occurred in this area. Victims who reach out for help from the anonymity of the hotline are not likely to report to law enforcement agencies. It is doubtful that the sexual assaults reported to all law enforcement agencies in the two counties would total 56.

Until victims of sexual assault can feel believed and safe when they tell about what has happened to them, the crimes of rape, incest, abuse and harassment will continue to be underreported. For this reason, I commend Senator Olympia Snowe and others on the Armed Services Committee for believing the courageous women in the armed forces who are coming forward with their stories.

Community education and training events were important outreach tools for RRS. Staff from the DA's office initiated a discussion with Walker in May about co-facilitating a training for area police officers on rape evidence collection and working with victims. The subsequent three-hour training was held at the Orono Police Department in late June. Because of Walker's earlier employment as Penobscot County Clerk, RRS was able to maintain the good rapport that Mullen-Giles had begun with personnel in the DA's and Sheriff's offices and with the Commissioners, all in Penobscot county.

Since some of the RRS funding through DHS was dependent on the Legislature, Walker thought it was essential to provide outreach and education about RRS programs to state representatives and senators in the two counties. What became an established practice every two years in January, following an election the previous November, was to send a congratulatory letter to each of the 31 members of the Legislature in the

RRS catchment area. A copy of the current Annual Report was included with each letter.

RRS was one of 30 exhibitors at a Community and Resource Fair sponsored in Greenville in July. Tents on the lawn of the C.A. Dean Hospital housed information tables from a variety of area health care providers and social service agencies in Piscataquis County, where RRS was still trying to establish a presence. Continuing to attend Resource Exchange monthly meetings in Dover-Foxcroft, Walker learned about the Fair and staffed the RRS table, giving away free brochures and other merchandise (coffee mugs, magnets, bumper stickers) which had been ordered years before and stored at the office. Few people turned out for the event, but it was "not a complete bust" because of contacts made or renewed.

Walker traveled to Dover-Foxcroft once a week, beginning September 23rd, to participate in recertification training sessions which were sponsored periodically by Womancare. Taught by Ginger Hutchins, the twelve 2.5 hour evening classes helped Walker learn more about the unique situations experienced by people affected by domestic abuse and the services they needed. Offered primarily for public school teachers who could earn recertification credits for their attendance, the sessions also provided good networking opportunities for RRS in Piscataquis county schools. Walker presented information about sexual assault at one of these recertification classes.

The last week in September was Rape Awareness Week at the University of Maine. A committee on which Walker represented RRS had been meeting for several months to plan the events, including a graffiti board at the Memorial Union where members of the campus community were invited to write their thoughts and ideas about rape and sexual assault. A brown bag lunch discussion, "Listening to the Victims of Sexual Assault," was facilitated by Walker during the week. Updates on statistics and "date rape drugs" were provided to "a small but receptive audience" that talked about myths, prevention, and hotline services.

Because of the increasing presence of RRS in the communities, a decision was made to print business cards with the hotline number vertically displayed under the logo. Addresses and telephone numbers for the two offices were also listed in teal on the light gray cards printed by Bangor Letter Shop. Board members, volunteers, and staff were all given multiples of these cards to distribute to individuals or at events. When an email address and a Web page were available in early 1998, stickers with this information were affixed to the backs of the cards.

In mid-March, Walker was privileged to attend the sixth annual National Student Conference on Campus Sexual Violence at St. Cloud State University in Minnesota. Campus Advocates Against Sexual Assault at St. Cloud was the local organizer of the event. The theme of the Conference was "Ending Sexual Violence: Commitment, Conflict, and Endurance." In her journal at the end of the conference, Walker wrote that she "picked up lots of ideas, and was very impressed with the quality of student leaders from around the country." Although she was familiar with the Clothesline Project of T-shirts decorated by survivors of domestic violence, she had not seen red and blue T-shirts designed by rape and incest survivors, respectively, until this event. Some red and blue T-shirts were subsequently decorated through the years by RRS group participants. Each shirt depicted a particular woman's experience, creating a visual display bearing witness to violence against women.

Lanphere-Ames left RRS just before Walker went to Minnesota, and shortly before O'Brien was due to take maternity leave. No longer having an employee in Piscataquis county, Walker made a point of being present in the Dover-Foxcroft office at least once a week to check messages, pick up mail, and network with Womancare staff and community members. She also attended monthly meetings of Resource Exchange and the Domestic Abuse Task Force, both in Dover-Foxcroft. Similar to the Task Force that met in Bangor, the presence of RRS at the table appeared to be welcomed by all participants.

One of the tasks which Walker completed was the delivery of Sexual Assault Awareness Month posters to the schools in Piscataquis county. RRS held the first poster contest early in 1997, copying an idea from another Maine sexual assault center. Encouraging students to create artwork that would appeal to other teenagers was a goal of the contest. Guidelines for the posters, including size, had been drawn up and distributed early in the year to art teachers in high schools throughout the two counties. The winning entry from a student at Bangor High School became the property of RRS. Poster-size (11"x15") color copies of the sole entry were made at Bangor Letter Shop and delivered by RRS staff to all high schools and colleges throughout the two counties in March.

Being upstairs in the RRS office at Womancare helped establish a great rapport and working relationship with that project's staff, especially during brown bag lunches in the group room. Walker was intentional about collaboration with both Womancare and SR because the issue of violence against women was too important for turf battles.

Sexual Assault Awareness Month

Although a committee had been meeting regularly at the RRS office to plan for Sexual Assault Awareness Month, including the poster contest, the most activity in April took place on the University of Maine campus with student leadership. RRS was part of a Rape Awareness Week subcommittee of the campus Rape Awareness Committee that planned the events. A journal entry noted that April 18th was "terribly cold and wet for a TBN March, but we went around campus anyway, and the rain did stop while we walked. I am so impressed with the students with whom I have worked on the march. It has been a great experience for me to lose some of my cynicism about young people."

Another long editorial by Walker, "Confronting Sexual Assault," was published in the April 19th edition of the BDN. The impetus was Sexual Assault Awareness Month:

> Sexual assault refers collectively to several violent crimes perpetrated, mostly by males, against both females and males of all ages. Rape, incest, child sexual abuse, sexual harassment—all are forms of sexual assault which occur with frightening frequency in the Bangor area.
>
> One in three women and one in six men will be sexually assaulted in their lifetime. Eighty-five percent of the assaults will be perpetrated by an acquaintance of the victim: date, neighbor, husband, friend, family member. Only 26 percent of rapes are reported to law enforcement agencies. A slightly higher percentage of victims will seek medical attention, though the risks are high for injury, infection, disease, and, for female victims, pregnancy. Recent studies are showing that a disturbing number of teenage pregnancies are the result of incest or rape by an older man, often a family member.
>
> Myths about sexual assault prevent victims of these crimes from seeking the help they need. Our reluctance to talk about anything

sexual, except in a joking or embarrassing manner, contributes to a victim's hesitation in reporting a sexual assault. Prevention programs in the public schools are also hindered by the widespread acceptance of myths about sexual assault, and by the mistaken belief that "sexual assault doesn't happen in this school or community."

The primary reason for our reluctance to confront sexual assault is the myth that "rape is sex." All crimes of sexual assault are crimes of violence. Sex is the weapon. Perpetrators dominate and overpower their victims by force and by threats. A victim's body is violated without consent, and repeated "no's" are ignored. Threats of greater harm to the victim, including murder, if she or he tells anyone about the assault, are frequently made by the perpetrator. It is simply wrong to equate such violence with sex, just because the same body parts are involved.

Another myth which is damaging to victims of sexual assault is that people "ask" to be raped by what they are wearing, how much they drink, or where they go. This myth makes sexual assault the only violent crime where the victim is blamed for what happened to her or him. Her dress was too short, his jeans were too tight, he was drunk, she should not have gone to his room alone—all of these victim-blaming statements focus attention away from the criminal act which has occurred. The most common feeling experienced by victims is one of guilt that somehow she or he could have prevented the assault. This myth which blames the victim only increases these guilt feelings, and reinforces the reluctance to report the crime. Can we really be serious in believing that anyone would "ask" to experience the physical and emotional trauma of rape or incest?

Recent cases of alleged rape in the sports world, and the confusing situation of rape accusations and counter-accusations in the military, have focused attention on a third myth: victims claim they are sexually assaulted to get even with the perpetrator, or to get attention for themselves. In actuality, false claims of rape and other forms of sexual assault are no more likely to occur than false claims of any other crime. It is estimated that less than 2 percent of claims of rape are unfounded. Listening to and believing the victims of sexual assault, and countering the myths, are ways that each of us can help to end these violent crimes and to bring some sense of healing to the victims.

Jennifer Dodge, a hotline advocate who had taken the fall RRS training in 1996, wrote a companion editorial that was published in the same edition of the BDN to highlight Sexual Assault Awareness Month. Both Dodge and Ann Hartman were hired by Walker in May to assist part-time with volunteers and office tasks during O'Brien's maternity leave. Walker had asked advocates to consider writing something for publication as part of RRS plans for the month, and Dodge was the only person who responded. She wrote:

> *When you ask any woman the chances are she'll tell you her greatest fear is being unable to defend herself from a rapist. This fear will be realized for one in three women at some time in their lives. Millions of women take self-defense courses each year in the United States and even those who don't have some strategy for self-protection. Some won't walk alone after dark, some install security systems, and an increasing number of women own handguns. But what is wrong with this picture?*
>
> *The problem reaches farther than most of us can bear to look. We shield our eyes from its glare, we turn our back and run to the false security of pepper spray and dead-bolt locks. Caution is so deeply ingrained in our daily lives that most of us don't realize how restricted our freedom is. Let alone get angry at it. The problem is the belief that living in fear is just part of being a woman. That it's something we must accept if we are to survive. That we shouldn't expect men to stop sexually assaulting women, so we must tailor our needs to meet theirs. That if a woman has let down her guard for a moment and been victimized, then it is her fault for not protecting herself.*
>
> *Perhaps it is easier to teach women how to protect themselves than it is to teach men not to rape. Perhaps we think women are more receptive to being told what to do than men are. Perhaps that tired old "boys will be boys" attitude persists. Yet no matter how much self-defense we learn, we can never feel totally prepared to stop a rapist. Manufacturers of self-defense products know this as well as women do. They prey on our fear, encouraging us to buy guns for that extra measure of security.*

When it comes to stopping rape, women are always at the mercy of men. We can learn self-defense tactics, prosecute rapists and scream for an end to violence, but we are ultimately dependent on men to stop rape. And yet we find ourselves trying desperately to stop it ourselves. We learn it is our responsibility not to be raped. We learn it is our responsibility to protect ourselves. And few ask, "When will it be men's responsibilities not to rape?" As long as we expect women to control an uncontrollable situation such as this, we can expect no end to the atrocities.

Learn self-defense if it makes you feel safer. By all means lock your doors and don't walk alone after dark. Don't leave yourself at the mercy of an attacker. But also look at the big picture. As a society, we need to refocus our energy on stopping rape where it starts—with a lack of respect for women. No self-defense course or security system can change this.

Hotline Volunteers

Notices about the need for volunteers appeared in successive issues of *The Weekly* during June and early July. The free advertising was available every Thursday when this supplement to the BDN was published: "Rape Response Service [*sic*] in Bangor needs volunteers for its round-the-clock Hotline which helps victims and their significant others. Call 941-2980 for an application and more information." When prospective volunteers completed the application, they were asked where they had heard about the opportunity, and many stated "*The Weekly.*"

The summer issue of *The Rape Response Reporter* described the importance of volunteers at RRS. Walker wrote: "I have said many times that this agency would not exist without our volunteers. The editing of this newsletter, for example, is the work of a volunteer, and I thank Jen [*Dodge*] for her efforts. During the first six months of 1997, volunteer hotline advocates have provided 4456 hours on the hotline, taking shifts 'round the clock every day. At a conservative $6.50 per hour, this contribution of time is worth $28,489 to Rape Response Services. One advocate who has been with us for almost three years has contributed over $15,000 worth of hours.

"Volunteer hotline advocates also accompany victims to the hospital on request, or through the court system. A thirty-five hour training course is required before a volunteer can take shifts on the hotline. Anyone reading this newsletter who is interested in becoming a hotline advocate may call the office now for an application; the next training will begin mid-September."

Assisting at the Bangor office during the summer was Debra Ellis, a student in human services at UC in Bangor, who completed a three-month internship under Walker's supervision at RRS. She was present at the office for one or two eight-hour days each week when Walker was also there. Her responsibilities included answering the telephone, putting newspaper clippings into scrapbooks, and completing assigned readings. Because of the summer placement, Ellis was unable to take the volunteer training until fall and could not take hotline shifts until then.

In mid-May, a MECASA Executive Directors' two-day retreat was held at a bed and breakfast, the Fairhaven Inn, in Bath. One of the tasks accomplished at this event was the revision and editing of several sections of the volunteer training manual, now titled "Help and Healing." The highest priority updates were the legal information sections to keep them current with changes in Maine law. Each Director read and rewrote separate portions of the manual; copies of the revised book were available early in 1998.

Several policies were adopted by the RRS Board through the years because of directives from MECASA or DHS, or due to suggestions from staff or advocates. The Policy on Illegal Drugs was approved by the Board in May to address what was then becoming a more apparent societal problem. Woolley provided assistance with developing this policy because of her employment at another social service agency:

> *The possession, use, manufacture, dispensing, or distribution of illegal drugs (heroin, cocaine, marijuana, LSD, steroids, etc.) is prohibited at any time in the RRS office, while taking hotline shifts or backup shifts, and as part of any RRS activities. "Illegal drugs" does not mean the use of drugs under a valid prescription. Employees and volunteers known to use, possess, manufacture, dispense or distribute illegal drugs are liable to public law enforcement actions and disciplinary action. Employees and volunteers who violate the illegal drug policy will be subject to disciplinary action by RRS. The severity of the imposed sanctions will be appropriate to the violation; possible sanctions include suspension,*

probation, dismissal, restitution, official censure or reprimand, referral for prosecution, participation in a rehabilitation program, and other actions that RRS deems appropriate.

Copies of all policies relevant to clients and the hotline were distributed to new advocates at the end of the training. New advocates and employees signed and dated one copy of each policy, which was retained in the personnel file if an employee or in the advocate's file. A second copy was kept by the employee or advocate.

School-Based Programs

The school-based education program in the two counties had suffered from the upheavals at RRS during the previous year. In addition to community education and outreach, school presentations were a vital part of the RRS mission.

One of the frustrating financial scenarios for all the sexual assault centers relative to school-based education was the state's decision to funnel a huge increase in sexual assault prevention money (earmarked for educational programs) from the federal PHHSBG into the coffers of the Maine Department of Education (DOE) instead of granting it to MECASA. Trying to reverse this decision had been ongoing since the previous August when Marty McIntyre, Executive Chair of the MECASA Board, made a presentation to the Bureau of Health in DHS about each center's school programs, plans, and the need for more money to reach more students. Both DHS and DOE saw their decision as a way for the rape crisis centers to gain access to the schools, because if sexual assault prevention was not in the health education curriculum, MECASA member educators would have no reason to be there either. Representatives from the DOE had already met with MECASA EDs early in January to begin a collaboration based on the Maine Learning Results for elementary and secondary schools. The health education curriculum goals specifically mentioned violence prevention at each grade level, and MECASA member centers were in place to write learning objectives and provide classroom presentations and/or teacher training sessions.

During 1997, RRS developed learning objectives for sexual assault prevention programs in middle and high schools, grades five through twelve. Copies of these objectives were sent to every school in the two counties with an introductory letter before the 1997-98 school year began. The letter mentioned the availability of RRS to provide classroom presentations. What was of utmost concern to MECASA was how classroom teachers would handle disclosures of sexual violence if they alone presented the sexual assault prevention material in the classroom.

Personnel Changes

Before she returned from her maternity leave early in September, O'Brien expressed a desire to focus on educational presentations in the schools, and Walker concurred. O'Brien became the part-time School-Based Educator as the new school year began. Prior to this time, RRS did not have a consistent presence in the public schools despite the preparation of learning objectives. O'Brien worked hard to change this and was invited to make presentations in many Bangor area school districts. Walker was able to fill requests for undergraduate classes at Beal College in Bangor, the University of Maine, Husson College, Eastern Maine Technical College (EMTC), and for staff at the Bangor Area Homeless Shelter.

After O'Brien made her decision, two part-time positions at RRS were advertised: a Volunteer Coordinator in the Bangor office and an Outreach Coordinator in Dover-Foxcroft. The advertisement for the Volunteer Coordinator position in the BDN in late August mentioned the "opportunity to work with committed group of volunteers." The position was part-time with prorated benefits, and "volunteer experience was a plus." The Outreach Coordinator in Piscataquis County was advertised in *The Eastern Gazette* and *The Moosehead Messenger* as well as the BDN: "Part-time, prorated benefits. Outreach to schools and community groups. Must have public speaking skills and ability to work independently. BS degree preferred. Training will be provided. Reliable transportation required."

Resumes and a cover letter for the Outreach Coordinator position were to be sent to Walker's attention at the Dover-Foxcroft office. After interviewing several candidates in both the Bangor and Dover-Foxcroft offices during the first week of September, the two part-time positions were accepted by Norma Allen. She had volunteered at Womancare and lived partway between the two RRS offices. Although unplanned, the two positions becoming one was a good decision that benefitted both Allen and RRS. A journal entry mentioned that Allen "landed in the midst of a whirlwind and took it in stride." Her title was Volunteer [Bangor]/Outreach Coordinator [Dover-Foxcroft], and she would split her time between the two offices.

Decisions about hiring and firing employees were delegated to Walker by the RRS Board of Directors; she only had to keep the Board informed about these actions and usually sought the advice of the Board President before deciding. New employees received a memo from Walker, spelling out job title, hours, rate of pay, details of health insurance coverage, and noting that RRS positions were covered by both workers compensation and unemployment compensation insurance as required by Maine law.

Every person hired at RRS was expected to complete the volunteer training in the early months of employment, if possible. Allen was able to take the fall training which had been set up and facilitated by Hartman, with some assistance from Walker. Another one of the trainees, Angel MacLaren, was a social work intern whom Walker supervised for the remainder of the school year.

Annual Report and End-of-Year Fundraising Letter

Another Annual Report, fiscal year 1996-97, was printed by Bangor Letter Shop as soon as the financial records were audited. Income totaled $94,662, including $67,448 from DHS and grants from the Lois Gauthier Trust and the Haymarket Fund. The grant from the Lois Gauthier Trust was specifically designated for financial support to victims and survivors who could not afford to pay for counseling sessions. At the request of a hotline caller, Walker researched the availability of grants and submitted an application to the Trust. Individuals who wished to utilize these funds for their counseling sessions were approved by the RRS Board of Directors after submitting a written request. A thank you note from one recipient's mother remained on Walker's RRS bulletin board for several years, reminding her that such efforts were a valuable part of the RRS mission.

Statistics in the Annual Report were compared to the previous fiscal year, with two fewer clients served (173). Sixty-one sexual assaults occurred, an increase of eight. The hours of community education, including schools, had increased from 72 to 209, with an increase of over 2000 in the number of participants. Board officers remained the same as the previous year, but there was a smaller list of members, with both Partridge and Roberts leaving the Board. Estler ended her long-time service as a Board member by year's end. Nineteen new hotline volunteers had completed training, including two social work interns. Walker could not praise the hotline volunteers enough, noting in her journal that "advocates dropped like flies all day in terms of not being able to take shifts for the next five weeks. Many away, some having problems and need break. But the ones left really came forward and filled all the slots! What a great bunch!"

The November end-of-year fundraising letter was signed by Woolley and Walker:

> *Your financial support has enabled Rape Response Services to significantly expand our outreach into the middle and high schools of Penobscot and Piscataquis counties. During the month of October, for example, we reached more than 450 students with programs focused on creating safe dating relationships. Our collaborative effort with the Maine Department of Education is making sure that sexual assault prevention is incorporated into the health education curriculum which local school districts are now developing.*
>
> *As a result of our outreach into the schools, more individuals have called the hotline during the past fiscal year. Creating a safe place for victims and survivors to report the crimes of rape or incest continues to be a major focus of this agency. We rely on a strong group of volunteers who staff the hotline all day, every day, and provide more than $70,000 worth of unpaid services during the year. Grants received this fall will allow us to increase our outreach to area college students, and to northern Penobscot county.*
>
> *It is a pleasure at the end of another year to thank you for your support of this agency. Whether you have given a direct donation, or have contributed to the United Way or to one of our fundraising efforts, we could not do what we do without people like you who give generously of your time and money.*

Enclosed with the letter, in addition to the response card and envelope, was a list of the 68 businesses and individuals who had contributed items and services to the Fall Festival Auction. A sentence at the top of the list encouraged readers: "If you have an opportunity, please express your appreciation for their support." The Grasshopper Shop, Bangor Mall, and Penobscot Paint were also recognized on the list for donating gift certificates which were presented to the poster contest winner in April.

For the first time, the agency was represented at the annual Festival of Trees held during the first weekend in December. The YMCA in Dover-Foxcroft charged a nominal fee for electrical outlet access and floor space on which a decorated Christmas tree could be placed. This event gave RRS another way to be present in the greater Piscataquis County community. As noted at the beginning of the year, outreach into the outlying areas of the two counties was a goal of RRS; many opportunities toward realizing this goal were provided throughout 1997.

1998: CELEBRATING TEN YEARS

The new year began inauspiciously with Ice Storm '98. Because of widespread icing and power outages, the RRS office was closed for a week in early January, as were many other businesses and public schools throughout Maine. Hotline services were still available to callers during the storm. Despite the weather, Walker observed in her journal on January 21st that there was a "good group of advocates and great staff at RRS, so feel as if we're doing well."

Internal storm clouds had hung over the center for a few years until August 25th when a former employee's lawsuit was finally heard in Bangor District Court. Walker attended the court proceedings with RRS pro bono attorney, Joe Baldacci, who presented arguments before Judge Jeffrey Hjelm. The basis for the claim was unpaid unemployment compensation. A motion by the opposing attorney to attach assets was especially troublesome.

Walker's journal recorded on August 25th: "A true disaster at court today. I fear for our future after the verdict, as I don't know where we will get the money." No verdict was rendered on the 25th, but Baldacci was informed the following day that the former employee was awarded more than $4600, including interest and court costs. Count II of the complaint (failure to pay wages in a timely fashion) was thankfully decided in favor of RRS because "the court does not regard unemployment benefits paid by the State to an unemployed person to constitute 'wages.'" The damages could not be paid with state funds, nor could they be paid until after the auction on September 9th because there were insufficient reserve funds. Interest continued to accrue in the interim. Although RRS did not prevail in court, Baldacci earned accolades for providing pro bono legal services during the entire time period. The agency could not have afforded to pay an attorney.

Sexual Assault Awareness Month

The resolution of the lawsuit was one of the notable moments at RRS during this tenth anniversary year of operation. An Open House and Reception at the office on the first day of April commemorated the decade that followed the filing of the Articles of Incorporation in 1988. Averill in "The Standpipe" featured RRS on that day: "Rape Response Services of Bangor and Dover-Foxcroft reminds you that the theme for Sexual Assault Awareness Month, which begins today, is 'Rape is not an April Fool's Joke.' To celebrate the 10th anniversary of Rape Response Services, past and present board members and advocates will be recognized at a public reception at 5:30 P.M. today at 157 Park St. in Bangor. The event also kicks off the RRS Web page for rape awareness.

"Other honorees at today's reception will be Orono High School senior Mike Landry, who won the second annual Sexual Assault Awareness Month poster contest. Landry's poster will be reproduced and distributed to all high schools and colleges in Penobscot and Piscataquis counties for display during April. Erica Cooper and Darcie Joy Burgoyne, both students at Hermon High School, finished second and third, respectively. Prizes were donated by Momma Baldacci's, Penobscot Paints and the Grasshopper Shop.

"RRS thanks judges Donna Gormley of WLBZ Channel 2, Tasha Jamerson of WABI-TV Channel 5, and Ric Tyler of WVII-TV Channel 7." Walker noted in her journal that inviting judges from the three local television stations meant that "we got some good exposure on TV for the poster contest," when the judging occurred on Friday, March 13th.

The reception was "well-attended and fun." Woolley purchased a cake from Cakes by Jan, who reproduced the RRS logo in teal on white frosting and wrote the words, "Congratulations Rape Response Services for 10 years of service to the community." The more than 50 poster contest entries received were displayed in the hallway outside the office, where a guest book was maintained by Allen. All three poster contest winners and their family members were present, reason enough to celebrate because only one entry had been received the previous year. The event, Walker observed, "did not require an inordinate amount of prep time but got some good publicity" on television. Floral bouquets were received from Board members, Womancare, and the Mabel Wadsworth Women's Health Center.

Sexual Assault Awareness Month brought the publication of a guest editorial in the BDN. On April 14th, Walker authored a piece titled, "Politics confuses sexual violence battle":

> *Sexual harassment is much in the news recently because of Paula Jones' lawsuit against President Clinton. This has led to investigations of other sexual improprieties in which the president has allegedly engaged. Making the cover of the weekly news magazines is a seemingly endless stream of women who have stories to tell about Clinton's sex life and their part in it.*
>
> *Furor about the sexual appetites of our nation's leaders is nothing new, and will not end with this president or these allegations. What is new, and hurtful to those of us in the violence against women movement, is the criticism that we are not rallying around Paula Jones and Monica Lewinsky et al., as we rallied around Anita Hill and other survivors of sexual violence.*
>
> *Pitting one woman against another, or one woman's group against another, is behavior engaged in by both men and women. Such behavior serves only to foil collaboration and to undermine the efforts made to promote zero tolerance for violence against women. It appears as if women and men think that power is finite, and when one person or group has power, another person or group will have to do without. What isn't realized is that power is strengthened, not weakened, by collaboration, by people working together to achieve a common goal.*
>
> *Those who have seized upon the Paula Jones' lawsuit, including the plaintiff herself, appear to see it as an issue of power over the president, perhaps even the power to bring Clinton down. They are not looking at the broader implications of what the lawsuit is saying to the millions of women who have legitimate claims of sexual harassment in their everyday workplaces. What is also not looked at is the fact that none of these women who were allegedly involved with the president were forced by him to do anything against their will. Each apparently consented to go to a motel room or to the Oval Office, unlike millions of victims/survivors of sexual violence who did not consent.*

And so to criticize those of us in the movement who have not jumped on Paula Jones' bandwagon is to drive a wedge among women, to force a split just when this country was starting to make a united statement that violence against women is not acceptable. Sexual violence is defined as a lack of consent; all the women allegedly involved with the president had an opportunity to deny consent and did not. Judge Susan Webber Wright's ruling legitimizes what many women have been saying since the Jones' case first emerged: This is not sexual harassment. Crude behavior, no doubt, is evident in all of the allegations, but the sexual advances were not continued when consent was denied by the women involved.

Such confusion and divisiveness, endlessly reported, allow sexually harassing and sexually violent behaviors to continue. The bottom line is a disservice to women who do have legitimate claims and are afraid to come forward because of the adverse publicity. And whether men are supporters or opponents of the president, they can continue to justify their violent treatment of women by laughing off the Washington scene as a media event. The gains we have made to educate men and women about sexual violence have not been well-served by these allegations.

The invitation for the annual Stay-at-Home Ball, held early in April instead of February, noted that it was "in celebration of Sexual Assault Awareness Month and the Tenth Anniversary of Rape Response Services." WEZQ 92.9 continued to support this event with music from 7:50 to 10:50 P.M. and for the first time aired public service announcements taped earlier by some of the syndicated radio announcers. The Ball provided: "An opportunity for you to remember the victims and survivors of sexual assault who have received assistance from Rape Response Services during the past ten years, and to help us move forward into our next decade."

Several other celebratory April events figured prominently in the Spring 1998 issue of *The Rape Response Reporter*. Walker created the two-sided newsletter using a software program on the new laptop, and had color copies made at Bangor Letter Shop. Her column began:

This special issue is sent to our supporters in celebration of Sexual Assault Awareness Month. The Reporter is combined in this mailing with the first newsletter from the Maine Coalition Against Sexual Assault. Rape Response Services is a member of the Coalition, and works collaboratively with the other nine centers located around the state.

April introduces our new Web page for rape awareness. Created by Carey Nason, one of our volunteer advocates, with financial assistance from a VAWA grant through the Maine Justice Assistance Council, the Web page is designed specifically for area college students, is accessible to anyone at http://www.mint.net/rrs/ and comments are welcome. The new e-mail address for Rape Response Services is rrs@ mint.net and the new FAX number is 941-2982.

RRS is pleased to be an allocation agency of the United Way of Eastern Maine. This status assures us of a grant of $5,000 to assist in our school-based education program. Wendy O'Brien, the part-time School-Based Educator, is busy during the school year doing class presentations in middle and high schools throughout Penobscot County.

The overall objective of this program is to educate young people about the crimes of rape, incest, harassment, and all other forms of sexual assault. Our agency believes that education is the only way to prevent the alarming incidence of these crimes. Specific learning objectives have been developed for grades five through eight and grades nine through twelve. These objectives include awareness about sexual assault, safety in relationships, available resources, and ways to help others.

Norma Allen provides school-based education programs in Piscataquis County schools as part of her Outreach Coordinator position. Since October 1, 1997, the beginning of our fiscal year, Rape Response Services reached 1,732 students in almost every area high school.

We are also working with the Maine Department of Education to be sure that sexual assault prevention is included in the new health education curriculum which local school districts are encouraged to develop. Representatives from Rape Response Services are available to work with community groups which are being organized to discuss curriculum development. We will also present teacher in-service programs on request.

Hotline Volunteers

The need to recruit more hotline volunteers was always evident, and now there were opportunities in both Millinocket and Bangor. On February 9th, Averill's "The Standpipe" column in the BDN publicized RRS in bold print: "Rape Response Services seeks phone volunteers":

We spoke last week with Kathy Walker, executive director of Rape Response Services of Bangor and Dover-Foxcroft, about the need for volunteers to work the organization's 24-hour hot line. RRS has a core group of "about 16 people" who volunteer for the hot line service, she said. But, of that number, only one is male. "We always like to have more volunteers, but we really like to have more male volunteers," she said. To become an RRS hot line volunteer requires participating in a 35-hour training session. That training, three hours per night, runs March 23rd through April 23rd. The sessions are Monday and Thursday evenings in Bangor.

Areas covered by the training include rape trauma syndrome, counseling skills, crisis intervention, social attitudes, and legal and medical issues. Volunteers then become advocates and are asked to sign up for weekly, eight-hour shifts. However, the program runs on a pager system so the advocate can work from his or her home. Prerequisites for becoming an RRS volunteer advocate include good listening skills and a caring manner.

A similar notice appeared in the February 14th edition of *The Weekly*. That article noted that "an effective Advocate will also have the ability to empower the sexual assault victim/survivor or those affected by sexual assault." This training was the first that Allen organized as Volunteer Coordinator. Walker was responsible only for the crisis intervention sessions on April 9th and 23rd, and the exit interviews the following week.

About this time, as noted in *The Weekly* article, RRS began to consistently refer to each caller and client as a "victim/survivor." As Walker explained in the crisis intervention presentations, the caller is the victim of a crime and has also survived that crime. RRS hoped that this language would empower the clients to think of themselves as more than victims. RRS was pleased to note that this terminology was also adopted by MECASA and the other centers.

The Katahdin Times on March 31st announced: "Victim services, support coming to tri-town area." This article stated:

> *Statistics show that one in three women will be raped in their lifetime. A rape occurs every 1.3 minutes in this country. Rape is a violent crime and is the only crime where the victim is blamed.*
>
> *April is Sexual Assault Awareness month. Rape Response Services (RRS) and the Katahdin Area Response Effort for non-violence (K.A.R.E.) are working together to bring services and support to victims in the Millinocket, East Millinocket and Medway area. Educational and training opportunities are planned throughout 1998.*
>
> *RRS in Bangor accepted more than 45 calls from Northern Penobscot County during 1996. Given the facts that RRS has no visible presence in this area, and that victims are reluctant to report an assault, the number of calls indicates a clear need for victim services. Because services will be community based, victims will receive the immediate and direct benefits of an increase in both services and support.*
>
> *Volunteer advocates play a very important role in the success of implementing and increasing services. During the next two weeks an invitation to participate in the volunteer advocate training project is extended to anyone who is sincerely interested in becoming involved. All applicants will be interviewed and screened by Kathy Walker, Executive Director of RRS. For more information or an application call K.A.R.E. member Sally Danforth at 723-9536 or Kathy Walker at 941-2980.*

By the time interested applicants for the training were screened, summer had arrived. Danforth and Walker made the decision to postpone volunteer training in Millinocket until September.

Money Matters

Good news from MECASA was received twice during the year. The DMHMRSAS grant was reauthorized for FY'99, beginning on July

1st at the full-year amount for each center, $17,767.60 plus an additional $1000 to provide mental health training for advocates. This meant that Veits could be paid a stipend instead of volunteering her hours. Paid for backup shifts beginning in May were volunteers Kellie Holmes and Barb Ames and staff members Allen and Walker.

A brochure published during the year by MECASA described the new mental health hotline services in detail and listed each of the centers' information. Without being exclusionary, the directors wanted to assure callers and providers that the focus was on people with a mental illness who had also experienced sexual violence. The document cautioned: "This service is not a substitute for DMHMRSAS crisis system services or any other service intended to respond to specific mental health related issues."

A listing of how the statewide hotline had been enhanced appeared in the brochure as follows:

- *Support line is able to handle a greater volume of calls from survivors with mental health problems.*
- *All support line advocates complete additional training specifically addressing trauma and mental health and responding to survivors who have mental health problems.*
- *All MECASA sexual assault centers assess the training needs of advocates and provide ongoing training opportunities so that they are able to address the special needs of survivors who have mental health concerns.*
- *There are two levels of advocates on call at all times. The first level of advocates responds to calls initially. The second call advocates are available* [as on call backup] *to provide support to survivors who have more complicated needs and/ or use the support line more frequently* [Level II callers].
- *All sexual assault centers have licensed clinicians available to advocates for clinical supervision.*
- *All support line advocates are volunteers who have completed a comprehensive 40-hour training course on sexual violence issues including topic areas such as: rape, incest, child sexual abuse, cult and ritual abuse, domestic violence, suicide, crisis intervention, role of law enforcement*

*and the criminal justice system and medical intervention.
Many are peer advocates.*

- *All support line advocates are evaluated at the completion
of training as to their ability and appropriateness to staff the
support line.*

Each center had to agree to meet these criteria before receiving the
funds from MECASA. Mandatory training to work with the population
identified for the trauma survivor support line was provided by the
University of New England (UNE) to RRS and other centers' staff and
interested volunteers. Because of Walker's degree in social work, the
RRS hotline training already incorporated many of these new MECASA
requirements, and she presented the crisis intervention portions of
each hotline training. The length of the training increased to 40 hours,
including time for reading the manual. RRS instituted a procedure
whereby only individuals who had received the mandatory training from
UNE would take the paid backup shifts on the hotline. Each center had
Level I and Level II advocates, the latter also known as paid backup.

The "Level II callers" on the enhanced hotline became known
throughout the state, and their names and telephone numbers were made
known to the answering service. When Level II callers contacted the RRS
hotline and identified themselves, backup persons were paged instead of
the on call volunteers. By the end of the year, one caller in particular had
utilized the RRS hotline many times for several hours each call. Walker
noted in her journal: "A long day with more calls on hotline from long-
winded person. I took one as third shift in early A.M., then I took over
for O'Brien and Allen in early P.M. Was stressed out but then realized
that this is why we exist, that the hotline is our primary service."

A second piece of good news from MECASA was the result of a
special directors' meeting in May to allocate additional PHHSBG funds
that would be funneled this time through DHS to MECASA centers
instead of to DOE. Earlier in the fiscal year, RRS had received $7750
from an increase in PHHSBG funds through DHS, in addition to the
annual allocation of $3402 from PHHSBG. When still more PHHSBG
money became available for FY'98 only, the MECASA directors present
at the May meeting voted to give RRS $10,567 of this additional amount.
Seventy-five percent of the new funds had to be spent on middle and

high school education. Proposals that each center made for the new funds helped to determine the amount allocated, with recognition from MECASA that RRS had many schools to reach in its catchment area. Although the fiscal year was almost completed, Greenlaw told the directors that the additional funds could be carried over in the new DHS contract.

These additional funds meant that O'Brien's position could be increased to full-time to provide school presentations in southern Penobscot and Piscataquis counties. She also initiated and staffed on-site services at several high schools, at Shaw House for homeless youth, and at Penobscot Job Corps. The schools provided a room and advertised hours when O'Brien would be available to meet individually with students who wanted to talk one-on-one about sexual assault issues. At the same time, Allen became the full-time Client Services Coordinator in Bangor, paid partially with funds from the DMHMRSAS grant.

A Community Presence

An increasing nationwide awareness of "drug-facilitated rape" resulted in an invitation for Walker to speak at a conference, "Rohypnol and Other Drugs Used to Facilitate Rape," sponsored by the District of Maine United States Attorney's Office and the University of Maine's Department of Public Safety. Held in March at the University, this afternoon event attracted over 100 people from around the state and resulted in a three-hour training videotape of all the speakers. The tape was to be used with first responders, law enforcement personnel, and victim services agencies.

Walker spoke for 30 minutes about the "proper treatment of victims of sexual assault." Sharing the stage with her were Florida State Prosecutor, Attorney Robert Nichols, and Florida Detective David Robshaw, who were nationally recognized experts on investigating and prosecuting drug-facilitated crimes. Other speakers included LeaAnne Jameson, Maine Drug Enforcement Prosecutor; Robert Dana, University of Maine; William Browder, First Assistant U.S. Attorney for Maine; and Jay McCloskey, United States Attorney. While the extent of the drug use in Maine was difficult to determine, this conference was a first attempt to bring Rohypnol and other "date rape drugs" to the state's attention.

In a follow up to the March Conference, Walker wrote a "Dangerous 'date rape' drugs" guest editorial on May 11th for the BDN. (Note: An almost identical editorial by Walker was published in *The Katahdin Times* in May 2001.) Walker's editorial began:

> The *"date rape drug" of choice has always been alcohol. Getting a person drunk and then raping her or him is a familiar story. That such an action is against the law has not stopped it from happening, primarily because the perpetrators of such crimes threaten their victims about reporting to the police or telling anyone. Victims and survivors of rape are also likely to blame themselves for getting drunk, and society is all too willing to agree with them.*
>
> *In recent years there has been increasing information about new date rape drugs. Seen at first in the southern part of this country, Rohypnol and GHB are now making their way into Maine. Both drugs are illegal in the United States, something which makes them all the more appealing to those who would use and abuse them.*
>
> *Rohypnol is available in pill form; GHB is a liquid. Neither can be detected when put in a beverage. Both take effect within 15 minutes of ingestion, and cause a person to feel drowsy, to pass in and out of consciousness, and to have impaired muscle control.*
>
> *And these side effects are what make both substances useful as date rape drugs. If an unsuspecting victim drinks a beverage, any beverage, into which one of these drugs has been placed, within a short period of time the victim is only semi-conscious, if that. Loss of mobility of arms and legs is also common. Such a state makes a person ready prey for the rapist who slipped the drug into the drink; he knows the victim will not be able to resist the rape that he has planned.*
>
> *The rapist also is aware of another side effect of the drugs: the victim will not remember what happened to her, as both substances cause amnesia. Even if the victim of a drug rape has some recollection, or some physical symptoms that suggest a rape, the rapist can often get away with denying everything.*
>
> *Of the two substances, GHB is, if possible, the greater of two evils. Rohypnol is a controlled substance under federal and state law, and is manufactured in pill form in 1- or 2-milligram dosages. GHB, on the other hand, can be made at home—directions are available*

on the Internet. The two basic ingredients are engine degreaser and lye. Because there is no way of knowing what proportion of ingredients was used to create one dose of GHB, the danger of serious side effects, even death, from this drug is greatly increased over Rohypnol. Both drugs are illegal to use and distribute in this country, and severe penalties exist for rapists who administer any drug, including alcohol, against another person's will with the intent to commit a sexual assault. Never accept a beverage from a stranger. If there is any suspicion that a date rape drug was administered, get medical attention, including a urinalysis, immediately.

In addition to volunteer trainings and the Rohypnol conference in March, many opportunities to provide community education were presented to RRS during the year. Walker facilitated a workshop, "Listening to Victims/Survivors of Sexual Assault," at the "Health in Our Hands" conference in April, sponsored by the Mabel Wadsworth Women's Health Center and held at the University of Maine. The description of the one-hour session was: "The trauma of sexual assault effects [*sic*] the physical and emotional health of many of us and our family and friends. Being listened to and believed is often the first step toward healing."

Community education in the form of letters to the editor in the BDN continued throughout 1998. Hartman wrote a guest editorial, "Marital rape is wrong," that was published in the BDN on May 7th. She was identified as a "volunteer advocate with Rape Response Services and a Master's of Social Work candidate at the University of Maine," and wrote:

As a volunteer at Rape Response Services, I have talked to many survivors of the awful crime of rape. Fortunately, these women and men have contacted our hotline for support and information after their frightening and devastating experiences. Through this volunteer work, I have found most people are raped by someone they know, and many are raped by the person who is supposed to be their closest friend, partner, and family member—their spouse.

Marital rape is a serious problem. An estimated 14 percent to 25 percent of married women experience forced sex at least once during their marriages. Even though many people believe marital rape to be a significantly less serious crime than rape perpetrated by a stranger, research has shown that women raped by their husbands are just as likely to suffer from a variety of psychological problems as women raped by strangers or other types of acquaintances.

Until recently, the law in Maine protected husband rapists, claiming that a man could not rape his wife. It wasn't until 1989 that the Maine Legislature made spousal rape a crime. However, marital exemptions to parts of the gross sexual assault, sexual abuse of a minor, and unlawful sexual contact laws still remain on the books. For example, a marital exemption exists in the gross sexual assault law if the victim is under the age of 14 and the perpetrator is an adult. In Maine, we don't often hear of a child of that age being married to an adult. However, just this year a 24-year-old Waterville man was indicted on gross sexual assault charges because of his sexual relations with a 13-year-old girl. His lawyer is quoted as saying the man planned to try to get a judgment in probate court for a marriage license and a possible ruling that would avoid the felony rape charge. In this case, the gross sexual assault law, instead of protecting girls, is harboring rapists.

It is crucial that we eliminate the marital exemptions from Maine's sexual assault laws. We need to eliminate the false implication that rape under certain circumstances is justifiable because rape is a heinous crime under any circumstances. Join us in contacting our Maine legislators to introduce a bill that would enable a victim of rape, married or not, to have legal recourse.

A deputy DA in Caribou, John Pluto, wrote a follow-up letter to the editor in which he disputed Hartman's belief that Maine statutes contained a bias against marital rape. Pluto noted that a jury in Aroostook County had recently convicted a man of this crime. He wrote that if a minor were legally married to an older man, the laws about forcing sex without consent would apply as in any other relationship. Pluto did not believe that further changes in the statute were needed.

Written by Walker and titled "Rape and consent," a letter published on June 22nd addressed the issue of consent which always raised a lot of questions, especially among young people:

It should not surprise us that young men like the student at Bates College express anger that the responsibility for avoiding charges of rape/sexual assault rests with them. The underlying issue, of course, is consent. Both rape and incest are crimes under Maine law, which is based on the concept of consent. If one party does not give consent to the sexual act or is incapable because of age or impairment of giving consent, the act is a crime charged against the second party. Impairment includes being intoxicated. It is also illegal to give someone alcohol or drugs and then rape her.

Giving consent implies communication. Talking about confusing signals of dress and body language is encouraged. Stating a clear "no" and respecting that "no" are responsible actions by both parties. The "no" may be stated on the first date, on the twenty-first date, even after marriage, and still demands the respect of the person who hears it.

Young men sometimes bring up the issue of male-bashing when their responsibility in a sexual relationship is addressed. What they forget or overlook, however, is that the weapon in the crime of rape is ultimately their responsibility. And young women raise the issue of victim-blaming. They feel as if they are unfairly criticized for their dress, for what they drank, for walking alone. When the crime of rape is reported, arresting the rapist is more difficult because of many victim-blaming ideas ingrained in our society.

The opposite of victim-blaming, however, is not male-bashing. Both are attitudes which cloud the issue and prevent honest communication. Communication implies responsibility. A responsible male will ask for and receive consent before and during a sexual relationship. A responsible female will expect her clear "no" will be respected before and during a sexual relationship. Neither party will take advantage of the poor choices sometimes made by the other, but each will be aware that poor choices can lead to the crime of rape.

What constituted sexual harassment was another issue which raised questions and concerns among adults in places of employment. Although RRS had publicized the availability of sexual harassment training for several years, no requests for such training had been made up to this point in Walker's tenure. This changed in May when she presented a two-hour workshop for the staff of MERT, a day program in Bangor for people with developmental disabilities. The acronym was the initials of the founder and ED, Mary Ellen Rush Thibodeau. Walker had met with her two weeks earlier to plan the session which "was well-received with compliments, a good, diverse group."

Rank and file union members also met in May for an "Introduction to Union Counselor Training" conference sponsored by the United Ways of Maine and the Maine AFL-CIO. The purpose of the conference was to provide attendees with information about community services, how to make referrals, and how to handle specific problems. Francine Stark from SR, and Walker presented a one-hour afternoon workshop titled "Crisis—Personal and Family" which was facilitated by DA Almy. One of the first events in recent memory where representatives from SR and RRS collaborated, this would not be the last. "Just being together is a step in the right direction," Walker wrote in her journal "and if I preach collaboration, I practice it too."

The second annual clinical training conference sponsored by the Office of Trauma Services in the Maine DMHMRSAS was held in Portland for two days in October. Over 650 people attended the conference which was open to survivors, families, professionals, and "others interested in learning more about the effects of trauma on the minds, bodies and spirits of its victims." Attendees would learn how to respond effectively to the needs of persons who had been sexually and/or physically abused and then retraumatized by professionals and institutions. Walker served on the planning committee.

"Violence, Trauma and Recovery: Responding to the Impacts of Interpersonal Violence" was the theme of this conference, at which Walker presented a 75-minute workshop, "Sexual Assault: A New 'Epidemic?'" The description of the session stated that it would: "explore the increasing interest in sexual assault as a public health issue. Viewed as an 'epidemic,' it has begun to generate both dollars and attention. What this might mean in terms of prevention efforts in Maine will be discussed." The "workshop went okay," Walker wrote, "but I had too much stuff, not enough time for discussion."

Earlier in the year Walker had responded to a Request for Proposals (RFP) to provide training on child sexual abuse detection and prevention for the Staff Education and Training Unit at DHS. Her proposal to present the six-hour session was accepted. In November, she gave the first of what would be two or three trainings each year for DHS personnel in various towns and cities around the state. Venues were usually hotel conference rooms. A stipend of $400 per session provided extra income for RRS. Walker noted after the November session that "evaluations were positive, and people seemed to be receptive." A combination of videos, lecture, small group discussions, and lots of handouts marked this and all future sessions. It became Walker's practice at each training or community event to begin her remarks by noting that there were likely to be survivors of sexual violence in the audience. She encouraged everyone so affected to call the hotline, and always made sure that brochures with the statewide toll-free number were available, as she often presented these trainings outside the RRS catchment area.

"Violence and women" was the heading for Walker's November 4th letter to the BDN:

> *A respected and beloved physician was murdered in his home, presumably for providing abortions, a legal action in all states, in addition to other obstetrical and gynecological services for women. A woman who was raped while comatose in a nursing home gave birth, although no one realized she had been raped or was pregnant as a result of the rape. A woman was shot and killed by her estranged husband a day after she made the choice to file for a divorce.*
>
> *Where is the outrage that violence against women, and violence to prevent women from making choices, occurs in this country every day? Are we so bombarded with violence on the news and in television shows or movies that we feel speaking out will not make a difference? Or do we believe that somehow this violence does not concern us?*
>
> *Murdering an abortion provider takes away every woman's right to choose what to do with her own body. Rapes and acts of domestic terror also take away this right. Violence against women impacts us all. It is time to speak out collectively against the erosion of women's rights which is occurring one murder and one rape at a time.*

MECASA and the Maine Coalition to End Domestic Violence (MCEDV) collaborated at a November event to highlight "Our Coordinated Community Responses to Ending Violence Against Maine Women & Children." Held at the Black Bear Inn in Orono, the day-long conference featured workshops and table exhibits, and was attended in part by staff and volunteers from sexual assault centers and domestic violence projects around the state. The purpose was to network, learning from each other. Other collaborators for the event included the Maine Ambulatory Care Coalition, Maine Commission on Domestic Abuse, DOE, DHS, Maine Department of Public Safety, General Medical Center (Portland), and the Muskie School of Public Service. Proposals to present workshops had to be submitted in advance to the planning committee for selection.

RRS was accepted to present part of a workshop and also a table exhibit which featured the first website for a rape crisis center in the state. Walker's journal noted that she was "pumped up by our collaboration with Womancare, the only two [*disciplines*] who presented together." This workshop, "Collaboration to Provide School-based Services in Penobscot and Piscataquis Counties," was proposed by Womancare and presented by Sandra Harmon, staff member there, and Allen. A handout provided at the workshop described the benefits of this collaboration:

> *...a natural outcome of the relationship between Sandra and Norma over a number of years. Prior to her employment at Rape Response Services Norma had completed the training at Womancare and volunteered there as part of a school practicum. Rape Response Services has office space at Womancare and conversations around education led to an offer from Sandra to combine presentations on domestic violence, dating violence and date rape and sexual assault. The more the possibility was discussed, the more sense it made. By combining presentations, there would be less overlap and conflict of information presented. Teachers, who were already pressed for time, would be saved valuable time when meeting with two people at once to discuss and schedule presentations.*
>
> *The joint presentations were offered in the following manner: domestic violence on the first day, the second, dating violence, and on the third day, date rape and sexual assault. The collaboration*

between the two agencies has been a positive experience and has saved time for staff at Womancare, Rape Response Services, and schools, while providing the same quality services for students that schools in the Penquis area have come to expect of each agency.

This format for school presentations was to continue between RRS and Womancare in Piscataquis County and in later years, between RRS and SR in Penobscot County. The early partnership between RRS and Womancare in the schools was a new concept for centers in other parts of the state to consider.

Outreach into Northern Penobscot County

Finally being able to provide services in northern Penobscot County was another cause for celebration during the tenth anniversary year of RRS. Walker met early in the year with Marie Arant at Millinocket Regional Hospital and Chief Warren Nelson at the Millinocket Police Department, and then went to East Millinocket to meet with Gerald "Twig" Cramp, Police Chief, and Peggy Daigle, Town Manager. Purposes of the meetings were to update everyone on the VAWA grant status and to enlist their cooperation in the training pieces for medical and law enforcement personnel. "A profitable and pleasant day in the Millinocket area," Walker noted in her journal. "Received well by everyone I met and moving forward at last on the VAWA grant in northern Penobscot county."

In mid-July, a job listing for a School-Based Educator was placed by RRS in the *Lincoln News* and *The Katahdin Times*, both weekly newspapers serving northern Penobscot County. The notice read: "Part-time position available 8/31/98 in northern Penobscot County. The successful applicant will present educational programs in public schools and for community groups. Bachelor's degree required. Teaching experience preferred. Excellent pay; some benefits. Training provided." Cover letters and resumes were to be mailed to Walker's attention by July 30th. To be certain that RRS hired someone from the targeted area of Penobscot County, an advertisement was not placed in the Bangor newspaper. During the first week in August, Walker interviewed two women for the position and hired Gale Patchell of Millinocket.

The impetus for moving ahead with the Millinocket hiring was the volunteer training to begin there in early September as part of the VAWA grant. Volunteers would be trained to accompany a victim/survivor to the area hospitals or to the District Courts. The training could be less extensive (three hours once a week for three weeks) than that in Bangor because the volunteers would not take shifts on the hotline, but instead would be paged to go to the hospital. Focus of the training was on evidence collection, the rape protocol exam, and responding to the victim/survivor. Part of one training session was spent in the ER at Millinocket Regional Hospital so volunteers could become familiar with that setting. Each trainee was given a complete copy of the MECASA manual which they were expected to read. All pagers in the Millinocket area were programmed by Com-Nav with identical telephone numbers. The on call person was paged to respond to hotline calls from the Millinocket and Lincoln hospitals. A backup person usually had her pager turned on, with the same telephone number, and could be reached if the on call person did not respond.

Walker facilitated the training at the office space which RRS would later rent from Liz Denney, LCSW in East Millinocket. Patchell took this training as well as the longer session in Bangor, and was provided with a computer and printer to work out of her home. Nine hotline volunteers, including Denney, McGillicuddy, and Danforth, and two nurses (Dorothy Budge and Julie Nason) completed the sessions. Walker's journal recorded on September 28th that she "finished up Millinocket training with a good session for a great group. I have really enjoyed being up there."

The efforts in the Katahdin area received a lot of excellent publicity in *The Katahdin Times.* An article on October 20th specifically focused on Patchell's hiring and was accompanied by a photo of Danforth, Patchell, and Walker reviewing education materials. Earlier in the month, on the 6th, reporter Barbara Waters wrote "Volunteer advocates to help victims of rape, sexual assault":

> *In less time than it takes to read this news story, another woman somewhere in America will be raped. U.S. Department of Justice compiled statistics bear this out: as the clock ticks away, somewhere in America every two minutes a woman is raped or becomes a victim of sexual assault. As if that were not enough, the FBI estimates that 72 of*

every 100,000 females in the U.S. were raped last year.

Least one think rural Maine and the Katahdin region are immune to this, one need only reflect on the fact that at least 60 of the rapes that occurred last year in the Piscataquis/Penobscot County area were reported to Rape Response Services of Bangor and Dover-Foxcroft. But, in far too many cases, rape victims are silent victims, not reporting their rape from the belief that it is a personal, private matter or from fear of reprisal.

But new efforts are underway in the Katahdin Region, the aim of which is not only to educate people, but to provide services locally for those who may be victims of rape or sexual assault. Through a collaborative effort between Rape Response Services and KARE (Katahdin Area Response Effort for Non-Violence)—and as a result of funding provided by the Maine Department of Human Services—a school-based educator has been hired for northern Penobscot County.

Filling this part time position is Millinocket resident Gale Patchell who, once her training is completed, will be available— beginning next month—to make classroom presentations in all school districts from Howland north. Her topics can include, but are not limited to safe dating relationships, dating violence, harassment and communication skills. All of the schools in her area have been advised of her availability. Her role, she emphasized, is not as a counselor.

"Hiring someone locally has been a goal of Rape Response Services," observed Kathy Walker, executive director. "Gale has a knowledge of the area which someone from away does not have, and she has already established good contacts with the local school districts."

Patchell is available to speak with businesses and civic organizations about this new school-based program or about sexual assault issues. She may be reached at 746-3876 or at PO Box 377, Millinocket [the KARE mailbox]. Of her new role in the Katahdin region, Patchell observed, "This is definitely a way I can help people." She will be available to speak to students. She hopes this area of concern, as schools build and change their curriculum, will become a regular part of the curriculum of schools in the future. Patchell received a bachelor of science degree from the University of Maine a year ago, with a major in elementary education and a minor in psychology. During the past school year, she was a substitute teacher, ed tech and tutor at Opal Myrick Elementary School in East Millinocket.

But above and beyond this, another significant new effort, a team approach to rape and sexual assault has been undertaken cooperatively by KARE and Rape Response Services. One facet of this team approach got underway late last month, when several women began their training as Rape Response Services Volunteer Advocates— under the auspices of KARE and Rape Response Services—a service until now only available in the Bangor area. There are four additional persons who would like to become trained volunteer advocates. The goal is to have 12 to 15 trained volunteer advocates.

Once these individuals complete their intensive 10-hour training, they will serve as resource and support persons for sexual assault victims/survivors, their families and significant others. The advocate's role will include involvement in a hospital emergency room, interaction with the local police, and/or involvement in the court system.

They will have knowledge—and the ability to articulate that to victims and families—of the procedures involved in a medical examination for sexual assault, the legal procedures and the resources available in the community. They will play a support role in all those procedures and serve as a sounding board for victims/ survivors through the hours following a sexual assault and will help those individuals examine the options open to them.

These volunteers will be on call to go to the hospital to be with a victim. The team approach to this issue also will include intensive training of law enforcement officers [which] will include: an overview of sexual assault and its impact on victims/survivors; an introduction to the services available in the Millinocket area; a discussion of appropriate responses to victims/survivors of sexual assault, including children; procedures for collecting evidence; information on Maine law pertaining to sexual assault cases; and to promote collaboration in the treatment of sexual assault victims/survivors. Additionally, rounding out the team approach, are two nurses from Millinocket Regional Hospital, Julie Nason and Dorothy Budge.

Once the team members and services are all in place locally, KARE and Rape Response Services will mount a campaign to educate people to report rape and sexual assault and to refrain from hiding behind a wall of silence. Sally Danforth, one of the organizers of the 10-year-old KARE organization, is pleased that at last a certain level of service will be available locally. She recalls several years ago accompanying a rape victim to Bangor and spending four hours there with that individual. "That's when I thought how great it would be to have something (services) here," she observed. She takes a great deal of satisfaction in the fact KARE's perseverance paid off.

Those currently being trained as Rape Response Services Volunteer Advocates are from all walks of life—housewives, professionals, teachers, etc.—and all are offering their time for a variety of reasons including: the opportunity to help others, the fact that providing services early on prevents long lasting effects, and making services available where they are needed. The training of advocates, law enforcement personnel and nurses is being made possible through a grant recently awarded to Kathy Walker of Rape Response Services, the author of that grant. The grant runs out June 20, 1999.

Part of this grant will fund the printing of brochures detailing services that are available in the area. KARE will be responsible for the distribution of this brochure. KARE also plans to educate the communities about these latest efforts by eventually going out into the community to speak at meetings of various organizations.

Printed by the Lincoln Press in teal, pink, and gold on glossy white paper, the tri-fold brochure mentioned in the October 6th article was the first tangible evidence that the grant was in place. "Sexual Assault Victim Advocate Services provided by Katahdin Area Response Effort for Nonviolence and Rape Response Services" drew attention to the front of the brochure, along with the logos for the two agencies.

Inside, each of the three sections highlighted what was being offered to the region:

- *Sexual Assault Nurse Examiners: Millinocket Regional Hospital has certified Registered Nurses who have specialized training in the collection of forensic evidence. They offer professional expertise to victims/survivors throughout the rape protocol examination. Survivors are encouraged to seek medical assistance as soon as possible.*

- *Trained Volunteer Advocates: The Katahdin area has trained volunteer advocates on call 24 hours a day. The volunteer advocate is available to serve as a resource and support person for the victim/survivor, his/her family, and significant others. The advocate's role is to provide compassionate support during the rape protocol examination, and to assist in the interaction with local police officers, or the court system. Information about future volunteer training sessions in the Katahdin area may be obtained by calling 746-3876 or 941-2980.*

- *Education: Education and consultation are available to schools and to community groups in Northern Penobscot County. The School-Based Educator at Rape Response Services provides presentations which focus on sexual assault and sexual harassment. For further information or to arrange a presentation, please leave a message at 746-3876.*

Annual Auction and Awards Night

What became a highlight every year at RRS was the annual auction, a primary focus of the Summer 1998 edition of *The Rape Response Reporter*. Averill's September 1st column in the BDN reported: "Rape Response Services expects successful auction. Last year's event was so successful that planners of the second Fall Festival Auction and Awards Night hope to far exceed the $4,500 raised during the first event in 1997. The auction begins at 5:30 P.M. Wednesday, Sept. 9th, at Jeff's Catering in Brewer. According to RRS executive director Kathy Walker, the goal for this year's fundraiser is $7,500. RRS has received 'an incredible number of items' for the auction, Walker said. 'In fact, we just received a signed and numbered otter sculpture from Forest 'Toby' Hart of Monroe.'"

The *Rape Response Reporter* mentioned that Sue McKay was returning again as the auctioneer. Music during the silent auction would be presented by the singing trio, "In Our Midst" (Edie Beaulieu, Susanne DeGrasse, Jean Boutot). Autographed items for the live auction included photographs from Katie Couric and Rosalyn Carter, a signed basketball from the Women's National Basketball Association (WNBA) team, the Detroit Shock, books from Gary Larson and Michael Feldman, and an Eric Carle poster.

Moosehead Furniture in Monson generously donated two maple dining chairs, the first of several years of support. Gifts of pottery from Tricia Largay at Monroe Salt Works continued to delight auction attendees. Lovely rugs from Saliba's in Bangor were popular items each year. Handmade creations and gift certificates rounded out the list of 43 items for the live auction plus at least 50 for the silent auction. Averill noted in her column: "For those early holiday shoppers, this may be just the night, and just the place, to get a lot of that pre-holiday 'work' done."

Jeff's Catering lent itself well to the auction setup, with narrow tables covered in white cloths around the perimeter of the room for the silent auction items. RRS had learned from the previous year how to organize the items and the bidding. Round tables in the middle of the banquet room accommodated guests, who could view live auction items arranged on a stage area. Jane Clayton assisted McKay by carrying the live auction items around to the tables so bidders could have a close-up view. The RRS Board and McKay decided on the order in which the items would be auctioned, and a printout with each item and donor was provided to the more than 100 guests. Estler was presented with the Janet Badger Volunteer Award by Badger and Woolley. Recognized for "her dedicated service to the agency for the past ten years, she was instrumental in the start of Rape Response Services a decade ago, and recently completed a long tenure on the board of directors, where she took a leadership role in developing personnel and board policies."

In addition to the auction and Ball, other fundraising events and donations provided some very welcome funds for RRS during 1998. The World's Largest Garage Sale, sponsored by WLBZ-TV Channel 2 in the Bangor parking garage in June was "not nearly as bad as I was told," noted Walker in her journal, "and we made over $400!" Volunteers, staff, and Board members all contributed items for the sale. Miller's Discount Store in Brewer held an employee "dress down" day every month and chose six organizations each year to receive the funds collected at these events. In November, RRS received a check for $30 in a letter that stated the Miller's employees "hope that this donation will help your group in their endeavors."

Annual Report and End-of-Year Fundraising Letter

The Annual Report for 1997-98 listed the same Board officers as in previous reports, with new Board members Judith Groth, Paula Johnson, and Bev Uhlenhake joining Greaney. All statistics outlined in the report showed large increases. There were 133 more hours of service on the hotline for 236 clients, 63 more than the previous fiscal year. The hours of school-based education had increased to 209, reaching 3417 students, an increase of over 2000. Sixty-four sexual assaults had occurred in FY'98, three more than in FY'97. Twenty-one hotline volunteers had received training in Bangor, enabling RRS to maintain a core group of over 25 on call advocates. The DHS contract provided income of $84,992, with an additional $32,732 in grants, fundraising, and from UWEM. Salaries and benefits for four employees was the largest expense at $64,315.

Woolley and Walker both signed the December 1998 "Dear Friend" letter. By the time this letter was mailed, new stationery had been printed with a letterhead that provided contact information for the two offices, Bangor and Dover-Foxcroft. The letter stated:

> As we near the end of our tenth anniversary year, it is a pleasure to gratefully recognize your continued support of Rape Response Services. Whether you have given a direct donation, or have contributed to the United Way or to one of our fundraising efforts, we could not do what we do without your generous gifts of time and money.
>
> Your donations during the past fiscal year enabled us to double our educational efforts and reach more that 3,400 students in the middle and high schools of Penobscot and Piscataquis counties. Having a presence in each of the school districts in the two counties provides students with an opportunity to learn about safe dating relationships. We also provide a weekly drop-in site at some area schools. Collaborative school presentations with Womancare, the domestic violence center in Piscataquis county, were a ground-breaking initiative for both agencies.
>
> A focus on prevention efforts in the schools is only part of the programs which your dollars help to support at this agency. Victims and survivors of rape and incest continue to receive care and attention

from our dedicated volunteers on the twenty-four hour crisis hotline. Our grant-funded training program means that volunteer advocates are available for the first time in northern Penobscot county to accompany a victim/survivor to Millinocket Regional Hospital. Another grant helped to get our Web page online.

For ten years, with your help, this agency has been making a difference in the lives of many individuals. Thank you for again considering a donation to Rape Response Services as part of your year-end giving plan. A response card and envelope are enclosed. We invite you to use the reverse side of the response card if you wish to honor someone with a special holiday gift.

The year concluded with a decorated tree set up in the snow outside the Piscataquis Regional YMCA for the annual Festival of Trees. Labeled the "Tree of Tears," it was donated by Rising Fields tree farm and decorated with laminated silvery tear drops, white and teal bows, and a laminated teal star on top, all coordinated by Allen.

Despite the financial setback of the lawsuit and delays in implementing the VAWA grant in northern Penobscot County, the year overall turned out to be a positive one for RRS. By the end of 1998, 22 advocates were available to take hotline shifts in Bangor, and an additional nine were on call for the first time ever in northern Penobscot County. Thanks to excellent print media coverage, the website, and many training opportunities, people in the two counties and beyond were learning that sexual violence was not acceptable.

1999: RRS INVOLVEMENT WITH
SEX OFFENDER NOTIFICATION

A statewide program that had surfaced during the previous year moved to the forefront: sex offender notification. With the help of key community players, RRS established a precedence in the state for procedures to use when the community notification of sex offenders occurred.

Steve Onacki, one of six sex offender specialists with the Maine Department of Corrections (DOC), began meeting with Walker in May 1998 to discuss community concerns about registered sex offenders being released from Maine prisons and moving to various locations in the state. Megan's Law, which precipitated the state's interest in sex offenders, was passed by Congress and signed by President Clinton on May 17, 1996. The law required states to register individuals convicted of sex crimes against children because these individuals posed a high risk of reoffending. In addition, the new federal law required states to make private and personal information about sex offenders available to the public. The interest of the government in public safety was seen as more important than the privacy rights of convicted sex offenders.

Onacki and Walker had met at a workshop which pertained to the Maine Sex Offender Notification and Registration Act. The Maine Legislature had enacted this law in 1996, requiring anyone convicted since 1992 of sexual crimes against a child under the age of 16 to be registered as a sex offender with the DOC when released from prison. The length of the registration period varied. An assessment of the sex offender's degree of risk to reoffend was part of the law. The conditions of probation were based on this risk profile which varied greatly depending on many factors, including imperfect research into what caused one individual and not another to repeat the crime. High profile cases in other parts of the country, where released offenders had committed new crimes of rape, increased the apprehension in Maine. Onacki asked RRS to collaborate with him in training law enforcement officers about the impact on any victim/survivor when an offender was released.

By early 1999, more than 250 registered sex offenders had already been released into Maine communities. An additional 150 were in prison, and were required by law to register when they were released in the next two years. State law required each police department to have a system in place for notifying residents when a registered sex offender moved into a community. Some communities held notification meetings; others notified neighbors by going door-to-door. While registration of sex offenders was a worthwhile effort, those who were required to register were only a small percentage of the total number who raped or committed acts of incest. Many rapists and sex offenders who were released from jail did not have to register, either because they committed the crime before 1992, or because their victim was age 16 or older at the time of the rape.

Onacki and Walker became part of a team which helped to facilitate many sex offender notification meetings throughout the two counties during 1999. Usually someone from the local police department and sometimes local legislators also sat at the front of the meeting room and fielded questions from the large, irate crowds. The most common questions asked at these meetings were, "Why does the sex offender have to move here?" and "Why can't we restrict where they live?" Participating in these notification meetings was an initiative unique to RRS, thanks to Onacki and later to Detective Jameson at the Penobscot CSD. Onacki opened the meeting with information about the sex offender, where he or she (at least one was a female) was living, and restrictions, if any, in the terms of probation. Photos and basic information about the individual were provided, similar to the wanted posters that used to appear in post offices. RRS brochures and other materials were also available.

Walker's presentation which followed always opened with the recognition that some people in the audience might have been sexually abused as children and that this meeting might trigger unpleasant memories for them. She described the RRS hotline services and encouraged people to call. Her next statement, "This person is probably the safest sex offender in your town," usually elicited some "yeah, right" comments. She then went on to explain that everyone in the room had a picture of the offender and could easily identify him or her, unlike the many sex offenders who lived in the communities and had never been caught or convicted. The thought always crossed Walker's mind at these meetings that some of the audience members could very well have been sexually abusing children.

The remarks Walker then made were focused on parents and teachers in the audience. She stressed that communicating with children was the key to keeping them safe from sex offenders. Telling children that no one had a right to touch the parts of their bodies which would be covered by a bathing suit was a key part of this communication, as was using appropriate terminology for these body parts. Walker always acknowledged in all presentations and trainings how difficult yet important it was to use correct terms for so-called "private parts." When children heard someone say, "Don't tell anyone," this usually meant they should tell someone. Walker also encouraged adults to allow children to be comfortable talking about anything, including people with whom they were uncomfortable, even if they were family members. Teach children to trust their instincts, she advised, and use this community notification as a "teachable moment."

Local law enforcement department personnel who were present at the meetings invited residents to call if the sex offender appeared to be violating the terms of probation, if any. Sometimes, for example, an individual could not have any contact with children under a certain age, or could not be seen within a specified distance of an elementary school. An offender who was doing such things was to be reported to the police, who would in turn notify Onacki.

One of these community notification meetings was held in Millinocket early in February. Walker noted in her journal that the "townspeople are understandably upset about the sex offender living there, really aren't hearing anything above their anger." For this reason, Walker always offered to return to the community and present an educational program specifically for parents. K.J. MacLean of *The Katahdin Times* reported on March 13th about a follow-up program:

Having a convicted sex offender move to Millinocket has shattered a lot of myths surrounding what kind of person sexually abuses children, according to the director of Rape Response Services. "People often think of a stranger in the bushes waiting to jump out at you," Kathy Walker said. "The fact is that 85 percent of children are sexually abused by someone they know. It could be a date, an uncle, a husband, a brother, or a neighbor."

Walker, along with other area counselors, told a group of more than 30 people in Millinocket recently, how to talk to their children about sexual abuse and sex offenders. The meeting was a follow up to a public hearing held in early February when convicted child molester Richard Withee, Jr. moved to Millinocket. It was explained that most children are tricked or manipulated, not forced, into sexually abusive activity, and often the children end up blaming themselves.

"They ask themselves, 'why did I do that, or why did I stay, or why didn't I run, or why did I go back,'" one counselor stated. "If we can just remove the blaming part." Kathryn Klein [RRS volunteer], a counselor with a practice in East Millinocket, said making sure children understand what's appropriate and what isn't appropriate as far as touching is concerned is good information. "To explain it, I say the private area is the part covered by your bathing suit."

Klein said it was important to stress that whenever the child is touched in a way they don't like, or that confuses them, they should let the person know, by saying no. "They need to do whatever it takes to get out of that situation. They should scream, scream loud... someone will notice."

As a school guidance counselor for the past 20 years, Deborah Drew said she has never worked with someone who has been raped by a stranger. "Over and over again I have worked with children who have been raped by someone they knew." The Stearns High School counselor advised the group to talk with their children about sexual abuse, saying children have a tendency to clam up, because what scares them more than anything else is that they might not be believed. "More often than not, they do not lie about this," Drew stated. "Give them guidance about who they should talk to."

While communication is key, it was stated, parents can run the risk of creating hysteria, if they go overboard. Talking tips, identified in information circulated include:

- *Use comfortable language: try to use specific names for all the parts of the body. Children need to know that all the parts of the body are healthy and normal.*
- *Minimize "scary" conversations: Balance the talk about bad or uncomfortable touch by also talking about positive, nurturing touch. Encourage children to think about different types of touch and to ask questions when they feel confused.*
- *Listen to the child's questions and responses: Ask children to explain what they think certain terms mean. Then, if necessary, provide an accurate definition.*
- *Develop the child's support system: With the child, list people they know and can trust. The list may include parent(s), relatives, friends, friends' parents, faith leaders, teachers and counselors. Places such as the police department, child protective services, rape centers or mental health centers are also resources.*

"Children need security," Walker said. "But they don't need a tremendous amount of unfounded fear. It's not a one-time conversation, it's on-going." Rape Response Services, which has an office in Millinocket, has a 24-hour hotline for victims, survivors, family and friends, at 1-800-310-0000.

Another sex offender notification meeting in Glenburn in June brought out "heat, mosquitoes, and 150 or more angry residents. Some people just don't want to get it," Walker wrote in her journal. "I share some concerns, but the ones they don't know are more dangerous. Crowd in Millinocket was less hostile." Again, Walker offered to present a follow-up session for parents. Scheduled in mid-July in the evening, Walker "planned on 100, only 20 showed up—how blind we are to sex offenders in our midst."

By the end of the summer, two additional sex offender notification meetings had been held, in Hampden and Corinth. After one event, Walker noted that "registered sex offenders seem to occupy more and more of my time: a newspaper interview [*The Weekly*] and a meeting in Hampden. Every community thinks it is, or should be, immune." A follow-up parent education night in Hampden attracted only two people and prompted the comment, "Denial is alive and well when it comes to sexual assault," in Walker's journal.

Another sex offender notification meeting in Glenburn brought out 75 people in September. Walker observed that it was the "same old, same old, with people asking the questions over and over, as if we can make the world safe." While trying to be empathetic with the concerns expressed, she noticed that those in attendance at this meeting and at others were not listening to the questions already asked or the answers given, because much was repetitive. This was the first meeting co-facilitated with Detective Jameson from Penobscot CSD.

One final sex offender notification meeting in 1999 was held in late December in Garland. Walker noted in her journal that this was a "milder crowd [*of 55 people*], still concerned. Two people came up to me at the end of the meeting and disclosed their own sexual abuse, and I encouraged them both to call the hotline." An interview that afternoon with Susan Faloon on 106.5 FM generated a lot of radio air time leading up to the meeting.

Being a part of these community meetings was an opportunity unique to RRS. Onacki and Detective Jameson deserve credit for always extending an invitation to RRS to participate. Walker's presentation remained the same: acknowledging that some audience members were victims and encouraging them to call the hotline, then segueing into the need to talk with children about sex offenders, especially the ones not identified. Not only were these meetings an opportunity to raise awareness about child sexual abuse, but the presence of RRS at the table made sure victims' needs were addressed by highlighting the services available to them. Brochures with the hotline number were always distributed to attendees.

An unfortunate consequence of the notification law became more evident as time passed: victims were discouraged from reporting sexual abuse by family members or friends if the perpetrator could be convicted and required to register. The trauma experienced by a victim of rape was apparently seen as less important than the stigma experienced by the rapist when identified as a registered sex offender. Even when reports were made, pleas to reduce the offense to a lesser charge that did not require registration as a sex offender were often made, or perpetrators took their chances with a jury trial. A trial meant that the victim might be called to the witness stand, and defense attorneys were often able to reduce the rape to a "she said, he said" scenario, casting doubt in the jurors' minds and making them reluctant to convict and require registration.

Sexual Assault Awareness Month

The primary focus of *The Rape Response Reporter,* spring edition, was another RRS initiative, "Take a Stand," a new April event. "It takes a whole community to end sexual assault" was the theme for activities during the month in Penobscot and Piscataquis counties. Newsletter readers were invited to "Take a Stand Against Sexual Assault" at one of four locations (Bangor, Dover-Foxcroft, Millinocket, University of Maine) on April 30th, beginning at 7 P.M. "Not a march or a speak-out, 'Take a Stand' is both a literal and a symbolic action," the newsletter noted. "By standing for about an hour, we will be making a statement that our communities have zero tolerance for sexual assault. Refreshments will be served at each location, and ribbons symbolic of the event will be distributed."

With four employees, RRS was represented at each of the Stands: Patchell in Millinocket, Allen in Dover-Foxcroft, O'Brien at the University, and Walker in Bangor at the corner of the Airport Mall parking lot on Union Street. The Mall owners required RRS to obtain a rider on the insurance policy specifically to cover liability for the event. Cupcakes to distribute at each location were made by students in the culinary arts program at Region III Vocational School in Lincoln. Each cupcake was frosted with "Take a Stand" in teal lettering on white icing. RRS was billed for the ingredients. Punch was donated by McDonald's.

By this time, the sunflower from the Web page had become the new symbol or logo for RRS. A sunflower appeared on the front of the spring edition of the newsletter. Allen created letter-size posters with the outline of a large sunflower and the words, "Rape is a power trip, not a passion trip!" around the flower's center. "April is Sexual Assault Awareness Month" circled the petals. Information about each individual "Take a Stand" event was included under the sunflower, and black and white versions of the poster were distributed throughout the two counties. Four large white vinyl banners with a sunflower on each end and bold lettering, "It Takes a Whole Community to End Sexual Violence," were made at Young's Canvas Shop, one for each Stand. Colored 5" x 7" sunflowers were also created with "Zero Tolerance for Sexual Violence" printed on the petals and the names of various schools (Lee Academy, Central High School, Dexter High School, for example) in the center circle. O'Brien and Patchell took these sunflowers to the schools during April, inviting each student and teacher to sign her or his name on a sunflower. These signed sunflowers, displayed on a school hallway bulletin board, declared "Zero Tolerance for Sexual Assault."

Additional publicity about "Take a Stand" was included in a guest editorial Walker wrote for the April 24th/25th weekend edition of the BDN:

> *April is Sexual Assault Awareness Month. Once a year the issues of rape, incest, harassment and child sexual abuse are given increased attention.*
>
> *But for the millions of survivors of sexual assault, both female and male, April is just another month in their long journey toward healing. A first step in healing comes in talking about a person's sexual assault. Often this talk is triggered by news stories about rape or incest. The reports about rape being used as a weapon in Kosovo are horrific in their depictions of brutality. And we are dismayed when these rape victims are denied access to contraceptive methods which might help them avoid the cruel results of the rapes.*
>
> *But rape as a war crime is actually more comfortable to discuss than the sexual assaults which occur daily in Maine. Society still embraces the myth that rape is perpetrated by strangers: soldiers assaulting women in enemy territory, child abductors, the stranger in the bushes. We want to believe that these are the rapists, and that if we can protect ourselves and our children against strangers, we will be safe.*
>
> *In actuality, only about 15 percent of perpetrators of sexual assault fall into these categories. The overwhelming majority of sexual assaults are committed by men (and in a few cases, women) whom the victims know—dates, acquaintances, husbands, fathers, neighbors, uncles. That someone in a trusting relationship can sexually assault another is something we don't want to believe. And because we don't want to believe, we blame the victim: She was*

"asking for it" by wearing a short skirt, or drinking too much, or he "asked for it" by going to a gay bar. We would not think of blaming the women in Kosovo for the rapes which are occurring there. Rape is no less horrific, no less brutal, when the rapist is not a stranger.

Rape used as a weapon in war is a crime against humanity, and we are outraged by the soldiers who commit such acts. Where is the outrage against the Lincoln County commissioner who was convicted of molesting a young boy? Where is the outrage over the light sentences given to sex offenders, sentences which release them quickly into our communities to offend again? Where is the outrage when people right in our own communities continue to blame the victim by saying that she or he was "asking" to be raped?

Walker concluded the editorial by inviting readers to participate in "Take a Stand": *Stand to show your support for victims and survivors. Stand to express your outrage over the rapes in Kosovo and in Maine. Stand to demonstrate that the communities of Penobscot and Piscataquis counties have zero tolerance for sexual assault.*

All four Stands were held outdoors on a beautiful spring evening. Television and radio coverage was good both before and during the Stand. Walker noted in her journal that "today was gorgeous, a perfect one for 'Take a Stand,' and as a first attempt, we attracted over 100 people to the four locations. It was a good month overall, and we continue to make an impact, while uncovering even more opportunities where work is needed."

A select number of invitations was mailed for the volunteer recognition dinner and annual meeting of RRS, the first since 1996. Held at Katahdin Hall on the campus of Eastern Maine Technical College (EMTC) in April, this event was attended by volunteers from the Bangor and Millinocket areas, Board members, and staff. Allen created very attractive invitations in teal and gray and printed them at the office. The food service students at EMTC provided the meal. Walker described the event as "great food, and everyone seemed to have fun." Gifts were provided to the volunteers, a tradition which continued for several years.

Another April event with which RRS became involved for the next few years was the Piscataquis Region Chamber of Commerce Business Expo in Guilford. For a small fee, floor space was available on which to place a table and display from RRS. People who stopped at the table were invited to tie red, blue, or teal ribbons on a silver-painted tree branch. Red represented survivors of rape, and blue was for survivors of incest. Those who tied teal ribbons on the branch were showing their general support for RRS. This display, along with free candy, became a popular trademark at other events in the two counties.

The spring edition of *The Rape Response Reporter* which described the Stand also noted the importance of RRS volunteers: "Looking at the assets of Rape Response Services, a person can easily see that our volunteer hotline advocates are crucial to the work that we do to assist victims and survivors of sexual assault. 'We could not do what we do without our volunteers,' says Kathy Walker, Executive Director. 'They provide over $70,000 worth of volunteer hours each year to this agency.'

"Volunteers are on call by pager or telephone for eight hour shifts, round the clock, every day of the year. Norma Allen, Client Services Coordinator, keeps track of the schedule, and maintains statistical information about hotline calls and volunteer hours. 'At the present time,' reports Norma, 'we have five volunteers who have contributed more than one thousand hours each to Rape Response Services.'"

A dedicated group of 21 advocates, many of whom had been with the agency for three years or more, prompted Walker to observe in her journal that the volunteers would "pack the room" if all could attend each monthly advocates' meeting. "Room was full of advocates," she noted, "and it is great to think how far we have come in three years, getting RRS back on its feet and expanding in new directions." A welcome addition to every meeting was a cake from Hannaford or Shaw's grocery store to celebrate any advocates' birthdays that occurred during the month. Birthday cards were also mailed to each advocate every year.

Money Matters

A high note for RRS during Sexual Assault Awareness Month was an unexpected $2500 check from the Stephen and Tabitha King Foundation. The Kings had supported RRS for several years with monetary donations and auction items, and this was the largest unsolicited gift.

Beginning in mid-year, staff members who took backup shifts were paid a stipend ($130 per week or $31 per shift) for their time, thanks to additional funding of $1666 from DMHMRSAS to each center. Volunteers Bean and Ames had been receiving a stipend since the beginning of the year from the enhanced hotline money.

As more federal money became available through DHS for rape crisis centers, a subcommittee of MECASA directors, on which Walker served, devised a funding formula to equitably distribute the additional funds. This formula took both population and square miles of coverage area into account, as well as whether the center was free-standing or part of another agency. At that time, all centers except the two covering Washington/Hancock and Aroostook counties were free-standing. While RRS had fewer people living in the catchment area than centers in the southern part of the state, the formula factored in the 7000 square miles for which RRS was responsible in the two counties.

Included in the formula were also the hours of service to clients and hours spent in educational presentations, both school- and community-based. The MECASA Board of Directors held at least one "stat summit" to be sure that all centers were recording statistics in the same manner. One change, for example, clarified that "contact" measured interaction and not people, so that three people in an office working with one client meant one contact and three client hours. Points were also awarded in the formula for whether or not each center's Board of Directors did fundraising, and for the percentage of the center's total budget that was not funded by the state. The latter not only encouraged fundraising activities but also rewarded centers for becoming more self-sufficient and less reliant solely on government funding. Percentages in the formula that would apply to all new allocations from DHS through the years included:

- 58% of the total new allocation for the base
- 8.4% each for population and geographic area
- 16.8% for service hours
- 8.4 % for fundraising efforts

The new formula was approved by the MECASA Board and endorsed by Greenlaw and his supervisor, Jeannette Talbot, at DHS just in time to allocate an additional $173,000 in CVAP/VOCA for fiscal year 1999. RRS received $18,070.74 under the formula, one of the higher allocations, broken down as follows:

- Base: $10,726.00
- Population: $1,890.61
- Geographic area: $2,806.13
- Service hours: $1,296.00
- Fundraising: $1,352.00

Although the RRS Board was involved in fundraising, non-government funds in the budget were only 30% of the total. Except for the annual auction, Board members had minimal involvement in fundraisers. The Stay-at-Home Ball, for example, held again in February 1999, generated good publicity on WEZQ 92.9, raised the usual $2000 from loyal donors, and required only office work to mail invitations and to hand-write thank you notes, something Walker made sure was done to acknowledge all donations. The RRS logo was printed by Fast Forms in teal on the front of the cream note cards that were used.

A Community Presence

Presentations to various groups and classes seemed to fill the year's calendars for all staff members. Despite the presence of O'Brien and Patchell in many schools, no posters were received for the annual contest, which was discontinued after this attempt due to lack of participation. In addition to classroom presentations, "The Yellow Dress," a theatrical performance about dating violence, was presented during assemblies at Penquis High School in Milo, Foxcroft Academy, and John Bapst High School in Bangor. RRS collaborated with both Womancare and SR to facilitate student discussions following the performances.

RRS was invited to speak at a University of Maine Women's Studies class and to do staff training at Aspenledge, a group home in Hampden for troubled teens. Walker's journal noted that she "tried to convince a Women's Studies class that rape is real, not sure that I did but got their attention with help from Tori Amos on CD ("She Cried No") and video. We don't want to believe we are vulnerable."

Speaking to a group of 26 women at Penobscot Valley Industries in Bangor was an experience that prompted Walker to write, "How sad to know that many of them are survivors, or will be victims in the future." These individuals who were developmentally disabled appeared to understand Walker's use of a hula hoop to demonstrate boundaries. She also spent a very emotional morning with employees at a social service agency in Bangor who wanted to process and learn how to respond to the rape of a co-worker the previous weekend. Months later, this rape was one of the few in the Bangor area that was successfully prosecuted, resulting in a conviction.

At the end of April, Walker presented six hours of training at the Best Western in Millinocket for DMHMRSAS. Titled "Working with Adult Survivors of Sexual Abuse in the MR *[Mental Retardation]* Population," the workshop attracted people from northern areas of the state who worked with those who were mentally challenged. "Despite a malfunctioning VCR and the hostility of a few males in the audience," Walker wrote in her journal that she "felt by the end that it had gone well, though I am always amazed at the prevalence of myths, and at peoples' speaking them out loud." After staying overnight in Medway, she presented another three-hour training the following day. Held at the Millinocket Regional Hospital for nine law enforcement officers from East Millinocket and Millinocket, this training fulfilled one of the requirements of the VAWA grant which had to be wrapped up by June 30th. DA Almy, Closson from the DA's office, and Detective Jameson assisted in the training. "A successful two days," Walker wrote in her journal.

Two DHS-sponsored six-hour training sessions for DHS employees on a new topic, "Adult Survivors of Sexual Assault," were taught by Walker in Portland and Augusta. Many disclosures were made at the Augusta session, and everyone was encouraged to call the statewide hotline number. Staff trainings for several other agencies were provided during the summer. Not as long as the DHS-sponsored sessions, these shorter versions offered an introduction to RRS and basic information on sexual assault. The Charlotte White Center in Dover-Foxcroft and a group of case managers in Bangor were among the training recipients. Training on how to respond to child sexual abuse was requested during three weekly lunch hours for the employees of Hilltop Daycare Center in Bangor. RRS also collaborated with Womancare to present six hours of training about domestic violence and sexual assault for clergy in the Dover-Foxcroft area. Churches in Bangor (Unitarian/Universalist [UU] Society, Grace UMC) later requested sermons about sexual violence or presentations for women's groups (Redeemer Lutheran).

Walker's remarks whether she spoke in church or in the community always began by acknowledging those in attendance who were survivors of sexual violence and encouraging them to call the hotline. Her sermons then continued:

> *I must confess that it is with some trepidation that I stand before you this morning. Although I have stood in this place before, my trepidation this morning comes more from the subject matter. Not that I am reluctant to talk about the subject. But how many times have we heard the words rape and incest spoken from the pulpit? Worship is seen by many as an opportunity to escape from the world for an hour, to be free from thoughts of the violence that pervades our society. Who am I to rock the boat, to interject unpleasant topics into what may be our only peaceful, restful part of the week?*
>
> *The church universal has for too long been silent about the issue of sexual violence. By our silence I believe we are condoning it. By not speaking out against sexual violence, we are saying that it doesn't happen here. We are denying the reality of the many, many women, and some men, who come through these doors.*
>
> *How can we respond to Bathsheba and Tamar* [Biblical women who were raped] *in our midst? The first step is naming the violence. Rape and all other forms of violence against women have historically been seen in two ways by the church: punishment for the past sins of the woman, and a sign that she is not a good Christian. By naming the violence, we are breaking the silence which has prevented women from coming forward with their stories of rape. We are encouraging women to name the violence which has happened to them.*
>
> *Another way to respond is to hold the perpetrators of violence accountable for their actions. We don't want to believe that rapists are part of our faith community. We don't want to believe that the man sitting in the next pew today might be raping his stepdaughter tonight. We don't want to believe that the woman who comes to church occasionally is being raped by her husband. And if by chance we find out that these men are accused of being perpetrators of violence, then we make excuses for their behavior, or we buy into their excuses. We blame the victims. We talk about "forgiving and forgetting."*

There can be no forgiveness when there is denial. By the church's failure to hold perpetrators accountable, we are feeding their denial. When the church does not speak loudly and clearly against sexual violence, we are denying the reality of the many victims in our midst.

Requests for sexual harassment trainings continued to be received infrequently. Twenty employees at Overhead Door Company in Bangor were present for a two-hour session, after which Walker's journal recorded that she "tried to make a difference by telling 18 men about sexual harassment." She always provided sample copies of harassment policies that the business could adopt, and also had small groups read various examples, reporting back to the entire group whether these scenarios constituted harassment. Lively discussions usually ensued.

RRS joined "concerned women and men nationwide and around the world to protest an Italian judge's decision to dismiss a rape case because the victim was wearing jeans. Saying that jeans are too tight to be removed without the assistance of the person wearing them, the judge declared that the rape was a consensual act." This item in *The Rape Response Reporter* (summer edition) noted that signatures and statements of protest were written on a pair of jeans by RRS staff and volunteers. The pair of jeans was sent to the Italian embassy in Washington, D.C. along with jeans from MECASA and other sexual assault centers around the country.

The summer edition of *The Rape Response Reporter* also advertised the upcoming Auction and Awards Night and other RRS activities. "School-based program makes a difference for young people" headlined a column about O'Brien's and Patchell's work in the schools. Because "education was the key to the prevention of sexual assault, RRS was active during the past school year in twenty-eight middle and high schools, representing all school districts within our two counties. On-site programs were started at Central (East Corinth) and John Bapst High Schools, and classroom presentations were made in grades six through twelve, reaching a total of 4,562 students." The article continued:

The Health Club at Central High School requested that Rape Response Services provide information about how to support someone who has been sexually assaulted. Students asked a variety of questions, and were concerned about the many ways in which sexual assault could impact a person's life. "As a result of this request at Central," says Wendy O'Brien, School-Based Educator, "I am pleased to report that students at Central are committed to zero tolerance for sexual violence."

Melissa Caruso and Lisa Parent, two Central students, displayed our "It Takes a Whole Community to End Sexual Violence" banner, and requested that students sign their names on sunflowers on which was written "Zero Tolerance for Sexual Violence." Hundreds of sunflowers were pinned up with the banner where all could see this wonderful display of support.

In the northern part of Penobscot County, Rape Response Services made first-ever presentations in Howland, Medway, and at Katahdin High School. Gale Patchell, School-Based Educator in that area, reports, "The information was well-received by students, and everyone wants me to come back."

Classroom presentations focus on the differences between healthy and unhealthy relationships, on definitions of sexual assault, and on how to access services. A special word of appreciation is extended to all of the faculty members and administrators who have supported the presence of Rape Response Services in their schools.

Small boxed areas of the summer newsletter advertised both goods and services from RRS. One mentioned clothesline pins that could be purchased at the Grasshopper Shop and Rebecca's in Bangor. Handmade by Bonnie Shelley from Ithaca, New York, the pins in a variety of colors represented T-shirts made for the Clothesline Project and were a best seller for several years, earning RRS eight dollars for each pin sold. Another boxed area encouraged readers to call about staff training for community service agencies. Sessions from four to six hours in length were available, focused on working with an agency's clients who had been sexually assaulted as a child or an adult. There was no charge for this training, but donations were appreciated. RRS had also been certified by the Maine Criminal Justice Academy (MCJA) to provide training for law enforcement agencies. A third boxed area noted that RRS funding was received in part from Penobscot County, the city of Brewer, and the towns of Hermon and Milford. Millinocket had discontinued the annual allocation earlier in the year; Milford had added RRS to the town's budget.

New RRS brochures were designed and printed during the year, replacing the blue documents that had been reprinted at least once since 1991. A cream-colored tri-fold with lettering in teal, highlighted by lilac, the brochures were developed by the staff as a group, as were all informational materials produced at RRS. Attention was given to language, making sure the words chosen were understandable to a diverse audience, and repeating some words for emphasis. Unlike the previous brochure, lots of open space was left, and simple icons of a gavel and a telephone receiver were prominent. "Legal," "Medical," and "Other" were the three sections inside the brochure. Bulleted points for "Legal" were:

- *Hotline Advocates at Rape Response Services can discuss options, and can be available for investigative interviews and court appearances.*
- *Reporting the crime of sexual assault is the choice of the victim/survivor.*
- *Any decision about criminal charges is made by the District Attorney.*

For "Medical," the listed points were:

- *Hotline Advocates at Rape Response Services can discuss options, and can be available at a hospital or clinic.*
- *A rape protocol exam is suggested within 72 hours for collection of evidence.*
- *Medical assistance is available at hospitals, clinics or doctors' offices.*

The "Other" points were:

- *Hotline Advocates at Rape Response Services are available 24 hours a day for on-going support.*
- *Information about support/education groups can be accessed by calling the hotline.*
- *Rape Response Services can provide information about additional community resources (counselors/therapists, attorneys, victim/witness advocates).*

A back panel of the brochure repeated the hotline and the TTY numbers that were included on the front. Sheriffs' department numbers in the two counties were provided, as was 9-1-1 for a local police department. The final panel listed all that RRS provided under "Client Services," "School Programs," and "Community Relations."

Annual Auction and Awards Night

The primary purpose of the summer newsletter was to advertise the annual Auction and Awards Night in September at Jeff's Catering. Averill's column headlined this event again in the August 28th/29th BDN: "Each year, noted local sculptor Forest 'Toby' Hart has donated a bronze piece to be auctioned," she began. "This year's third annual event is no exception, as Hart has donated a small bronze moose for the benefit. RRS executive director Kathy Walker is proud of Hart's commitment to this cause and even prouder to boast she believes this year's contribution 'is the best ever.' Other names that should catch your attention are those of Maine summer resident John Travolta, who has donated an autographed photograph, and actress Drew Barrymore, who has donated two autographed photographs.

"Last year's event raised $7,000 and Walker is hoping to exceed that amount this year. A goal of nearly $8,000 is not unrealistic considering the event 'becomes more popular every year, and ticket sales are going very well,' she said. Additionally, the list of donations for the auction continues to grow, with approximately 150 items to bid on including a handmade quilt, stained glass wall hangings, pottery and gift certificates. 'What really is wonderful is all the auction items are donated,' Walker said of individual, business and community support for this find-raiser. The evening is underwritten by RRS benefactor Sawyer Environmental Recovery Facility, and friend of RRS, the firm of Sargent, Tyler and West." For the first year, corporate sponsors for the auction donated cash amounts at various specified levels and received free tickets to the event depending on the level of giving. Table tents highlighted the support of these underwriters.

McKay again capably served as the auctioneer, and "In Our Midst" provided music during the silent auction. Badger and Woolley presented the annual award to Rancourt who had been a faithful volunteer for five years, donating 3876 hours on the hotline. A maple coffee table from Moosehead

Furniture, overnight accommodations at Maple Hill Bed & Breakfast in Hallowell, a year of homemade desserts, ten dozen holiday cookies—all generated lively bidding from a crowd of more than 100 people, many new to RRS. The auction had excellent media coverage and was good publicity for RRS, with live television broadcasts from the event. Over $7500 was made. Walker always spoke at the auctions, thanking people for coming, mentioning the sponsors and all the donors, introducing Board members and staff, and especially highlighting the volunteers.

Personnel Changes

The RRS staff commitment Walker had noted earlier, unfortunately, was to be short-lived. Allen left the center in September, just before fall training began. RRS was able to pay Bean an additional stipend for assisting with the training, an arrangement that would continue for many years. At this and all future RRS volunteer trainings in Bangor, Millinocket, or Dover-Foxcroft, a video produced by Sexual Assault Response Services (SARS) in Portland was used. Titled "Hope, Help and Healing," this twenty-minute production, completed in April 1998, featured a SARS advocate and was moderated by Kim Block, a television news reporter. The video highlighted the important role of advocates at rape crisis centers.

After one of the first nights of the fall training, Walker observed that "We have probably the best group of new advocates ever," and she was "energized by their enthusiasm." Several volunteers who completed this training, a "record number," remained with RRS in various capacities for several years, including Alcinda Hall, Shannon Sheehy (a social work intern), Angela Fileccia, and Marianne Fricke, wife of Larry Lussier who had taken the training in a previous year. He continued to be a valuable part of RRS, available to speak with male hotline callers or go to the hospital with a male victim, even when given a last-minute notice.

RRS group facilitator training was held at the Northeast Occupational Exchange (NOE) offices in Lincoln on two Saturdays in September and October. O'Brien and Holmes, who had co-facilitated a rape support group at RRS the previous year, were the trainers. Providing these sessions was another part of the VAWA grant, and Walker was able to pay the trainers a stipend. Participants in the training were RRS volunteers from Millinocket and Bangor who wanted to facilitate support groups; very few people from Millinocket were able to attend.

In November, Walker advertised, interviewed, and offered the vacant Client Services Coordinator position to Karen Martin. At this time, O'Brien was given the title of School Services Coordinator to reflect her increased responsibilities for on-site services in various schools. Martin had not taken the hotline training and was unable to sign up for hotline shifts before the following spring.

Annual Report and End-of-Year Fundraising Letter

The Annual Report 1998-99 again listed Woolley as Board President and Veeder as Treasurer. Harrison remained on the Board and was replaced as Secretary by Uhlenhake. Other returning Board members were Greaney, Groth, and Johnson. Sharon Closson was a new member. She had left her position with the DA's office and was a big help at the RRS office, cleaning, filling in on the phone, and doing stats after Allen resigned.

Two hundred ninety clients received services in this fiscal year, an increase of 54. Because of the enhanced hotline services, the total hours of service increased by 560. Sixty-four sexual assaults occurred in FY'99, no change from the previous year. Two hundred forty-five hours of school-based education reached almost 5000 students. According to the annual report, 27 on-call hotline volunteers in Bangor and nine in Millinocket constituted the largest group in RRS history. An additional three volunteers, inactive from the hotline, were available for special projects. The state DHS contract provided income of $115,089. Fundraising and donations gave RRS a total of $16,289, including Stay-at-Home Ball income of $2995. Grants provided another $32,107. Personnel expenses were the largest at $107,911. Rent, insurance, telephone, and travel totaled $33,087.

The fundraising letter at the end of the year noted the record number of students reached by RRS in middle and high schools and the all-time high number of hotline volunteers. "Support groups are once again being offered," wrote Woolley and Walker in the upbeat letter, which also contained a list of 71 individuals and businesses who had donated items and services for the auction. New initiatives during the year, including the sex offender notification meetings and "Take A Stand," helped to create more visibility and support for RRS throughout the two counties, support that was especially evident at the annual auction.

2000: THE BENEFITS OF CHANGE

Personnel changes at both RRS and MECASA occupied a lot of Walker's time in the first year of the new millennium. Change was inevitable in social service agencies where wages and benefits were lower than in the private sector. In addition, the stress of facing the reality that rape occurred even in rural areas of Maine could lead to burnout for both staff members and volunteers. Although training sessions did not gloss over this reality, actually answering the telephone and being totally present for a victim/survivor took a toll. Self-care was stressed at RRS; sometimes this meant taking another position or a break from the hotline.

Martin left the center early in the year. Facing the spring hotline training without her was not a problem because Bean assisted again. The training sessions got underway at the same time that O'Brien and Holmes were co-facilitating a support group for survivors of incest. Walker provided supervision after each support group session throughout this year and her tenure at RRS, either in-person for Bangor groups or on the telephone. This supervision provided an opportunity for the co-facilitators to discuss issues that arose in group and to brainstorm ways to address these issues.

Closson continued to help out at the office, causing Walker to be complacent about hiring Martin's replacement. Sarah Mullen, a Bangor High School graduate and a college student, also assisted at the office during the summer, cataloging the RRS library and creating an annotated bibliography of what was available. She read at least part of all the books in the office bookcase and helped to weed out some of the less-useful titles. Amy Junkins, a client of one of the Bangor volunteers, helped with dusting, vacuuming, recycling, and other projects to gain some work experience.

Interviews for the vacant position were finally conducted by Walker in June, and Jennifer Pease accepted the offer to be Client Services Coordinator. She brought enthusiasm, laughter, and creativity to the Bangor office at a busy time when all three were in short supply. One of her initiatives, which far outlasted her tenure at RRS, was *Our Monthly Advocate,* a four-page newsletter which she produced and distributed at each advocates' meeting or mailed to those not in attendance. Containing interviews with staff and advocates, news items, quotes, advocates' birthdays, and statistics, this popular document was later reduced to two pages and also included recipes contributed by RRS personnel.

Walker became executive chair of the MECASA Board of Directors in the fall. Cyndi Amato, the former MECASA ED, had resigned her position the previous year to become ED at SARS in Portland. Walker served on the MECASA Board's personnel committee which was fortunate to hire Elizabeth Ward (later Ward Saxl) to fill the ED position.

Patchell left RRS in mid-August. In September, Walker conducted interviews at the East Millinocket office of RRS, and invited two people back to the office for a second interview. O'Brien and Pease joined Walker for the latter, when the two candidates gave presentations. All staff members were pleased that Robin Carr of Lincoln accepted the position of Community and School-Based Educator in northern Penobscot County.

Sexual Assault Awareness Month

Copying an idea from Womancare and SR, RRS had wooden nickels made in time to distribute at several events during April. "Rape Response Services" surrounded a sunflower on one side of the disc, with the hotline numbers on the reverse side. The word "RAPE" with a dark slash through it was centered inside the circle of numbers. These became very popular items to distribute at community and school events for the next few years.

The tenth Stay-at-Home Ball in April had a new twist: during the evening hours from eight to eleven, Walker was invited by DJ Dave Russell to join him at the WEZQ 92.9 studio in Brewer. Her journal entry noted: "my debut as a disc jockey went well, a few glitches, but lots of fun. And we even got two calls, one a pledge and one a promise. Wonder how many people were listening?" More than $2000 was raised, as the community increasingly demonstrated support for RRS and the clients.

Later in April, the space for the annual meeting and volunteer recognition dinner was provided at Penobscot Job Corps. State Senator Robert "Buddy" Murray, who was to become a Maine District and Superior Court Judge, spoke about new legislation related to sexual assault. Murray was the Senate chairperson of a commission which recommended a ground-breaking change in Maine law (Public Law Chapter 719) that directed the Department of Public Safety to develop a standardized forensic examination kit for rape protocol exams. This change also mandated that the Maine Victim's Compensation Board would pay for all forensic examinations conducted on or after November 1, 2000. A victim of sexual assault was no longer required to report the crime to law enforcement before the state would pay for the exam. The standardized kit would be provided by the state to hospitals throughout Maine. MECASA had played a key role in affecting these changes in Maine statutes.

O'Brien participated on a rape awareness panel at the University during April, covered by *The Maine Campus* on April 28th. "The discussion began," noted reporter Joe Gunn in the article, "with O'Brien presenting an overview of her work and that of Rape Response Services, which is a 24-hour-a-day, seven-day-a-week sexual assault crisis hotline manned by a staff of volunteers. The staff also serves as a resource for those who know someone who has been the victim of sexual assault and wish to support their loved one. As the school services coordinator at Rape Response Services, O'Brien has traveled to countless middle, junior-high and high schools throughout the state [*sic*] and tries to end apathetic or insensitive attitudes towards sexual assault and the victims of sexual assault." Other panelists spoke about consent, myths, sexual assault of men, and the "stigma that surrounds the victims."

At the end of the month, Walker's journal noted that another "Take A Stand" attracted "a faithful group of thirty-five [*in Bangor*] on a cold, windy night." Stands were held in Dover-Foxcroft, Millinocket, and Bangor, and the publicity, especially radio coverage, was "great" before and during the event. A TBN march and rally on the Orono campus the previous week attracted "more students than [*Walker had*] ever seen" at such an event.

A Community Presence

Attempts were ongoing throughout the year to educate the public about the reality of sexual violence and the services provided for victims. One way to do this continued to be through the newspaper. A January 25th letter from Walker to the editor of the BDN was titled, "Rape isn't glamorous":

> *A made-for-TV movie aired last week, "The Mary Kay Letourneau Story." Subtitled "All-American Girl," this movie tells the real-life story of the married schoolteacher, Letourneau, who has an affair (and two children) with a male student, beginning when he was 13.*
>
> *There is nothing "all American" about Letourneau. She is a rapist. Someone who is 13 is not legally capable of giving consent to a sexual relationship. Under Maine law, this is rape, or gross sexual assault. Letourneau was jailed for the crime she committed.*
>
> *Below the age of 18, boys and girls are sexually assaulted in equal numbers. The rapists are almost always in a position of authority or trust: teachers, coaches, family members, bus drivers. Rape is never a way for either gender to learn about sex.*
>
> *Making a movie of Letourneau's crime, and showing it on primetime television, glamorizes what she did. This in turn does a great disservice to anyone who has ever been victimized by a male or female rapist. There is nothing glamorous about sexual assault.*

Thirty students and faculty members at UC in Bangor (now the University of Maine at Augusta, Bangor campus) attended a ninety-minute presentation about date rape and dating violence. Walker observed in her journal: "I was 'winging it,' but O'Brien told me we have been doing this too long to 'wing it.' It was nice to just pull out an outline and do ninety minutes of talking."

A few days later Walker presented a six-hour DHS training in Augusta titled, "Introduction to Child Sexual Abuse." Despite feeling that she was not prepared enough for this new topic, the 27 participants wrote positive evaluations. That same evening she faced a crowd of 250 people at Hermon High School for another sex offender notification meeting where, according to her journal, she "got more passionate than

I usually do, about excusing men as pedophiles." A line of people waited to talk after the meeting and provided "supportive comments."

Another sex offender notification meeting was held in Newburgh a few weeks later. Follow-up parental information sessions at both locations were a "waste of time." By summer's end, many fewer people turned out in Hermon for yet another meeting to learn about another sex offender who had moved into the community. Walker observed a "small group this time, but some powerful disclosures from parents about their children's abuse still didn't stop two young mothers from plotting to drive this particular guy out of town."

The Maine Attorney General's (AG) office sponsored a two-day conference in May at the Samoset Resort in Rockport. Focused on interpersonal violence, the workshops were presented by invitation to MECASA directors and MCEDV staff members. Conference attendees included law enforcement officers, DA and AG office employees, and victim service programs from around the state. On the second day, Walker assisted in presenting two ninety-minute workshops, "Drugs Used to Facilitate Rape" and "Sex Offenders in Our Communities." Her journal recorded "mostly preaching to the choir," but "my workshops both went well and attendees learned something, according to evaluations."

Later in the month, Walker actually drove to Presque Isle and back in one day (324 miles) to present another DHS training session on child sexual abuse. She was surprised that the evaluations were good because it was "not my best." After presenting on this topic for the first time back in March, she had planned to revise the outline but had not taken the time to make the changes that she felt were necessary to improve the content.

When the 1999 state crime statistics were released in June 2000, rapes reported to police had risen by 19.2%. A front page BDN article on the 28th by Ordway quoted Walker:

> "We're hoping that this shows that people are more willing to report to police. I really feel that the majority of this increase is due to a willingness to report. Although in looking at our figures and talking with other centers across the state, we feel that there are more young women between the ages of 13 and 17 being raped."
>
> Walker said her center had seen an increase in calls from teen-age girls reporting they had been raped and said there also had been

cases in which the use of "rape drugs" such as Gammahydroxybutryate (GHB) and Rohypnol have been suspected.

In the article, both Bangor Police Chief Donald Winslow and DA Almy backed up Walker's assertion, with Almy noting that "his office currently is waiting for laboratory results in another case in which drugs are suspected of being used on the rape victim."

Ordway's article continued:

> *Walker said there was an increase in stranger rapes in southern Maine, but that such rapes are rare in eastern and central Maine. "Our statistics at the center are showing an increase in reports from younger people ages 13 to 17 and most often it is by someone they know who is likely to be about five years older. We've had cases in which the victim describes an experience which makes us suspect date-rape drugs, but we've been unable to substantiate it because the drugs leave the system very quickly." Officials said they would be watching rape statistics closely to see if the trend increases.*

This article is an example of how RRS had become the go-to place for Bangor-area television, radio, and newsprint reporters who wanted a comment on breaking news stories about sexual violence.

During the summer, O'Brien trained students at Penobscot Job Corps to be peer educators. She had started the RRS relationship with Job Corps the previous year. The students were planning to develop rape awareness projects on their campus. O'Brien and Sue Hamlett, a SR educator, also met during the summer to plan shared presentations in public schools. Dating violence, sexual assault, and healthy relationships were the topics to be covered in high school classrooms. This was the first of many such collaborative efforts by educators from RRS and SR.

Money Matters

A highlight of the year was the first annual production of "The Vagina Monologues," presented in February as a benefit for RRS by the Student Women's Association (SWA) at the University of Maine. Scheduled on Valentine's Day ("V-day"), the event was postponed for a week by snowstorms. Eve Ensler had written the script for off-Broadway theatre in 1998, and had initiated the V-day campaign, according to the program brochure, to "end sexual violence against women and to proclaim Valentine's Day as the day to celebrate women and demand the end of abuse." Eighteen separate and powerful monologues were performed by students and community members, including RRS volunteer Hall.

Publicity about the fourth annual Fall Festival Auction and Awards Night headlined both Averill's column in the BDN on August 22nd and the summer RRS newsletter. "RRS executive director Kathy Walker called Monday morning," Averill wrote, "to announce that another new item has been added, and that's 'a Standard Otter Kayak from Old Town Canoe.' Among the highlights of the auction will be a small bronze fox, signed and dated by sculptor Forest 'Toby' Hart of Monroe. Attendees will also be able to bid on an end table from Moosehead Furniture, 10 pounds of lobster delivered by Delwin Faulkingham, and pottery from Monroe Salt Works. Helping sponsor this event are Sawyer Environmental Recovery Facility of Hampden, the Bangor Daily News and Pro Realty." Sargent, Tyler and West later became a sponsor. Other consistent supporters of the auction included Bangor Savings Bank (BSB) with a $50 savings account, and Quality Jewelers with lovely necklaces valued at $200 or more.

"Walker said the admission to the fund-raiser is kept low [*reduced to $5 per ticket*] for a very specific reason. 'An auction is not good if you don't have people coming,' she said. 'We like to have bidders and buyers there, so we keep the cost as low as possible since this is our biggest fundraiser of the year. We have some really nice items this year, and they continue to come in on a daily basis.' Those who've attended this fundraiser previously will be happy to learn that, back by popular demand, will be the unflappable Sue McKay as auctioneer." McKay outdid herself by donning a Green Bay Packers' "cheese head" which had been donated by Board member Groth, a Packer fan. Programs for the live auction were created by Pease. "In Our Midst" again provided musical entertainment.

A follow-up article in *The Weekly* on September 15th noted: "Joseph Baldacci of Bangor is this year's recipient of the Janet Badger Volunteer Award. In presenting the award, Executive Director Kathy Walker said the attorney has been providing pro bono legal services to the agency since 1991. The Janet Badger Volunteer Award is presented annually at the Fall Festival Auction and Awards Night and was named in honor of a longtime volunteer at Rape Response Services. Another person receiving recognition was Rick Vigue, owner of Rebecca's in downtown Bangor, for selling the clothesline pins with no markup for the shop. The fourth annual event generated gross receipts of $9,200, far exceeding the goal. Walker said financial as well as emotional support is key to the staffers and volunteers." Over 125 guests attended the auction, demonstrating outstanding support for RRS in the community.

Hotline Volunteers

The Rape Response Reporter (summer edition) also noted that fall advocate trainings would be held in both Bangor and Millinocket. Carr and Pease, as new employees, participated in the two trainings. Three social work interns in Bangor, (Jessica Shirley, Liz Swartz, and Nichole Clark) all proved to be invaluable assets for RRS during the school year. In addition, new volunteers Nicole Booker and Stormi Ames were to become an important part of RRS for several years. Bean assisted Walker again with the Bangor sessions; Walker facilitated those in Millinocket. Over 30 volunteers total in Bangor and Millinocket had Walker observing: "I feel fortunate we have so many volunteers, as most other centers do not." The last Bangor advocates' meeting of the year had 19 in attendance.

Annual Report and End-of-Year Fundraising Letter

Another Annual Report for fiscal year 1999-2000 listed the same officers as in previous years. Nita Wainwright and Hartman were new Board members, with Johnson and Harrison both ending their terms. Closson, Greaney, and Groth remained on the Board. Harrison had received special recognition at the auction for her service to RRS. Seven fewer sexual assaults occurred in FY '00, but the number of 57 was still way too high for the two counties. Over 500 hours of school-based education reached 5800 students. The website had 6700 hits.

Money from the state contract with DHS was lower than in the previous fiscal year at $105,000. Fundraising, donations, and the United Way generated total income of over $30,000, again demonstrating outstanding community support as RRS continued to fulfill its mission in the two counties. Personnel expenses of $120,500 included wages and benefits for the four employees. The value of all the volunteer services was conservatively estimated to be over $88,000 in FY'00.

An article in the BDN on October 27th described an increase in the UWEM allocation: "A $7,500 grant…will help educate students about the facts of rape. The funds specifically support their school-based educator and a school services coordinator. The educators talk to all classes in Penobscot and Piscataquis counties to present information regarding current issues about rape and dating violence. Kathy Walker…says of the program, 'The only way that rape will be eliminated is to educate young people that rape is a crime and to teach them that violence does not have to be part of a relationship.'"

The end-of-year fundraising letter from Woolley and Walker briefly touched on all the highlights and described O'Brien, Carr, and Pease as dedicated staff members. Collaboration with both Womancare and SR in some school presentations was mentioned. An attached list of 104 businesses and individuals who donated items to the auction encouraged readers to express appreciation for the support.

By the end of the year, it was apparent that personnel changes had strengthened RRS, especially in the Millinocket area where community outreach and school programs were expanded under Carr's leadership. Many volunteers in both Bangor and Millinocket were available around the clock to respond to calls on the hotline. Services to a victim/survivor had not been affected by the goings and comings of staff or volunteers.

2001: VIP

T he possibility of an increase in state funding occupied many hours and discussions throughout this new year. A subcommittee of personnel from sexual assault and domestic violence agencies had worked during the previous year with legislative leaders and a lobbying firm (Moosewood Associates) led by Betsy Sweet to discuss strategies for increasing funds. As chair of the MECASA Board, Walker took an active role in these efforts, traveling frequently to Augusta to attend planning meetings, testify at hearings, buttonhole legislators, and speak at legislative committee meetings. Governor Angus King had included support for domestic violence prevention in his budget proposal, and Sweet convinced both MECASA and MCEDV that only by collaborating would anyone obtain any additional funding.

The proposed legislation, Legislative Document (LD) 524, also known as the Violence Intervention & Prevention Act (VIP), was introduced on January 10th by Rep. Patrick Colwell of Gardiner, the House Majority Leader, and asked for $4.8 million. Funds in the bill were earmarked for direct services to victims, school-based prevention, community safety, and infrastructure support for sexual assault centers and domestic violence projects. One hundred forty-four legislators signed on as co-sponsors of LD 524. The last major increase in state funding to combat violence against women had been passed 15 years earlier. A selling point for the bill was that is requested just $4.00 per person in Maine.

Walker's letter to clarify the funding in the bill had appeared in the BDN on the day of its introduction. The letter referred to a January 5th BDN article which had mentioned only domestic violence beneficiaries, and was titled "VIP Treatment":

I want to clarify that the proposed $4.8 million would benefit sexual assault centers as well as domestic violence projects throughout Maine. Called the Violence Intervention and Prevention Act (VIP), this bill provides funding to increase prevention efforts in the schools and crisis services for victims and survivors. As Rep. Colwell stated, the bill provides a "holistic approach" to everyone who is affected by the crimes of sexual assault and domestic violence.

Members of the public are invited to attend a press conference regarding VIP at 11 A.M. today in the Hall of Flags at the Capitol in Augusta. We are grateful to both Rep. Colwell and to Gov. Angus King for proposing additional funding to fight the crime of interpersonal violence. Thanks also to the legislators who have already agreed to co-sponsor this legislation. Additional information about the press conference or the bill may be obtained by calling 941-2980.

Despite the collaborative work between MECASA and MCEDV on the legislation, the press tended to focus more on domestic violence than sexual assault. Exactly the same article appearing in two different newspapers illustrated this difference with "Sex-assault victims back bill" headlining it in one and "Victims put face on domestic-violence bill" in the other.

Walker, in her journal, noted that she was "totally pumped up by the press conference for the funding bill: speakers, crowd, and press interest." RRS volunteer Booker gave compelling personal testimony at the press conference:

I'm a student at the University of Maine, and I volunteer at Rape Response Services in Bangor. I am here today to offer my support for the VIP bill. I firmly believe that funding is needed to expand the education our children receive here in Maine. I feel that the education we currently provide is lacking in areas concerning social issues such as domestic violence, sexual assault and rape. These are issues of prevention, issues of intervention, issues of self-esteem and most importantly, issues that affect our children. And so we need a comprehensive educational program to address these issues. By comprehensive, I mean a program that begins in grade school with lessons about self-esteem. Lessons about actions that are not okay. Lessons about ways to say no. And lessons about how to get help.

A comprehensive program that builds on itself year after year and introduces new issues as they become age appropriate. Parents are often hesitant to expose their children to this type of education. Why? Because parents want to protect their children from harm and the crimes of the world. But I believe that educating our children and teaching them how to prevent these crimes is truly the best protection we can offer. Studies show that by educating our children, we can help them identify these crimes and prevent them from happening.

These crimes are happening every day in our communities. I can attest to this because I travel around and give rape education talks whenever I can. In every place that I speak, women and CHILDREN, yes young children, come forward with the crimes that have been committed against them. The rapes, the sexual abuse, the incest. It is all here in Maine. In the brief time that I speak to these students, I bear witness to how education is needed. During my last talk, three girls from just one grade came forward with their rapes. Three interventions in one hour. And I'd bet even more crimes were prevented in that hour. The need is here. Our children need to be protected. Through this bill for Violence Intervention and Prevention, we have a chance to help and protect our children. By supporting this bill, you can protect our children through education. I urge you to join me in educating our children, the children of our communities and our state. Thank you. [emphasis in original]

Early in April both Angel Tyler [formerly MacLaren], a RRS volunteer, and Walker testified at the hearing on the VIP bill before the Appropriations Committee. Three months after her initial euphoria, Walker wrote, "hearing on funding bill was disappointing in terms of turnout and state money problems." Speaking from personal experience, Tyler was identified in *Kennebec Journal* and *Portland Press Herald* articles by Paul Carrier the following day (April 3rd) as one of "the three victims who put a human face on a problem. When she was 17, Tyler said, she met a 22-year-old man who was 'everything a young girl could want in a boyfriend.' But first impressions proved to be devastatingly wrong. Tyler said her boyfriend raped her in the bathroom of a friend's house, stalked her and eventually threatened to kill her, forcing her to leave Maine for a time. 'He took away my pride, self-worth and any control I had over my life,' Tyler said."

As a member of the collaborative committee that had been working for several months on the proposal, Walker's testimony focused on the direct services element of the funding, while other committee members addressed the remaining elements:

> *Senator Goldthwait, Representative Berry, members of the Committee, my name is Kathy Walker, and I am the Executive Director of Rape Response Services, the sexual assault crisis center that serves Penobscot and Piscataquis counties. I want to thank you for your consideration of LD 524, and I especially want to thank the Committee members who signed on as co-sponsors of this bill. Your support affirms the work that we do in sexual assault and domestic violence agencies throughout the state.*
>
> *A portion of the funds requested in LD 524, $1.1 million, would help our agencies increase our direct services to victims of sexual assault or domestic violence. We estimate that an additional 3,355 individuals, who are not now receiving services, could be assisted with this portion of the funds.*
>
> *I want to spend a few minutes talking about what we mean by direct services. For domestic violence projects, people immediately think of shelters or safe homes and hotlines. And for sexual assault centers people also think of hotlines. Shelters or safe homes and hotlines are a crucial part of the services we provide. All of the sexual assault and domestic violence centers rely on volunteers to take shifts on our hotlines, and I have been known to say many times that we could not do what we do at Rape Response Services without our volunteers. But volunteers must receive extensive training of 40 hours or more before they can take hotline shifts, training provided by paid staff. And when most would-be volunteers are employed outside the home during the day, when the issues presented by our hotline callers become increasingly complex, it becomes more and more necessary to staff our hotlines, especially during the day, with paid employees.*
>
> *Direct service also means support and/or education groups for victims and survivors of sexual assault or domestic abuse. Support groups are facilitated by one or two trained employees, and meet weekly for a specified period of time.*
>
> *Another form of direct service is what is commonly known as*

on-site. Sexual assault and domestic violence centers provide on-site services at schools in their catchment area. This means that a staff person from the center is available at the school at a specified day and time each week. Students access this on-site service for one-on-one support regarding their own sexual assault or dating violence issues. Support groups for survivors are also facilitated within the school setting by personnel from domestic violence or sexual assault centers. Some domestic violence projects provide on-site services at hospitals and at DHS child protective locations.

Direct services that are unique to sexual assault centers include accompaniment to the hospital and advocacy during the rape protocol exam. This exam is an invasive and lengthy procedure which some have said is like being raped all over again. The role of the sexual assault advocate, whether a volunteer or an employee, is to be present in the exam room for the entire four or more hours required to gather evidence. Direct service in these situations means holding the victim's hand, preparing her or him for what is going to happen next, and making sure that the victim is treated with respect by the medical and law enforcement personnel who are also present.

Housing for victims is a form of direct service that is unique to domestic violence projects. We have already mentioned shelters and safe houses. In addition, projects provide transitional housing opportunities for longer-term safe housing than can be provided at a shelter. Emergency shelters are another form of direct service provided for victims of domestic abuse and their children.

Both sexual assault and domestic violence centers provide direct services within the legal system, accompanying individuals to court, assisting with protection from abuse orders, being present during interviews with law enforcement officers, observing the court process. A new initiative of some sexual assault centers is the Sexual Assault Response Team or SART that combines advocacy, medical care, and legal issues in a coordinated approach to the victim of rape.

Children are often victims of sexual or domestic abuse. Direct services are provided to them as well. Domestic violence projects offer shelter to a woman's children as well as to her, and often provide childcare while assisting a woman with paperwork. A sexual assault advocate is sometimes called to be present during the medical exam of a child who has been sexually abused.

Last year the twenty sexual assault and domestic violence centers provided one or more of these direct services to 18,500 individuals throughout the state. We know that many more individuals, particularly in the rural areas or in the ethnic communities, are in need of these direct services. Please help us to reach them by funding LD 524. Thank you for your consideration of this bill.

Statistics from Walker's testimony were included in the *Journal* and *Herald* articles referenced earlier. Scarce state funding was evident as the Appropriations Committee deliberated on LD 524 during the remainder of April. Some Committee members suggested that the 20 separate agencies could be combined for greater efficiencies. Walker was quoted in an April 25th BDN article by reporter Mal Leary about the Committee meeting where this suggestion was made: "Victims of sexual assault often see themselves as different from victims of domestic violence," Walker noted. "She said a recent study based on the consolidated system in North Carolina indicates separate structures work best. 'When the agencies are combined into one, survivors of sexual assault often feel that they have no hotline, that they have no services, because they do not see themselves as survivors of domestic abuse.'

"Walker also said the board members of Maine agencies are all volunteers, as are those who answer the hotline phones. She said funding is mostly reserved for professional staff to provide direct services and improve prevention programs. 'It makes sense for us to do coordinated programs, and we are,' she said. 'We do coordinated school programs with Women Care [*sic*] in Dover-Foxcroft and with Spruce Run in Bangor.' She said there are 116 schools in the two-county area served by her agency, with the equivalent of 1½ full-time educators to provide prevention programs. LD 524 would provide more staff for school-based domestic violence prevention programs and additional sexual assault prevention efforts."

Two days later, Leary wrote in the BDN: "The Legislature's Appropriations Committee unanimously endorsed a $4.8 million-a-year measure, even though the price tag exceeds all the cash left if the panel's proposed current services state budget is adopted." Walker's journal noted that she was "glad to be in the room" for the vote. Senator Mary Cathcart and Representative Sharon Libby Jones, both from the RRS catchment area, were on the Appropriations Committee and wholeheartedly supported the legislation. Representative Colwell called this an important first step, and Senate Republican Minority Leader Mary Small of Bath said she was "personally willing to vote for a tax increase to fund the measure," and was "not the only one in her caucus that would support raising new revenues to pay for this program."

Leary noted that "Supporters were thanking lawmakers after the vote, and were clearly elated at the show of support for the legislation. 'It's an important step to get a unanimous report out of Appropriations,' said Kathy Walker. 'We are working behind the scenes to come up with a source of funding.'" Although Walker was the only person quoted in these two articles, the headlines still focused solely on domestic violence.

In July, word was received about the VIP funding allocations. Reporter Ben Baker covered the news in the *Piscataquis Observer* on July 11th:

> *Despite a tight budget year, domestic violence and sexual assault treatment and prevention programs throughout the state are slated to receive new funding. "We were a presence they could not ignore," said Kathy Walker of Bangor's Rape Response Services, referring to the many hours she and other domestic violence and sexual assault workers spent in Augusta during the last two weeks of the budget debate. "I really think that we made a difference by being there day after day," Walker said. "They had promised at the beginning of the session, when 144 legislators signed on as co-sponsors, that there would be funding. We were there every day as a presence to remind them."*
>
> *Though a victory, the amount of funds provided in the budget is significantly less than the original bill had asked for. Walker said that the total asked for over two years had been $9.6 million, or $4.8 million total each year. As funded, the amounts come to $1.2 million in the first year and $3 million in the second. These funds are to be shared by domestic violence and sexual assault programs across the state. Walker said that the reduced funding amount will mean some reassessing of needs within her agency. Establishing a Rape Response Services office in Dover-Foxcroft remains a priority, she said.*

Cindy Freeman-Cyr of Womancare in Dover-Foxcroft said that when the money becomes available on October 1, her organization will receive between $65,000 and $75,000, whereas Walker expects Rape Response Services to receive about $32,000 [in actuality, $26,600 the first year, $66,600 expected in second]. *The difference in amounts, Walker said, is because when the* [VIP] *coalition looked at what its service needs were, it was found that domestic violence projects serve three times as many clients as sexual assault programs. "We went into the funding request knowing that for every dollar that sexual assault projects received, domestic violence* [projects] *should receive three dollars," she said.*

The exact amount a [sexual assault] *program receives is decided by a funding formula, which takes into account the population and square miles covered by the program, as well as service hours, hours spent on hotlines and in support groups, and how much fundraising is done by the organization. The more each program raises for itself, Walker said, the more points they get under the funding formula. "We're encouraging our agencies not to rely solely on government support," she said.*

In addition to the funds agencies throughout the state will receive because of this bill, Walker said that the campaign had some non-monetary benefits. "Number one, the issues of sexual assault and domestic violence received a lot of media support this whole legislative session," she said. "We were on TV, in the paper—we were out there." The other main benefit of the campaign was the collaboration between the sexual assault and domestic violence centers. "We have not always collaborated," she said. "[This time] we were at the table together, we did this together. I think we can take pride in the fact that we are collaborating."

RRS hosted a celebration of the passage of the funding bill by inviting staff members from both Womancare and SR to the Park Street office for refreshments and conversation on an August afternoon. Twenty-seven people attended. Before the collaboration on the legislation, such an event would probably not have occurred, but after sitting at the negotiating table together, a lot had been learned about mutual goals and needs.

A press conference and candlelight vigil were held in Bangor to kick off domestic violence awareness month on the first day of October, and to celebrate the passage of LD 524. Ordway reported on the event in the following day's BDN: "It's the biggest infusion of state funds that the organizations have received from the state in 16 years, according to Kathy Walker, executive director of Rape Response Services, which operates in Penobscot and Piscataquis counties. It was about half of what supporters were hoping for when they first submitted the $10 million legislation, but in the tempestuous and turbid final days of the legislative session, when a $300 million shortfall saw dozens of spending programs tossed aside, supporters were happy with what they got. For Rape Response Services, it means an actual office in Piscataquis County and maybe a small raise and some benefits for workers who have had neither."

Both U.S. Congressman John Baldacci and Representative Colwell were in attendance at the Bangor event. Colwell had words of praise for Bangor area legislators and program administrators for their tenacity. He also, however, referred only to domestic violence, as did the Congressman, as recipients of the funds. Ordway wrote: "Walker has been around for awhile and she's heard a lot of promises and a lot of speeches from politicians vowing to end domestic violence [*Walker mentioned sexual assault too*] in Maine. Colwell, she said, is different. 'To have a House majority leader get it...,' she paused, 'well, I think that's a very big deal. Of course he didn't get it right away, but he does now.'"

Baker's article in the October 5th *Piscataquis Observer* mentioned the T-shirts that were on display at this celebration in West Market Square, attended by about 50 individuals. He wrote: "One of the speakers during the gathering was Kathy Walker, executive director of Rape Response Services. Walker was deeply involved in pushing for the passage of LD 524, and spent many hours in Augusta during the final days before the budget's passage, lobbying and reminding legislators of their promise to provide funds for fighting domestic violence and sexual assault. 'Every day a private trauma takes place...throughout the state,' Walker said, comparing the private nature of abuse to the very public trauma the country had experienced on Sept. 11. 'It might be called rape, it might be called battery, it might be sexual abuse against children. We are here tonight to say the trauma must stop.'"

Hotline Volunteers

Funding concerns could not diminish the reality that volunteers continued to be the lifeblood of the agency, with 18 attending the January advocates' meeting and prompting Pease to write in *The Monthly Advocate*, "We've got an enormous group now and I LOVE it!" Averill's column in the BDN on March 14th quoted Pease about the upcoming advocate training. Pease had taken the course and told Averill it was "all-encompassing. Rather than being a program only for sexual assault victims or survivors, it is the type of course from which everyone benefits, she said. 'I learned so much about the community and what services are available. I got so much out of that. It's a wonderful course for anyone to take for the knowledge it provides.' Of course, RRS wants people to take the course who will use it in the hotline program. But, as Pease pointed out, once volunteer advocates have completed this course, they will have a much greater understanding of, and appreciation for, the variety of services their community provides those in need."

Pease initiated a new volunteer training feature which continued for many years: agency showcases. Put together to highlight local organizations, the first group consisted of representatives from Womancare, SR, Katahdin Friends, Inc. (KFI), Shaw House, and SpeakOut!, all of whom spoke about the client populations they served. A second group from Eastern Maine AIDS Network, Penquis Community Action Program (CAP), Mabel Wadsworth Women's Health Center, and the Bangor Sexually Transmitted Diseases (STD) Clinic helped to familiarize new advocates with medical resources that were available to the victim/survivor.

The process of annual advocate evaluations which were a requirement of the MECASA quality assurance standards was started by Pease. Evaluations were primarily an opportunity for the Client Services Coordinator and each advocate to touch base annually and discuss the hotline experiences. Suggestions for any improvements RRS could make were always welcome. Each advocate also had to present both a valid driver's license and proof of car insurance when she/he completed the initial training, or at an advocates' meeting. Copies of these two documents were retained in the advocates' individual files along with their applications and signed copies of RRS policies.

Personnel Changes

Late in the previous year, Walker had met several times with Renate Klein, assistant professor of human development at the University of Maine, to discuss her idea of submitting a VAWA proposal for a Safe Campus Project (SCP). When VAWA was reauthorized by Congress in 2000, more funding was earmarked for prevention programs on college campuses. This collaborative effort between Klein and RRS was awarded a $300,000 grant for two years with a portion going to RRS for a full-time campus-based staff person. Administrative expenses for RRS were also included. The purpose of the grant was to look at and improve the campus response to crimes against women by developing stronger collaboration among campus and community resources. Campus policies were to be reviewed with an eye toward better advocacy and support for victims. Training opportunities and printed materials for both students and staff members would be developed. Not since 1994 had RRS received funds for campus work.

The first of several staff changes that occurred during the year was, therefore, the good news that Nason had accepted the position of SCP Coordinator. Robert Dana, the Dean of Students on campus, met with Nason and Walker and agreed with the decision that she be hired. Nason had continued to be involved with the agency since designing the Web page, although too busy to take hotline shifts. Her new office, located on campus in East Annex, was provided by the University. As a grant-funded RRS employee, Nason attended all RRS staff meetings. A Safe Campus Task Force was established with campus and community representatives, including RRS and SR. Checks for the Safe Campus grant were paid to RRS by the University. Under Nason's leadership, SCP blossomed into a vital University presence until Nason resigned in 2012. (Note: After 2005, when VAWA funding was discontinued, SCP was funded by the University and became part of the Women's Resource Center, with oversight provided by Sharon Barker.)

Early in March, O'Brien left the agency. From her RRS start as a social work student in 1995, O'Brien had weathered a lot of changes personally and professionally. Although not trained as a teacher, she had established a solid footing for the school-based program at RRS and was ready for a change. By now, Carr had enough experience in the schools to take over some of the workload, especially the commitments already made with teachers.

By the end of September, Pease had also left RRS. Booker agreed to assume the Client Services Coordinator position for 20 paid hours per week as a field experience for her college degree, and was able to facilitate the advocate training that was already underway. Pease had moved out of the area, returning for some of the training sessions, and both Bean and Rancourt assisted Booker. Once again, the RRS volunteers outdid themselves. In her final edition of *Our Monthly Advocate*, Pease wrote to all: "Never lose sight of the fact that the work that each of you does is priceless. Yes, Kathy tries to guesstimate the value each year, but really none of us can."

School-Based Programs

The presence of RRS in public school classrooms throughout the two counties had initially been undertaken by O'Brien, who welcomed assistance from Carr in northern Penobscot and Piscataquis county schools. Before she left RRS, O'Brien took the initiative, with assistance from Carr and Pease, to produce Volume 1, Issue 1 of a *Rape Response Education Newsletter* that was mailed in March to teachers, principals, and superintendents throughout the two counties. A lead article was focused on a collaborative effort between SR and RRS to present and evaluate a dating violence prevention program at Central High School where Mike Hatch was the health teacher. The forty-minute daily sessions over an eight-day span were designed to teach students how to identify the signs of an abusive relationship, power and control, and physical, sexual, and emotional abuse. Learning how to obtain help for themselves or a friend was also included. A pre-test, post-test, and three-month follow-up to assess student learning were designed by O'Brien and Hamlett at SR. This evaluation was a component of outcome-based measurements required for continuation of the United Way funding. The results of the tests were compiled and presented as part of the UWEM reapplication process.

Another article in this education newsletter highlighted work that Carr was doing with Peer Counselors at Stearns High School in Millinocket. These juniors and seniors met with Carr to learn about how they might be support persons for victims and survivors of sexual assault. The positive impact of a supportive peer was stressed, because students often did not feel comfortable disclosing sexual assault to an adult. An editorial in *The Katahdin Times* on February 20th alluded to the peer program: "Prevention was very much on the mind of Rape Response Services when it hired an educator more than a year ago to go into the area schools to educate the region's youth regarding sexual harassment and abuse." Also included in the education newsletter was information about recent U.S. Supreme Court rulings regarding school liability for sexual harassment, and upcoming April events at RRS.

When Carrie Congleton was hired in July as the School-Based Educator to replace O'Brien, she hit the ground running. A former RRS volunteer and an education graduate from the University of Maine who worked as an elementary school teacher for two years, Congleton introduced herself in a late-summer letter to teachers and administrators. A bullying prevention program for elementary grades was developed by Congleton and Carr, both of whom also utilized the RRS learning objectives which were linked to the Health and Physical Education portion of the Maine Learning Results for all grade levels. RRS printed three separate brochures for teachers and administrators in grades K-4, 5-8, and 9-12, describing this alignment. A section of the brochure mentioned that RRS educational presentations could include topics ranging from good touch/bad touch, bullying, sexual harassment, dating violence, and sexual assault, and could be tailored to meet the individual needs of each school. Programs could also be offered to parents and teachers.

These brochures were mailed to school personnel in the RRS catchment area. "To define boundaries," an RRS objective in grades 3-4, was linked to Maine Learning Result E-1: "Use appropriate communication and listening skills to enhance health." Maine Learning Result C-5 for grades 5-8, "Demonstrate ways to avoid or change situations that threaten personal safety," was linked to the RRS objective, "to engage students in a discussion about safe relationships with peers and family." Creating the objectives and distributing the brochures was a project unique to RRS, and increased the credibility of the education program in area schools.

Carr and Congleton also worked diligently through the next several years to make classroom presentations informative and fun. Congleton completed evaluations at seven middle and high schools between August and December and compiled the results to satisfy requirements for both DHS and UWEM related to performance-based objectives. Ninety-two percent of the 261 participants in grades 9-12 felt that the amount of information was "just right;" 87% thought the speaker was neither too fast nor too slow but "just right." Students learned how to support a survivor (70%), what consent means (85%), not to blame the victim (70%), "I have choices" (80%), and the RRS hotline number (85%). Almost 50% wanted to have RRS available in the school (on-site) for support and guidance.

Some of the comments written on the evaluation forms by these students further emphasized the importance of the school-based initiatives:

- *The RRS presentation helped me help one of my friends get help after she was date raped this past summer.*
- *It was important for guys to know that not only girls get raped.*
- *I learned a lot about it, and know now to ask girls before just doing stuff.*
- *The one thing that I really got out of the presentation was when it was stated "It's not your fault," I think that's really important. I know people who have blamed themselves and it is pretty sad.*

Sexual Assault Awareness Month

April, Sexual Assault Awareness Month, began with a guest column that Carr wrote for the April 1st edition of the *Katahdin Times*. Titled "The facts about sexual assault," the article began:

> *Statistics state that one in three women and one in seven men will be a victim of sexual assault in his/her lifetime. Sexual assault is defined as rape, incest, child sexual abuse, and sexual harassment. One in three women and one in seven men is a shockingly high number, but you may not be feeling shocked after reading that statistic. You might be thinking "this could never happen to me" or "nothing like this could happen in my community." You might be thinking that you could pick a child molester out of a crowd, or that rapists lurk in dark alleys waiting to attack strangers. You might be thinking that people who are sexually assaulted ask for it by the company that they keep, the clothes that they wear, or the alcohol that they consume. You might be thinking that you aren't an attractive target for an attacker because of your age, gender, or physical disability.*

If you are holding on to any of these beliefs, you don't have the facts. It is happening right here in this community, and YOU are at risk. It is impossible to pick perpetrators out of a crowd. A very small percentage of violators have mental illnesses, and the larger majority has average to above average intelligence.

You may not want to believe anyone that you know could be a rapist, especially not anyone that you trust. However, statistics also state that 84% of victim/survivors know their attackers. You may also want to believe that your behavior keeps you safe. You may believe that by dressing conservatively, walking only in daylight, and limiting your alcohol intake mean you are immune to this crime.

Society has perpetuated the idea that sexual assault is about sex. The fact is that sexual assault is about power and control. It is unfortunate that it involves the sexual parts of the body, and so it gets confused and we think that we can do something to control it or protect ourselves. That is why it is so easy to blame the victim. It is easy to see that when you think about sexual assault as a crime motivated by power and control it makes sense why anyone can be victimized.

The elderly may be targeted because of the predictable schedules that they keep, impaired eyesight, or a smaller circle of family and friends. Children may be victimized because they are taught to obey and trust adults, and that only strangers need to be feared.

Those are the facts. It can happen to anyone, even you. Victims are not to blame. Sexual assault is a brutal crime based on power and control. But it is not hopeless. You can do something about it. Maybe it is time that you stopped buying into the myths about this crime. Maybe it is time that you educated your children and encouraged education in your schools. Maybe it's time that you told your children that violence is unacceptable. Maybe it's time to get help for yourself or someone that you love who has been victimized.

You have the power to change things. Rape Response Services is an organization in your community that you can turn to for help and support. Take a leap, make the call. The month of April is Sexual Assault Awareness Month, now is your chance to make a change in your life. [emphasis in original]

April events in which RRS was involved included the annual Stay-at-Home Ball which was "hosted live by Dave Russell and Kathy Walker," according to the invitation, and generated one called-in donation. Ward was the featured speaker at the annual meeting and volunteer recognition dinner provided by Penobscot Job Corps students at their facility. A TBN march and rally were held at the University of Maine with almost 200 people in attendance. Nason and the SCP staff organized the event which also included a candlelight vigil and speak-out. Tyler spoke earlier in the week at a "Responses to Rape" panel on the University campus about services available to survivors. A display table was also set up again at the annual H.O.P.E. Festival in Brewer.

At all of the April events and for the next several years, RRS distributed rolls of Smarties candies which were attached to a yellow business card decorated with small sunflowers bordering "SMART." This acronym, created in response to the drugs used to facilitate rape, was borrowed from a website:

- "Sip only from cans you open.
- Monitor your drink constantly.
- Avoid drugs and alcohol.
- Refuse drinks from punchbowls.
- Throw away if it tastes funny."

The reverse side of the card was printed with "Rape Response Services for questions and concerns about sexual assault" and included the hotline number, all within a border of tiny sunflowers. Advocate Hall assembled about 700 of these popular candy handouts in 2001.

MECASA held its annual April tea at the Blaine House, with Governor King as the guest speaker. Walker as MECASA Board Chairperson had the privilege of introducing him (in his own home!):

> *Governor King, Senators and Representatives, honored guests, friends, it is my pleasure to welcome each of you to this kickoff of Sexual Assault Awareness Month. Today is a celebration. But it is a celebration tempered by the sobering reality that everyone in this room has been affected in some way by the crime of sexual assault. Whether you call yourself a victim or a survivor or a victim/survivor,*

whether your loved one or friend has been sexually assaulted, whether you volunteer your time or are employed at a sexual assault crisis center, your experience of sexual assault has changed the way you view the world.

I want to speak just a minute about the word "survivor." The popular TV series that bears this name has certainly gotten the word "survivor" a lot of attention. But the real survivors are the people in this room, the people who call our hotlines, the people who attend our support groups. The "survivors" on the TV show volunteered to be participants. There is nothing voluntary about sexual assault. The "survivors" on the TV show earn monetary prizes even if they lose. There are no big bucks for survivors of sexual assault. And so to the real survivors in this room, I say, "I'm glad you survived. We are here to support you. We believe you. And thanks for being here today."

It is now my pleasure to introduce our next speaker, who really needs no introduction. But when I spoke just a minute ago about no big bucks available for survivors of sexual assault, I am happy to say that Governor King is trying to change that. For the first time, I believe, a Maine Governor has included in his Part One budget an amount specifically earmarked for sexual assault and domestic violence prevention. And Governor King has been willing to talk openly and often about the devastating impact of the crimes of sexual assault and domestic violence. We thank you for your initiatives, Governor King, and for your willingness to join us here today.

After the Governor's remarks, the annual Make a Difference Awards were presented by MECASA. Mentioning that she was now speaking as RRS director, Walker again used a TV show analogy:

If you're at all familiar with the TV show, "Who Wants to be a Millionaire?" you know that when a contestant gets into a tight spot and cannot answer the question, he or she has one chance to call a "lifeline" for the answer. The recipient of the Make a Difference Award is that lifeline for me and for the other directors of sexual assault centers in Maine.

Steve Greenlaw is our DHS Contract Specialist. That is his official title. But Steve is much more than a title. Steve is the champion of our sexual assault centers in the DHS bureaucracy. Steve is a helpful and calming voice at the other end of the line when we have questions about our contracts. Steve is the person who either knows the answers or gets right back to us with the answers. Steve is generous in his praise, patient with our delays, and gentle in his corrections. Like I said, Steve is our lifeline. Steve makes a difference by helping each of the ten centers and the coalition do our jobs in a better way.

Walker concluded the program by reminding the audience: "each person in this room has the opportunity to make a difference in the lives of those affected by sexual assault."

Nason's letter to the editor about sexual assault awareness month and the annual "Take a Stand" was published in the weekend (April 21st/22nd) BDN:

> *April conjures several images such as springtime, warmer weather, and of course, mud. As noted in a Department of Justice report, a college campus which has 10,000 female students could experience more than 350 rapes a year. If this number were scaled to fit the University of Maine, which has roughly half that amount of female students, it can be speculated that UM has 175 rapes a year. That's an astonishing number.*
>
> *In 1999, there were two forced and one unforced sexual assaults reported to Public Safety* [at the University]. *Does that mean there were only three rapes on campus? In the same Department of Justice report, it is noted that only 5 percent of all rapes are ever reported to police. Victims of sexual assault often feel guilty for their rapes and blame themselves.*
>
> *There are several things one can do to support those who have been sexually assaulted with the most important being to believe the victim/survivor's story if he or she comes to you for help, to offer support without making choices for the survivor, and to allow a survivor to talk about his or her experience without judging.*

The national website CAVNET (Communities Against Violence Network) featured "Take a Stand," which was again held in Millinocket, Dover-Foxcroft, and Bangor in late April, covered by all three television stations. A total of about 55 individuals attended the three events, promoting sexual assault awareness in the communities where they were held. Baker from the *Piscataquis Observer* was at the Dover-Foxcroft Stand and wrote on May 2nd:

> *The event, called Take a Stand, allows people to show by their very presence that sexual assault in any form is unacceptable. The demonstrations are sponsored by Rape Response Services of Bangor, and are the brainchild of Kathy Walker, executive director of the organization. Stands were held in Bangor and Millinocket in addition to Dover-Foxcroft. This is the demonstration's third year in Dover-Foxcroft.*
>
> *"We don't want people to feel they have to go to Bangor," Walker said of the wide-spread locations. She noted that the Stands are alternatives to "Take Back the Night" marches and speak-outs held elsewhere. After attempts at marches received little response in Bangor, she picked up on the comment of a student helper and decided to develop the Stands. "A Stand is an alternative to marching," she said. "We encourage people to speak if they want to, but it's not a speak-out."*
>
> *Participants stood for about an hour, discussing the needs of sexual assault victims in Piscataquis County, and what more could be done to prevent such crimes. Donna Runnels, victim witness advocate for the Piscataquis County DA's office, noted that raising awareness about the presence of such crimes in the area is key. Though the turnout for the Stand is not as great as it could be, Walker is hopeful for the future. "We may be small, but we're mighty," she said.*

The eight enthusiastic participants at the Stand in Dover-Foxcroft appeared in a photograph to accompany the article. Holding one of the RRS banners on the steps of the Congregational Church, "They were there to make clear one thing—that they have zero tolerance for sexual assault in their communities," according to the caption under the photo.

A Community Presence

Community education and training events were scheduled regularly throughout the year. Region V (Penobscot and Piscataquis counties) police training was presented by Walker in Hampden in

February for 35 officers and in March for University of Maine Public Safety in collaboration with SCP. RRS was certified by MCJA to present these trainings so attendees from law enforcement agencies could receive credit. The two and a half hour sessions included information about the rape protocol exam, collection of evidence, role of RRS advocates, and registered sex offenders. Most of the 28 municipal or county law enforcement departments in the two counties were represented at one or more of these Region V trainings through the years.

Walker also presented another DHS six-hour training in Bangor in March. "Introduction to Child Sexual Abuse" was the focus for the 24 participants. She had "changed my whole sequence since last time," according to her journal, and received positive evaluations. Her introductory remarks expressed the wish that "no one should have to be introduced to child sexual abuse."

RRS was invited to participate during the year in two sex offender notification meetings in Etna and Glenburn. Walker's experience at these events was part of the impetus for an op-ed that appeared in the BDN on July 17th. In response to another column earlier in the month, Walker wrote:

> Patt Morrison's op-ed column expresses her incredulity over the charges of child molestation brought against her friend, comedian Paula Poundstone. This incredulity, unfortunately, is what all victims and survivors of child sexual abuse face when they try to tell someone about what is happening. The same incredulity is evident in the ongoing discussion about fingerprinting of teachers. We do not want to believe that people we know, our friends, our co-workers, our teachers, our neighbors, are guilty of sexually abusing or harassing another person.
>
> It is much easier to cast doubt on the person who is trying to tell his or her story of sexual abuse. It is much easier to believe that perpetrators of sexual abuse and harassment are the strangers in our communities, the people we don't know and would never want to know, the people we can avoid.
>
> State Sen. Peter Mills, in speaking last month against the repeal of fingerprinting, told about three clients he represented in his law firm, all of whom were convicted of child sexual abuse. Sen. Mills told the other senators that these people, these convicted child

abusers, were no different in appearance or in community position or in any other way, from anyone in the Senate chamber. But we want to believe they are different, because how else could they commit the criminal act of child sexual abuse?

Child abusers rely on this societal denial to get away with what they do. They know that we would never suspect them, and they know that we would cast doubt on anything that a child might say against them. And just for good measure, they usually are adept at adding threats to their abuse, the threat of retaliation if a child should ever think of getting up courage enough to tell. It does take a great deal of courage for anyone, child or adult, to come forward and report sexual abuse or harassment, knowing that there is already a strike against you that no one will believe what you have to say. Kudos to those who have the courage to tell, and to those who listen and believe.

In late October, a DHS training, "Working with the Sexually Abused Child," was presented in Bangor. Walker noted in a journal entry: "My six hours of training was terribly disorganized and off-the cuff, but the 32 foster parents and others gave it high marks. I changed my opening to talk about learning from each other, and that is exactly what happened, with me as facilitator providing some basic info or reinforcing. Number of troubled kids out there is horrendous."

During the late summer and fall, the Maine Department of Behavioral and Developmental Services (DBDS, formerly DMHMRSAS) held planning sessions in Augusta for a conference scheduled in Augusta in late November. Jennings, still the Director of the Office of Trauma Services, now in the new department, was the force behind this third attempt at "Connecting Trauma, Substance Abuse and Mental Health," the theme of the conference. Because of the funds that sexual assault agencies continued to receive from the new department, MECASA had a seat which Walker filled at the planning meetings.

The workshop which Walker presented on the first day of the conference was titled "Working with Adult Survivors of Child Sexual Abuse." A description of the workshop in the brochure stated: "participants will gain an understanding of the trauma of sexual assault and some of the best ways to help survivors. Someone who can listen and believe what has happened to them is often most helpful to survivors.

Information about resources for both the survivor and the caregiver will be shared."

Another letter to the editor from Walker appeared in the November 27th BDN:

> *Bravo to the jurors in Ellsworth who convicted Eugene Merchant of gross sexual assault. They saw through the smoke screen of consent and other defense tactics without being privy to the information that the defendant had already been convicted of the same offense against another person in 1986.*
>
> *Bravo to the victim who took the stand and held firm in spite of suggestions by the defense attorney that she had not acted like a "typical" victim. Drinking with someone is not an invitation to be raped. And there has never been a profile of how a victim of rape should respond. Response to the trauma of rape takes many forms. The courage of both the victim and the jury to convict this rapist sends a welcome message to other women and men who have been raped that they will be believed.*

Annual Auction and Awards Night

A Summer 2001 edition of *The Rape Response Reporter* headlined the upcoming fifth annual auction early in September. A small bronze moose from Hart and a five-foot maple bookcase from Moosehead Furniture were two of the live auction items, along with a signed copy of a novel by Mainer Monica Wood, whom Walker had met earlier in the year. New auction underwriters included Veeder and Longtin, CPA (Certified Public Accountant), and Groth & Associates.

A bidding directory for the auction, developed by Pease, listed the expanded RRS staff of six, and new Board officers. Both Woolley and Veeder had left, but continued to support the auction. Groth was Board President, Wainwright, Treasurer, and Hartman, Secretary. New members, Elizabeth Allan and Shellie Morcom, joined Greaney and Uhlenhake on the Board. McKay again called for bids on the 54 live auction items, a number that all agreed in later years was too many. A quilted wall hanging, stained glass pieces, quilts, and a made-to-order Santa Claus were among the handmade items. Bidding was lively for all food items, including a pie per month from Frank's Bakery, ten dozen holiday cookies from Martha Naber, and one delectable dessert per month from the RRS Board members.

Two advocates, Bean and Hall, were surprised to receive the Janet Badger Volunteer Award for donating hundred of hours on the hotline, at trainings and for other RRS projects. Badger was always present to present the award given in her name. Kim Miller and friend provided musical selections during the silent auction. Despite having more items to auction and more people in attendance (120), plus a longer list of underwriters, the auction raised just over $9700, five hundred more than the previous year. "I know that is good," Walker observed in her journal, "but I always have visions of so much more."

Money Matters

Other fundraising events to benefit RRS and to raise awareness occurred throughout the year. Shannon Sheehy presented RRS with a check for $100 from Wal-Mart, where she was employed. The company donated this amount in recognition of the time she spent volunteering at RRS, after Walker signed a form to verify the hours.

A production of "The Vagina Monologues" was presented on the University of Maine campus by SWA on Valentine's Day. Intended for presentation at colleges and universities, the Monologues raised both money and awareness. An article in *The Maine Campus* by Beth Haney on February 16th, reported: "The Vagina Monologues was performed to a packed Minsky Recital Hall, the second year this play has been done at the university. Kathy Walker from Rape Response Services gave an introductory speech. She reminded the audience that one in three women and one in seven men are survivors of sexual assault. That is why performances like the Monologues are so important. 'In talking comes healing,' Walker said."

In the Katahdin area, Carr and Danforth were busy on February 14th distributing carnations donated by Millinocket Floral to area businesses. The flowers were part of a Valentine's Day event organized by Carr to promote public awareness about sexual assault and domestic violence. A card attached to a ribbon on each carnation provided RRS hotline numbers and additional information.

The Maine Campus on March 2nd printed an advertisement for an event to benefit RRS: "Tonight at 6 P.M. the brothers of Beta Theta Pi will be holding their 8th annual sleep out with this year's proceeds benefitting Rape Response Services of Bangor. The brothers will spend the night sleeping in cardboard boxes on the front lawn. Raffle tickets will be sold to raise money for Rape Response Services, and remarks will be given by the organization and by Officer Deb Mitchell. All are welcome to this chemical free event. Please show your support for Rape Response Services."

An article by reporter Doug Kesseli in the weekend (March 3rd/4th) BDN reported on the Friday event:

> *While most people sought warmth and stayed indoors Friday night, dozens of University of Maine students huddled around a bonfire, weathering bone-chilling temperatures in order to promote a cause. In a stark reminder of life's harsh realities, the members of Beta Theta Pi fraternity have been holding winter sleep outs for eight years, promoting a greater need for awareness and action on curbing homelessness and domestic abuse. This year, the nearly 40 Beta brothers were to stay outside from 6 P.M. Friday to 6 A.M. Saturday to draw attention to sexual assault. The night, like the subject it is intended to raise awareness about, wasn't easy.*
>
> *Beta chapter president Dan Chadbourne, a sophomore, acknowledged that the need to promote sexual assault awareness was worth the sacrifice of one night in the bitter cold. "Even if three people say 'Hey, I'm going to be a little more educated on this,' then it was worth everything we did," he said. "Hopefully, many people— much more than three people—would be willing to be a little bit more educated."*
>
> *The timing was, it turned out, unfortunately appropriate for taking up the issue in light of a warning the campus issued earlier this week that two women had been assaulted on campus. It was the first time in two years that the university had issued a crime alert. But for every sexual assault reported, many others go unreported, acknowledged Deb Mitchell, a University public safety officer, who is often a primary investigator in sexual assault cases reported on the campus. One in three women is sexually assaulted in their lifetimes, yet only one in three women report the assaults, she said at Friday's sleep out. Hence the need for more coordinated programs*

and projects such as the sleep out.

"I think it shows that men are coming together...men are willing to promote that awareness as well," said Carrie [sic] Nason of Rape Response Services, which will receive an estimated $1,250 that was raised through a raffle of prizes collected by the fraternity. Several university sororities also raised money for the project and showed up for support Friday. That men are and need to be involved is important, Mitchell pointed out. "The ones that we need to teach prevention to are the men, because they are the only ones that can actually prevent sexual assault," Mitchell said, acknowledging that women also must be educated on how to lessen their chances of being sexual assault victims. Mitchell thinks the fraternity's involvement helps fraternities get out from under a long-held stereotype that most rapes on campus occur in frat houses. They don't, Mitchell asserted. Most occur in dormitories.

Money was not the only welcome gift at RRS. Items such as sweatpants and sweatshirts and office equipment had been donated through the years. The donation of a much-needed, used full-size refrigerator was made at the end of 2001 by David and Barbara Shaw. This easily fit into the office kitchen, replacing the apartment size unit that had been there, and providing ample room for storing staff lunches, snacks for training, and food for the occasional advocates' potluck meal or holiday party.

Annual Report

Another Annual Report for the fiscal year that ended on September 30th recorded 60 sexual assaults had occurred, an increase of three over the previous year. Over 250 hours of service had been provided on the hotline to 240 clients, with a consistent number of over 30 advocates in Bangor and Millinocket. RRS presented more than 330 hours of community and school education programs, reaching 5200 individuals. The state contract provided income of $122,300, with fundraising and donations at an all-time high of over $20,000. The conservatively estimated value of volunteer services exceeded $88,000. Personnel expenses accounted for almost $162,000.

Because of staff changes and paid backup, a record twelve W-2 forms were typed and distributed to current and former RRS employees at the beginning of 2002 to reflect work completed in 2001. Bean and others had previously been paid for backup as independent contractors, but another look at the rules for this employee category necessitated a change. Although these individuals could choose the shifts when they were on backup, the shift hours and mobility of the people on backup were determined by RRS and meant that the employees were not completely independent.

The year had been filled with new initiatives at both the state and agency levels. Looking ahead to 2002, RRS was hopeful that increased funding initiated by the VIP legislation would allow expansion of programs to reach more people in the outlying areas of the two counties.

2002: A SART/SANE APPROACH
TO VICTIM SERVICES

The main focus of 2002, SART/SANE, an initiative which began in Minnesota and was endorsed by MECASA in 1996, is best understood by events that occurred at RRS in previous years. SANE was the acronym for Sexual Assault Nurse Examiners, designated forensic RNs who had completed specialized training in conducting the rape protocol exam. These nurses were trained to also provide crisis intervention counseling, testing for sexually transmitted infections, emergency contraception, and drug testing if a drug-facilitated rape was suspected. A SANE could be subpoenaed to court as an expert witness in rape cases.

MECASA brought Rebecca Campbell, RN to Maine from Minnesota in October 1997 and several times during 1998 to provide week-long training sessions for RNs who wanted SANE certification. Campbell was the impetus behind the nationwide SANE program. By sponsoring the training, MECASA made sure that the role of advocates in the rape protocol exam was not overlooked. MECASA directors presented a portion of each SANE training, chosen by proximity to where the sessions were held. Two nurses from Millinocket Regional Hospital, Budge and Nason, and several from the Bangor area, including Shellie Morcom at the University's Cutler Health Center and Laurie Eddy at Penquis Health Services (part of Penquis CAP), completed the earlier trainings. A training at Penquis Health Services in Bangor in mid-September 2001 had 14 trainees, and Walker presented the piece on advocates' roles and responsibilities at this session.

A Sexual Assault Response Team (SART) was officially comprised of a SANE, an advocate, and a law enforcement officer, and was seen as a way for the victim/survivor to receive coordinated care in a timely manner following a rape. The sole focus of the SART could be on the victim/survivor throughout the exam and the police interview, resulting in, it was hoped, more convictions of rapists. Prior to the implementation of SART/SANE, many medical personnel were reluctant to perform the rape protocol exam in the ER for two reasons: lack of training, and the amount of time required (as much as four to five hours) to complete the exam. Hospitals welcomed the availability of an on call SANE who could devote her time to the collection of evidence. An advocate was part of SART to answer questions, to provide emotional support for the victim/survivor during the exam, and to speak up if necessary for the best interests of the victim/survivor.

The SART Advisory Committee in Bangor had scheduled monthly meetings since 1998, initiated and convened by RRS. Different from the three-person team that mobilized in the event of a rape, the Bangor SART provided an opportunity for local law enforcement officers, representatives from the DA's office, nurses, and RRS staff members to discuss procedures then in place and to review earlier cases. Many SART programs around the country were coordinated by rape crisis centers instead of hospitals; this was the model endorsed by MECASA and eventually by DHS. RRS had been taking steps to implement this approach and would move forward with the help of a VAWA grant.

In August 1999, Walker had reluctantly submitted an application for VAWA funds to underwrite a SART/SANE effort at Penquis Health Services. RRS and Eddy, supported by the SART Advisory Committee, had been working on an idea to take the rape protocol exam out of the impersonal ER at the local hospitals. Walker's reluctance to write the grant was due primarily to her belief that there were too many unknowns in the proposal, a premonition, perhaps, of what eventually evolved. The full amount requested, $20,600, was approved in November 1999, she noted in her journal, "more than I've ever competed for!" This money, of course, could be used only for grant purposes, but Walker had learned to insert an amount for "administrative expenses" into each application.

By the time Pease was hired as Client Services Coordinator in June 2000, RRS had sufficient leftover funds in the personnel budget to hire Closson as the first SART Coordinator. Closson, who had been volunteering at the office, assumed the part-time temporary position to help establish the Penquis Health Services site. In February 2001, Tyler was hired as the full-time SART Coordinator at RRS, paid with an increase in funds from the DHS contract because of support for the initiative at the state level. Tyler moved into the office that Closson had established at Penquis Health Services; RRS paid rent to Penquis CAP for this space. Almost $13,000 of the VAWA grant was used to purchase a colcoscope with an attached camera for photographing the internal bruising that occurred during a sexual assault. Thanks to Eddy's enthusiasm, a suite of rooms for the exams, in addition to the office space, had been set aside, and was outfitted with an exam table from Penquis Health Services plus other supplies purchased with grant funds. Besides the exam room, the suite included a shower, bathroom, and waiting room.

RRS was the first center in Maine to consider performing rape protocol exams outside a hospital setting. The goal of the RRS plan was to create a more caring environment away from the hospital ER, a place where the sole focus could be on the victim. A contract between SANEs, RRS, and Penquis Health Services was drawn up. The SANEs were expected to be on call for three or four 24-hour shifts per month, to carry a pager provided by RRS, and to maintain their own malpractice insurance. Time while on call would be unpaid; a flat rate of $100 would be paid for each exam performed at the site. The SART Coordinator would prepare an on call schedule three months in advance. According to the original plan, the site at Penquis would be operational by late 2000 or early 2001.

What was not factored into these plans was the difficulty in maintaining a SANE group that was large enough to fill the on call schedule. Classroom training was only the first step in a long process before SANEs could receive certification. Tyler worked with Bangor nurses throughout 2001, trying to help them become certified. Performing a specified number of pelvic exams, observing several sexual assault cases and the testimony of expert witnesses in court, and assisting with a specified number of rape protocol exams, were difficult to schedule when the nurses were also employed full-time at area hospitals.

Before the SART Advisory Committee meeting in February 2002, it had become evident to all players that the dwindling number (six or fewer) of available SANEs meant the site could not open as planned. All the details still had not been worked out about how to access the site during non-business hours and on weekends, and this was a stumbling block for law enforcement officers. Too many unanswerable questions loomed over the establishment of the Penquis site, including quality assurance standards and liability. How would the summer schedule and vacations for the nurses be handled? What contractual relationship, if any, would the site have with the two hospitals in Bangor? Could RRS obtain a medical liability insurance rider for nurses who were not covered elsewhere? Who would pay the $100 for each exam? Despite the best intentions of many individuals, these issues proved to be insurmountable.

By the time the plan was scrapped early in 2002, several nurses at each of the Bangor hospitals had become certified SANEs and agreed to be on call for rape protocol exams at the hospitals. They were willing to go to either hospital, but questions arose as to how they would be paid, who would cover their insurance, and who would provide medical direction if the nurses were not at their own ERs. Colleen Lemon and Dottie McCabe, registered ER nurses and SANEs at St. Joseph and EMMC, respectively, were valuable assets for the Bangor SART, as was the DA's office and Dr. Erik Steele at EMMC. The colcoscope was eventually sold for $1500 to Dr. Elizabeth Weiss who took it to a clinic in Nicaragua.

Although disappointed that plans for a community-based site did not work out, the SART Advisory Committee continued monthly meetings, facilitated by Tyler. A two-page quick reference guide for advocates to use with a victim/survivor was developed by RRS and the Committee members. The key purpose of the guide was to inform the victim/survivor of options, with a detailed listing of the advantages and disadvantages of reporting to law enforcement. Provided under the question, "Do they want to report?" and the statement, "Encourage reporting, remembering the choice is theirs," the advantages of reporting were:

- *Better chance of gathering more evidence if done ASAP*
- *Less deterioration of evidence, especially drugs or alcohol*
- *Can tell story once to SART*
- *Get initial work done and over*
- *Healing process can begin with telling story*

The disadvantages listed on the reference guide included:

- *Telling might cause more trauma if victim/survivor not ready*
- *Very intrusive questions will be asked*
- *May feel as if on trial*
- *Waiting to report makes investigation more difficult*

In addition to exploring the advantages and disadvantages, either on the telephone or at the hospital, the advocate was reminded in the guide to explain that the victim/survivor could choose to have anyone or no one in the hospital room, besides the SANE, at any time during the exam.

If clothing was needed to replace what was removed from the victim/survivor for evidence, the advocate was advised in the guidelines to call the person on backup who would deliver clothes to the hospital unless the advocate carried bags of donated clothing in her car. Transportation for any victim/survivor needing a ride from the hospital could be arranged with a local taxi service by calling the RRS ED for authorization to bill RRS. Telephone numbers for all the police and sheriff departments and hospitals in the two counties were listed at the bottom of the guidelines, as well as the toll-free number for Spurwink, an agency in Portland which had expertise in examining child victims of sexual assault.

The SART Advisory Committee also had an opportunity to view the new evidence collection kit that had been obtained from the state for rape protocol exams. Requiring a statewide standardized kit, instead of the variety used at different hospitals, was part of a legislative action in 2000, but developing the new kit had been a long process at the Maine Crime Lab. The new kit when used during a rape protocol exam could be stored at room temperature for up to six months unless there was a urine specimen (for drugs) which had to be frozen, or a blood tube (for alcohol) which had to be refrigerated. The completed evidence kits were stored by the law enforcement agency in the municipality where the rape occurred until the victim/survivor decided whether or not to report the rape. If a report was made, the kit was sent to the Maine Crime Lab for testing.

The rape protocol kit consisted of one or two boxes and contained a multitude of labeled paper envelopes and bags into which samples were deposited. Implements for collecting each sample, such as tweezers and cotton tips, were also included. Evidence of a rape could be found in the following areas, and each had a separate envelope or bag:

- Oral swabs and smears
- Nasal swab
- Nasal mucous sample
- Fingernail clippings or swabbing of both hands
- Blood collection (finger prick)
- Head hair sample pulled from five areas of the scalp
- Foreign material collection (clothing)
- Debris collection (dirt, foreign hairs, leaves, fibers)
- Dried secretions (blood, saliva, ejaculate)
- Pubic hair combing
- Pubic hair sample (pulled)
- Genital/penile swabbing
- Rectal swabs and smears
- Vaginal swabs and smears
- Cervical swabs and smears
- Miscellaneous evidence (tampons, etc)
- Urine specimen if suspicion of rape drug within four days
- Blood alcohol specimen if suspicion of rape drug within one day

An advocate from RRS did not go to the hospital except at the specific request of the victim/survivor. When at the hospital, the advocate was able to provide a basic overview of the exam, with more details described as each step was done. Once the exam was underway, the nurse focused on collection of evidence and could not leave the room for any reason in order to ensure that no one contaminated the evidence. Sometimes an advocate was asked by the nurse to obtain something outside the room, such as warm blankets for the victim/survivor. A nurse was required to keep the completed evidence kit in her or his possession until turning it over to a law enforcement officer in the municipality or jurisdiction where the rape occurred. In most instances, an officer arrived at the hospital to pick up the kit as soon as the exam was completed, even if the victim/survivor at that point had not decided whether to report the rape.

Providing trainings for local law enforcement officers became a new focus of the SART Advisory Committee, which developed objectives for this training:

- *To provide an overview of sexual assault and its impact on victim/survivors*
- *To discuss appropriate responses to victim/survivors of sexual assault*
- *To review procedures for collection of evidence (including interviewing)*
- *To provide information about recent changes in Maine law*
- *To promote collaboration in the treatment of sexual assault victim/survivors*
- *To provide information on what options are available to victim/survivors*

An overview of sexual assault and RRS opened these training sessions, and the importance of law enforcement officers in sexual assault cases was emphasized. This outline had been used in previous trainings, sometimes with an additional piece about registered sex offenders added, and would be used in subsequent years.

Sexual Assault Awareness Month

April was busier than in previous years, with some new activities added and new twists on others. The Stay-at-Home Ball was hosted live again on WEZQ 92.9 with Dave Russell and Walker. This year Averill provided publicity on April 5th in the BDN:

> *Rather than going out for a good time this weekend, Dave Russell, program director for radio station 92.9 WEZQ, hopes you will keep your keys in your pocket and use what's in your wallet for something different. Russell hopes you will tune in to the station's annual Stay-at-Home Ball, which airs from 8 to 11 P.M., and enjoy an evening in the comfort of your own home while helping those in need.*
>
> *Funds raised through the Ball benefit Rape Response Services of Bangor, and RRS executive director Kathy Walker will be joining Russell live, on the air, for the broadcast. "Listeners are encouraged to make a donation to RRS, and can do so by calling the WEZQ*

Listener Line," Russell wrote. "We're encouraging folks to take the money they would have spent going out on a Saturday night and donate, instead, to Rape Response Services."

Sheri Lynch and Bob Lacey of the syndicated "Bob & Sheri Show" also taped public service announcements which aired on WEZQ 92.9 in the days leading up to the Ball and during the event itself. Two calls came in to the station during the evening.

The MECASA Blaine House Tea, which featured a presentation of the annual Make a Difference Awards, was again held in Augusta. Maine House Speaker Michael Saxl and Maine House Majority Leader Patrick Colwell were the award recipients. Walker's remarks as executive chair of the MECASA Board began:

> *As I thought about what I would say today, many ideas popped in and out of my head. Last year I mentioned a couple of television shows and said that the real survivors are the people who call our hotlines, not those on the TV show. My natural inclination this year is to mention the trauma of September 11th, saying that for victims and survivors of sexual violence, every day is a September 11th. But that analogy has been overused.*
>
> *So let's think for a moment of the phrase, "make a difference." MECASA gives these annual awards to celebrate people who make a difference. Before rape crisis centers were established back in the seventies, acts of sexual violence were not discussed, were not prosecuted, and were blamed on the victim/survivor. A grass roots movement was started by a few women in California and Washington D.C. who were determined to make a difference. And from their efforts thirty years ago, we have sexual assault or rape crisis centers in every state.*
>
> *For many years, child sexual abuse by priests in the Catholic Church was not discussed, was not prosecuted, and was ignored. A few men, when they reached adulthood, were determined to make a difference by speaking out about the sexual abuse that they experienced as children in the church. And from their efforts, others are finding the courage to tell their own stories, and the church is listening.*
>
> *To the women and men in this room who make a difference*

by telling your own stories of sexual violence, I say thank you. Thank you for your courage and your persistence in the face of disbelief and victim blaming. To the men and women in this room who make a difference by listening and believing the stories of sexual violence, I also say thank you. Thank you for the services you provide and for the support you offer.

My husband grew up on a farm in Vermont. His family had a team of workhorses named Pat and Mike who were always pulling together. Sometimes they pulled a plow to break new ground. Other times they pulled a rake to gather up the hay. After being taught a few simple commands, like "gee" for turning right and "haw" for turning left, Pat and Mike worked together for many years, focused on getting the job done, whatever that job entailed.

Today we honor our own Pat and Mike. A team. Workhorses. Committed to getting the job done. Together they have broken new ground by gaining passage of the Violence Intervention and Prevention Act last year. Together they worked to rake in the votes this year so that our funds would not be cut.

At the beginning you might say that our Pat and Mike had a little difficulty in understanding the "gee" and "haw." They seemed to get the "gee," the domestic violence part okay. But just as "gee" and "haw" have to go together, so did domestic violence and sexual assault have to go together when it came to passage of the VIP bill. And it was the "and sexual assault" that came a little harder for our Pat and Mike. Now they have been taught so well that they sometimes say "sexual assault" before adding "and domestic violence."

It is my very great pleasure to present our annual Make a Difference awards this year to House Speaker Mike Saxl and House Majority Leader Pat Colwell. Thank you for the work you have done to make a difference in the lives of everyone affected by sexual violence. Thank you from everyone in the Maine Coalition against Sexual Assault. Thank you, each of you, for attending this celebration. Thanks to the people in this room and many others, acts of sexual violence are discussed, are prosecuted in increasing numbers, and are not always blamed on the victim/survivor. Give yourselves an award each time you make a difference in the life of someone affected by sexual assault.

A "really nice" RRS annual meeting and volunteer recognition dinner was held in mid-April at the UU Society building right across Park Street from the office. April was also Volunteer Appreciation Month. State Representative and Bangor City Councilor Pat Blanchette was the speaker, sharing some of her life experiences. The potluck meal was provided by Board members and staff, who also set up and decorated the tables. Gifts for the advocates this year were made by ladies from Grace UMC. These clear glass dinner plates had sunflower fabric decoupaged on the back, and were accompanied by a poem Walker wrote:

Sunflowers
standing tall and strong
seeking the sunlight
surviving wind and storms
symbol of hope and resiliency

Survivors
standing tall and strong
seeking the sunlight
shouting "NO! NO! NO!"
sustained by hope and resiliency

Printed under the poem on a sheet of sun-drenched paper were the words: "Thank you for volunteering your time at Rape Response Services where the sunflower symbolizes our commitment to supporting victims and survivors of sexual violence."

"Take a Stand" was held again at three locations (Bangor, Dover-Foxcroft, Millinocket) near the end of April. About 25 people attended the event at Cascade Park in Bangor despite snow earlier in the day and a raw, cold wind. Two television stations covered the Stand, where teal ribbons and wooden nickels were distributed.

School-Based Programs

Publicity for "Take a Stand" was the primary focus of the Spring 2002 edition of *The Rape Response Reporter,* which also reported on new hires at RRS, and highlighted the work of Congleton, Carr, Nason, and Tyler. Eighty-nine sexual assaults had reportedly occurred in the two counties during the previous calendar year, with males being the victims of five and strangers committing nine.

Statistics for school-based programs during 2001 recorded 3655 students reached by in-school presentations, grades K through 12, and 774 students by SCP at the University. Programs for elementary school students were offered for the first time in 2001. Training was provided to 403 professionals. Carr and Congleton had done an "excellent job" presenting data about the school-based education program in front of the UWEM review panel which determined continued funding. They also received accolades from the Maine DOE for "excellent" teacher workshops offered statewide on behalf of MECASA.

As evidenced by these statistics, education programs in the schools and communities were increasing in both number and quality. Carr had been working during the school year with the civil rights team at Stearns High School in Millinocket on an eight-week bullying prevention program for second graders at the local Granite Street Elementary School. She described this endeavor in *Our Monthly Advocate*:

> *Students are learning about how to identify their feelings and the feelings of others, using "I messages" to communicate their feelings to each other, defining bullying situations, and recognizing safe adults to talk to about bullying. These concepts are being taught through games, role plays, books and interactive activities. The kids seem to look forward to seeing us every week and they really look up to the high school students. They all have stories to tell about what has happened to them at school and they want advice about how to handle bullying and teasing. This seems like something that really matters to the kids and is important in their everyday lives. I am glad we've had the opportunity to do this and I am hoping to expand this program into other school systems in the future.*

Workshops presented by Walker in April reached a total of 55 people at the Maine chapter of the National Association of Social Workers (NASW) annual conference and at the University of Maine child abuse conference. At the University, a video, "The Healing Years," which Walker used as part of the DHS training sessions, was shown and discussed. The Women in the Curriculum panel on consent during

Sexual Assault Awareness Week in September on campus attracted 18 individuals and generated an "awesome" discussion. A TBN speak-out and march concluded the week with almost 250 people in attendance. Red tape depicting a "rape free zone" encircled the mall and was worn as a sash by participants. Colorful red, teal, and blue ribbons fluttered in the cool breeze. People walking through the mall during the week had been invited to tie a ribbon to clotheslines attached between trees. Earlier that day, decorated T-shirts in red, yellow, and blue, collected and loaned by MECASA, were displayed in the Union where RRS handed out teal ribbons and brochures. Yellow T-shirts depicted experiences of child abuse.

Summer Sunderland, a graduate student in social work doing her field experience at SCP, was supervised by Walker and organized the week's events. She worked with Nason at the Safe Campus office which had officially opened earlier in the year. After thanking everyone for attending the speak-out and march, Sunderland spoke about rape statistics and stated: "Society still wants us to think it is strangers doing the raping." The April 22nd article in *The Maine Campus* continued to quote Sunderland: "We women in particular are taught to live in fear and to fear the night…what kind of life is it to live in fear and to live locked in the prisons of our own homes, which is where the majority of the violence is happening anyway. This is not a life of freedom, and it is not okay to live like this."

Walker's remarks at the speak-out noted the many levels at which sexual assault exists, including not only gender but class, race, and sexual orientation. "Rape is everyone's issue. It is not a women's issue. It is not a men's issue." She thanked the men on campus, including Beta Theta Pi for the sleep out and Sigma Phi Epsilon for their Brothers Against Rape program. Allan, a new RRS board member, and Barker both spoke about stopping the violence, before turning the microphone over to the many individuals who wanted to tell their own personal stories.

Money Matters

Celebration of the increased state funding through VIP was short-lived, as the Governor's budget deleted the second year's allocation. Early in the year, Walker appeared again before the Appropriations Committee, speaking on behalf of the ten sexual assault centers:

We appreciate the support of our work that was evident in the last legislative session when $4.2 million was allocated over the biennium for sexual assault and domestic violence projects. I am here today to give you some highlights about the ways in which the sexual assault centers have been utilizing our share of the $1.2 million available in this first year. I am also here to urge the members of this Committee to restore the full $1.8 million that has been cut from our funding in the Governor's budget for the second year. Without the full funding of $3 million for the second year, we will be unable to sustain the services and programs and infrastructure changes that we have been implementing since October 1st. None of the twenty projects and centers in domestic violence and sexual assault is new, nor are our programs. Last year you recognized the need for us to do more.

September 11th changed our world forever, and has certainly made your responsibilities as a Committee much harder. But for victims and survivors of sexual assault, every day is a September eleventh. They must live every day with the trauma and terror of being sexually assaulted or battered by someone whom they knew and trusted. And it is for these courageous survivors, women and children throughout the state of Maine, that we request the restoration of our funding.

Since the beginning of our fiscal year in October, the ten sexual assault centers have been making good use of our share of $1.2 million. What is most striking to me is the increase in direct services to the very rural areas of our state. Offices have been opened for the first time in Washington and Piscataquis counties, providing outreach to schools and community groups about the services available for those affected by sexual assault. Students at schools in northern Franklin county are now receiving services. Women and children in parts of Oxford county can now access services on a regular basis, not just in an emergency as before. And the Loring Job Corps at the top of Maine now has a drop-in program for victims and survivors of sexual assault.

Direct services and school-based prevention education programs often overlap because of the large number of students in our schools who have experienced a sexual assault. One center *created a Youth Services Program that has provided support to sixty adolescent survivors since October 1ˢᵗ. This Program includes drop-in services and support groups at area high schools. Two other centers are developing adolescent support groups in their areas of the state.*

The number of students reached by our school-based prevention education programs has anecdotally increased with this funding. I would be happy to provide you with the official numbers when the October through December first quarter [of fiscal year] statistics from all ten centers are available. I will also provide copies of our learning objectives that are directly tied to the Maine Learning Results.

Three centers have increased the number of programs presented in elementary and middle schools. Two of these three centers provided bullying prevention presentations to more than 750 students in grades K through five. An educator in rural Penobscot county works with the civil rights team at a local high school to take bullying prevention classes every week into the elementary grades in that community. Drop-in hours have been established at Colby College and at the University of Maine.

Community-based prevention education programs underway with this funding include consultation with the Micmac tribe in Aroostook county, trainings for law enforcement and medical personnel in Franklin county, and volunteer trainings in Piscataquis and Oxford counties. Several centers will utilize the skills of their school-based educators during the summer months to provide education programs for community groups.

In addition to programs, part of the funding increase was targeted toward capacity building. Five of the centers were able to increase the hours worked by some of their employees, offering not only more time for programs and services, but also increasing the employees' opportunities for full-time benefits, and decreasing their necessity to find other part-time jobs. A goal was set by the centers to increase all salaries to a minimum of $25,000. This funding has enabled us to work toward that goal and, in some centers, to achieve it. A substantial increase in health insurance premiums for many of the centers was met without "breaking the bank," a crisis that we could not have handled as well without the additional funding.

While all of the efforts undertaken represent a major step *forward, we remain far from ending the problems of sexual violence in Maine. Many communities are still not receiving the services they need. Planned expansions in prevention education and crisis services must happen in order to make real progress. We make a promise to the victim/survivor of sexual assault that someone will always be there when a call is made to our hotline. We worked hard with you last year to achieve a promise that $3 million would be available to help us provide services and programs throughout the state. Please keep your promise so that we may keep ours.*

Later in the session, Walker met one-on-one with Maine Senate President Mike Michaud (now U.S. Congressman) about reinstatement of the second year funding, and termed the meeting "worthwhile." The second-year funds, however, were not reinstated in the budget.

Fundraising events and grant writing continued, therefore, to be a focus throughout the year, and were seen as opportunities to raise both money and awareness. As in past years, the "Vagina Monologues" and the Beta Theta Pi sleep out were held at the University of Maine to benefit RRS. The performances of the Monologues were sold out on each of the three nights, and Walker preceded each performance by offering the hotline number for anyone whose memories of assault might be triggered by what was performed. She also told the audience that RRS advocates were in attendance to process any issues. Twenty-six red carnations were delivered by Walker backstage to the cast members before the second night. The RRS share of the proceeds from the Monologues was $2700, with SR receiving the same amount.

A Beta brother, Jasper Hotchkiss, was quoted on March 21ˢᵗ in *The Weekly*: "Rape Response is something we caught onto because they have a really tight budget, and we wanted to do something to better the local community. We like supporting a cause that most people might think a fraternity would not usually support." The brothers of Beta raised $1400 for RRS, topping the previous year's amount of $1276.

A grant of $7604 from the Agnes M. Lindsay Trust enabled RRS to purchase a Savin 9922DP Digital copier with an auto feeder, duplexing and cabinet. This money was also used to purchase three Gateway 300C desktop computers with Microsoft Windows XP operating systems and 17" monitors. The new copier replaced the one purchased in 1995 with

Lindsay funds, and new Gateways would supplement the two obtained with VAWA funds in 1997. Walker's old Gateway could not handle the Peachtree accounting software program to be installed by the RRS accountant. The office was wired for Internet access by consultant Jon Falk. A domain name was chosen (raperesponseservices.org), and all staff in all offices were provided with up-to-date desktop computers and their own email addresses. State income and unemployment taxes could be e-filed, as could the DHS reports.

Good news was also received from Stephanie Leonard, Administrator of the Stephen and Tabitha King Foundation. The grant that Walker had proposed, "Prevention Resources for Teens," was funded in the amount of $3000, slightly less than requested. Leonard's letter concluded with the words, "Congratulations on the award, and continued success with your good work." The money was used to update and print on glossy paper a "Teen Talk" brochure that had first been developed in 1998.

The redesigned brochures were colorful with computer-generated stick figures dancing in many poses. One section of the tri-fold brochure listed hotline numbers and the website address, as well as individual RRS office numbers. Sexual assault myths and the corresponding facts were provided in another section. Statistics about sexual assault and what to do if someone you know had been sexually assaulted filled two additional sections. Telephone numbers for the two Sheriff's Departments, the two DA's offices, SR and Womancare, and Shaw House were also included. A listing of what RRS could offer completed the final panel of the brochure. Special care was taken to keep the language simple and easily understood by a wide audience.

Another portion of the King Foundation grant enabled RRS to purchase multiple copies of the teen novel *Speak* by Laurie Halse Anderson (New York, 1999) and distribute these to each of the 53 high school and middle school libraries in the two counties. Still in print, this acclaimed novel is about a girl who is raped in a high school janitor's closet by a star athlete, and depicts her struggle to speak out about the assault. The books were ordered through Book Stacks in Bucksport where one of the RRS advocates, Judy Somes, was employed. A bookplate inserted in the front of each book noted that this was a donation from RRS with support from the King Foundation, and included the hotline number.

Two thank you letters were received by RRS, one from Susan Grant, the Assistant Librarian at the Foxcroft Academy Library, and the other from Jane Van Arsdale at Orono High School. Both individuals expressed appreciation for the copies of *Speak*. Grant wrote: "Hopefully, someone who needs to 'speak' will because of the strength this book provides them." The book was "almost constantly in circulation" at Orono High, Van Arsdale wrote, concluding her letter by stating: "We are thankful for all of the services you provide and have posted your toll free confidential hotline phone number so students and faculty members can make use of your services should there be need." An email was also received from Eve Salley, library assistant at SeDoMoCha Middle School in Dover-Foxcroft, thanking RRS for the "kind donation" and concluding: "I have read it and it is a very good book."

Preparations for the annual auction consumed most of Walker's time every August, and 2002 was no exception. Save-the-date postcards were sent instead of a newsletter to 500 people on the mailing list. Hart donated a small bronze bear cub sculpture, and Moosehead Furniture gave a large maple-framed mirror. Sharon Versyp, coach of the University of Maine women's basketball team, offered one lucky bidder the opportunity to be an honorary coach and to obtain four tickets to a game on February 1st. A website design and hosting package from Rainstorm Consulting, who hosted the RRS website, and an hour-long children's photo session with photographer Michele Stapleton, were two of the unique donations. "Women with Wings," an a cappella group of which Veits was a member, provided musical selections during the silent auction. Sponsors of the event were Pine Tree Landfill, BDN, Veeder & Longtin, CPA, Pro Realty, and Sargent, Tyler & West.

Board members listed on the auction program included Groth as President, Darlene Bay, Treasurer, and Hartman, Secretary. Only three others remained, Allan, Greaney, and Morcom. Despite Walker's concerns during August, plenty of items were received, with 53 in the live auction, about ten more than McKay wanted. A pleasant surprise was the $10,067 in gross proceeds, the highest ever! The CPA firm of Jane and Chuck Veeder and Chris Longtin received the Janet Badger Volunteer Award to recognize the many years they had performed the annual financial compilation for RRS, without charge, and their assistance with the auction. Special recognition for their support of the Stay-at-Home Ball was given to the WEZQ 92.9 duo of Dave Russell and Dorian Daniels.

Personnel Changes and Plans

Interviews for both the Client Services Coordinator position in Bangor and the newly-funded (by VIP) part-time Community Outreach Coordinator in Piscataquis County were conducted in January. The top two candidates for each were invited to a staff meeting where they gave short presentations on a topic related to the jobs. By the end of the month, Sue Currie of Brewer accepted the Bangor position and Lisa Snide of Milo assumed the position in Dover-Foxcroft. Walker wrote that she had "never had new employees be as happy as they were when the jobs were offered." They were the only two people to take the advocate training, taught by Booker, which began in late March, as three prospective volunteers dropped out. In early February, arrangements were made to rent office space at the Penquis CAP building in Dover-Foxcroft.

On a Saturday early in May, a long-awaited four-hour planning retreat for RRS was held upstairs at the Peace and Justice Center across Park Street from RRS. Ilze Petersons again facilitated the event, which "celebrated our growth and did some serious work of looking ahead." Four board members, four volunteers, and all seven staff members attended.

The last five years of changes at RRS were celebrated. In the area of staff and space, these highlights included:

- Increase from one full-time and two part-time staff to five full-time and two part-time, respectively
- Additional office space: East Millinocket, University of Maine, Penquis Health Services
- More stable office space in Dover-Foxcroft
- New computers for all staff
- Paid clinical consultant
- Presence in northern Penobscot County
- Active member of MECASA
- New photocopier
- Computers networked at Bangor office
- Access to email for all staff
- Two to three social work interns each academic year
- Increased length of advocates' service

- All hotline shifts covered by both on call and paid backup
- Advocates co-facilitate training and support groups with staff
- Trainings held consistently in spring and fall

Participants then listed all the services that had increased over the previous five years, some as a result of the VIP funding:

- Hotline in Millinocket
- Paid backup
- Support groups
- Support group facilitator training
- School presentations at every grade level, K-12
- Trainings for DHS and law enforcement personnel
- Presence on University of Maine campus
- SART in Bangor
- Web site
- Newsletter twice a year
- Annual report
- Participation in community notification meetings
- Support line for consumers of mental health services
- Increased media coverage of activities and issues
- Resumption of office in Dover-Foxcroft
- Community education activities, including discussion programs for parents, comments at auction
- Annual "Take a Stand" event in three locations

Sources of funding had also increased over the past five years:

- $80,524 budget in 1997; current budget, $260,117
- United Way allocation agency status
- VAWA grants
- Increase in state funding via VIP
- Annual auction
- Corporate sponsors for auction
- SCP grant
- Agnes Lindsay Trust grant
- Stephen and Tabitha King Foundation grant

- Stay-at-Home Ball
- KARE funding of internet connection for East Millinocket office
- Sale of clothesline pins
- End-of-year letter
- DBDS funds
- Dress-down days at businesses
- Donations from schools for presentations
- Events on campus ("Vagina Monologues," Beta Theta Pi sleep out)
- Clothing donations for hospital calls
- Beanie Baby raffles
- Corporate match for hours provided by employees who are volunteers
- In-kind services donated by advocates, accountant, attorney
- Volunteer hours donated by Board members not included in above

After the celebratory listings, issues to consider in each of the three areas (staff and space, services, funding) were raised by the group. Under the broad category of staff and space, the issues generated for further consideration were:

- Paid advocates
- Therapist on staff, full-time or part-time
- Continuing education for staff
- Board/staff interaction
- Improved office space in East Millinocket
- Hotline and advocate meetings in Dover-Foxcroft
- Continuing education for advocates

The issues to consider under the broad category of services included:
- On-site services in schools
- Underserved populations
- Community education
- Training for school personnel

- Training for professionals

Possible sources of increased funding were also listed:

- Grant writer on staff
- Capital campaign
- Attracting young donors
- Matching gifts from employees of large corporations
- Buy sunflowers for $1.00 to display in store windows
- Road race and/or skiing/snowboarding fundraiser

Issues chosen as priorities by the group were:

- More interaction between Board members and staff
- Improve East Millinocket office
- Increase continuing education for staff and volunteers
- Community education
- Underserved populations
- Grant writer
- Sunflowers
- Road race/winter event.

Petersons concluded the retreat by addressing each of these priority issues in turn and focused on the when and who. Carr, Congleton (who became Moring in July), and Snide assumed responsibility for community education/underserved populations, and agreed to complete a feasibility study by May 2003 with a plan in place by December 2003. A sunflower campaign would occur in April 2003, planned by Currie, Bean, and Tyler. Fileccia would explore by October 2002 the feasibility of a road race. Having a grant writer in place within five years was the task that Rancourt and Somes agreed to explore. Continuing education and more Board/staff interaction were seen as Walker's responsibilities, with help from staff.

The long-range results of the retreat were mixed. The feasibility study for reaching underserved populations was not completed, and having a grant writer did not become a reality. By mid-June, however, Carr had located a new office space, a storefront in East Millinocket with a large front room and window, a smaller room behind it, and a bathroom beyond that. The rent was reasonable. An open house at this new office was held later in the year with good attendance from the community. Invitations were printed in teal on the inside of the RRS note cards, and a notice appeared in the *Community Press*. State Senator Steve Stanley from Medway was one of the attendees.

Snide left RRS in early June; by early August, Kathy Dixon-Wallace accepted the vacant part-time position in Dover-Foxcroft. "I feel good about staff at RRS," Walker wrote in her journal in August, "and I told them that. We are doing good work!"

As staff numbers and the use of email increased, an email policy for staff was adopted by the RRS Board. Parts of the extensive policy demonstrated how seriously RRS took this new technological capability:

> All the electronic, communication, and computer equipment, systems, software and services, including but not limited to email (collectively, the "Electronic Systems") are the property of RRS. All communications, data, records, files and other information (collectively, the "Information") created through the use of, or retained in, the Electronic Systems are RRS property. RRS makes the Electronic Systems and the Information available to its employees solely for conducting RRS business. All passwords and codes used in conjunction with the Electronic Systems and the Information are the property of RRS. Employees should regard email as another form of written communication. Nothing should be said in an e-message that would be inappropriate, improper, or unsuitable to state in a written memo. The Confidentiality Policy at RRS applies fully to all information within the Electronic Systems. Employees may disclose information obtained from the Electronic Systems only to authorized individuals.

A Community Presence

Despite the good news that SCP received VAWA funding for another two years, Nason and Allan were embroiled in an alleged sexual assault case at UMaine. Two football players were suspended for their part in an off-campus incident that occurred in June. Allan served as chairperson of the five-member Student Conduct Code Committee which heard the case in late September as part of the campus judicial affairs process and determined that the suspension was warranted. A three-person appeals committee upheld this Committee's decision late in October.

Allan's positions on the RRS Board and as advisor to Men Can Stop Rape on campus were called into question by attorneys for the players, claiming that Allan was not impartial. University of Maine President Peter Hoff defended Allan's integrity by stating to the BDN's Pete Warner on October 26th /27th: "She has a very bright future and I will not allow her prospects to be tarnished by unwarranted attacks on her qualifications and her character." No criminal charges were brought against the players, primarily because the alleged victim and her family did not want to go further with the case. Nason had been working with the latter individuals throughout the process, demonstrating the value of the SCP, and Walker noted in her journal: "I'm proud of Carey's role."

The case generated a lot of publicity and sympathy for the football players. Walker's interview with Grover at WABI-TV Channel 5 and her letter to the BDN on October 2nd attempted to remind readers of the victim in this case without naming anyone directly:

> *It takes courage for someone to report being sexually assaulted. It takes courage to go through the rape protocol exam. It takes courage to relive the sexual assault every time the incident is described to medical, law enforcement or judicial personnel. It takes courage to endure the inevitable victim blaming that occurs when the crime of sexual assault is reported. It takes courage for the victim-survivor to face the reality that the sexual assault has changed her or his life forever. Rape Response Services supports the right of anyone who has been sexually assaulted to talk about the trauma and to be believed.*

Attention continued to be focused on the suspended players during the football season, prompting Walker to submit another letter to the BDN on November 18th in response to an op ed earlier in the month:

> *James Varner is the latest person who is attempting to generate sympathy for the suspended University of Maine football players without any consideration for the confidentiality of student conduct code hearings. These proceedings are held in private to protect the rights not only of the victim and the defendant, but also of those who*

make the decision.

Who is going to want to come forward and report a sexual assault on campus knowing that all the details will be aired in the press? Who, in fact, is going to want to serve on a conduct board in the future, knowing that their entire background will be aired, as if they are the accused?

One in three women and one in seven men will be sexually assaulted in her or his lifetime. If we are not the one in three or the one in seven, it is more than likely that we know someone who is. These statistics tell me that it would be almost impossible to find someone who does not have some personal experience or knowledge about rape. Are we going to exclude anyone with knowledge about rape from serving on a campus conduct board? If so, where will we find people who have no knowledge or experience with it?

Let's show some consideration for all victims and survivors of rape whenever a statement is made regarding this particular case or any case. Every time an article is printed, a person who has been raped is forced to relive the experience all over again. It is much easier to blame the victim or to cast doubt on the hearing process than it is to admit that rape happens.

Despite this case, SCP was ready to enter a new two-year funding cycle and could report great strides, including the establishment of two men's groups that were committed to promoting a safe environment for all as well as challenging many of the myths surrounding rape. Men Can Stop Rape, a group based in Washington D.C., was providing consultation through the SCP grant. Nason had also reviewed and rewritten the campus sexual assault policy and had developed policies on stalking and dating violence. A website was up and running for SCP, and victim advocacy drop-in hours were offered. Trainings for residence hall staff and presentations in first-year classes were ongoing efforts.

Moring was instrumental in helping to develop a "Community of Caring Lecture Series" that was offered one night per month at Brewer High School. Two forty-minute topics ranging from dating violence to bullying, from high blood pressure to asthma, were offered concurrently, followed by refreshments and a repeat of the sessions. Advertised for students, parents, and staff members, this collaborative effort among

RRS, Riverview Primary Care, and Brewer High extended throughout the school year. Drop-in hours at both Project Atrium in Hampden and Shaw House in Bangor were arranged by Moring to reach the at-risk youth population at each location. Presentations at Mountain View Correctional Facility for juvenile offenders, located in Charleston, were also made.

Staff trainings for Shaw House and for MERT employees, as well as United Way presentations during the annual campaign and a repeat of the Womancare recertification training for teachers, made the days and evenings busy and continued to reach new audiences for RRS. Another DHS training, "Working with Adult Survivors of Sexual Abuse," was attended by 24 people in Augusta, and evaluations were positive. Ninety-four people at the annual meeting in Bangor of the Maine Bureau of Elderly and Adult Services listened to Walker's presentation about sexual assault and the elderly. A dialogue at NOE with 24 clients with disabilities prompted Walker to write in her journal: "awesome hour at NOE with group of clients, talking about sexual harassment thanks to a mutual client's suggestion." Having our clients tell others about RRS meant the center was doing something right.

Fall volunteer training at RRS, co-facilitated by Currie and Bean, brought Tamar Mathieu, director of the Penquis Law Project, into the fold as an advocate. Dixon-Wallace also completed the training. Walker and other staff members continued to take hotline and backup shifts.

Sex Offenders

Sex offender notification meetings, while not as frequent, were still scheduled throughout the year. The *Lincoln News* reported on July 18th about one held in Mattawamkeag. Carr and Walker attended, along with Detective Jameson from Penobscot CSD and Paul Kelly, the offender's probation officer. About 25 residents gathered outside the municipal building, waiting for the doors to be unlocked and swatting black flies. Probably everyone heard Walker ask Carr, while waving her arms around to keep the flies away, "Why would anyone want to live in Mattawamkeag?" Carr never let Walker forget this rhetorical question, or the fact that Walker's credibility at the meeting was undoubtedly compromised by it.

The article in the *Lincoln News* by Chris DeBeck quoted Walker as saying there were two reasons for her presence at the Mattawamkeag meeting: "First, the fact that a convicted sex offender has moved into town might trigger some people to recall abuse they suffered as a child. Secondly, she said she understood the anxiety parents might have about having a sexual offender move into town. 'You have a right to be nervous,' she said. 'I can tell you that this particular sexual offender is practically the safest one in Mattawamkeag. You know what he looks like, you know where he lives. It's the people you don't know are abusers that you need to be concerned with.' She added that many sexual offenses follow the pattern outlined in this case, where trust is built up first before the assault takes place." Walker mentioned the hotline, local educational programs for children of all ages, and left brochures and wooden nickels.

In August, Walker returned to Corinth for the second sex offender meeting there, with only 21 people in attendance this time. No one from the community attended a meeting in Greenbush in late September, and it was easy to conclude that people from some communities were becoming complacent about this issue and had moved on to other concerns. Corinth held its third sex offender notification meeting in November, attended by 53 residents, more than twice the number at the August event. Detective Jameson and Walker had facilitated enough of these meetings around Penobscot County to make a good team.

Two letters in the BDN focused on the same issues as the sex offender notification meetings. A letter from Walker about the looming scandal of child sexual abuse by priests in the Roman Catholic Church appeared in the February 28th BDN:

> *What disturbs me most about the decision of the Roman Catholic Diocese to release the names of priests who have sexually abused children is not the numbers. It is well known that convicted child sex abusers are only a small percentage of the people who get away with this crime every day. And it is also well known that many persons who sexually abuse children have many victims before being caught. The numbers of priests and the numbers of victims are shocking but not surprising.*
>
> *I am disturbed, however, by the continued denial that child sexual abuse happens in Maine or anywhere else. We deny it by blaming the victim, by suggesting that a 15-year-old could have said*

no. We deny it by suggesting that the celibacy of the priesthood is a reason for these criminal acts. We deny it by not wanting to hear or believe the words that the victim/survivor of child sexual abuse wants to tell us.

Child sexual abuse is an issue of power and control. People sexually abuse children because they can, and because they can get away with it. These priests have used their positions of authority to change the reality of a child's life forever. And when we deny that priests can be sex abusers, when we blame the victim, we continue to deny the reality of the victims in our midst.

"Rape is always a crime" was the title of the second BDN letter (August 17th/18th) from Walker:

I agree with Susan Jacoby (BDN 8/12) that we talk about rape more than we did 30 years ago before the feminist movement. There is room, however, for still more improvement in how we treat those who have experienced rape. A stranger abducted and raped the two young women in California. We believe them because these rapes, by a stranger, are the way we want to believe that rape happens. And if women don't put themselves in situations where strangers can abduct us, then we also want to believe that we will be safe from rape.

But the reality is that strangers perpetrate only about 15 percent of all the rapes that occur. All the rest of the rapists are people who are known to the women or girls whom they rape. Sometimes these rapists hold positions of authority, like priests or teachers or coaches or are sports heroes or other public figures. In these cases, we seem to hold women to a higher burden of proof than when the rapist is a stranger. We make statements like, "She had been out with him before," or "She was drunk and was asking to be raped." We are much more likely than in stranger rape cases to blame the women who have been raped, rather than the rapists.

So, while I agree we have come a long way in the past 30 years, we still have a long way to go before "no" means "no" to any unwanted sexual encounter. Rape is a crime regardless of the relationship between the two people involved.

Annual Report and End-of-Year Fundraising Letter

The Annual Report highlighted the fiscal year ending September 30th. Kim McKeage had joined the Board at the beginning of the school year. Income received from the state contract was $160,870. The largest expense was for personnel at $189,860. The value of in-kind services from volunteers was $93,550.

At this time, new RRS stationery was printed, listing all five offices on the letterhead with addresses and telephone numbers for each. The SART office at Penquis Health Services, the SCP office, and the East Millinocket office were added to the Bangor and Dover-Foxcroft listings under the larger RRS heading with hotline numbers. Groth and Walker co-signed the end-of-year fundraising letter, printed on this new stationery, and mailed in December:

> *Your generous financial support of Rape Response Services is helping us make a difference in the lives of women, men and children throughout Penobscot and Piscataquis counties. Individuals who experience the trauma of sexual assault know that our trained volunteers and staff will provide compassionate services and support that are not available from any other agency in this area. Without our help, the victim/survivor of rape would have to face the medical and legal systems alone, and would have no one to call at two o'clock on a Saturday morning when nightmares about the rape prevent sleep.*
>
> *During the fiscal year that ended on September 30, 2002, a record number of 74 sexual assaults occurred in these two counties and were reported to our hotline. We hope that this increase reflects the fact that more individuals who have been raped are reporting the crime to us because they know they will be believed and not blamed. But we also know that rape continues to occur at an alarming rate, particularly among young women below the age of 25. A total of 187 individuals received help from Rape Response Services in FY'02, representing 352 hours of service from volunteers and staff.*
>
> *Everyone who works or volunteers at this agency is committed to prevention of the crime of sexual assault. Expansion of our educational programs into the elementary schools in the two counties has occurred with great success. During FY'02, 1,421 students in*

grades K-4 participated for the first time in one of our classroom presentations. The Safe Campus Project at the University of Maine reached 1,861 students in classroom settings. Middle and high school programs, some offered in collaboration with other agencies [Womancare and SR], continue to be available, educating 4,249 students, grades 5-12, in FY'02. Our mission is the focus of what we do: "to offer hope, understanding, support and advocacy" for those among us who are directly affected every day by the trauma of rape, incest, or child sexual abuse. Please be as generous as you can in helping us fulfill our mission.

A busy year of staff changes, grants, community and school education programs, and some long-range planning, contributed to a sense that RRS was fulfilling its mission in the two counties. Despite the failure to develop a community-based SART/SANE site at Penquis Health Services, this venture too had increased the collaboration among previously disparate organizations.

2003: A SPECIAL 15ᵀᴴ ANNIVERSARY AUCTION

T he passage of 15 years since the rebirth of RRS was highlighted by the seventh annual Fall Festival Auction and Awards Night, held in September at Jeff's Catering. A very special guest, Governor John Baldacci, was in attendance. Walker had sent an invitation to his office early in the year, and did not know for certain that he could attend, because of his schedule, until he walked through the door, preceded by security personnel. His support of efforts to reduce violence against women, both as Congressman and Governor, and his Bangor roots, convinced the RRS Board to extend an invitation to this anniversary event. The Governor made some remarks to the audience, and Walker interrupted to remind him to include "and sexual assault" after "domestic violence." The good-natured camaraderie between Governor Baldacci and Walker elicited many laughs from the audience, and led to his auctioning off a lunch at the Blaine House in Augusta for $250 and a gift certificate to Momma Baldacci's restaurant. He also assisted in awarding the Janet Badger Volunteer Award to Danforth, and a new Teal Ribbon Award to Mike Hatch and Bruce Morse. These men, health teachers at Central High (Corinth) and Bangor High, respectively, were instrumental in the ability of the school-based educators to gain access to the ninth grade health classes for week-long presentations in collaboration with SR.

Pine Tree Landfill, Husson Park Associates (formerly Pro Realty), BDN, and Sargent, Tyler & West continued as sponsors with many new businesses added: Veazie Veterinary Clinic, WABI-TV Channel 5, the "Rock Team" at ERA Dawson Bradford Realty, Mayo Regional Hospital, and NOE. "Women With Wings" again provided musical selections during the silent auction. The printing of tickets was donated by Fast Forms. Several media venues (Bangor *Chamber News*, BDN, *The*

Weekly, Coffee News, and *News & Views* of the Peace & Justice Center), publicized the auction. A live on-site interview before the auction with WABI-TV Channel 5 told viewers they still had time to attend the event. Forty items in the live auction, capably managed again by McKay, included a "Kruzer" kayak from Old Town Canoe, a "Trek" mountain bike, overnight accommodations at several inns, a small bronze otter from Hart, Stephen King's signed novel, and many handmade creations. When everything was totaled up the following day, gross proceeds were $13,747, a new high for this event. The ticket price had increased to $8 each or two for $15.

Shelley Farrington, a reporter for the *Community Press* in Millinocket and Danforth's daughter, wrote about the auction in the September 9th edition under the heading "Millinocket woman recognized for her volunteerism with RRS":

> *An evening of anniversary and recognition took on new meaning for a Millinocket woman as she was honored for her dedication and volunteerism. Sally Danforth was given the Janet Badger Volunteer Award by Rape Response Services Executive Director Kathy Walker during the organization's Seventh Annual Fall Auction and Awards Night, Sept. 3rd, at Jeff's Catering in Brewer. "This is presented to someone who has volunteered above and beyond to this agency," Walker said. "The really neat thing with this is that we present it but the volunteers don't go away, they continue to be there. Sally has been a volunteer since 1996, when we first opened an office (in the area) and before that she was one of the leaders of KARE. Words don't describe the kind of volunteer Sally Danforth is," she continued. Visibly surprised by the award, Danforth said she didn't really think she had done anything special. "Doesn't everyone do this?" Danforth asked. "You do what you can and you give back."*
>
> *After the event, Robin Carr, RRS community and school based educator for the region with an office in East Millinocket, said she appreciates Danforth's efforts more than she can say. "She really cares about the people of her community," Carr said. "She does things at the drop of a hat without even thinking about it. We couldn't do this without her. She's really been instrumental in getting the word out and making talking about it (rape and sexual assault) less taboo."*

Walker also used the event to award the organization's first ever Teal Ribbon Award recognizing individuals who "do special things for Rape Response Services. These are people in the community who aren't necessarily volunteers but have done special things for our programs." "We're very grateful for what you've done for us," Morse told Walker and the crowd when accepting the award, "we're honored but we didn't do anything." Carr again applauded Morse and Hatch for "their willingness to put educators in the system and talk about the issues."

The event marked the fifteenth year RRS has been providing services to Penobscot and Piscataquis Counties. "This is bittersweet," Walker said to the approximately 150 people at the event including Gov. John Baldacci, "if we've been in business for 15 years then we should've done away with rape but we haven't. But what we have done is raised awareness and put the crime of rape in the public eye. Fifteen years ago we never would've had this kind of attendance at this event or the services we have, or the volunteers we have in Penobscot and Piscataquis counties. Your presence here gives voice to those who have been raped or the victim of sexual violence."

Baldacci thanked Walker for the invitation to the auction because it gave him a chance to thank her for all her work in the field of domestic and sexual violence. He commended Walker's dedication and leadership in keeping the topic in the public eye for all these years. "We've got to make sure the enforcement is there," Baldacci said, "and that law enforcement remains sensitive to the issue and that counselors and volunteers are there. These are important issues and that's why I'm here, to raise awareness and to raise money. But we, as policy makers, need to keep these issues in the forefront and make our state the best place to live. Thanks to Kathy again and all the volunteers."

Money Matters

Money issues continued to plague RRS into the new year, including late checks from both DHS and the University of Maine. Walker wrote in her journal: "working with our clients is a less stressful part of my job than wondering about the money each pay period." When the DHS checks for the previous September (!) and December had still not been received by payday on January 15th, Walker informed Greenlaw and Talbot at DHS that she had to close the RRS doors the following Monday. Sharing such information with the staff brought tears and anger, and the crisis was temporarily averted when both checks were deposited. When funds were finally received, Walker was able to implement two percent pay raises for all staff members, thereby alleviating the earlier angst and giving each staff member (except Nason who was paid under a separate grant) between $12.26 and $12.39 per hour. (Note: Three years later, in 2006, per hour wages had increased minimally to a range from $13.01 to $13.15. Despite the best efforts of legislators and donors, sexual assault centers remained poorly funded.)

Fundraising events sponsored by other organizations to benefit RRS were always welcomed. Performances of the "Vagina Monologues" at the University of Maine raised money ($2736) and awareness for both RRS and SR. A $2600 check was presented to RRS after a dinner at the Beta Theta Pi house, proceeds from their tenth annual sleep out. A "Rock Against Rape" concert was sponsored on campus by Sigma Phi Epsilon fraternity and provided $500 to RRS. Walker was also pleased when the Hermon Town Council voted to increase the annual RRS donation from $200 to $500. Attending the Council meeting when the social service line of the Hermon budget was discussed was something Walker did each year because the Councilors cut donations to agencies that were not represented. The annual Stay-at-Home Ball also celebrated the fifteenth anniversary of RRS, and was broadcast live again on WEZQ 92.9 in April with Dave Russell and Walker.

The sunflower campaign which was discussed at the 2002 retreat was implemented during April, thanks to Currie and Bean, and was a first-time success, raising $129. Speedy Print of Bangor donated 5"x7" white cardstock with an outline of sunflower petals and "WE CARE" printed in the yellow center of the flower. Bright green leaves and stem were intersected by the words "I give my support" above a line for a signature. "Rape Response Services" at the top and the hotline number at the bottom completed the card. Advocates asked a few stores in the two counties, and the store owners agreed to offer the sunflowers to customers for one dollar each and to place the signed sunflowers in the store windows. In addition, the Exxon station in Milo held a raffle during April that raised $56, and the sale of stickers and other items at the annual

H.O.P.E. Festival brought in $63. Walker provided two six-hour DHS staff trainings during the year, for 15 people in Bangor in January and for 16 in Augusta in May, each earning $400 for the agency. As Currie noted in *Our Monthly Advocate*: "every dollar helps."

"Designing Women," a local craft guild, held their fine crafts and artwork show and sale in November, with the two dollar suggested donation at the door going to RRS. Janyce Boynton, who later became a hotline advocate at RRS, was a member of the guild and displayed at the show a quilt she designed and made to help herself heal from rape. An October 30th article in *The Weekly* quoted Boynton as deciding "to show the quilt because she believes that rape is still such a taboo issue— and that it's important to break the silence and secrecy surrounding it." Walker wrote in her journal about the "event that required minimal work on our part [*and*] raised $1200 for RRS. And raised awareness as well, equally important." Many attended to view the quilt and picked up RRS brochures and wooden nickels.

Sexual Assault Awareness Month

As in past years, Sexual Assault Awareness Month activities required both time and attention during April. Walker's remarks at the annual Blaine House tea were focused on denial:

> *Despite our best prevention and education efforts, rape is still a subject that people do not want to discuss or acknowledge. Juries still blame the victim and acquit the rapist. Our agencies are not allowed to participate in what are promoted as "family events" where children will be present. Communities rally around football players and refuse to believe that they are capable of raping someone. The Air Force Academy denies the allegations of rape at that facility. Survivors are told to "just get over it."*
>
> *Alice Sebold is perhaps not a familiar name, but her personal story is all too familiar to the people in this room. She is the author of a novel that has been on the <u>New York Times</u> best-seller list for more than six months. It is the fictional account of a young girl who was raped and murdered by a neighbor, and who is now in heaven looking down on her fractured family. I believe that this is the first novel about rape to occupy such a commanding presence on the best-*

seller lists. Sebold's agent was quoted in the <u>New York Times</u>: "Rape is one of the subjects people have a knee-jerk reaction to. A number of publishers expressed distinct misgivings [about the book], though readers have obviously not had similar problems." Alice Sebold has made a difference, and her story has resonated with the millions of people who not only put her book on the best-seller list but also have kept it there.

Many people in this room make a difference just by doing their jobs day after day. I want to say think you to volunteers, staff, Board members, and others who are affiliated with local rape crisis centers in any capacity. Our presence throughout the state makes it more difficult for people to be in denial that rape happens. We are also the only agencies in Maine that focus exclusively on victims and survivors, both female and male, of rape and all other forms of sexual assault, whether it occurred today, or many, many years ago.

Later in the program, Walker made concluding remarks: *I began my remarks today with some rather discouraging comments about how much our society is still in denial that rape exists. We cannot negate that reality. But you have heard many stories about how people in this room and beyond have made a difference. By speaking out, by offering support, by listening and believing, by educating and writing, by saying "NO" to rape, by wearing teal ribbons, we are also saying "NO" to the denial of rape. And we are making a difference!*

Six new advocates (Paula Copeland, Laurie Sokoloski, Steve and Glenna Dean, Jaime Gradie, and Donna Runnels) took the training in Dover-Foxcroft, facilitated by Dixon-Wallace, early in 2003, creating a group similar to that in the Millinocket area that would accompany individuals to the hospital and to court appointments. A six-year goal of having volunteers in Piscataquis County was finally achieved. Carr facilitated training at the East Millinocket office for three new advocates (Jane Frost, Joann Dickinson, and Robin Stevens) who joined the pool of committed individuals in that area. Two new advocates had recently completed the Bangor hotline training, co-facilitated by Currie and Bean, with Sheehy and Hall also attending the sessions and assisting with role plays.

The annual advocates' recognition dinner was held again at the UU Society building. Twenty-six people attended the dinner, including Board members, and advocates from all three regions. Each advocate was given a molded plastic teal ribbon pin with a tie tac back that could be worn during April and would last longer than the cloth ribbons.

This recognition dinner occurred in the middle of Sexual Assault Awareness Week at the University where Nason coordinated a variety of activities in collaboration with RRS, SWA, Athletes for Sexual Responsibility, Brothers Engaged Against Rape, UMaine Men's Education Network, Public Safety, Greek Peer Educators, and several sororities and fraternities. Nason was quoted in the April 7th issue of *The Maine Campus*: "It's been the most awesome experience working with all these people."

"Take a Stand" events were held indoors at three locations (Brewer High School, Katahdin Region Higher Education Center in East Millinocket, and the Congregational Church in Dover-Foxcroft) at the end of April. Teal inserts to publicize the events were included in the Stay-at-Home Ball invitations mailed in March. Shirts from the MECASA Clothesline Project inventory were displayed at each place, and participants had an opportunity to make their own small paper T-shirts. Another commemoration of the 15th anniversary of RRS, these indoor Stands attracted the least number of participants for the fifth year of this event.

New this year for all the community events were printed business cards to which a cloth teal ribbon was pinned. The card asked people to "please wear this ribbon to support victims and survivors of sexual assault." Statistics about one in three women and one in seven men being sexually assaulted in their lifetimes were printed beside the ribbon along with "Rape Response Services provides support to everyone affected by sexual assault." Hotline and telephone numbers, a sunflower, and the words "Make a difference" appeared on the back of the card. The cards were designed by staff and printed at the office.

Walker's letter to the BDN editor on June 9th reiterated concerns about the prevalence of rape while mistakenly believing that the war in Iraq had indeed ended. She wrote:

> *Another Sexual Assault Awareness Month has come and gone. April was different this year because of the war in Iraq. Sexual assault crisis workers often compare the trauma of rape to the trauma of*

war. Both traumas are forms of extreme interpersonal violence.

But this war in Iraq has made evident the differences between war and rape. This war was in our faces day and night, constantly on television, covering the front page of daily newspapers, evident in flags and yellow ribbons everywhere. Thousands of people marched in protest against the war in Bangor and around the world.

We talk about the war, and we support our troops. We still do not talk about rape, and we still blame the victims and survivors of rape for what happened to them. April is over. The war is over. Imagine the difference we could make if people had rallied against rape during April, as they did against the war. Imagine teal ribbons, the color for sexual assault awareness, hanging from mailboxes and signposts. Imagine news stories about rape that are so pervasive that we demand an end to this crime.

The reality is that rape and other crimes of sexual violence continue to occur daily, even as the war in Iraq has ended. This interpersonal violence occurs right in our midst, not in some far-off country. Maine crime statistics for 2002 show a 20.2 percent increase in rapes reported to law enforcement; over the past four years there has been a 70 percent increase in reported rapes in Maine. Although people may be more willing to report a rape to the police, rape is still occurring at an alarming rate.

Where is the outrage? Where is the willingness to take a stand against rape, as we took a stand against the war? Where is our willingness to speak out, to demand an end to the trauma of rape?

Quality Assurance Standards

In early July, a Quality Assurance (QA) Subcommittee of MECASA comprised of two center directors, Sue Hall Dreher (from the Brunswick center) and Donna Strickler (from the Augusta center), and a staff person from MECASA, Melissa Pendleton, came to RRS for the QA site visit. Documents had been prepared and sent to this subcommittee in advance of the visit. For several years MECASA had been developing standards, finalized in September 2001, which each center was expected to meet. No penalties were in place for failure to comply with the standards. RRS received a certificate after the site visit for successful compliance with the Standards.

"Sexual assault crisis centers value empowerment and promote the dignity and respect of all persons," was a statement of philosophy on the opening page of the document that delineated the QA standards. "Specialized services have been developed based on the belief that persons who have been sexually assaulted have the right to determine their own response to the assault(s), and the immediate availability of crisis intervention and support services helps to facilitate their recovery process."

Program standards were spelled out for crisis intervention services, Level II services, volunteer recruitment and training (a minimum of forty hours), volunteer management, community education services, school-based education services, support groups, and group facilitator training (a minimum of ten hours). Confidentiality standards were listed in a separate section, and included the prohibition of cordless and cellular phones for confidential calls. Some coalition standards included the expectations that someone from each center would attend MECASA meetings, and that centers' activities outside their catchment areas would be discussed with the appropriate center.

A final section related to organization standards required each center to have a Board of Directors of at least seven members. The Board would have active committees for fundraising, personnel, and nomination. Documents to be maintained for each center included articles of incorporation, by-laws, personnel policies, Board minutes, job descriptions, and financial records. RRS met most of the standards except for Board subcommittees and a well-defined record when individuals were screened out of training.

One of the policies that was required and adopted by the RRS Board just prior to the site visit addressed client records: "All client records including client contact forms and printouts of phone numbers and names from answering service, are confidential. Only the Executive Director and Client Services Coordinator at RRS have access to these records. Client records are maintained indefinitely in a locked file cabinet at the Bangor central office." A locked file cabinet was purchased for this purpose and maintained by Currie in a corner of her office under the Fax machine.

Another policy that was written at the same time dealt with "Activities Outside Catchment Area," and stated: "It is the policy of RRS to refer all hotline callers and others from areas outside Penobscot and Piscataquis counties, to the sexual assault center in the caller's area. Callers are provided with the hotline number and/or office number for that center. If the caller is in an immediate crisis, the person taking the call may provide support before making a referral. With the caller's permission, a call may be made to the appropriate center on behalf of the caller, requesting that a follow-up call be made by that center." RRS advocates were provided with a list of the other centers, their geographic areas, and both office and hotline numbers. Some centers had discontinued their separate hotline numbers and relied on the statewide number to direct calls to the appropriate center.

After another center had received a subpoena for client records, all centers developed a subpoena policy: "When records, staff, or volunteers are subpoenaed, RRS will make every effort within the limits of the law to carry out the client's desired response to the subpoena. The advice of the RRS Attorney will be sought before any action is taken regarding a subpoena."

An equal opportunity policy was extracted from the personnel polices and formatted in the same manner as all the other policies which were provided to both volunteers and staff. The policy stated: "RRS is committed to a service and working environment fully inclusive of the population it serves. Thus, RRS will not discriminate, and will fully comply with applicable laws prohibiting discrimination on the grounds of race, color, religion, sex, sexual orientation, national origin or citizenship status, age, handicap, or veteran status in employment and services."

A Community Presence

Leary reported in the BDN on July 21st about the recently released Bureau of Justice statistics on violent crime in Maine. He mentioned the underreporting of sexual assaults, and quoted Walker: "'In our experience, most rapes go unreported,' said Kathy Walker, executive director of the Bangor-based Rape Response Services. 'But I have a theory on why there are more being reported than there used to be.' Walker said Maine joined a national trend in the 1990s of establishing sexual assault response teams that allow a victim to tell her or his story once. The team includes counselors and medical personnel as well as law enforcement. 'There are still a lot going unreported, even with all the efforts being made to encourage reporting,' she said.

"Applying the national study to Maine, it is likely more than 600 rapes occurred in Maine in 2000, not the 318 reported to police. The study also asked respondents why they did not report a crime. The most frequently stated reason (23 percent) for not reporting a sexual assault was that it was a private matter. The second most frequent reason (12 percent) was a fear of reprisal. 'There are a lot of reasons,' Walker said. 'One we hear is the fear of being blamed and the self-blame. And we hear all the reasons they mention in the report.'"

The following day, an editorial in *The Katahdin Times* addressed concerns about the rape of an elderly Millinocket woman who was assaulted in her home earlier in the month. Aaron Miller in the "From the Editor" column reported:

> *In towns stretching from Lincoln to Mount Chase, about three to five rapes are reported each year to Rape Response Services, a non-profit agency that has offices in Bangor, East Millinocket, Dover-Foxcroft and Orono. Of those reported rapes, only 20 percent are reported to police, according to the executive director Kathy W. Walker.* "Often sexual assault or rape involves someone the victim knows," *Walker said in an interview Friday.* "There is fear of retaliation, a fear of their name being spread over the community and a fear of being blamed." *The victim in this case* [in Millinocket] *was brave enough to put embarrassment and any fear of retaliation aside. Rape victims who are beaten are more likely to come forward, according to Walker. When a victim is not beaten they are less likely to report the crime. Keeping rape quiet makes a tragic situation even worse.*
>
> "My advice for people is to find someone to talk about it— sooner than later," *Walker said.* "Research says if we stuff our feelings and ignore it, it usually comes back in other ways such as nightmares or flashbacks." *People began locking their doors—a measure one lifelong resident did for the first time last week. Some people couldn't sleep. The crime served as a big wakeup call for many who learned no community is immune to such a nightmare.*

Walker's letter which appeared on the same day in *The Katahdin Times* as the editorial addressed the reality of rape even in small communities:

A front page article in the July 15 edition of The Katahdin Times *describes a burglary and rape that occurred in Millinocket during the previous week. Rape is a trauma not only for the person who experiences this horrible crime, but also for the community in which the crime occurred. We want to believe that our small towns are safe from such traumatic events.*

Living in a small town means that everyone knows, or thinks they know, all the details about the event. Confidentiality is often breached because by talking about the person who was raped, we think we can distance ourselves from rape and believe we can prevent it from happening to us.

A person who has experienced the trauma of rape needs first and foremost to be believed and to be supported by the community. Reading about a rape that has occurred may also trigger memories in other people who have been raped or sexually assaulted in the past. Talking about the experience is the first step toward healing from the trauma of rape, and being a good listener is the best way to help someone who has experienced this trauma. A 24-hour hotline (1-800-310-0000) is offered by Rape Response Services to anyone in the Katahdin region who needs support or help in healing from any form of sexual assault, regardless of when it occurred. Additional services and materials are also available at our local office in East Millinocket (746-3876).

Just a few short weeks later on August 8th, Walker was compelled to write an op ed piece for the BDN titled "'Rape Song' is not laughing matter":

In a review of "The Fantasticks" currently playing at Penobscot Theatre, one of the songs is titled "It Depends on What You Pay." That's a euphemistic title for what is known as the "Rape Song." The lyrics to this song contain such phrases as, "…you can get the sort of rape you'll never ever forget," repeated over and over again. There are also descriptions about types of rape: "comic rape," "romantic rape," "drunken rape," "military rape," and more.

I walked out of the theatre [on August 1st] before the song had ended. Singing about rape, laughing about rape, suggesting that someone might pay to have his daughter raped, are just not acceptable behaviors today in any venue. And this production exhibits an appalling lack of sensitivity to anyone in the audience who has ever been raped or sexually assaulted. I am well aware that "The Fantasticks" is the most successful musical in world history, running for more than 40 years in the same theatre. "Try to Remember," another song in the play, is a wonderful addition to our memory bank of songs from the past. In Director Mark Torres' notes, he refers to the play as helping us remember "a time when the cares of the world seemed a world away."

And there was a time, 40 years ago, when rape was not talked about, when theatre patrons could pretend that it didn't happen to them or to anyone they knew. A song about rape might have been funny then because people had no idea about how often it occurred or how devastating the impact could be. Rape was seen as more of a seduction with a scandalous hint of violence. The assumption was that rape definitely did not happen to anyone with money enough to patronize the theatre.

Today, organizations such as Rape Response Services work with hundreds of women and men, young and old, from all socioeconomic levels, who were raped or sexually abused yesterday or a decade ago or 40 years ago. We also present prevention programs in the public schools, trying to convey to our young people that rape is a traumatic and unacceptable crime, not a laughing matter. What contradictory message does the "Rape Song" give to these same young people who are in the audience at Penobscot Theatre? Is any theatre that continues to produce this show aware of the message it is providing someone who is trying to heal from the trauma of rape?

More than any of Walker's other pieces in the BDN, this one generated several supportive comments from people on the street and in the bank, especially from women who wished they had also walked out of the theatre when the song was sung. Walker had written in her journal on August 1st: "I did not want to believe what I was hearing but found lyrics on Internet."

Some new community education and outreach efforts were undertaken during the year. RRS, the Bureau of Elder & Adult Services in DHS, and the Trauma Services Office of Program Development in DBDS, collaborated to produce "Guidelines for Facilities: Sexual Abuse of Vulnerable Adult Populations." This nine-page document was developed with extensive input and editing from Walker and Jennings, in response to incidents that had occurred at some group homes.

The RRS brochures were slightly redesigned and printed during the 15th year, as the supply from 1999 had run out. Changes were primarily cosmetic; colors and words remained the same, and staff members chose new graphics to separate the sections. Once again, staff working as a group agreed by consensus on the redesign as they did on all informational materials produced at RRS, including posters and revisions to the website.

RRS initiated a court watch program in late summer. First proposed during Allen's years at the agency, this was an opportunity to track data and to be a presence in the courtroom when sexual assault cases were on the docket. Domestic violence projects had been active in court watch programs for several years. Now that RRS had sufficient staffing to take on new endeavors, court watch became one of Tyler's responsibilities.

Another collaborative effort began with area UMCs to provide "Safe Sanctuaries" training that was required for clergy members and lay people in the local churches. Twenty-seven people from at least seven churches attended the first event in Houlton. Sexual abuse revelations in the Catholic church created the impetus for other denominations to get people talking about child sex abuse, background checks of Sunday school teachers, and mandated reporting.

A mandated reporting policy in effect since 1996 at RRS was updated substantially by the end of 2003, specifically stating to whom the reports would be made. Because allegations of abuse in the church had not been reported, there was a renewed emphasis in Maine on who was a mandated reporter. Walker stressed this responsibility at all DHS trainings and Safe Sanctuaries presentations, and provided copies of the RRS policy to encourage churches and social service agencies to adopt their own.

The revised RRS policy began:

> Any incident of present abuse or neglect, including sexual abuse, of a child (a person under the age of 18) must be reported to DHS or the DA's office by RRS. At the beginning of a conversation with anyone under

18 or suspected to be under 18, RRS Advocates and staff are advised to say that they are mandated reporters. If the RRS Advocate or any other representative of RRS is told that the alleged perpetrator of the abuse is currently the parent, guardian, or custodian of the child, or has responsibility for the child's health or welfare, whether in the child's home or in a day-care or other facility, then a call will be made to DHS. The person providing the information may also be encouraged to report to DHS.

If the RRS Advocate or any other representative of RRS is told that the alleged perpetrator of the abuse is someone other than the parent, guardian, or custodian of the child, or is someone who does not have responsibility for the child's health or welfare, then a call will be made to the DA's office in the county where the abuse occurred. The person providing the information may also be encouraged to report to the DA's office. If the RRS Advocate or any other representative of RRS is told by someone over the age of 18 that the alleged perpetrator of her/his abuse currently is responsible for the health or welfare of children under the age of 18, then a call will be made to DHS. The person providing the information may also be encouraged to report to DHS.

Reporting requirements for RRS Advocates and other representatives consist of a telephone call to the Executive Director or the Client Services Coordinator. This call should be made as soon as possible after the information is obtained; if the information is received on a weekend, the Executive Director or Client Services Coordinator should be called at home. It is the responsibility of the Executive Director or the Client Services Coordinator to report the information to DHS or the DA's office in a timely manner. The RRS Advocate is encouraged to make a follow-up call to the RRS office to verify that the appropriate report was made. (Note: The responsibility for reporting abuse rested with the person who first heard the allegation, but not all Advocates were comfortable with calling in a report.)

Sex Offenders

Sex offender notification meetings continued to be held in several Penobscot county communities throughout the year. Corinth hosted its fourth in July with 52 people in attendance. First meetings in Lagrange in September and Clifton in October attracted a "large crowd" to the former and 41 residents to the latter. A follow-up meeting for parents in

Clifton later in November seemed to indicate that other issues had taken precedence in the ensuing month because only five women attended. Eleven people showed up for the final meeting of the year in December in Etna. Detective Jameson and Walker presented the information each time as if the room were full.

As the state considered changes in the registered sex offender notification law, Walker met with Chiefs of Police Don Winslow in Bangor and Steve Barker in Brewer to obtain their perspectives on the current law. Neither of these cities had scheduled community-wide meetings and had chosen the option of notifying residents by distributing flyers door-to-door in the immediate neighborhoods where the offenders lived. Winslow felt that this minimum standard of notification to abutters and schools was sufficient, and observed that meetings would not work because of the transient nature of the sex offender population in Bangor.

Barker did not want to receive any more mandates from the state, but believed there should be a statewide uniform system of handling notifications. Better risk assessment of the offenders was needed, he observed, and he questioned who would follow up on registration once probation ended. Some sex offenders were not on probation. Walker did not disagree with any of these observations, which she then shared with Ward Saxl at MECASA who was working with the Maine Department of Public Safety on proposed changes. That there was no uniform state system was evident, in that RRS was the only center involved to such an extent in community notification meetings.

Personnel Changes

At the end of July, RRS was struggling again with personnel issues, as Dixon-Wallace left the agency. Classified advertisements for the position appeared in the BDN in late August:

> *Community Outreach Coordinator, Rape Response Services, F-T position available immediately in the Dover-Foxcroft office. Job responsibilities include coordination of volunteer program, and presentation of educational programs and trainings for the prevention of both sexual assault and child abuse. Position requires ability to work independently, public speaking and computer skills. Position will be filled when qualified candidate is found.*

By mid-September, four candidates had been interviewed by Walker, two finalists had made a presentation at a staff meeting, and Joyce Perry of Dover-Foxcroft had accepted the position. The team was now in place that would stay with RRS during the remainder of the years when Walker was the ED.

RRS was able to fund this position at full-time when Perry was hired because of a subcontract entered into with Penquis CAP to utilize child abuse prevention funds. The two organizations were part of the Child Abuse and Neglect Council (CAN) which met monthly in either Penobscot or Piscataquis county. Cheri Snow at Penquis CAP and Walker agreed that this collaboration would make the best use of available money for both sexual assault and child abuse prevention efforts. A nine-week parenting program to prevent child abuse and neglect was already in place for men incarcerated at Charleston Correctional Facility, and Perry assumed responsibility for these classes. Mandated reporting trainings held twice a year for teachers and a support group for parents of adolescents were also expected. Carr became involved in the Parents are Teachers Too (PATT) initiative in Lincoln. For several years, sexual assault centers had been encouraged to be part of the local CAN councils; now Perry also attended statewide meetings of the Maine Association of Child Abuse and Neglect Councils (MACANC) in Augusta.

The Rape Response Reporter

More than 700 copies of a longer six-page edition of *The Rape Response Reporter* were mailed in August, highlighting some of the work done by each staff member, with articles authored by them. Moring wrote about evaluating school-based programs:

> *During the past school year, educators at RRS presented over six hundred school-based programs for students in grades K-12. As the programs grow and develop every year, so do the ways in which we evaluate what students learn during our presentations. For students in grades K-8, I rely mostly on oral questions and responses to evaluate student understanding. For high school students, I use a pre-test/post-test form that includes the following statements:*

- *Sexual assault is a part of society that cannot be changed.*
- *A person has to say no for it to be rape.*
- *Physical force is used to commit rape.*
- *Strangers commit most sexual assaults.*
- *Women in their twenties are at the highest risk for sexual assault.*
- *You cannot legally give consent when under the influence of drugs and/or alcohol.*

Students are asked to respond to these statements on a four-point scale: 1 for agree and 4 for disagree. This brief test is given just before and immediately after a presentation. I then compare answers from both tests to measure any difference in student responses.

For example, the following results are from a class of ninth graders taught this spring at an area high school. One of the greatest changes in responses was to Statement 6. During the pre-test ten students answered 1 for agree compared to sixteen students who answered 1 in the post-test, a total change of six students. There was also a large change for Statement 5. During the pre-test one student answered 4, compared to nine students who answered 4 on the post-test, a total change of eight students.

Results vary from class to class. Some statements like 1 and 2 do not demonstrate a significant change from pre-test to post-test. This is a preliminary attempt to measure the outcomes of our school-based programs, to demonstrate that our presentations are having an impact on the attitudes and beliefs of students. I consider it to be a work in progress and welcome suggestions.

Carr's topic in the newsletter was "reaching out to elderly victims of sexual assault," a follow-up to what had recently occurred in the Millinocket area:

We live in a society filled with stereotypes about sexual assault. Even advocates and staff who are educated about the issue can feel some initial surprise when answering a hotline call or arriving at the hospital to find an elderly person on the other end of the phone or behind the closed door. The elderly victim/survivor often conveys feelings of shock and disbelief. "What did he want from me?" "I am an old woman; I don't understand."

Our culture teaches us that sexual violence is about sexual desire. We hesitate to believe what the motive really is: to gain power and control over another person. Accepting that reality means accepting that no one is immune from sexual crimes. Accepting that reality means that even a person whom our society may not deem as "sexually desirable" can be victimized. We are all at risk, no matter what our age or level of ability may be.

While victims/survivors of all ages have some similar concerns, there are unique concerns for persons who are elderly. Often a recent rape is not the first experience that an elderly person has had with sexual violence. Many remember experiences of incest and sexual abuse that occurred in their childhoods. Many find themselves telling those stories of abuse for the first time. Many realize that their recent rapes have unearthed memories nearly a half century old. These memories may be overwhelming to elderly persons. They have never spoken about these past abuses until now. No one ever knew. No one talked about things like that. There were no words, ways, or resources to help them find their voices.

Older persons often face the aftermath of rape with physical injuries and limited support systems. They usually must return to the place where the rape occurred, their own home. They may be living in nursing homes, assisted living facilities, or have home health care. Care providers often are not educated about how to provide assistance without retraumatizing their clients.

While the concerns that older persons may have following a sexual assault can be complicated, there are many things that can be done to reach out and support an elderly person we know who has been sexually assaulted. Listen. Convey important messages such as "I believe you" and "It is not your fault." Discuss any concerns that the person may have, without assuming that you know what those concerns are. Help the person brainstorm ways by which she or he could feel safer and in control. This might mean helping the person to discuss with caregivers how she or he would like to be touched and approached. It might also mean helping to create a support network to include friends, family, neighbors, clergy members, counselors, and a rape crisis hotline.

Help her or him access services by providing all available information and allowing the victim/survivor to guide the process. Offer to provide transportation or make phone calls if necessary.

Encourage care providers and health care facilities to train their employees about appropriately and respectfully working with elderly victims/survivors to avoid retraumatization. If the assault occurred within a healthcare facility, or by a person providing home health care, take immediate steps to report the incident to the appropriate authorities and agencies. Together, we can reach out to provide support to victims and survivors of all ages.

Currie's contribution to the newsletter reported on the fall volunteer training that would begin in Bangor:

Many people wonder what an advocate at Rape Response Services does. After the successful completion of forty hours of training, each person is provided with a pager. All advocates are expected to attend one meeting per month where they sign up for at least one weekly shift on the hotline. The shifts range from six to nine hours in length. Calls to the hotline are directed by the answering service to the on call advocate. A backup advocate is always scheduled as well, to ensure coverage and support at all times. If you are looking for an opportunity to volunteer, and have excellent listening skills, Rape Response Services is the place for you. Join our team of dedicated and caring volunteers.

Attracting more volunteers in Bangor was essential to maintain a number sufficient to fill hotline shifts. Staff members in Bangor received an hour of compensatory time for each shift they took that could not be filled by a volunteer. By the end of September, three junior social work students, including Brooke Gordon and Nicole Norman, and three members of Brothers Engaged Against Rape (BEAR) at the University of Maine, including Joe Sargent, were taking the training that Currie had mentioned in the newsletter. Bean again co-facilitated with Currie, and Hall filled in for one week.

An article by Nason in this edition of *The Rape Response Reporter* focused on men:

Many of us have been exceptionally fortunate to have some great men in our lives and some great women as well. Conversely, we probably all have known people who have a less than desirable character. A few men committing atrocities reflect horrendously on all men. The work of rape prevention, and on a larger scale, anti-violence work, is often labeled as a woman's job. Historically, it has been women doing this work. One of the philosophies about women in this field is that if men are the perpetrators of violence, women need to be the responders. Women are the victims of these crimes more than ninety percent of the time; more than ninety percent are committed by men. Given these statistics, a huge debate continues about where men fit into the rape prevention picture.

If we begin to build barriers by stating that only women can do this work, and men cannot, we are defeating our own purpose and mission. Men speak the best to men. And women can benefit from the positive influence of positive men. Male survivors are often forced into the dark, not allowed to speak out about their abuse. The recent scandalous cover-ups of male child sexual abuse within the church have brought much of this to light. But there is still more ground to be covered. Male survivors fear being labeled, having their sexuality attacked, their credibility and masculinity challenged. They battle with the belief that a man who is raped is no longer a "real" man. If a woman perpetrated on a man, who will believe him? Men are supposed to want sex. That's what society tells them, and that's the message that society reinforces in advertising and the media.

Women in general, seemingly from the point of birth, are taught to be victims. Society views victimhood as more acceptable for a woman than a man. From early childhood, women are not taught to be vocal, to state their opinions and thoughts, to say NO when they are being treated unfairly, or to stand up for themselves. They are shown that the way to be a "proper woman" and a "good little girl" is to be nice, to not ever talk back, to be quiet, to look pretty, wear lots of pink, be virginal, keep thin, and never, ever be rude. Being rude translates into not ever saying NO at the risk of offending someone. Just as women are set up for immediate failure, so are men. Men and boys are taught to be boisterous, to fight, to demand what they want, to command respect, to be providers, to be unemotional, to objectify women, and to be highly successful at whatever they do. When we expect men to behave badly, they do. These gender stereotypes and life lessons do far more damage than good. And they serve to separate women and men from being able to live and work together within the framework of equality.

The original question still remains: what about the men? If we do not provide a place for male survivors, and men in general, to speak and to share their thoughts and concerns, what are we doing? We who fight oppression then become the oppressors. We would never say we were oppressors. It is contrary to our mission to marginalize others. If we squelch or squander the voices of others, we are self-defeating. Men, just as women, want to be validated and supported. Male survivors, particularly, long to be validated, heard, and know that they are not alone.

There are men who really "get it" and are working to make this a safer community for all of us. Men who "get it" show up in the most surprising places. Maybe they are surprising places because we overlook them when they have been there all along. Maybe we are the ones who are not giving men a place. This is not to say we should have diminished expectations of men and their behavior. We should expect and demand that perpetrators of violence, regardless of who they are, be held accountable. Let's not forget, however, that abuse, rape, incest, bullying, harassment, and violence do not just affect women; they affect men as well. Men are survivors of violence themselves, men are bystanders who see it happening around them and feel powerless, and men have partners who have been directly affected. There is a place for them: working side by side with others to stop violence. A place where they can be believed, heard, encouraged, and supported. [emphasis in original]

Tyler's contribution to the newsletter covered self-defense:

How do people protect themselves? Some buy a dog (big, mean), a security system, or even a gun. These all can be good strategies, especially if they work for you. I believe, however, that your best security lies within yourself. Knowledge is your power and your best self-protection. There are many ways you can gain this power. *Numerous martial arts programs or kick boxing classes are available to satisfy the need for knowledge. To become proficient, you must invest time and money; these programs also require a certain skill and/or agility level.*

My knowledge about these programs is limited, so I will describe what I know: RAD for women. Rape Aggression Defense (RAD) Systems Inc. is a self-defense program for women, children, and most recently for men. RAD is all about education. We believe that ninety percent of self-defense is risk awareness. Most likely, if you are aware of risks or potential danger, you can avoid the situation. For ten percent of the situations that you cannot avoid, then what? Then you decide what will be your best option to get out of that situation safely. Women have many options, such as fighting, running away, talking your way out, or complying. Society needs to remember that these are the options for the one who is being attacked, and are not to be critiqued by someone who was not there.

RAD classes discuss risk awareness and teach physical options. We call these "tools for our tool box." This is where most of the education comes in. Many of us know what our risks are but not what our bodies are capable of, because we are never taught. In RAD, the techniques were designed for the average woman to learn and execute fairly easily. Many of the movements are based on gross motor skills and how to optimally use your body to achieve the most power. Many women discover how easy the techniques are, but most importantly, they realize the amazing strength they never thought they had. Not only physical strength, but mental and emotional strength as well.

We discuss these techniques as options because some are just not available. To those who have physical limitations, such as arthritis or even a broken hand, a particular technique cannot be used. You then dig into your "tool box" for another option. The RAD techniques are not power or strength based. Knowledge is the element of surprise. Those who choose to attack women do not believe that women can protect themselves, and RAD teaches us to prove them wrong. RAD is not about becoming the aggressor. The main goal is to escape that dangerous situation. Many are afraid that self-defense means to go and beat up on someone, but that is simply not true. We discuss what is and is not appropriate.

With all the physical options to choose from, RAD also acknowledges that one option is to comply. We stress survival. If you feel that compliance is your only option for survival, then you are doing what is best for you, and no one has the right to tell you otherwise. This is your life, and no one else's. For me, the most important part of the program is when the students educate themselves on their new abilities. The education builds confidence which in turn decreases the likelihood of being attacked. Can we guarantee that you will not be attacked? No. But hopefully, you will have more tools available to you. Is it the best program for you? Maybe, but maybe not. I encourage you to research all self-defense programs to find what is best for you, and then find the instructor within that program who will meet your needs.

Annual Report and End-of-Year Fundraising Letter

The Annual Report for the fiscal year ending September 30, 2003, listed the same Board officers, plus new members, Beth Brown and Sunderland. Bay resigned from the Board and from her position as Treasurer a month after the auction. Keeping Board members was as difficult as retaining staff at RRS. Volunteers continued to provide almost $100,000 worth of donated services to the agency. Hotline statistics showed a decrease of nine reported sexual assaults from the previous fiscal year. The total hours of hotline service were 271 provided to 159 clients. Six hundred fifty-six hours of prevention programs reached 13,666 students in grades K-12 and college. The state contract provided $178,350. Personnel expenses again were the largest fiscal category at $210,800.

Over 400 copies of the end-of-year letter were mailed in December. Signed by Groth and Walker, the letter began:

Fifteen years ago, in October 1988, Rape Response Services was incorporated as the sexual assault center serving Penobscot and Piscataquis counties. Rape and other forms of sexual violence were not discussed in public then, and when discussion did occur, victim-blaming statements were usually heard.

Has much changed in the years since that incorporation date?

We at Rape Response Services believe that changes have occurred, thanks in large part to the generosity of donors like you. Your support this year is more important than ever, as we face the uncertainty of government funding.

The crimes of sexual violence are discussed more often, whether in the media, in community forums, on college campuses, in school classrooms, or at our annual auction. Services are readily available for anyone who has experienced rape, and may include a caring volunteer on the hotline, or accompaniment to the hospital and police station. Local offices in East Millinocket and Dover-Foxcroft provide assistance for women, men and children in the rural areas of our two counties.

These vital services are not provided by any other agency in this area. Fifteen years of being a small, non-profit business have taught us, however, that collaboration with agencies doing similar work is vital to our success. In addition to the Safe Campus Project at the University of Maine, other ongoing collaborative projects include school presentations with Womancare and Spruce Run, and child abuse prevention efforts with Penquis CAP. Working together with other agencies, and with your continued support, Rape Response Services will be sure that the voices of all victims and survivors of sexual violence are heard for the next fifteen years and beyond. Please consider a gift of $15 or more in commemoration of our anniversary year.

Several high notes marked 2003 as the 15th anniversary year of RRS. The efforts of a small group of volunteers back in 1988 had planted the seeds for a viable organization that was still committed, first and foremost, to serving each victim/survivor in Penobscot and Piscataquis counties.

2004: OUTSTANDING COMMUNITY SUPPORT FOR RRS

Moving into the new year with a full staff and many volunteers in place at RRS was a phenomenon that had not often occurred in the center's first 15 years. Everyone recognized, however, that this was not a reason to be complacent about the future.

Sexual Assault Awareness Month

One of the ways to combat complacency was to create new events that would commemorate Sexual Assault Awareness Month in April and increase awareness of sexual violence at the same time. An evening candlelight vigil at Grace UMC in Bangor in mid-April was one such occasion. Sponsored by RRS and area UMCs, this meaningful event was attended by a small group of women and men. The pastor at the host church, Rev. Grace Bartlett, and Walker put together the service using the story of Tamar from the second book of Samuel. Vignettes composed from what hotline callers had shared with RRS were read aloud by participants in the vigil, which also included songs, prayers, and a silent meditation when candles could be lit at the altar.

Carr attended a meeting at which the seven members of the Millinocket Town Council adopted and personally signed a Proclamation that was probably the only document of its kind ever produced in the RRS catchment area. Resolve #5-2004 stated:

> *WHEREAS one of every four women, and one of every seven men, experience sexual assault at some point in their lives and one of every four girls and one of every six boys will be sexually abused before the age of 18; and,*

WHEREAS, the number of reported rapes in Maine increased by 19.2% in 2003 and the substantiated cases of child abuse and neglect reported in Maine in 2003 increased to 2,477; and,

WHEREAS, the direct and indirect costs of these crimes to the individual and our communities exceed billions of dollars annually; and,

WHEREAS, April is both Sexual Assault Awareness Month and Child Abuse Prevention Month that let people know about resources available to anyone who has experienced crimes of sexual violence or child abuse, including Rape Response Services at 1-800-310-0000 and its various school and community educational programs, direct services, and prevention programs;

NOW, THEREFORE, BE IT RESOLVED that the MILLINOCKET TOWN COUNCIL, in Council assembled on April 8, 2004, does hereby proclaim that April 2004 is Sexual Assault Awareness Month and Child Abuse Prevention Month in the Katahdin Region and that all citizens, parents, governmental agencies, public and private institutions, businesses, hospitals, and schools in the Region are called upon to support all efforts by Rape Response Services that will encourage an end to crimes of sexual violence and child abuse and neglect.

Also on April 8th, Carr, Danforth, and the Stearns High School Civil Rights Team promoted community awareness at the Millinocket Regional Health Fair with another new event. The interactive hit of the RRS display at the Fair was the opportunity for children to plant sunflowers in paper cups to carry home. A lot of printed information was also given out to the adult participants. Perry and the Dover-Foxcroft advocates staffed a table at the Business Expo in Guilford in early April, when many people accepted the invitation to "Tie One On," adding red, blue, or teal ribbons to the "tree." Mr. Paperback in Dover-Foxcroft agreed for the first time to display sunflowers, posters, and books related to sexual assault in one of their storefront windows during two weeks in April.

RRS had developed a large tri-fold stand-alone display board with input from all staff members. In demand at several locations during the month of April, the board added a new dimension to the events at which

RRS displayed information. Gordon was a social work intern at DHS as well as an advocate; she borrowed the board to make a presentation about RRS for 70 people with whom she worked in the Bangor DHS office. Having advocates who were willing to generate publicity for the hotline and the agency was something for which the staff was very grateful.

Nason and Walker co-facilitated on the subject of consent and sexual assault at the annual conference of the Maine chapter of the NASW in mid-April at the Samoset Resort in Rockport. The proposal to present an interactive 135-minute workshop was accepted by the planning committee and attended by 50 social workers. Walker's journal entry observed that it was "well-received and lots of fun," one of the few times she had an opportunity to do a presentation with a staff member.

Another mid-April event was the Annual Meeting and Volunteer Recognition Dinner held again at the UU Society building. Lussier, a Reiki instructor at his Lakeside Healing Place and a former volunteer, spoke at the dinner about managing stress and self-care. Donations of food for the dinner were received from Frank's Bakery, Bangor Rye, Olive Garden, Captain Nick's, and Sam's Club, all in Bangor; Paradis Shop 'n Save and Pastry Paradise, both in Dover-Foxcroft; and The Store in Orono.

It was Walker's pleasure at the annual Blaine House Tea sponsored by MECASA to present a Make a Difference Award to Jennings:

> *When given a bio similar to what I have in front of me for Dr. Ann Jennings, I feel as if I am either delivering a eulogy or introducing a keynote speaker. I could mention that Ann is currently sharing her expertise about trauma-informed systems throughout this country and beyond as a consultant for SAMHSA* [federal Substance Abuse and Mental Health Services Administration]. *I could mention that Ann initiated and directed for eight years the first state system Office of Trauma Services in this country, right here in Maine. I could also mention the many articles and books that she has written or edited. In all these ways she has Made a Difference.*
>
> *But I want to mention something about Dr. Ann Jennings that is not in her bio. Ann is a very creative person. My experience is that creative people tend to be disorganized. But Ann is creative even in her disorganization. She carries the biggest datebook that I have ever seen, longer and wider and fatter than anyone's. And she checks it*

occasionally, certainly giving the appearance that she is organized!

The awesome thing about Ann is that her heart is as big as her datebook. It's a hundred times bigger when being creative about ways to help victims and survivors of sexual assault. The Office of Trauma Services, the annual Trauma Conferences, the partnership since 1996 between DBDS and MECASA, are all cutting-edge, make-a-difference actions that began and were nurtured because of Ann's creativity. At the core of all these actions, at the center of Ann's creative being, are her commitment to ending sexual assault and abuse in Maine and beyond, and her commitment to providing ongoing support and services to victims and survivors.

"Take a Stand" was held on the last day of April at only one location, in Bangor at Borders Books, which also hosted Benefit Days for RRS on April 30th and May 1st, donating 15% of pre-tax purchases to anyone who presented a special coupon, an event that raised $312. The Clothesline Project was displayed, and participants, a few more than the previous year, could again design their own paper T-shirts. Publicity for the Stand and the Ball appeared in the Bangor *Chamber News, News & Views* of the Peace & Justice Center, *The Weekly,* and BDN. A small teal flyer about the April events was again included wih the invitations for the Stay-at-Home Ball. The Ground Round in Bangor held dress-down days to benefit RRS, providing a $150 donation. Raising money was an added bonus of community awareness events.

A Community Presence

Collaboration with the Penobscot Nation led to Walker's presentation of a 2.5 hour workshop on "Talking with Children about Sexual Abuse: An Informational Opportunity for Parents, Grandparents, & Caregivers." The Penobscot Nation had received a VAWA grant and formed a Violence Against Women Task Force the previous year. RRS and SR were both members of the Task Force which met monthly. Erlene Paul, a social work classmate of Walker and the Director of the Penobscot Nation Department of Human Services, and Esther Attean, another social worker, were also Task Force members who had been instrumental in writing the grant. Seventeen women and men attended the workshop in mid-January. Topics covered included victim-blaming, male victims, sex offenders, mandated reporting, and sexual aggression by girls.

A BDN article by reporter Diana Bowley on April 12th described a new initiative in Piscataquis County:

> *Area professionals have joined together to form a Penquis Region Sexual Assault Response Team to provide care for victims of violence. The team includes professionals from local, county, and state law enforcement organizations, the Office of the District Attorney and victim-witness advocate, Rape Response Services, and hospital emergency department nurses, according to Detective Lt. Scott Arno of the Dover-Foxcroft Police Department. The focus of the team is to improve the overall response, investigation and prosecution of cases, as well as provide care for the victims of sexual assaults.*
>
> *"Our efforts will provide for the complete care of a victim-survivor who is subjected to violence of this nature," Arno said recently. He added the team hopes to increase reporting of these crimes so offenders will be exposed and deterred from reoffending. The team also plans to provide more public education about sexual assaults. While SART groups exist throughout the state, this is the first of its kind in the Piscataquis and southwestern Penobscot County region, according to Arno. Since April is Sexual Assault Awareness Month and Child Abuse-Neglect Prevention Month, SART encourages the public to participate in any activity that will create awareness about these issues.*

Minutes of the Piscataquis County SART Advisory Committee recorded representatives from the Maine State Police, Mayo Regional Hospital, the Dover-Foxcroft police department, and the DA's office in attendance, in addition to Perry and Shaw.

Receiving grant funds from Penquis CAP for CAN meant that RRS had a seat at the monthly meetings of the SCAN (Suspected Child Abuse & Neglect) committee at EMMC. These late afternoon gatherings brought together a diverse group of hospital personnel, Maine Department of Health and Human Services (DHHS, formerly DHS) employees, and others to review de-identified cases of children who were hospitalized.

The SART Advisory Committee in Bangor continued to meet monthly with good representation from local law enforcement departments. Hannah Pressler from Spurwink in Portland provided training in June for 52 officers from throughout Maine about signs to look for in suspected child sex abuse cases. Shaw (formerly Tyler) coordinated this four-hour afternoon event at the University of Maine. Dr. Lawrence Ricchi at Spurwink was the only person in the state qualified to perform forensic exams on children under the age of 15, or to advise a SANE on the telephone about how to proceed. He was in Bangor once or twice a month to conduct exams and was frequently called as an expert witness by the DA's office.

RRS was part of a Bangor Jail Diversion Coalition which received a grant in October from the Maine Department of Public Safety to fund two Crisis Intervention Teams (CIT), one at the Penobscot County Jail and one at the Bangor Police Department. Members of a CIT were trained to determine if an inmate was suicidal and to work with offenders who had a mental illness. Believing that the voice of the victim/survivor needed to be heard at every table where offenders were discussed, Walker attended Coalition meetings beginning in the spring. For the same reason, RRS was involved in a Re-Entry Committee which met at Bangor Mental Health Institute and planned for the release of juvenile offenders into the communities.

A community presence for RRS was also evident throughout the year in letters to the editor or newspaper articles. Titled "Rape really happens," the letter from Walker in the September 11th/12th weekend edition of the BDN began:

> *The only surprise about the Kobe Bryant case was that the end didn't occur sooner. I was amazed at how much abuse the alleged victim continued to endure from the media, from the public, and from the very court system that was supposed to protect her. Did anyone threaten to kill the alleged rapist? Of course not, but there were death threats against the young woman.*
>
> *When allegations of rape are made, the defendant has two common lines of defense: "I wasn't there," or "It was consensual." Bryant readily admitted to being there, and continues to maintain that the sexual encounter was consensual. No one except the two individuals will ever know for sure what occurred in that hotel room. Those who think they know, who are quick to blame the woman, and*

to say that she was only looking for money, have no more knowledge of what occurred than I do.

This is the dilemma with all rape cases. Only two people are present when a rape occurs. To convince a jury that a rape was really consensual sex is much easier than convincing a jury that this innocent-looking man seated in front of the judge could be a rapist. The woman who alleged that Bryant raped her is a victim of our society, a society that refuses to believe that rape happens. She knew that the odds of being believed were against her, just as anyone else who has ever reported a rape knows this reality. These odds have not stopped women and men from coming forward in the past, nor will this case stop them. Rape Response Services (1-800-310-0000) will be there to support them, to listen and to believe. If only the rest of society would do the same.

Ordway quoted Walker in her usual thought-provoking column in the BDN on October 22nd about prisoners who received flu shots and porn. "For Kathy Walker," she wrote, "who deals daily with rape victims in her role as director of Rape Response Services, it's another example of offenders' rights taking precedence over the rights of victims. 'Some of these victims can't afford health care, let alone worry about a flu shot. They can't pay their light bill let alone subscribing to a magazine.' With research showing a strong relationship between pornography and sexual assault, Walker finds it unwise to allow incarcerated sex offenders to receive pornographic material." Penobscot County Jail was an exception to the new DOC rules and did not allow any publications which contained nudity.

Money Matters

A mini-grant of $2091 from the Maine Safe and Drug Free School initiative had been provided late in the previous year to create materials for a collaborative effort between the eighth-grade health instructor in Milo, Carr at RRS, and Angie Alfonso, the Teen Advocate at Womancare. Beginning on October 23, 2003, and ending on May 20, 2004, the program "specifically addresses the early adolescent behavior of peer pressure and acceptance of others," according to the grant application. "It teaches and promotes a healthy life style and school climate with tolerance towards the acceptance of differences within the school body. Suspension rates related to harassment investigations and incidences of smoking in school will be reduced."

The plan was to provide each of the 82 students with a pre-program survey at the beginning and a post-program survey after the completion of the 17 forty-minute lessons, over 11 hours of classroom instruction. Learning objectives to be addressed included the effects of risky behaviors, ways to avoid or change situations that threatened personal safety, analysis of media influences, and demonstration of conflict resolution strategies. At the end of the program, each student was to do a comprehensive presentation highlighting specific areas of the lessons.

The "Vagina Monologues" and the eleventh annual Beta sleep out were again held in February to benefit RRS. The sleep out raised $1500 and generated publicity in the BDN and *The Maine Campus.* "Hundreds join to combat rape" was the headline in the latter on February 23rd. Noting that many people who had attended the hockey game at the nearby arena stopped by to offer support and money, staff writer Heather Cox quoted Nason: "Beta has consistently organized this and drawn people together not only from campus but from the community at large to take a stand on the issue. I think Beta's done a great job showing it's not just a woman's issue."

Eric DeGrass, Beta philanthropy chair, observed: "Rape is such a serious issue on college campuses nationwide and it needs to be stopped. We want people to know how important this cause is to us. It's not so much that Rape Response is a worthy recipient as it is that we are privileged to be involved with such an organization that does such positive things for this community, and, more importantly, this campus." The article was accompanied by an image and the words "It takes a whole community to end sexual assault" from the RRS website.

An interview with Walker by Kristin Saunders, sports editor at *The Maine Campus,* was published after the event on February 26th. "The event is important because it is sponsored by an all men's organization and shows the community that rape is an issue," Walker noted and continued, "the event sends the message that not all men are rapists and that there are lots of men who want rape to stop."

The long interview and article included a discussion of RRS and the anti-sexual violence services provided. Procedures for becoming a volunteer and for being on the hotline were discussed in the article:

> *Volunteers keep the program running. Walker said a total of 15 volunteers currently staff the 24-hour crisis hotline. She said in their around-the-clock phone coverage it is estimated they donate about $100,000 in wages. "We could not do what we do without our volunteers," Walker said. "Our major goal is to give a person who has been raped choices. We help a person work through the options."*
>
> *Walker emphasized that the impact of the volunteers can be felt by the victims because they will take five hours out of the day to sit with a victim at the hospital, reassuring them that they are important and there is someone who cares about them. "It's invaluable, awesome, all those words," Walker said. The funds raised from the Beta Sleep Out will be used throughout the organization, including for a new curriculum. According to DeGrass: "We continue to support them because we feel that fighting sexual assault is still a worthy cause and needs our continued support."*

The sleep out and RRS also received nationwide publicity in the March 4th online newsletter, "Speaking Up: The Family Violence Prevention Fund's News and Tips for the Domestic Violence and Sexual Assault Communities." Under Maine news, the website quoted the February 23rd BDN article. Kyle Webster, a Beta brother, noted online: "Rape is one of the most serious issues on any college campus. The purpose of the sleep out is to show that guys are not only willing to raise money to fight against it, but also willing to make a stand against it. People see what we're doing and get the message that rape is not acceptable."

Over 600 invitations to the annual Stay-at-Home Ball were mailed in mid-March. Held early in April and hosted again by WEZQ 92.9, the Ball experienced a few changes: Rick Andrews had replaced Russell at the station, and the hours were from 7 to 10 P.M. Walker joined Rick live on the air and was pleased to be given more of an opportunity to make comments in a commercial-free format. A pleasant surprise was a telephone call from Russell, who had moved to Pennsylvania and listened to the Ball online. This annual event raised $3000, more than usual.

Addressing the funding issue in mid-May in her journal, Walker observed that a MECASA discussion about possible new directions for centers was "precipitated by me because of a fifty percent cut in the DBDS money on July 1st." It also appeared that RRS was going to lose the CAN funds from Penquis CAP, necessitating a potential cut in Perry's hours, although Walker had already included the $6000 in the new DHHS contract. She thought MECASA needed to look at ways in which to consolidate centers and/or services before the state forced this, or required combining with domestic violence projects. RRS was involved in one meeting in late July with the Ellsworth and Aroostook center directors, and in mid-July Walker facilitated a meeting of center directors in central Maine, but nothing came of this regionalization idea at the time. Checks from DHHS continued to arrive late, sometimes by two or more months. Running a small non-profit organization was not for the faint-hearted.

A welcome bright spot in the financial situation occurred when the Stephen and Tabitha King Foundation awarded RRS another grant in late May for the printing of 5000 posters with tear-off sheets. A requested amount of $3800 was provided in full to cover the printing done by Fast Forms. All public places in the two counties were to receive posters by the end of the year. RRS had run out of the previous posters which had been reprinted at least once. The new staff-designed creation was eye-catching in bright teal with a stylized gray and black sunflower. "We Will Listen" in black letters outlined with white on the top was followed by smaller black letters "If you want to talk about…" and a listing of Rape, Incest, Child Sexual Abuse, Sexual Harassment, Other Forms of Sexual Violence, each pointed to by a sunflower petal. "It's Never Too Late To Call" appeared under the sunflower. "Call Rape Response Services for Free and Confidential Support, Referrals, and Information" and the toll-free number were printed on the bottom of the poster beside the tear-off sheets. (Note: As this book is written in 2013, the posters are still displayed throughout the catchment area.)

Personnel Changes

Moring's hours were reduced to 30 per week for the months of June and July to save money when schools were closed for the summer. When she returned, almost 80 letters were mailed by Carr and Moring to school contacts throughout the two counties. Walker had to inform Veits that RRS could no longer pay her stipend after July 1st because of the pending cut in DBDS funds. Veits would continue as before, volunteering her time as clinical consultant to RRS, and attending advocates' meetings and trainings, where she presented a session on self-care. The cut in funding necessitated a change from paid backup hours for Bangor staff to compensatory hours, one hour for each backup shift taken. Carr's and Perry's hours also had to be cut in October because of the loss of CAN funds from Penquis CAP. Perry's full-time position was reduced to 30 hours per week.

As expected, Nason left RRS employment at the end of 2004 when the second round of VAWA funding expired, and the Women's Resource Center, under Barker's leadership at the University of Maine assumed responsibility for SCP. RRS continued to receive some SCP funds through the University for consultation on curriculum development. The work on campus had led to more collaboration between RRS and SR, including a staff person from the latter paid with grant funds and working under Nason's supervision. Nason completed the SR hotline training, and Tina Roberts from SR began monthly meetings with Walker.

Early in the year, Walker had made the decision to retire from RRS in two years. May 2006 would be when she left if all went according to plan. In hindsight, perhaps the public announcement to staff, advocates, and Board, in that order, was premature and could have waited another year, but giving everyone time to prepare the groundwork for her replacement was uppermost in Walker's mind at the time.

Support Groups

A two-part support group for women who had experienced rape, incest, or child sexual abuse began in Bangor early in April, co-facilitated by Currie and Shaw. This group met two nights a week for six weeks, with the second part beginning in August and continuing for an additional five weeks. Staff members (except Moring) requested and received six hours of group facilitator training led by Shaw and Nason so they could lead support/education groups in their own offices. Volunteer Sokoloski and Perry then co-facilitated a group at Womancare beginning in late March, and Walker provided supervision via conference call after each session. In June, Nason and her husband hoped to begin a once-a-week support group for men who had experienced sexual violence. Although often requested through the years, this group again did not materialize when one of the two registrants dropped out at the beginning. All of the support groups in 2004 utilized the Trauma, Recovery, and Empowerment Model (TREM) for which training and materials had been provided by DBDS. One of the RRS guidelines for groups was to close them to newcomers after the first session. Groups at RRS were not therapeutic, offering education and support only, with a variety of activities and exercises.

Completed in March was the spring advocate training for three volunteers, again co-facilitated by Currie and Bean; six new advocates participated in the November training. Becky Reed, who worked at the Penquis Law Project, emerged from these sessions as a long-time RRS supporter. At the same time, Perry finished training for two volunteers in Dover-Foxcroft. Each Bangor training alternated between having a staff member from Womancare or SR attend a session and present information on domestic violence. Currie continued to arrange for informative speakers to attend the monthly advocates' meetings, not only to provide information to those in attendance, but also to publicize RRS in the Bangor social service community.

Sex Offenders

News about sex offenders appeared frequently in both state and national media. The *Community Press* in Millinocket published a guest column by Carr on March 9th titled "It takes a whole community to end sexual violence":

> *Lately it is impossible to turn on the radio or television without hearing another report of a child that has been abducted, exploited, or abused. These stories can be extremely disturbing to hear. However, they can prompt us to take a more active role in attempting to keep our kids safe. Talking with your children about sexual abuse is an important step toward increasing their safety. Like most parents you probably have many questions about how to do that. It isn't easy. As parents, we want to protect our children. We don't even want them to know there are people out there who would want to hurt them. However, not discussing sexual abuse with your children leaves them vulnerable. Here are some tips to get you started:*
> - *Teach children accurate names for all of their body parts. They can be introduced during discussions about personal hygiene. It is important that kids know all of the*

correct names. *If they ever need to report being touched inappropriately, they know the words to use.*

- *Include rules about body safety with all of your other safety rules. It is as important as knowing about poisons, what to do in case of a fire, or how to cross the street. Let children know that the private parts of his/her body should only be touched by an adult to help keep them clean or healthy, such as parents helping with baths, or the pediatrician for a check-up.*
- *Avoid telling kids that only strangers are dangerous. It is important to know that in 85% of sexual abuse cases, the perpetrators are known to the victims. Instead of saying strangers are dangerous, talk about situations that are dangerous.*
- *Help children understand and trust their feelings. Ask them if they have ever felt "funny" or like they should stay away from someone. Explain that when you have feelings like that, trust them. Tell a trusted adult how you are feeling.*
- *Discussing these issues may make you feel uncomfortable; if so, let your children know that. Chances are they can tell by your body language anyway. It is okay to say that you feel uncomfortable, but you don't mind that feeling because you want your kids to talk with you about anything they need to. Otherwise, your body language may be saying "Don't tell me" while your voice is saying "Talk to me about anything."*
- *Don't encourage behavior that can leave kids vulnerable. Examples may include saying "Always do what adults tell you to do" or "Don't hurt Uncle Joe's feelings, hug him good-bye." Children need to learn how to say no when they don't want to be touched. They need to have permission to tell us who or what they don't like and why.*
- *It is most important to keep in mind that if your child discloses abuse, it is vital to believe him/her. Children rarely make up stories of this nature. Report the abuse, and reach out for services. There are many people that can help. For more information please call Rape Response Services at 1-800-310-0000.*

Sex offender notification meetings continued to be scheduled in towns throughout the RRS catchment area. Two more meetings in Corinth, in early February and early July, were attended by 26 and 25 residents, respectively. They heard a shortened version of Walker's presentation because the audience members had "been there, done that" so many times. The people who attended these subsequent meetings were not as interested in general information as in specific details about the particular offender, but Detective Jameson and Walker stuck to the traditional format.

A meeting in Charleston in late July addressed the fact that two offenders had moved to town. Twenty-seven people attended this meeting which was facilitated by the chairwoman of the Board of Selectpersons. One woman talked with Walker after the event about the ritual abuse that her daughter had experienced. Usually one or two disclosures about their own sexual abuse were made by attendees at the end of these sessions.

The Rape Response Reporter

The Summer 2004 issue of the *Rape Response Reporter* was formatted by Carr and sent before the eighth annual auction to 600 on the mailing list plus 150 school contacts, police chiefs, and UMCs where Safe Sanctuaries trainings had been held. Staff members again wrote informative and thought-provoking articles, beginning with Carr's "The Girl Nobody Knows":

> *We've all been there...blazing a path through the mall at a runner's pace frantically searching for a last minute gift. The first three stores you have tried produced no results, and you are calculating your next move, when all of a sudden, you see them. There they are, the **girls**. They look like they have just stepped off a page in <u>CosmoGirl.</u> They travel in packs, carrying bags from American Eagle and Abercrombie and Fitch, sending text messages on their cell phones, and tucking their freshly highlighted hair behind their ears to expose shiny gold hoop earrings. You know those girls. You have seen them a hundred times. You know all about them. There is something reassuring about seeing them here at the mall. You get the feeling that everything is right with the world. You admire their laughter and excitement, and long for the carefree feeling that they surely possess. Their lives are certainly perfect at this moment.*

I have had the privilege of getting to know some amazing girls over the past few years. I have met athletes, artists, semi-professional shoppers, writers, Goths, and skateboard enthusiasts. These girls have all been individuals with different passions and pursuits. They have each had their own unique qualities that have made them beautiful. They have all been growing and changing and figuring out the kinds of women they want to be. And they have all been survivors of sexual abuse, trying to figure out how to make it in the world while living with that reality.

At least one in four of those girls from the mall, the beach, or the skate park, are living with that same reality. Those girls are the ones that nobody knows. We don't want to see them. We would rather let their picture-perfect outward appearance show us who they are.

The truth is that the girl no one knows is struggling with some pretty tough issues. She is wondering if she should tell someone what has happened to her. Maybe she has told, and regretted it later, because it got reported to her school social worker, her parents, and DHHS. Her report set off a scary chain of events including statements, interviews, therapy visits, court proceedings, and maybe even foster care. Maybe she told, and no one believed her, not even her mom, who decided to keep dating the man that abused her. Maybe the sexual abuse is still happening, and she doesn't know how to make it stop. Maybe it happened a long time ago, and everyone in her life feels like she should be over it by now. She trusts no one, and is suspicious of everything. She seems happy and smiles all the time; it is exhausting. She keeps on smiling, however, because that is what she thinks others want to see: a carefree girl enjoying the best time of her life. She just wants all the memories to go away, but no amount of starving, cutting, sleeping around, drinking, drugging, or denying seems to make it happen. She is writing in journals, ripping up pillows, and talking to therapists, but she still can't forget about it. She feels all alone in the world.

As long as we ignore this girl, we can't be there for her. We can't support her, believe in her, or let her just be real for a while. And she really needs us. She needs us to listen to her concerns and not assume we know what they are. She needs our reassurance that even though she can't forget what happened to her, she can work toward *healing in her life. She needs to hear that she is strong, beautiful and courageous. She needs to see that we have faith in her, and that we think she is incredible. We need to accept who she really is, that she isn't just an image from <u>CosmoGirl</u>. She is a whole person with unique thoughts, feelings and experiences. She is a part of our family, our friend's daughter, a student in our class, a member of our church congregation, our co-worker, our babysitter. She's hurting, and though we've seen her a hundred times, somehow we didn't notice. We must have been looking at her freshly highlighted hair and gold hoop earrings.* [emphasis in original]

Currie wrote an article about volunteering at RRS, and Perry listed "Ten Ways to Show Love for Children" that she adapted from the curriculum she used with incarcerated fathers at the Charleston Correctional Facility. Moring began her article about sexual assault and minors in Maine with the comment: "Whenever I go into schools to speak about sexual assault, one of the topics students are most interested in is consent. Specifically, students want information on sexual acts involving minors that are against the law. This topic can be confusing for anyone, even for those familiar with sexual assault statutes. It is always helpful to me to revisit existing laws and to look at what changes, if any, have been made by the Legislature." She then went on to quote definitions related to crimes of sexual violence from the Maine Revised Statutes Annotated (MRSA) and to list various sexual activities that could or could not be legally engaged in by minors. Moring concluded by noting: "This quick overview of the sexual assault laws as they pertain to minors is for informational purposes only, and is not intended as a substitute for legal advice. Additional information or referrals to attorneys may be obtained by calling RRS."

Consent was a topic that interested both teenagers and adults. On February 13th, Walker's letter that addressed consent was published in the BDN, in response to articles in the newspaper that had appeared in late January:

It was interesting to note that both Marian Wright Edelman in her column, "Old South lingers in a legal lynching," and "Dear Abby" in "Dating could mean jail time," have written about consent and sexual violence. While I respect the writings of both women, I have concerns about the victim-blaming statements that they made in their columns.

Consent is the issue that students most want to hear about when Rape Response Services makes classroom presentations in the public schools. Young people might have a vague understanding that they need to get or give consent before engaging in sexual activity, but the law in Maine is confusing about the interrelationship between age and consent.

Responsibility always rests with the older of the two individuals, and if he or she is 18, consent for sexual intimacies with a younger person over age 14 must always be unequivocally obtained. A person under age 14 cannot give consent to sexual activity, period. It is always better to abstain than to assume that consent has been given.

Using a condom is not an indicator of consent. Young people are also confused because of the myths about rape that persist. "Women say no when they really mean yes." "Men are going to suffer physically or emotionally if they don't release the built-up passion." "She would not have gone to his room with him if she didn't want to have sex." "He had been intimate with her in the past." All of these myths allow us to make excuses for sexually violent behavior that is both unacceptable and illegal. These myths allow us to focus our anger not on the person who committed the crime but instead on the victim. I encourage parents and teachers to be sure our young people have information about consent. I also encourage each of us to be conscious of victim-blaming statements that we might have made about someone who has been sexually assaulted. Crimes of sexual violence affect us all.

"What is a Victim?" was Nason's contribution to *The Rape Response Reporter:*

Rape Response Services has been in business for over sixteen years. It is truly phenomenal that an entity based solely on the existence of rape victims and, essentially, rapists, is still needed in our communities. Educational programs historically focused on the victim as the one who needed to stop the attack, stop the rape, sufficiently resist. Legal language and definitions still ask the question, *"Did you fight back?"* One is led to think that the only true victim is attacked unprovoked by a stranger, and shows sufficient physical and emotional suffering to be deemed worthy of carrying the title of "rape victim." But rape victim has such a pejorative tone. No one necessarily wants that label.

What is your image of a rape victim? What are the first thoughts that come to your mind of a "true" victim? The lying woman is the prevailing myth of rape. Men cannot be victims is another myth. We don't want to believe that rape exists in our modern day society. If we can discredit a victim, it means we do not have to accept that this violent crime happens in our own community. We don't want to admit that we have a problem in our town, nor do we really want to examine our own beliefs and biases that contribute to the tolerance and acceptance of rape.

So who is the "true" victim? All of us. We all pay when rape happens. We pay financially through taxpayer dollars to support law enforcement, health care, and a court system. We pay to cover the costs of offender treatment and possible rehabilitation. We pay for jail time. We pay for the needed assistance a victim requires and deserves. And we pay even more when we don't do anything about rape.

There are opportunities for everyone to get involved to make our communities safer. Volunteer your time assisting and supporting victims of trauma. Believe when you hear a story about rape. Write letters to the editor. Speak up when you witness something that is really not okay, such as demeaning language and behavior. Encourage men to get involved in taking a stand against violence. Use your voice and actions to be a positive influence in our communities. As noted by Gandhi, each of us can "be the change you wish to see in the world."

Inserted in a boxed area titled "More Than Statistics" under Nason's article was the following: "Someone recently asked if RRS had served clients back in the sixties, clients who had been helped so significantly by this agency that they would be willing to share stories of that assistance in a public forum. The reality is that sexual assault agencies like RRS did not exist until the seventies, although crimes of sexual violence have certainly always occurred. Now agencies like RRS provide assistance to clients around the state of Maine every day. Clients put a face on the reality of rape. Clients help us understand that they are not statistics, that they have a name and an identity beyond the term 'victim/survivor,' and that they deserve to be believed and respected for their courage and perseverance."

School-Based Programs

Statistics were cited in the summer *Rape Response Reporter* for RRS program activity from January 1st through June 30th in 2004: 1220 students reached in grades K-4, 2056 in grades 5-8, 2189 in grades 9-12, and at the post secondary level, 2376 students. These were the highest numbers ever reached by the school-based educators and SCP. In November 2004 alone, 1414 students in grades K-12 heard RRS classroom presentations.

Results of school-based program evaluations compiled by Moring for the period from September through December showed increases in the responses that were "more than adequate" by the 111 students in grades 4-6 after classroom presentations on bullying. A student in grade five wrote: "Thanks for coming and talking to us!" "Bullying is bad!" noted a grade four student, while another in grade five observed: "People shouldn't bully each other." A grade six teacher commented: "I like that the subject of bullying is talked about by someone in addition to teachers and parents."

Similar increases were exhibited by 100 students in grades 7-8 following presentations on gender stereotypes. A student in grade eight wrote: "We understand more about harassment. Thanks for coming." "Thanks for the presentation," wrote an eighth grade teacher. "My students in this rural area do not have enough resources. Rape Response Services provides some of this support."

One hundred one students in grades 9-12 showed a 52% increase in the number of "more than adequate responses" to a question about identifying a few myths surrounding sexual violence. When asked to define consent, 85% percent of these students provided a "more than adequate response" after the presentation compared to 46% before. A grade ten teacher wrote: "We really find this service valuable to our health program." Students wrote some questions on the evaluation forms about helping others, and Moring followed up on these with the classroom teachers.

Evaluations in grades K-3 were done orally by Moring, who

asked the classroom teachers to record the answers that the students provided. Examples of the questions were "How does safe touch feel?" and "How does unsafe touch feel?" Students' answers ranged from "feel good" for safe touch to "really uncomfortable" for unsafe. A grade one teacher observed: "I love the way you talk to kids…age appropriate and worthwhile lessons." "They need to know it is ok to say no to a hug and that it doesn't mean they don't like you," wrote a second grade teacher. All of these evaluations were part of the performance-based measurements of programs funded by both the UWEM and DHHS.

Annual Auction and Awards Night

Publicity about the eighth annual Fall Festival Auction and Awards Night in September appeared in the September Peace & Justice Center newsletter, the BDN on August 27th, *The Weekly* on September 2nd, and the September edition of *Chamber News*. McKay would return again as the auctioneer. Continuing to underwrite the event were Pine Tree Landfill, BDN, Husson Park Associates, Veazie Veterinary Clinic, and Sargent, Tyler & West. New underwriters included Filene's, Mayo Regional Hospital, and St. Joseph Hospital, plus one anonymous "Friend."

Walker's appreciation was expressed in the September *Our Monthly Advocate* for supporting another successful auction which raised over $10,311. More than 200 items were donated by 150 businesses and individuals. These included "Joe Otter," a small bronze sculpture from Hart, and a signed copy of a Barbara Delinsky novel. The members of the 2004 men's hockey team at the University of Maine had signed a stick to be auctioned. Another kayak from Old Town Canoe and a 26-inch 6-speed bicycle had also been donated, along with the opportunity to sit in the flag stand at a Speedway 95 race and wave the flag to start a race. Hartman began the tradition of donating monthly bouquets of flowers from her garden, arranged and delivered to the lucky bidder, and had also obtained donations from businesses in Piscataquis County. Many handmade items, including "Dog and I" apparel that was modeled by Cynthia Rollins and her dog, were also popular.

New at the auction were door prizes courtesy of The Squire, Country Hearts, Bangor Mall, Marie's Flower Shop, and Hartman. Stickers found inside some of the bidding directories alerted the door prize winners to pick up the brown paper bag with the same number as their sticker. Ticket prices remained at eight dollars each or two for fifteen dollars.

A very emotional Lussier received the Janet Badger Volunteer Award for his many years of service, especially as a backup to be with or talk to men who wanted a male advocate. As noted in *The Weekly* on October 14th, Klein was the recipient of the Teal Ribbon Award because she "has been instrumental in establishing a firm presence for RRS on the University of Maine campus. The award is presented annually to an individual who makes a difference for the agency in a capacity other than as a volunteer." Walker described the auction in *The Weekly* article as an event that "generated crucial financial support for our agency and also provided emotional support from the community for our volunteers and staff."

Annual Report and End-of-Year Fundraising Letter

The Annual Report for FY'04 listed Board officers: Hartman, President; Greaney, Treasurer; and Brown, Secretary. Eddy had rejoined the Board along with new members Mike Hatch, Alan Stormann, and April Taylor. Groth and Sunderland had both left the Board in May, meaning a limited number of Board members was available to solicit items for the auction, because Stormann's job in public safety at the University of Maine prohibited this type of activity. In the Annual Report, the number of sexual assaults that were reported to the hotline was 17 more than had occurred in the previous fiscal year. Volunteers who took these hotline calls provided in-kind services estimated to be worth almost $111,000. March 2004 recorded a high for the year of 78.5 volunteer hours on the hotline, responding to calls from 76 individuals.

A face behind these statistics was the client from a long-ago (1996) Christmas Eve who appeared in Walker's office, looking for a safe place to stay. The Greater Bangor Homeless Shelter felt unsafe to her, and no other options were available. A safe house in Bangor for people who had experienced sexual assault had been discussed when the DMHMRSAS/DBDS funds first became available. Although a building had been located and initial services provided, the effort was not sustainable. Walker noted in her journal that she did what she could for the client, but "glimpses into the system of homelessness make me feel angry and hopeless."

According to the Annual Report, successful fundraising events and donations generated income of over $37,000, helping to create an increase of $2500 in the unrestricted fund balance. The agreement with DHHS provided $178,350 to RRS. Personnel expenses amounted to $223,000, with telephone and travel together costing $15,700. Insurance costs had increased to $34,000.

Hartman and Walker signed the end-of-year letter in December that highlighted a very busy year and was mailed to about 400 individuals. The letter began:

> *Thank you for your generous financial donations to Rape Response Services. With your help, this agency is able to focus on our mission: "to offer hope, understanding, support and advocacy" for every woman, man and child affected by sexual violence in Penobscot and Piscataquis counties. Our direct services to victims and survivors are not available from any other agency in this area.*
>
> *A total of 183 individuals received 453.5 hours of help from volunteers or staff at Rape Response Services in the fiscal year that ended on September 30, 2004. Many individuals also participated in support groups offered by this agency. A record number of 82 sexual assaults was reported to our hotline as having occurred during this twelve-month period. We hope that this increase reflects the fact that more individuals who have been raped are reporting the crime to us because they know they will be believed and not blamed. But we also know that rape continues to occur at an alarming rate.*
>
> *The second part of our mission—"to educate the communities"—is addressed by this agency's commitment to the prevention of sexual violence. During FY'04, 7,697 students in grades K-12 throughout the two counties participated in one of our classroom presentations. The Safe Campus Project at the University of Maine reached another 3,293 students. Collaboration with other agencies that provide school-based prevention programs is a priority at Rape Response Services. Please continue to be as generous as you can in helping us fulfill the two parts of our mission.*

Some housekeeping tasks had been accomplished by the RRS Board during the year. Original RRS By-Laws were amended once in 1997, twice in 2000, and again by the Board in early August 2004. This last amendment removed the requirement that two individuals had to sign all checks. The adopted language stated: "Two signatures are necessary on all checks over $5,000." In the earlier revisions, the ED was named as a non-voting Board member who was also the corresponding secretary. A Board "Chair" became a Board "President." Standing committees of the corporation were spelled out (financial/administration, public relations, fundraising, personnel, and clinical/training), with a minimum of two people, one of whom was a Board member, on each. Advocates could be Board members; no more than two advocates were allowed to serve at the same time. The annual meeting would be held in April.

Amendments to the original document had also spelled out the RRS purpose in Article II. The revised purposes were to:

a. help the victims of sexual assault deal with the initial trauma of the assault, recover from the experience and its aftermath, and return to normal life;

b. work to gain fair and non-judgmental treatment of sexual assault victims by professionals, such as doctors, nurses, psychiatrists, psychologists, police officers, attorneys, and judges; and the general public, such as family and friends, neighbors, co-workers, schoolmates, and potential jurors;

c. encourage a social climate in which every human being has the right to live without fear of sexual assault.

Article II continued to state that the purposes would be achieved by:

a. providing a crisis counseling hotline, and information and/or referral for victims of sexual assault;

b. developing a public and professional education program which will include a multi-media publicity campaign and public speaking;

c. working with law enforcement officers, mental health professionals and other service providers to increase and enhance their knowledge of, and skills in dealing with, survivors of sexual assault;

d. maintaining legislative involvement in bills related to the goals of this organization;

    e. working with legislators, members of the legal professions, and health care providers to modify court procedures which discourage sexual assault victims from reporting the crime and seeking other forms of assistance.

A Dissolution or Liquidation Article VII had been added at the end of the By-Laws. This Article described the process by which assets of RRS would be distributed if the center were permanently closed.

One of the busiest and most productive years in RRS history was at an end. Programs in the schools and communities were reaching all-time high numbers of participants. Despite the loss of Nason as an RRS staff member, SCP had achieved secure status at the University of Maine. Remaining RRS personnel looked ahead to continuing quality programs and initiating new ones in 2005.

2005: A PRESTIGIOUS AWARD

Increasing numbers of students reached by the school-based educators, and record numbers of monthly website visits, were highlights of another outstanding year for RRS. Over the previous several years, the center had established itself as a place for quality programs and services.

Recognition of this high quality was achieved in April when RRS received word that the center had been "selected as the recipient for the 2005 NASW-Maine Chapter Agency of the Year Award." The letter addressed to Walker from Catherine Stakeman, the interim Maine Chapter ED, further stated: "NASW-Maine is honoring you and Rape Response Services in recognition of the contributions to support and advocate for victims of sexual assault in Penobscot and Piscataquis counties." The award was presented to RRS at the annual NASW-Maine Chapter conference, held at the Samoset in mid-April. Walker was delighted to accept the plaque on behalf of all the staff members who were present at the luncheon. Walker's brief remarks were applauded by a standing ovation. The conference program described RRS: "The agency has grown its community presence through many activities, including appearances on the local news, coordination of special community functions during April's Sexual Assault Awareness Month, and representation at conferences and community gatherings. Kathy Walker, the Executive Director has maintained high visibility throughout our state by heading the Sexual Assault Coalition for the past four years."

Receipt of the award was publicized in *The Weekly* on April 28th: "An agency that receives the award exhibits excellence in promoting social work values for its clients, staff, and the community. RRS joins a prestigious group of agencies, both small and large, as the latest recipient of this award." The Bangor Chamber of Commerce *Our Members' News* also mentioned receipt of this honor.

Walker's contribution to the summer 2005 issue of *The Rape Response Reporter* highlighted the award and was titled "Everyone Working to Eradicate Rape":

> *RRS was honored in April to receive the Agency of the Year Award from the National Association of Social Workers (NASW), Maine Chapter. This award recognizes an agency in Maine that exhibits social work values toward clients, staff, and community. The recognition of the work that we do is deeply appreciated.*
>
> *Gary Bailey, NASW President, spoke at the conference in April when the award was presented. His thought-provoking remarks included a challenging question to the social workers in attendance: "Are social workers trying to eradicate anything?" Referring to earlier efforts of the profession to eradicate poverty or hunger, for example, the question provided RRS with an opportunity to remind the audience, "Yes, we are working to eradicate rape!" An impossible task? Maybe, because rape and other forms of sexual violence have been part of our culture, of every culture, from Biblical times to the present. How can one small agency hope to eradicate this crime?*
>
> *Prevention is a major focus of this agency's mission. And education is a key component of prevention. When people are educated about the devastating and life-long impact of sexual violence, they are more likely to believe the victim/survivor, and to disbelieve rape myths and victim-blaming comments. Our prevention programs are offered by our School-Based Educators in the public schools, grades kindergarten through twelve and in the local colleges. Prevention programs also are provided by our SART Coordinator at trainings for law enforcement officers and hospital personnel. Other prevention and education work at RRS is done through community meetings and media channels, via our website, and by word-of-mouth.*
>
> *Let's not discount the value of word-of-mouth, one-on-one prevention work. Each person reading this newsletter interacts every day with many others who may not understand that the victim of rape did not "ask for it." Challenge the victim-blaming statements*

that you hear. Remind people that minors cannot legally give consent. Exhibit zero tolerance for all forms of sexual violence in your words and actions. Never underestimate the power of one voice or of one small agency that believes rape can be eradicated.

Sexual Assault Awareness Month

Early in April, Walker drove to Guilford and took a shift at the Business Expo where 42 attendees tied red, blue, or teal ribbons on the tree that dominated the RRS display table. Two days later, she drove again to Piscataquis County and helped Perry arrange the Sexual Assault Awareness Month "simple and good" window display at Mr. Paperback in Dover-Foxcroft. Route 15 from Bangor to Dover-Foxcroft was becoming very familiar to Walker.

A half-hour presentation on date rape to a class at UC in April convinced Walker that RRS still had a long way to go in changing attitudes about sexual violence. She wrote in her journal that there is "so much misinformation out there about rape. Even the teacher had an attitude." The request to speak had come from a student in the class.

Currie had the idea to change from the annual dinner and advocate appreciation event to a "come when you can, leave when you must" evening at Grace UMC in mid-April. Individual stations were set up where advocates could get a massage or a manicure, learn about homeopathy for pets, obtain information about healing herbs, and eat desserts prepared by staff members. Called a "Volunteer Celebration," the event featured vendors from the community who gave their time to provide the services, and "no one wanted to leave." Walker made arrangements for the sign outside the church entrance to read "Thank you volunteers at Rape Response Services" on both sides.

This sign remained in place for a sexual assault awareness vigil and service later in the month, sponsored by RRS and area UMCs. Twenty-one people attended this second annual event of readings, prayers, and candle-lighting. "I wish I had done some tweaking of words in bulletin to be more inclusive," Walker noted in her journal, "as we had several men present." The story of Tamar's rape was again the basis of the service, at which people who attended were chosen to read the various parts.

Booths at the H.O.P.E. Festival, now at the University of Maine, and at the Millinocket Health Fair provided outreach and exposure for the agency in these communities, as did a TBN speak out and march at the University of Maine. Currie, Carr, Nason, and several volunteers participated in one or more of these events. Walker was quoted in the BDN coverage of the Festival on April 25th when she "estimated that 100 people visited the organization's display. 'We could not do this kind of outreach just by ourselves. We have tried to do that but we need to be part of a larger event.'" This statement was in reference to the discontinuance of the annual "Take a Stand" due to a significant drop in participation over five years.

Sex Offenders

Ordway wrote in the BDN on January 7th about sex offenders and a new treatment program that was to begin at the Maine Correctional Facility in Windham. She interviewed Walker for her column, mentioning that Walker was "going to towns throughout the county to talk to residents when notified that a sex offender is moving into the area. You know that one of the first questions she's asked is: 'What kind of treatment have they had?' Her answer, sadly and frighteningly, is 'none.'" The program at Windham was to last four years. Ordway noted: "It will take a few years, but hopefully someday Kathy Walker can sit among a group of concerned residents in a small Penobscot County town and provide them with exact details of the extensive treatment their new and feared neighbor received while in prison. There is no cure-all for this wretched crime, but today with the sex offender registry up and running and the new treatment program about to begin, Maine is taking steps in the right direction."

More than 1000 people heard about RRS on one late-April day when Walker participated in a panel at a Brewer High School assembly in the morning, and at a sex offender notification meeting at night in Dover-Foxcroft. Walker's journal recorded that the "usual ignorance" was evident at the notification meeting, "but it was good overall." Perry had made arrangements for the event, which attracted more than 130 people. She distributed flyers and had spoken to town officials about the importance of community notification. Walker was quoted in Diana Bowley's coverage of the meeting in the April 30th BDN: "'Every community has sex offenders, but most have never been caught.' The sexual offenders with whom the center deals are not the 'snatch-and-grab stranger rapist,' rather, they are men and women who have cultivated a relationship with a child long before any abuse takes place. 'This is a teachable moment, this is a good opportunity to talk with your children about being safe.'"

Grover's interview with Walker on WABI-TV Channel 5 about registered sex offenders early in May yielded some unexpected results: RRS became the target of the Dennis Dechaine support group, "Trial and Error." Dechaine had been tried and convicted more than a decade earlier for raping and murdering a young girl and was serving his prison sentence. His supporters throughout Maine and beyond continued to claim his innocence and petitioned the state on a regular basis for a new trial. In Walker's interview with Grover, she mentioned that denial is rampant about sex offenders, commenting that people do not believe that someone they know could commit such a crime. Because a request for a new Dechaine trial was again in the news, Walker offered this case as an example of denial, even by the sex offenders themselves.

When these comments aired on television a week later, RRS was bombarded with emails, phone calls, packages, and threats demanding to meet "or else." A letter was received from Dechaine at the Maine State Prison. Walker rejected several certified letters and packets which were sent to the office, addressed to her and to Board members, from members of "Trial and Error." One caller demanded financial information about RRS. The harassment continued through the end of June when someone in the group intercepted an unrelated email exchange between Stormann and Walker, after probably hacking into Stormann's campus account. During the entire time, Walker had notified both the Bangor and Hampden police departments, and had forwarded all emails. Unopened packages and letters were given to Grover at Channel 5, who offered to do a follow-up story about the harassment; the decision was made that such a move would only add fuel to the fire. Eventually, everything received was turned over to the Bangor Police Department. By mid-summer, nothing further was heard at RRS from "Trial and Error."

On June 9th, another letter from Walker was published in the BDN. Titled "Not always strangers," the letter began:

> *How close to schools should registered sex offenders be allowed to live? That is the sex-offender issue of the moment being debated*

in the Maine Legislature. What we are forgetting is that registered sex offenders are not the only child sex abusers who live in our communities, maybe even right next door to our schools. Many people who commit sex crimes against children have never been caught, convicted, or served time in jail, and therefore, have never had to register.

I continue to be amazed at how much we still want to believe that the stranger is the person who grabs our children and sexually abuses them. We don't want to believe that child molesters are usually relatives, friends, coaches, teachers, or neighbors who have established a relationship with a child long before abusing her or him. While no one wants to have a registered sex offender move into a community, parents can use this event as a teachable moment to talk with their children about keeping safe from any older individuals who may try to hurt them.

Focusing only on registered sex offenders gives us a false sense of security that we are doing all we can to keep our children safe. Let's focus our energies on what goes on inside the school rather than how far from the school someone may live. Educators at Rape Response Services are available to provide age-appropriate presentations for students, grades K through 12, and for parents. This school-based program, supported in part by the United Way of Eastern Maine, equips both children and adults with skills that help to counter the fear and anger generated by the release of registered sex offenders into our communities.

Walker's journal entry a few days later noted that RRS was "generating lots of comments these days." Following the publication of this letter, for the first time, she "got hate mail in response to my op ed. Unidentified sender using profanity."

Thirty-two residents of Dexter attended a sex offender informational meeting early in August. The event was prompted by the move of a registered sex offender from Corinna to Dexter, and the subsequent questioning of Dexter town officials about notification requirements in town. The "same old anger and misconceptions about sex offenders" were evident at the meeting, according to Walker's journal entry. Yet another registered sex offender had moved to Corinth earlier in the year, prompting Walker to observe in her journal that this meeting was "not a good one, as he was there with lots of defenders, hometown boy who got caught. No one dared speak, I fear."

Annual Auction and Awards Night

An exciting ninth annual Fall Festival Auction and Awards Night in September earned over $12,000 and attracted a huge crowd that filled over 16 tables. A decision had been made by the Board to raise the price of auction tickets from eight dollars to ten for one ticket, with two for $15, and the price for a table of eight increasing from $50 to $60. Publicity in both *The Weekly* and the BDN, including Averill's column, emphasized signed copies of novels by Stephen King and Barbara Delinsky. Returning underwriters included Pine Tree Landfill, BDN, Sargent, Tyler & West, Veazie Veterinary Clinic, Husson Park Associates, Mayo Regional Hospital and St. Joseph Hospital. New this year were WABI-TV Channel 5, Bangor Historic Track Inc, Machias Savings Bank, Merrill Merchants Bank, Eastern Maine Healthcare Systems, Groth & Associates, and Rainstorm Consulting. Many handmade items were again featured among the 42 live auction opportunities. Because of a disastrous fire earlier in the year at Hart's studio, he was not asked to provide a sculpture for this year's auction.

The highlight of the evening, as always, was the recognition of two individuals: Veits who received the Janet Badger Volunteer Award, and Grover, the recipient of the Teal Ribbon Award. Live coverage for the entire event was provided by WABI-TV Channel 5, Grover's employer. Walker had proposed to the Board earlier in the year that RRS honor Veits and Grover at what would be Walker's last auction. An article on October 6th in *The Weekly* quoted her remarks when presenting the award to Grover: "a strong ally for RRS in the local television market, helping us educate the public with informative and timely coverage of sexual assault issues." Veits, Walker noted, "is respected and loved by so many people throughout our area. The award is only a small token of our appreciation." The auction "exceeded our fundraising goal, and also provided an affirmation of the work done by volunteers and staff at this small, nonprofit agency." The article also noted that "Janet Badger, a longtime volunteer at Rape Response Services, assisted in the presentation," as she had done for each of the nine years.

RRS Policies

Several RRS policies were revised by staff and approved by the Board during the year. In response to the DBDS grant, an "Enhanced Hotline Services Policy" that had first been adopted in February 1999 was revised in January. The components of the policy were:

1. Enhanced hotline services at RRS are available to callers who have multiple, extended, or frequent contacts with the hotline, and to callers who have special needs (self-injury, suicidal, etc), linked to sexual abuse.
2. Calls which require enhanced hotline services are expected to take more time than regular hotline calls, but setting limits and offering a follow-up call are appropriate.
3. Callers who require enhanced hotline services may be given to the person on backup when the advocate who takes the initial call is unsure or uncomfortable about handling a call, or when she/he cannot spend the amount of time which a caller needs.
4. Training for taking enhanced hotline calls is incorporated into the regular volunteer training and the in-service training at RRS.
5. Documentation of enhanced hotline services is completed on forms provided by MECASA; compilation of the monthly forms from each center and transmittal to DHHS is the responsibility of MECASA.

The "Work/Advocacy Conflict Policy" had also been developed in February 1999, and was updated by the RRS Board in January 2005. Many advocates were employed at other social service agencies where the same clients might be seen. The Confidentiality Policy referenced in this Work/Advocacy Conflict Policy had been in effect since Walker took the training in 1994. The new policy read:

> As stated in the confidentiality policy, any information that comes to an Advocate through your association with RRS shall remain confidential, even if the information is about someone with whom you have an association at work. Any information that an Advocate receives at your place of work will not be shared with RRS, even if the information

is about a known RRS client. If an Advocate is asked to respond to a co-worker's client, because you are known to be an Advocate at RRS, you should give the requested information to the co-worker, but let your co-worker respond to the crisis, to avoid conflict of roles. If the client in crisis is your own, you will respond to the situation (not identifying yourself as an RRS Advocate), and use RRS as a referral as you would any other agency.

An Advocate may be called to the hospital in situations where you recognize the victim/survivor or a family member. You have the option of not identifying yourself as an Advocate and calling the backup person. Another option is to identify yourself as an Advocate and to discuss with the victim/survivor whether another Advocate would be more appropriate. Let everyone know that the circumstances are confidential regardless of what the decision is regarding an Advocate.

If an Advocate recognizes the name of a caller on the hotline, you should give the call to backup. During an Advocates' meeting while processing calls, if information is revealed about someone you know, you have the option of leaving the meeting. If you choose to stay at the meeting, any information is strictly confidential regardless of your relationship with the person whose situation is being discussed. If there are any questions about a case, or if circumstances arise that are outside of what is described above, the Advocate will contact the Executive Director of RRS or your Clinical Supervisor at work, using hypothetical situations for direction on how to proceed. An Advocate's association with RRS may be terminated if this policy is not adhered to.

A Community Presence

SCAN continued to meet monthly at EMMC. At an early February meeting, Walker's guest was Ann Lynn, who had flown in from Massachusetts to speak to the committee about a Child Advocacy Center (CAC). SACC in Lewiston had worked with Lynn to develop a CAC, just getting underway in that area. These advocacy centers in other states provided a child-friendly room in a building apart from the hospital or police station where alleged child victims of sexual abuse could be interviewed and examined. One-way glass in the room allowed others to observe the interviews. According to Walker's journal, Lynn "made a good presentation to SCAN about a CAC in our area."

Carr and Walker met in February at the Lincoln UMC where 23 people participated in a four-hour Safe Sanctuaries training. The group "was very open and receptive, and had done a lot of work on policies." An earlier session at the Hampden Highlands UMC attracted 15 people from six area churches who were "generous in donating $85 in checks and cash." In May, Walker met for an hour with a group of 18 people at the Park Street UMC in Milo to present information about child abuse. Different from the Safe Sanctuaries training, this session was more focused on policies that the church could implement. A $50 donation was made to RRS.

Some good court news occurred in early April when U.S. District Judge John Woodcock "ruled that the University of Maine system did not violate the right to due process" of the two former football players involved in an alleged sexual assault in 2002. An article by Judy Harrison in the BDN on April 12th summarized the case, and reported that Judge Woodcock ruled the players were "not entitled to a jury trial on their claims." The University had complied with all the "requirements outlined in case law" when college students face disciplinary charges. In answer to the claim that Allan was biased because she was a member of the RRS Board: "Woodcock wrote that 'it is difficult to take seriously the plaintiffs' claim of bias. There is not exactly a constituency in favor of sexual assault, and it is difficult to imagine a proper member of the hearing committee not firmly against it. To the contrary, the record of the hearing reflects, instead of treating the claim as proven, Dr. Allan's chairmanship of the hearing committee was characterized by even-handedness and neutrality.'"

Shaw's editorial, "Rape victims must be heard, believed, supported," was published in the June 22nd issue of the *Piscataquis Observer* following a trial during which both Perry and Shaw provided support to the victim/survivor. The woman did not want to write her story for the newspaper, but was willing to let Shaw quote her comments:

> *Recently our community declared a victory when a man was sentenced to prison for the crimes of attempted gross sexual assault and unlawful sexual contact. The conviction and sentencing is [sic] an obvious victory all in itself. The victory I am referring to is the one the victim/survivor can claim: she was listened to, believed, and supported.*

As she stated, "I am a 63-year-old woman who at the age of 61 became a victim of a sexual assault. I never thought I would be writing about this horrific experience." Many victim/survivors of sexual assault are ridiculed and shamed for choices that we all have a right to make. Society still blames the victim by judging the clothes they wear, how much they drank, or for taking a walk with someone they thought they could trust.

"I was violated. He took advantage of the trust I had in him. We victims often wonder what we did to have this kind of thing happen. I still have lots of fear but in no way will I let him ruin my life. There is no reason to give him that kind of power. I know I did nothing wrong and I will not take the responsibility for his actions," she testified.

Each person can make a difference by putting the blame where it belongs, on the perpetrator. Make a decision to listen, believe, and tell the victim/survivor it is not her or his fault. If you or someone you know has experienced rape, sexual assault, or child sexual abuse at any time, seek and/or encourage assistance from Rape Response Services. We are here to listen, support, offer referrals and options to anyone who has been affected by crimes of sexual violence. We will accompany the victim/survivor to medical appointments, law enforcement interviews, and through the court process. Call the confidential hotline at 1-800-310-0000 any time, day or night. Every victim/survivor deserves to be believed and supported. They don't deserve to be sexually assaulted or abused. Let us all help in the recovery process from sexual assault: listen, believe and support.

In mid-December, Walker facilitated a staff meeting at SR, at their request, to process a sexual assault that had occurred to one of their clients. This emergency crisis intervention was a "good interaction" that would not have occurred a few years earlier when the two organizations were not collaborating.

RRS occupied seats at the usual meetings (Resource Exchange, Domestic Abuse Task Force) and a few new ones throughout the two counties during the year. The latter included a community/school partnership in Lincoln and a health advisory committee in Mattawamkeag, with Carr involved in both. Trainings of law enforcement, social services staff, and medical personnel were held at several locations. By the end of the year, RRS brochures and the new posters had been delivered by volunteers and staff to 175 locations in the two counties, including medical and municipal offices. Increasing the community presence of RRS led not only to awareness about sexual violence but also to support for the victim/survivor and the center itself.

Money Matters

A vote taken at the February 2005 Board meeting authorized Walker to transfer the excess RRS funds, recorded in the FY'04 compilation as a $2506 increase in the fund balance, into the money market account held by American Express Financial Advisors. Board members present for the unanimous vote were Hartman, Greaney, Eddy, and Taylor. Unknown at the time, this decision was to figure prominently in the RRS financial situation by the end of the year.

Productions of "The Vagina Monologues" were again presented in February to benefit RRS, SR, and the Mabel Wadsworth Women's Health Center. Ten percent of the proceeds went to support Iraqi women. A major snowstorm compelled Walker to close the RRS offices for two days in February, and postponed the performances of the "Monologues" until the following week. Walker presented opening words at one performance, and advocates were present each night to process issues that arose for anyone in attendance.

Earlier in the week, Walker was a dinner guest at Beta Theta Phi and received a $1000 check for the proceeds from their annual sleep out. Almost 500 invitations were mailed to the annual Stay-at-Home Ball held on April 2nd with Rick Andrews and Walker co-hosting from 7 to 10 P.M. This signature event raised $2440.

Walker expected in mid-July that she would have to kick in the line of credit for the first time as the June DHHS payment was only $123, and neither the July DHHS payment nor the May check from the University of Maine had been deposited. Despite these worries, which she would be happy to leave behind, Walker wrote in her journal on July 15th that she "squeaked by with about $130 left in checking account and even cashed my own check." By the end of the month, there was still no money, and the line of credit was used to cover an $11,000 overdraft once all bills were paid. A month later she noted in her journal: "I needed to have the line of credit a long time ago, as it saves a lot of worrying over no money. RRS paid $65 in interest for a loan of $10,300."

Early in July, Walker completed the FY'06 contract and emailed the pages to DHHS well in advance of the deadline, feeling a sense of relief that this was the last such document she would have to prepare. The RRS Board had approved the contract budget and authorized Hartman and Walker to execute the agreement on behalf of RRS. The contract included the stipulation that RRS would receive $185,150 from the state: $20,191 (State Purchased Social Services or SPSS, formerly SFPSS); $83,248 (Social Services Block Grant or SSBG); $22,285 (Social Services Block Grant-Prevention Education or SSBG-PE); $36,571 (CVAP); $3202 (PHHSBG) and $19,653 (Rape Education Prevention Grant or RPEG). This total amount included $36,000 for SART. A local share match required for SPSS and CVAP was $12,706. The match was to be provided by 1412 hours of hotline advocates' time at $9.00 per hour. A revenue summary also included $8929 in government revenue from the DBDS contract, and $2000 from county/municipal funds. Program income was budgeted at $550 to be raised from schools and trainings. Restricted revenue of $36,789 (University) and unrestricted at $21,143 (fundraising) brought the total revenue to $267,267.

Expenses totaling $267,267 in the contract were primarily for wages ($167,190) and fringe benefits ($36,985) that included FICA, unemployment compensation, workers comp, and health/dental insurance. The hourly rates of pay ranged from $13.01 to $13.15 for the five employees; a stipend for Bean as paid backup was also included in the wages. Rent was $16,140 ($795/month in Bangor, $250/month in Dover-Foxcroft, $300/month in East Millinocket). Telephone (hotline, pagers, office phones, internet, website), and travel (to schools and other staff-related) were each budgeted at $6000. Client-related travel was estimated at $1500. Bonding and insurance totaled $5261 and included liability insurance, directors and officers insurance, and a renter's policy. Materials, supplies, and maintenance at $4150 covered maintenance contracts on two copiers, plus office supplies, postage, and the newsletter. An amount of $3375 was budgeted for the payroll service, $1500 for an independent auditor, and $6460 to cover coalition dues, fundraising, fees, dues, conferences, and advertising. Revenue, expenses, and employee positions were all six times higher than the FY'90 contract prepared by

Mullen-Giles 16 years earlier, although the contract pages looked the same. The local hotline presence which Mullen-Giles had worked hard to organize remained in place.

Walker wrote the contract, and all relevant portions of the narrative were reviewed by the appropriate staff members. The description of services that RRS offered read as follows:

> Services are provided out of offices in Bangor, East Millinocket, and Dover-Foxcroft to best serve the geographic area covered by RRS. The primary service is a 24-hour crisis hotline, staffed by trained advocates and supervised by trained paid staff who provide backup to every shift. All advocates and staff are provided with pagers. RRS maintains a pool of advocates who consistently take hotline shifts in the Bangor area (serving the entire two counties through the toll-free number), and provide accompaniment to hospitals, courts, and/or law enforcement departments. Additional groups of advocates in Millinocket and Dover-Foxcroft are available to accompany callers to the hospitals, to police interviews, or to court in their respective areas.
>
> Information about referrals to other agencies and to counselors is also available through RRS. Mental health practitioners are surveyed every two years to keep the referral list updated; each advocate has a copy of this list. A statewide collaborative effort with the Maine Office of Trauma Services has enabled RRS to include hotline services for persons who have a mental illness as a result of sexual abuse.
>
> A second service provided by RRS is education/outreach. Learning objectives for grades K through 12 have been written by RRS to conform to the key learning concepts of the Maine DOE health education curriculum. RRS collaborates with both Womancare and Spruce Run to provide presentations on dating violence. A website, developed and maintained by RRS since 1998, generates hundreds of hits per month. RRS maintains its own lending library of current books and periodicals in the Bangor office. A collaborative VAWA grant at the University of Maine supports education on campus.
>
> The third service provided by RRS is support/education groups for female and male survivors of rape and incest. Support groups are facilitated by either two staff members or a staff member and an advocate, all of whom have received group facilitator training.

Members of the support groups must have access to a therapist, at least for the duration of the group. Groups are held consistently throughout the year.

The SART program at RRS continues the collaboration with Penquis Health Services that provides office space for the SART Coordinator. This person works with the six hospitals in the two counties to develop protocols and provide training. Facilitation of Sexual Assault Response Teams and ongoing training of law enforcement officers are done by the SART Coordinator.

The number of units of service which RRS projected to provide under the terms of the contract was a total of 220 women, men, and children and 400 client hours, with the SART Coordinator projected to provide 100 of these hours to 20 individuals. Support group services recorded numbers of individuals separate from those served on the hotline. Six support groups at RRS were expected to meet during the contract year for 21 clients. One was to be in Piscataquis county, one for adolescents in northern Penobscot county, and one for males in Penobscot county. Activities that modeled emotional support and self-actualization were mandatory for support groups.

Everything other than direct services to victims included such mandatory activities as presentations and trainings to the faith-based community, to the healthcare field, and to the general community via TV/radio interviews and special events. Presentations to schools, newsletters, court watches, posters and brochures, and participation on statewide boards and committees, were all mandatory under the terms of the contract.

While the above items and two broad goals were generated by DHHS, the strategies to meet the performance measures had been developed by RRS. Goal #1 provided by DHHS stated: "Individuals affected by sexual assault and/or sexual abuse will be provided supports and services in order to minimize medical, physical, emotional, and legal trauma."

To achieve the measurement under Goal #1 that "100% of clients who request medical support and assistance will receive agency response and support within fifteen minutes," RRS strategies were:

- RRS will continue to be the lead agency in developing and maintaining SART/SANE programs in Penobscot and Piscataquis counties.
- RRS will continue to train hotline advocates for accompaniment during rape protocol exams at hospitals in the two counties.
- Hospitals in Dover-Foxcroft, Millinocket, Greenville, and Lincoln will continue to receive assistance in developing rape protocols.

Achieving a second measurement of "100% of clients will receive appropriate/relevant medical information on potential longer term medical consequences" would require the following strategies:

- RRS will continue to offer support/education groups for female and male survivors.
- Training at RRS for hotline advocates will include information about physical effects of sexual assault.
- Hotline advocates will make appropriate referrals to medical professionals.
- Training will be provided to medical professionals.

A decrease in emotional trauma was to be measured by RRS in three ways:

1. 100% of crisis calls will receive a return call within 15 minutes.
2. 75% of clients who participate in a support group will complete 6 to 12 weeks of support group services, and no more than 25% of support group clients will participate beyond 50 weeks.
3. 80% of clients who participate in support groups will give positive feedback regarding the support group's assistance in decreasing their emotional trauma (agency's client survey).

RRS strategies to achieve these three measurements were:

- RRS will staff and supervise a 24-hour crisis intervention hotline.
- Support/education groups will be offered for female and male survivors of rape and incest.
- Each group participant will complete an evaluation tool.
- Hotline advocates will receive training on crisis intervention, mental illness and developmental disabilities.
- RRS will participate in notification meetings when a registered sex offender moves to a community.

The indicator that legal trauma had been decreased would be measured by "100% of clients who request legal support and assistance services will receive agency response within 24 hours." The strategies listed by RRS included:

- MCJA-certified training of law enforcement personnel will be offered.
- Hotline advocates will receive training in legal issues relevant to sexual assault.
- RRS will continue to collaborate with Victim/Witness Advocates in the DA's office.
- RRS will continue to participate in sex offender community notification meetings.
- RRS will maintain a court watch program in Bangor and Dover-Foxcroft courts.

Goal #2 provided by DHHS stated: "Maine communities will have zero tolerance for the perpetration of sexual assault and sexual abuse." With the indicator being "zero tolerance," the measurement prescribed was: "A pre/post survey administered by the agency to education and training groups will demonstrate a positive change in community attitudes towards lower tolerances regarding sexual violence/sexual harassment (baseline % to be determined by agency)." RRS strategies were:

- RRS will continue to expand the educational efforts in the public schools.
- RRS will present at least one program in each school district in the two counties.
- Community education will include op ed pieces, radio/TV interviews, newsletters, and redesigned website.
- RRS will continue collaboration with domestic violence projects in some school presentations and performances of "You the Man."

A narrative written by Walker described in more detail how the community education and community response service areas would be measured:

The School-Based Educator in the Bangor office will provide classroom and assembly presentations on sexual assault prevention to each of the fourteen school districts in southern Penobscot and Piscataquis counties. At least seventy-five presentations will be provided in grades K through 4. Working relationships with contact persons in each school will be maintained and strengthened. On-site services will be continued in one shelter for area youth, at Mountain View Correctional facility, and will be available on request at area high schools. Evaluation forms will continue to measure outcomes via a pre-test, post-test. The results will be tabulated and shared with school personnel. Joint presentations on dating violence will be given in collaboration with Spruce Run at two area high schools.

The Executive Director will provide two sexual harassment training sessions for area businesses. Five United Way member agency presentations will be made to supporters and potential supporters in the business and medical community. Training for twenty DHHS staff and others will be offered in the area of child sexual abuse. RRS will participate in six community notification meetings for registered sex offenders in the two counties. In collaboration with the SART Coordinator, MCJA-certified training will be available to all police departments; a total of thirty officers will receive the training. The revamped website will allow for updating as needed. One meeting will be held with the Bangor area clergy group, and a vigil will be held in April at an area church. Training on child sexual abuse prevention for United Methodist clergy and laity will be provided at two area churches.

An outreach office at Penquis CAP in Dover-Foxcroft provides a space from which the part-time Community Outreach Coordinator is available to attend at least four area meetings each month, provide two trainings for nursing home staff and others, and be a presence in Piscataquis county. This person will supervise the advocates in Dover, and will work collaboratively with Womancare to avoid duplication of services.

All fundraising activities (auction, Stay-at-Home Ball, end-of-year letter) will include an educational component, either in the publicity, or at the event, or both. Two newsletters will be developed and mailed during the year to 600 persons. At least five media contacts will occur throughout the year.

A separate description of the work in northern Penobscot county followed:

The part-time Community & School-Based Educator in northern Penobscot County will provide classroom and assembly presentations on sexual assault prevention to each of the seven school districts in the area from Howland north. Relationships will be strengthened with the contact persons in each K through 12 school. At least one presentation will be made to a class or series of classes in each elementary, middle, and high school. Collaboration will continue with the Civil Rights Team at one area high school, and with Womancare staff in one northern Piscataquis County school district. Evaluation forms from both students and teachers will continue to measure outcomes.

Supervision of the advocates in the Millinocket area is provided by the Community & School-Based Educator, who will facilitate additional volunteer trainings as needed. Three trainings for nursing home staff and other social service agency providers will be offered. The collaborative effort with K.A.R.E. (Katahdin Area Response Effort for Nonviolence) to educate the communities will continue. Four presentations will be made to area clergy, parents, and to civic groups.

At the end of September, a "Rock Against Rape" concert was sponsored by Sigma Phi Epsilon fraternity at the University of Maine to benefit RRS. An estimated 1500 people attended the concert, at which Nikki Hopkins, a new social work intern at RRS, was quoted in the September 26th issue of *The Maine Campus:* "I would like to tell people rape is a serious issue, and that they should pay more attention to it. It happens to a lot of people, but not enough are educated about it." Other community members spoke out against rape at the event, including Mitchell of Public Safety and State Representative Emily Cain from Orono.

School-Based Programs

The ED's reports which Walker prepared monthly for the Board, following an example set by Burkhart/LeClair, were always headed with the RRS mission statement. She then broke down the mission statement and provided bulleted statistics under "to offer hope, understanding, support," "to offer advocacy," and "to educate communities." Monthly statistics were compared to the previous year in each category. Major benefits of these reports were the opportunities to visualize, on a month-by-month basis, how many people were being reached by the hard-working RRS staff members and volunteers, and to compare numbers to the previous year. Year-end statistics that provided only total numbers did not have the same impact. (Note: Unfortunately, all these monthly reports, including Burkhart/LeClair's, and all the Board meeting minutes until 2005 were apparently destroyed in the transition to Penquis CAP in 2008. Details in this chapter and the next are condensed from the monthly reports and minutes that remain.)

In March 2005 alone, for example, Moring and Carr made a total of 71 classroom presentations that reached 1552 K-12 students, a high for the calendar year. As many as 84 presentations were made in one month (November). Almost all of the numbers were higher than in 2004, and were in addition to the students reached by drop-in hours that Moring held at Penobscot Job Corps, in collaboration with SR, and at Shaw House, Mountain View Correctional Facility, and Acadia Hospital in the adolescent programs. The programs in the elementary schools, thanks to Moring's initiative, established RRS as a leader among other sexual assault centers throughout the state. Letters from Moring and Carr were mailed at the beginning of each school year to all public and private school principals in the two counties.

The publicity brochure for the new UWEM campaign mentioned RRS in a section titled: "Results Matter: We don't measure results by how much money we raise and distribute. We look at our overall impact in the specific areas that we have targeted and the lives and the communities we have improved. By measuring results, we can be sure the programs we support are really making a difference, and you can better measure how well your money is spent." Directly under this statement, to highlight the "Strengthening Children and Families" focus of UWEM, RRS was featured: "Rape Response's Sexual Assault Prevention in Public Schools program was presented to 2,359 students last year. After the program, 100% of the 4th-6th graders surveyed could identify examples of bullying and name two ways to help someone who is being bullied."

Success of the SCP at the University of Maine provided Moring with the incentive to implement programs and student leadership trainings at other area schools of higher learning. Photocopies of the new RRS poster were distributed in all the new student orientation packets at Eastern Maine Community College (EMCC) in Bangor to publicize the on-site hours that Moring had arranged. In place of the tear-off sheets on the poster, a printed notice read: "An advocate from Rape Response Services will be available to EMCC students on the first and third Tuesdays of every month from 5-6 P.M. at 120 Enrollment Office, Campus Center. Free and confidential."

Moring worked with the counseling center at Husson College to establish drop-in hours on campus four times during November and December. *The Spectator,* an in-house newsletter at Husson College, publicized this service:

> *We are extremely excited about the presence that Carrie Moring from Rape Response Services will have here. Carrie is an advocate for people who are or have been affected at any time by rape, incest, childhood sexual abuse, or sexual harassment. You don't necessarily have to be the individual who experiences sexual inappropriateness. This service is also intended for those who have family members or friends who have been involved with sexual trauma.*
>
> *The purpose of Rape Response Services is to give the individual who has been violated a sense of power and control over the situation.*

Carrie will be available for education about inappropriate sexual experiences. Not only will she discuss ways to help both female and male students stay sexually and legally safe, but also will explain how to proceed if an assault has already occurred. She will present options to students. These include legal options that are available to students, medical protocols, and assistance that is available during the time immediately following an assault. Carrie also has community resources to suggest for ongoing support.

The Rape Response Reporter

Over 700 copies of the summer newsletter were mailed or distributed in August to publicize the upcoming auction and other activities. A small box described the work that Carr-Slauenwhite (formerly Carr) was doing with Rainstorm Consulting to redesign the website: "A newly designed brochure-style website will provide more information and resources to the people of Penobscot and Piscataquis counties, including a feature that will allow the agency to post information about upcoming fundraisers and events. The current website was the first to be launched by a sexual assault center in Maine, and continues to receive hundreds of hits each month. It will still be accessible until sometime this fall when the new site will be launched. Please take the opportunity to log on to www.raperesponservices.org and check out the new look!"

Carr-Slauenwhite formatted and edited the newsletter again, and also wrote another thought-provoking article titled "Teens Under the Influence: Alcohol, Drugs, and Sex":

It's Monday morning. You're taking books out of your locker. Everyone in the hallway is quietly talking about the pit party on Saturday night. Who got really wasted, who got busted by the cops, and who was hooking up. You are trying to pretend you can't hear it. You are pretending you have something fascinating in the bottom of your backpack that is captivating your attention. You quickly gather your things and rush past the crowd, pretending you are late for an important class. All that you want to do is go home, and forget all about the party. All you want to do is pretend you were never there, and that nothing happened. Then you see him. He casually walks by you, not even acknowledging your existence. You are kind of relieved actually. What would you say to him anyway?

Unfortunately, this is a typical Monday morning for many teens. The number of teens that are partying, drinking, and doing drugs is staggering. Many of these teens are mixing sex with drugs and alcohol. In a recent survey of 15-24 year-olds done by the Kaiser Family Foundation, fifty percent said that "people their age" mix alcohol and drugs with sex "a lot." Over eighty percent of teens ages 15-17 said that their peers drink or use drugs before having sex either sometimes or a lot. In the same survey, over a third of teens and young adults said that their decisions about sex have been influenced by alcohol or drugs. Almost thirty percent have "done more" sexually than they had planned, as a result of drinking or doing drugs.

Another upsetting fact about this scenario is that it refers to a casual "hook up" with another person. An increasing number of teens states that they have or have had a "friends with benefits" arrangement with another person, have hooked up with someone, and/or know someone who has. No matter what language is used, it all describes the same situation: having a sexual relationship with someone with whom you don't have an emotional relationship. Much of the time, teens are engaging in these relationships while drinking or using drugs.

Making the connection between alcohol, drugs, and risky sexual activity isn't that difficult. It is hard to say which comes first, or that one leads to the other, but the facts show that for many teens, alcohol and drugs are closely linked to sexual activity. Many parents have had conversations with their teens about alcohol and drugs, and about the dangers of drinking and driving. Many parents, however, have probably not talked about the dangers of mixing sex with drugs and alcohol, even though the consequences can be just as life-altering. Teens get sent very clear messages about drinking and driving, but what messages are we sending about drinking and having sex?

It's not too late to initiate a conversation with a teen in your life about the party scene, drinking, and sex. Talk with her or him about some of the "hang-ups" of "hooking up." Ask, "What do you think the benefits really are in a 'friends with benefits' relationship?" Ask him or her to make decisions about sex when sober. Help them figure out how they can best stick to those decisions. Talk with her or him about how to show respect for another person, and how to get consent for sex…remind them that a person who is under the influence of alcohol or drugs can't give consent.

Moring's contribution to the newsletter was titled "A Year of Excellence in Education":

The education program at RRS has just completed a busy and productive year. In the greater Bangor area, we provided classroom presentations to 1,571 students in grades K-4, 1,307 students in grades 5-8, and 2,836 students in grades 9-12. An additional 3,533 students in grades 5-12 in northern Penobscot and Piscataquis counties received classroom programs presented by Robin Carr-Slauenwhite.

New activities are continually being added to the curriculum to make it more comprehensive. Evaluation tools for grades K-12 were implemented in order to accumulate raw data about the impact of our programs. Partial funding for the School-Based Education Program is provided by the United Way of Eastern Maine. Services to at-risk youth have increased during the past year. Programs and services are provided for young women at Mountain View Correctional Facility in Charleston. Residents at Shaw House have access to a weekly on-site advocate. A collaborative effort with Spruce Run provides bi-weekly programs at Penobscot Job Corps Center.

A plan is in place to expand the education and on-site programs to several local college campuses in September. Building on the success of the Safe Campus Project at the University of Maine, services will be offered at Husson College, Eastern Maine Community College, and University College, Bangor. As the RRS education program continues to expand, the youth who continue to be in need of our services remain at the forefront of our planning efforts. Sexual violence should never be suffered in silence. Any school or other youth organization that might benefit from RRS programs and advocacy is encouraged to call or email.

"A Powerful Presence in Piscataquis County" was written for the newsletter by Perry. She described the "wonderful" group of advocates in Dover-Foxcroft, and mentioned the RRS activities that had occurred in Piscataquis county, including child abuse prevention programs and the window display at Mr. Paperback.

Currie encouraged people to "Make a Difference in Your Community: Volunteer" by writing:

> *What a great group of volunteers we have at RRS! We offer volunteer possibilities in the Bangor, Dover-Foxcroft, and East Millinocket areas. The Bangor office covers all the hotline calls, and provides accompaniment to local hospitals, law enforcement offices, and to court. Volunteering at RRS is a rewarding experience for someone who is looking to be involved in her or his community.*
>
> *A forty-five hour training is offered twice a year, in September and April, at the Bangor office. Shorter trainings are held in Dover-Foxcroft and East Millinocket. Bangor advocates meet for two hours on the third Wednesday of each month in the evening to learn about current trends and changes, to process calls, and to offer support to each other. Advocates in Dover-Foxcroft and East Millinocket meet every other month. Pagers are provided to each advocate to allow flexibility in taking shifts and being on call. Advocates also help with tabling, brochure delivery, and with other activities during April, Sexual Assault Awareness Month.*
>
> *The next advocate training in Bangor will begin on September 15 and conclude October 24, running on Mondays and Thursdays from 5-8 P.M. A support group will begin on September 13 for nine weeks. If you are interested in being a volunteer at RRS, or if you would like information about support groups, please call or email.*

Hotline Volunteers

Advocates were always advised to use a secure telephone line when calling a client or when making any calls about a client, to ensure confidentiality. The preferred telephone at the time the first policy was adopted prior to 1994 was a corded landline phone. RRS Board members voted at their November 2005 meeting to revise the policy and allow the use of cellular phones. Cordless telephones were available in both analog and digital types, but analog could not be used for hotline calls because it did not provide a secure connection. A digital telephone could be used if the unit was fully charged, and if both call waiting and caller identification were blocked.

Several policies specifically related to advocates and volunteers were adopted or revisions approved by the RRS Board during the year. The "Policy on Active Status of Advocates," first revised in June 2002, began with a description:

> Responsibilities of advocates include talking to hotline callers, accompaniment to police or hospital, and follow-up. Advocates assist with hotline coverage on a twenty-four hour, seven day a week schedule. Advocates also may staff information tables at community events, distribute information in the communities throughout Penobscot and Piscataquis counties, and provide help as needed.

> Active Bangor Advocates are expected to:
> 1. complete the forty-five hour volunteer/advocate training
> 2. attend monthly Advocates' meetings, or schedule a one-on-one meeting with the Executive Director and/or Client Services Coordinator
> 3. take one or more hotline shifts per week

> Active Dover-Foxcroft/East Millinocket Advocates are expected to:
> 1. complete the fifteen-hour volunteer/advocate training
> 2. attend quarterly/monthly Advocates' meetings or schedule a one-on-one meeting with the RRS area staff person
> 3. take one week of on call or backup per month

> An Advocate may request a leave of absence from the hotline for no more than three months by calling the office and speaking to the Executive Director and/or Client Services Coordinator. If a leave of absence extends beyond three months, the Advocate will no longer be considered active, and will be sent a letter stating the reason and how to become active again. Advocates may end their affiliation with RRS through any of the following:
> 1. request of the Advocate
> 2. decision of the Executive Director and/or Client Services Coordinator, based on factors such as: poor attendance at

> Advocates' meetings, failure to meet with the Executive Director and/or Client Services Coordinator, unwillingness to take at least one hotline shift per week/month, or a violation of RRS Personnel Policies
> 3. failure to contact the Executive Director and/or Client Services Coordinator for three consecutive months

> Whenever a decision is made for an Advocate to not be involved with RRS, the Advocate will receive a written notice of their status and of what steps the Advocate can take to become active again. The Advocate will be required to turn in the pager. An Advocate who is not active for six or more consecutive months may be required to repeat some or all of the entire training before regaining active status. The decision to return to active status will be made after a meeting with the Advocate and the Executive Director and/or Client Services Coordinator.

For the first time, a distinction was made in the RRS policies between an advocate, who took hotline shifts, and a volunteer, who completed the training but did not want to be on the hotline. The "Guidelines for Volunteers" and the "Policy on Active Status of Volunteer" were similar to those for advocates, without mentioning hotline responsibilities. The Policy began with the statement: "A volunteer provides time by helping to support the work of RRS. Examples are staffing information tables at community events, distributing information in the communities throughout Penobscot and Piscataquis counties, or providing help with office tasks." A volunteer could request to be removed from the active list or could be removed due to failure to contact the RRS office staff for three consecutive months. Volunteers could keep current about RRS activities by attending advocates' meetings or contacting office staff. Any disclosures from members of the public to a volunteer while representing RRS were to be reported as soon as possible to the office for statistical purposes. Hours that volunteers spent representing the agency were recorded like hours on the hotline.

During four evenings at the end of June, RRS offered 12 hours of in-house group facilitator training using the TREM model, taught by Shaw, Nason, and Currie. Although no longer an employee of RRS, Nason volunteered her time to train group facilitators. Six advocates and staff completed the training and were available to co-facilitate groups: Nicole Hill, Theresa Lowell, Cindy Smith, Bean, Moring, and Hall. Moring and Currie began in August to co-facilitate a group of three in collaboration with Katahdin Friends Inc. (KFI) which had an office in the same building as RRS, and provided services for people with developmental disabilities. In addition to the KFI group, four support groups were co-facilitated during the year by various RRS individuals, both staff and volunteers, in Bangor and Dover-Foxcroft.

Eight new hotline advocates completed the spring or fall trainings, with social work students Nikki Hopkins (senior) and Anna Gardner (junior) in the latter group. Boynton, who had created the quilt displayed at Designing Women, was also part of the group. These new advocates joined what Walker referred to as a "large, loyal bunch" after the October meeting. Although inactive, Joe Sargent, who assisted with role plays at trainings, was available to talk with callers who requested a male advocate. The caller was to be asked if a follow-up call was agreeable, then Sargent would be contacted by backup to make that call.

Thanksgiving prompted Walker to write more than usual in *Our Monthly Advocate*:

> *Thanksgiving will be here in a week! Before giving in to the frenzy of eating and shopping, I like to take time for reflection on my reasons to be thankful. Obvious things like family, friends, good health, and home immediately come to mind. You have heard me say many times, "We could not do what we do without our volunteers." I hope each of you knows that this is another way of saying, "Thank you! Thank you! Thank you!" You all help me be very thankful that I live where I live and work where I work.*
>
> *The directors of the ten sexual assault centers in Maine recently held our annual retreat. Some of the directors were complaining about how many times they had to be on call on their hotline. Others suggested that before too long, "we will have to pay people to take shifts on the hotline." Almost every center except RRS has a shortage of hotline advocates, people like you who sign up every month to take shifts so that our staff members get a break from being on call. Thank you! Thank you! Thank you!*
>
> *I don't believe any center can make the claim, as we can, that*

our advocates stay with our agency for years and years of dedicated service. I'm thinking of Kristan who has been with us since 1994; Darlene since 1996; Sally, Kathy, and Jane in the Millinocket area since 1998; Gretchen and Alcinda since 1999. Thank you! Thank you! Thank you!

Some of you have joined our group of advocates more recently than 1999. Your willingness to sign up for shifts is also a cause for thanksgiving. Not only do we hold on to our volunteers, but we also recruit others like you who will stay with us for many years. Thank you! Thank you! Thank you!

Our hotline volunteers have always been called "advocates" in keeping with the practice throughout the state. Many people volunteer at RRS in a role other than advocate. They include: Board members; Carol, our clinical consultant; and all those who choose to volunteer in capacities other than the hotline (tabling, distributing posters, etc.) To everyone, volunteers and advocates, Thank you! Thank you! Thank you!

The ED reports for each month in 2005 provided Board members and others an opportunity to see just how busy the hotline volunteers were, often even busier than the same month during the previous year. A high for the year of 53 calls that required 30.5 hours of volunteer time was recorded in May. Some months had as few as 16 calls to the hotline. The enhanced hotline for callers with a mental illness consistently served from one to five individuals, often requiring more time from the RRS backup person who responded to these calls. As a relatively new phenomenon, the RRS website recorded as many as 4326 visits during April and from 2000 to 4000 visits in other months. A separate category was added to the DHHS statistical form for reporting website visits because other centers had followed the lead of RRS to create their own websites.

During this time, MECASA attempted to move forward with an online database of the monthly statistical reports. When Vyvyenne Ritchie left as the ED of Downeast Sexual Assault in Ellsworth, the statistical forms which had been mailed to her became the responsibility of Susan Koch at SACC to collect and compile into a calendar year spreadsheet. Copies of the forms were also mailed to the DHHS contract specialist.

These statistics were important not only to the state but also to MECASA for the annual revisions of the funding formula. Currie completed the hotline and group portions of the reports, and all staff members provided statistics for the community education portion. Walker typed and mailed the final document. Several MECASA-affiliated people had attempted to create database software. The cost of existing programs was prohibitive, and these often did not capture the information that was unique to Maine.

Personnel Changes

In preparation for the Board's ongoing discussion of transition planning for a new ED, Walker had prepared a list of the administrative tasks she performed at RRS:

- Budget
- Contract with DHHS
- Semi-monthly payroll and accounts payable
- Monthly payroll taxes
- Quarterly federal and state payroll tax reports and payments
- Annual W-2 and W-3 reports
- Annual 1099-Misc and 1096 reports
- Quarterly financial and narrative reports to DHHS
- Annual financial report to DHHS auditor
- Annual Federal Form 990
- United Way application
- Write all grant applications and requests for money from towns, etc.
- Deposit checks and reconcile checking account
- Sign all checks
- Purchase supplies and equipment for all offices
- Meet with insurance agent and complete all insurance applications
- Complete all staff evaluations and write memos to staff re: raises, etc
- Maintain employee files
- Maintain vendor files and contact vendors when services

needed
- Provide bi-weekly supervision for each staff member
- Facilitate staff meetings
- Participate in MECASA Board meetings, Augusta
- Maintain mailing list and complete all bulk mailings
- All paperwork for new employees
- Conduct annual United Way campaign at office
- Actively participate in planning and implementing fundraising activities
- Attend RRS Board meetings
- Write and review agency policies
- Write annual report
- Compile monthly program and support group stats and enter into database
- Preserve artifacts of RRS in scrapbooks
- Execute leases for office space in Bangor, East Millinocket, Dover-Foxcroft
- Advertise for and hire all staff
- Keep staff and Board informed about statewide and regional/local issues
- Write monthly ED report for Board and archives
- Develop and send agenda for Board meetings to members
- Help to recruit new Board members

Hartman attended a portion of a staff meeting without Walker to facilitate a discussion about the transition plans. A list of the most important characteristics that staff felt were necessary in a new ED was developed. The top priorities in descending order voted by the five staff members present included:

- Philosophy that we bring our services to rural communities and connect logistically to do good work (ED willing to go to satellite offices, upgrades on technology)
- Ability to do supervision and social work background—balance of personal support and clinical
- Not a micromanager—someone who has trust in staff

making own decisions

- Comfort with diversity of populations—not handing it off, but taking it on, meeting people where they're at, altering services and being creative (mental health consumers, men, elderly)
- MECASA—be able to deal with system issues state-wide as well as locally (politically savvy)

Other characteristics mentioned were:

- Knowledge of sexual assault issues
- Big picture person—media, organizational, meetings/ panels, fundraising/grant writing
- Frugal person
- Not someone who is completely hands off—availability to consult
- Someone open to learning what we do and offer ideas but respect staff knowledge
- Patience, flexible, accepting of staff, not going to do overhaul
- Someone who envisions staff and advocates having more access to board members (formally and informally)
- Understanding need for flexibility based on community needs
- Philosophy that we are not just an agency for women
- Commitment to finding populations that may be underserved—"our services are for everyone in Penobscot and Piscataquis counties"
- Not a consensus model and don't want to be one—want a leader who makes decisions
- Ability to model good boundaries (with staff, clients, community, and other agencies)
- Communication between ED and staff about big picture (good and bad)
- Ability to work with other agencies that can be challenging
- Someone who is truly invested in RRS and free and clear from other agencies

At a later meeting which Walker did not attend, the RRS board condensed these descriptions into their own list of characteristics for a new ED:

- Comfort and skill in dealing with the public
- Grant writing experience and/or knowledge
- Fundraising abilities
- Knowledge of sexual assault and its effects, and passion about the issue
- Attention to detail and ability to carry through on ideas
- Values
- Experience and knowledge of supervising a staff
- Willing to look at areas that need growth and help with it
- Bridge business and social agency work
- Assertive
- Willing to collaborate
- Compatible management style

Beginning to prepare for a smooth transition, Walker established the line of credit with BSB and met with a CPA, Ed Hopkins, in his office at 157 Park Street about doing the FY'05 compilation. The $50,000 line of credit at BSB cost $100 per year and provided slightly more than two-months' operating capital. Discovering that BSB would do payroll but not accounts payable for $50 per month, Walker initiated the Advanced Payroll System at BSB to begin January first, allowing also for automatic deposit of paychecks.

Prior to this time, health insurance premiums for RRS employees were paid in full. An increase in health insurance costs prompted a change in the personnel policies that was approved by the Board: "It is the policy at RRS that all full-time employees will be covered by health insurance. For health insurance purposes only, anyone who is employed 25 hours or more per week is considered full-time. RRS will pay 90% of the annual premium for health insurance, single coverage. The remaining 10% will be a payroll deduction for those employees covered by the RRS policy. Employees covered under another health insurance policy are required to provide annual proof of this coverage. Those employees so covered have the option of receiving monthly taxable dollars equal to 80% of the amount paid for a single premium, to be used at the discretion of the employee."

Personnel policies had initially been approved by the Board in October 1994, and were amended in March 1998, February 2001, and June 2001. Portions of the ten-page policies, especially the section titled "Ethics and Staff Standards," applied to both paid employees and volunteers, and covered such areas as confidentiality, boundaries, conflict of interest, non-discrimination, and substance abuse. Volunteers were provided with copies of the relevant portions at the completion of training. This section also specified: "media statements will be made, as appropriate, by the ED and/or Board designee. If a staff member, as a private citizen, wishes to make a public statement, the individual shall make it clear that s/he is neither acting in any capacity as an employee/ volunteer, nor is speaking for the agency."

Hiring procedures were covered in another section of the policies, and included a definition of probationary status (six months), regular full-time (40 hours per week), regular part-time (less than 40 hours per week), and temporary (specified, limited period of time not exceeding one year). Only temporary employees were ineligible for benefits, which were prorated for part-time employees. A two-week written notice of resignation was expected, and an exit interview would be conducted by the Board President and/or ED. Evaluation, disciplinary, and appeals procedures were spelled out in detail, especially for the ED, who was responsible for evaluating all other staff members at the end of their probationary period and annually in the anniversary month of employment. Disciplining and evaluating the ED was the responsibility of the Board. Personnel files were to be maintained in a secure location.

Twelve paid holidays were allotted to full-time employees with a prorated number for part-timers. In addition to the eleven regular observed holidays, a twelfth was designated a "day of choice" and could be Columbus Day, the employee's birthday, or Christmas Eve day. RRS in 1998 had instituted a policy of Paid Time Off (PTO) in lieu of vacation and sick time. PTO could also be used for personal or family business, or family emergencies. All requests for PTO had to be approved in advance by the ED or the Board. Only one month of PTO could be carried over into a new anniversary year, and unused PTO would be forfeited upon termination, as it carried no monetary value.

An extensive chart in the personnel policies delineated how much PTO the ED and the regular full-time and part-time staff would earn based on years of service. A new ED was eligible for five weeks or 200 hours in each of the first three years, reaching up to seven weeks after six years of service. Regular full-time employees received four weeks or 160 hours in each the first three years, and six weeks after six years. The policies also spelled out in detail how the PTO would be prorated for part-time positions that ranged from 10 hours per week to 35 hours. Paid bereavement leave of three days for full-time employees was also prorated for part-timers.

A section of the personnel policies dealt with office closings due to weather: "The ED or designee decides if the office is to be closed due to severe weather. If the office is to be closed all day, other staff will be notified prior to 8:00 A.M. Employees who cannot travel to the office as a result of severe weather conditions on a day when the office is open must notify the office prior to 9:30 A.M. No pay loss will result for any employee if the office is officially closed; the employee may work at home if s/he desires."

Other standard sections of the personnel policies covered injuries, family/medical leave, special educational leave, jury/court duty, and military leave. PTO accrued only during paid leave. In addition, the policies noted: "Training is an ongoing part of employment at RRS. The agency will provide in-service training for its employees when appropriate. All employees will be expected to participate in training activities from time to time as a means of improving job performance and the service of the agency." Employees were to receive written notice within 30 days of any changes made to the policies by the Board.

SART

Perry and Shaw had been working for several months with SART in Piscataquis and Penobscot counties to develop "First Responder Best Practices Guidelines for Sexual Assault." The tri-fold brochure was printed and distributed, with the support of a small grant from Penquis Resource Exchange, to all police departments in two counties. As noted on the front: "The Guidelines were created for officers as basic reminders of steps to follow when responding to sexual assault victim/survivors and to standardize the process." A description of a SART was also included: "Sexual Assault Response Teams promote multidisciplinary collaboration to create and maintain an effective victim-centered response to sexual violence." Across the top inside the brochure were the words, "Thank you for all you do." Printed on the back panel were telephone numbers to reach all the area hospitals, plus the toll-free RRS number, which was repeated in the center section.

"Attend to Victim/Survivor" was followed by the reminders to "approach victim in a supportive manner," and to "consider the physical and/or psychological trauma that has been endured." Other reminders were to "explain that you are there to help, and that the Victim/Survivor is now safe" and "assess safety and provide emergency medical aid." The officer could "encourage the victim/survivor to go immediately to the hospital for medical attention and evidence collection," and "if victim/survivor is declining to go to the hospital, encourage them to seek medical attention from their Primary Care Provider."

The very thorough brochure then highlighted evidence preservation: "Request that the victim/survivor not bathe, shower, douche, drink, smoke, brush teeth, urinate, defecate, wash or destroy clothing worn during the assault." The explanation to be given was that "there is a greater chance of collecting evidence" if these actions had not been taken, but it could also be stated that "evidence can still be collected if any of the above actions have been taken."

Protecting the victim's privacy was the next reminder. "If possible, limit traffic over police radio that would identify the victim/survivor," and "avoid questioning of the victim/survivor by multiple police officers." Officers were encouraged to hand out the RRS contact card and to make the victim/survivor aware of the toll free number. Securing and protecting the evidence included a reminder that there were multiple crime scenes: suspect, victim, clothing, and assault location (e.g.: bedding, seat covers, rugs). Complete contact information regarding the suspect and any witnesses was to be collected, as well as vehicle description if any, type of weapon if applicable, and direction of flight if relevant. As a reminder that the person reading the brochure was a first responder, the brochure noted: "unless you will be conducting the entire investigation, avoid unnecessary questioning of the victim and suspect." Answers to "who, what, where, when, how" were important in these first encounters.

The final inside panel reminded first responders to "avoid judgment or blame," and to "be supportive." Additional reminders included: "The crime of sexual assault may have occurred even if no visible evidence exists," and "Individuals will have varying emotional responses ranging from hysteria to a lack of emotion." An observational note could be made of the "victim/survivor's physical/emotional appearance, injuries, and damage to clothing," and of "any information that will be of value in establishing proof of compulsion or use of force, something that may not always be obvious."

Reminders for first responders at the hospital included "reassure victim/survivor." Noting that "trained medical/forensic personnel are available regardless of intention to prosecute," these individuals should be informed by the first responder of any evidentiary needs. The police interview would be conducted separately from the medical interview, so it was important to collect contact information for all persons present during the medical exam. If the suspect also required medical attention, the first responder was asked to "try to ensure that victim and offender do not see each other." When a urine sample was necessary because date-rape drugs were suspected, an officer's supervisor might need to approve this because storage requirements for the evidence collection kit were different if urine and/or blood samples were included in the kit.

Evidence storage practices were listed on the back of the brochure:

- "air-dry wet material prior to packaging
- use separate paper bags when packaging evidence
- do not use plastic bags
- seal bags with tape, not staples"

First responders were encouraged to photograph physical injuries and the crime scene. A suggestion could be made to the victim/survivor to return to the police department for additional photographs if bruising became more visible, or if the photographed bruises changed.

Annual Report and End-of-Year Fundraising Letter

The Annual Report for the fiscal year that ended September 30th listed Hartman as Board President; Greaney, Treasurer; Eddy, Secretary; and members Brown, Hatch, and Stormann. Taylor had resigned from the Board in June, and Brown moved out of the area and left the Board by the end of 2005. Recruiting new Board members was always an issue at RRS, as the agency struggled to maintain the minimum number of Board members (seven) as stated in the MECASA QA standards.

A decrease of 18 occurred in the number of sexual assaults that were reported to RRS as having occurred in FY'05. Five hundred twenty-two contacts had been made to the hotline by 163 clients who received 270.75 hours of service. School education and prevention programs reached 10,363 students in grades K-12 and college. The value of in-kind services provided by volunteers was conservatively estimated to be $113,758. Income for FY'05 included the DHHS contract at $178,350. Salaries and benefits ($197,745) were by far the largest expense. This appeared to be the last Annual Report prepared by RRS.

Appreciation was extended to RRS donors in the annual fundraising letter signed by Hartman and Walker, and sent in early December to about 130 individuals on the mailing list. The letter stated:

> *You are among the many loyal and generous donors to RRS over the past several years. Thank you for helping this agency grow into a safe and responsive place where anyone affected by sexual violence can find support every day and night of the year. Our education and prevention programs have also seen tremendous growth: in September 2005 alone, the school-based education presentations reached more than 850 K-12 students throughout Penobscot and Piscataquis counties. The majority of these students were enrolled in grades K-4.*
>
> *We wanted you to be among the first to know of some changes that are occurring at RRS. These changes, we believe, offer the possibility of continued growth for the agency, growth that is always focused on our mission.*
>
> • *Our website (www.raperesponservices.org) has been completely redesigned and revised to reflect the changing needs of the population that we serve. You're invited to log on and check out our new look. Feedback on the changes is welcome.*
>
> • *Our work that began as the Safe Campus Project at UMaine*

has a difference format, and is ongoing. Outreach to the other five college campuses has accelerated this fall.

- *Our Executive Director, Kathy Walker, will be retiring at the end of May 2006. After leading this agency through ten years of unprecedented growth, Kathy is going to pursue her hobbies of quilting, scrapbooking, genealogy, and travel. A statewide search will be launched in February for her successor. We encourage you to spread the word of this position opening to possible candidates. A master's degree and/or equivalent experience in managing a non-profit agency are among the requirements.*

These are difficult times with government funding cuts, with natural disasters throughout the world, and with the looming cold weather. Unfortunately, despite our prevention programs, women, men, and children continue to experience the trauma of sexual violence, and continue to need our services, services that are provided by no other agency in this area. We hope you will continue to be as generous with your year-end donation to RRS as you have always been.

As another year came to an end, a year filled with many high points, the question hanging over the center was: who will be the new ED? Board members, staff, and volunteers were all curious about how this change would impact not only RRS but each of them individually as well as the clients they capably served day in and day out.

2006: TRANSITION

Uncertainty marked the beginning of the new year for RRS. Not only did everyone wonder about who would replace Walker as ED, but the usual financial uncertainties continued to be evident. None of this, however, prevented RRS from initiating new programs and continuing all the successful outreach into the two counties.

Money Matters

The DHHS Department of Audit had notified RRS at the end of 2005 that the state expected to be paid, as cost-sharing, the $2506 in revenue over expenses that RRS had realized in the fiscal year ending on September 30, 2004. Although the Board had voted earlier in 2005 to place this revenue in the money market account, as recommended by Greenlaw, he had left DHHS in 2005. Noting that this represented 5.7% of the entire amount raised by RRS, the Board expressed frustration about being penalized for raising money, and directed Walker to appeal the decision. Journal entries recorded that she became "obsessed with resolving the situation in our favor." Greenlaw's replacement at DHHS "doesn't even want to get involved since it occurred on Greenlaw's watch." Walker's appeal letter "just asked for a chance to fix mistakes on reports that we did in good faith."

Early in January, Walker recieved the answer from DHHS to her appeal letter: the amount owed was reduced to $1990! With the Board's approval five days later, Walker sent a letter to Governor Baldacci, detailing concerns about the DHHS claim on the RRS funds, money which he had actually helped raise at the 2004 auction. Walker later received a couple of supportive telephone calls regarding the letter from Mullen-Giles, who was then employed in the Governor's office.

The uncertainty about this situation made Walker nervous when completing the FY'05 reports, wondering what claims would be made for cost-sharing. This angst, however, was lifted with a telephone call from the DHHS Department of Audit near the end of January, saying that RRS did not owe any money! Walker wrote in her journal: "letter to Governor Baldacci may have produced results at Audit." The FY'05 compilation which Walker could then finish showed net assets over expenditures of $650, and Walker was optimistic that these overages were not large enough for DHHS to consider for cost-sharing.

In early February, Walker submitted a grant proposal to the Agnes M. Lindsay Trust for upgraded office equipment totaling $4933. The last grant had been received in March 2002, and a three-year wait between proposals was required. A letter to Susan Bouchard at the Trust described the request:

- Toshiba Tecra A5-S516 laptop (includes Windows XP Prof) ($1248)
- Dell 1100MP projector for Power Point (3-yr warranty) ($829)
- Carrying case for laptop ($100)
- 512 Mb USB drive for laptop ($30)
- Wireless router for laptop ($75)
- Dell Dimension E310 Intel Pentium 4 Processor 521 (2) ($1418)
- Windows XP Professional for above (2) ($298)
- HP DeskJet 6540 printer ($130)
- QuickBooks Pro 2006 software ($180)
- Software licenses for laptop and new computers ($100)
- Estimated labor for installing above (15 hours @ $35/hr) ($525)

The letter went on to explain: "RRS currently borrows the equipment needed to provide PowerPoint presentations, but borrowing is not always convenient or possible as more trainings are provided. The two Dell computers replace two Gateways that were obtained in 1997, one for the Bangor office and one for the Dover-Foxcroft office. The printer replaces one that has been used in the Bangor office for many years and is leaking ink." Falk had consulted with Walker about the specifications, and CPA Hopkins recommended QuickBooks to replace Peachtree.

Beta Theta Pi hosted their thirteenth annual sleep out in mid-February to benefit RRS. Walker made remarks at the beginning of the event, and was interviewed on two television stations. Large posters advertising the sleep out were placed around the University campus and in surrounding communities. "Buy a ticket. Win stuff. Help Rape Response." appeared in large print at the top of the posters, with "Help us help rape victims" underneath. According to an article by Daniel Dumais in *The Maine Campus* on January 30th: "The Sleep Out hopes to not only raise money but also awareness in the community. In 2002, six cases of forcible sex offenses were reported to Public Safety. That number grew to seven the next year, and in 2004, it increased to nine. Kathy W. Walker, executive director of Rape Response Services, said, 'During the past 12 months, 55 sexual assaults were reported to this agency, fewer than in previous years, but still far too many. Beta is trying to reduce these numbers and to give a voice to the victims, and we are very appreciative of these efforts.'"

An article in the February 9th issue of *The Weekly* was written by Andrew Knapp, the public relations/philanthropy chairman of Beta. Titled "Fraternity 'sleep out' to aid rape crisis center," the opening words echoed *The Maine Campus* about the number of reported rapes at the University. Knapp noted that the 2005 event had raised $1000 and had attracted more than 300 individuals. Beta wanted to "surpass the money raised by last year's event by a substantial amount." Walker was again quoted: "This annual sleep out provides an excellent opportunity to raise awareness about sexual assault and the services provided by this agency. The commitment of the brothers and other community members is outstanding, generating extensive media coverage for both organizations." Averill's column in the BDN on the 16th mentioned the sleep out and quoted Walker: "Kathy Walker, executive director of RRS, reports the organization 'is honored' to have been chosen 'as the recipient of the funds' raised during the sleep out."

During the same weekend as the sleep out, another production of "The Vagina Monologues" was staged by SWA at the University of Maine to benefit RRS and SR. Walker was able to make opening remarks at all three performances during the weekend, and again presented carnations to the cast members after the last performance. Many events like this were the last ones Walker would be attending as ED; in her journal she observed: "each 'last time' gives me pause."

Walker's last appearance at a budget meeting of the Hermon Town Council in April resulted in an increase of $50 in their allotment, in honor of her retirement. The office equipment grant of $4933 from the Agnes M. Lindsay Trust was also awarded to RRS in April. At the end of May, Walker sent a follow-up letter to Bouchard:

> *As promised, I am providing you with an update on the office equipment grant of $4933 that the Trust generously provided to RRS last month. All of the equipment has been purchased and is operating, much to the delight of staff.*
>
> *The most accolades have been centered on the PowerPoint equipment (projector and laptop). Three staff members have received some training in the use of this equipment. One staff member has used it four times already to make presentations on Internet safety for separate groups of students and parents in the Greenville and Guilford school districts. These are two of our most rural areas of Piscataquis County, and the ability to reach people with this up-to-date technology has greatly enhanced our outreach offerings.*
>
> *A successful conversion has been made on the Executive Director's new Dell computer from Peachtree to QuickBooks, all thanks to the grant from the Trust. The remaining Dell is ready for use at one of the satellite offices as soon as the part-time staff member in that office has time away from doing Power Point presentations to be in her office.*
>
> *I will retire at the end of next week. This grant has allowed me to leave the agency knowing that the staff has the technology needed to move forward with a new Executive Director. Thank you again for this award.*

Personnel Changes

At the January Board meeting where Walker received approval to write the appeal letter to the Governor, transition planning began in earnest. Eddy agreed to draft the job ad for a new ED, and Hartman the job description. Hatch would develop a rubric for scoring the resumes. Interview questions were to be formulated by Greaney with Walker's assistance. A special Board meeting was scheduled at the end of February to score the resumes and choose candidates to interview, a meeting in which Walker agreed to participate. After that meeting, she would no longer be involved in the interview and selection process.

On the first day of February, Walker sent her official retirement letter to Hartman and members of the Board:

> *This letter is the "formal" piece of the discussion of my retirement that has been ongoing for several months. I hereby give notice that I am retiring as Executive Director of Rape Response Services, effective June 3, 2006. It is not expected that I will have a lot of vacation time to be used by that date. I will be available at the office for about a month to provide support to the new Executive Director.*
>
> *In mid-May I will complete ten years as Executive Director at this agency. They have been years of tremendous growth for Rape Response Services. I am pleased to have been a part of the exciting endeavors and new initiatives that have occurred during my tenure here. I appreciate the confidence that has been placed in me by current and past Board members, and I wish each of you and the agency all the best in future years.*

Despite the letter, the retirement became a true reality on the weekend of February 5th when the position opening appeared in the BDN, the *Maine Sunday Telegram*, central Maine newspapers (*Morning Sentinel* and *Kennebec Journal*), and on the RRS website. The advertisements cost over $1650 to run and all read as follows:

> *Executive Director*
> *Rape Response Services*
> *Rape Response Services, a sexual assault agency providing support and education for more than seventeen years to people affected by rape, incest, childhood sexual abuse, or sexual harassment, is seeking an experienced, energetic and talented leader.*
>
> *Applicants must have knowledge of and sensitivity for issues of sexual assault, and be supportive of the agency's mission. Excellent written and verbal communication skills, and strong organization, fundraising, and grant writing abilities are required.*

The successful applicant will have experience in managing a non-profit agency including financial management, supervision, and program development. A demonstrated ability to work collaboratively with diverse populations, community social service agencies, and law enforcement agencies throughout Penobscot and Piscataquis Counties is essential to this position.

Master's degree in related field preferred; bachelor's degree in related field required. Anticipated start date is early May. Send resume and letter of interest including views on sexual violence prevention to: Search Committee, Rape Response Services, P.O. Box 2516, Bangor, ME 04402-2516. Please respond no later than February 24, 2006. No phone calls please.

An "Update on Transition" was written by Walker for the February issue of *Our Monthly Advocate:*

Applications for the position of Executive Director are starting to arrive following the appearance of the ad in the major newspaper markets on February 4th or 5th. The last day for interested parties to respond is February 24th. On March 6th, the Board of Directors will meet to open and review the applications. I will be involved in that first look at applications, and then I will remove myself from any further input into the hiring process.

Interviews will be scheduled during March. The top one or two candidates will be invited for a second interview, following the format that we have used at the office for hiring other staff members. Each person invited back will be asked to provide a short presentation in front of Board and staff members and any advocates who would like to attend. These second interviews will be held in late March or early April. If any advocate or volunteer is interested in attending these second interview presentations, please notify Ann Hartman, our Board President, at 327-4676. Please call her directly; do not leave messages for her at the RRS office.

The final decision will be made by the Board of Directors after hearing input from staff and advocates. I am especially hopeful that advocates from the Millinocket and Dover areas will be involved, and will feel that they are a part of the hiring process. It is expected that a new Executive Director will begin work in early May. My last day of employment is June 3rd. I intend to work about a month in overlap with the new Executive Director.

Some people have asked about my plans for continued involvement with RRS. I will not volunteer on the hotline for at least a year or more, nor will I take on any other capacity at this agency, in fairness to the new Executive Director. You are all my friends, however, as well as being advocates/volunteers at RRS. Nothing will prevent this friendship from continuing with those of you who wish to stay in touch. I do not need to know what is occurring at the agency, but I will still be interested in each of you personally. You know how much I enjoy sending and receiving cards and notes!

Questions have also been asked about a retirement party for me. No one is planning to surprise me, thankfully! Ann is looking at the possibility of some event in April. Again, if you're interested in helping plan this, please get in touch with Ann. Thanks for your interest in supporting both RRS and me during this transition process.

A Board meeting early in March provided an opportunity to review the five applications that had been received for the ED position. Everyone had expected there would be more. Three candidates were selected for the first interview to be held later in the month. A salary range of $45,000 to $50,000 was discussed.

Ordway wrote about Walker's retirement in her April 7th BDN column:

When Walker was pegged 10 years ago to head RRS, she wasn't new to public service. She had served as the mayor of Hampden and as the clerk of Penobscot County. This week, I learned that Walker was preparing for her retirement. Since 1994, when she first took the volunteer training for RRS, she has answered the call from rape victims across Penobscot and Piscataquis counties. She has since taken the agency from a fledgling $60,000 annual budget to its $300,000 budget today. Back then, she was the only employee. Today she has five employees plus herself and 30 volunteers. Last year her agency reached 11,000 schoolchildren in the two counties, teaching everything from "bad" touching and "good" touching to gender identity and bullying issues.

For 10 years, I have watched her make compelling cases to lawmakers as she fought for strong laws to support victims of sex crimes and domestic violence. She wasn't always that way. "I remember when I first went to a middle school and this teacher said to me, 'You don't know how it is. These girls just ask for it in the way that they dress and act,' she recalled this week. "I remember looking at this teacher and saying, 'How sad it is for you and them that you think that way because if you think for even a moment that anyone is asking to be raped, then you really don't have a clue as to what rape really means,' she said. "That was a lot for me to say back then. Until that moment, I didn't think I had that kind of confrontation in me."

Walker has come a long way. Today she is a woman who composes letters to the editor in her head as she drives down the road. She becomes infuriated when people talk about sexual perpetrators as those who "fit the profile" and those who don't. Walker has managed to forge much-needed relationships with other agencies in the state and has been a tireless advocate for those who have suffered trauma. "Trauma can't be fixed completely, but talking helps," she said. Walker grew with her role as executive director of RRS, and the agency benefitted.

Hartman informed Walker early in April that Kim Roberts, the ED of MCEDV, whose office was directly across Park Street from RRS, had accepted the offer to be the ED at RRS. A journal entry on that date noted that Walker was pleased: "She is known, in the state and to me, and will carry the center forward." Roberts had moved from Maryland to assume the MCEDV position four years earlier, and was involved in many of the statewide groups in which Walker was also a participant. It was hoped that Roberts could participate in the advocate training which had just begun.

Words of welcome from Walker in the April issue of *Our Monthly Advocate* began:

The Board of Directors and I are pleased to welcome Kimberly Roberts, MSW as the new ED at RRS. Kim will begin her position here on May 15th and will overlap with my tenure for about two weeks. I expect to be done before Memorial Day, using a week of vacation before my "official" retirement date of June 3rd. Kim, we believe, has the enthusiasm, vision, and talent to guide this agency into the future. Several years ago, Kim was an intern at her local rape crisis center, staying on as a volunteer after the internship ended. She took the training then and performed all the tasks that our volunteers do, including hotline shifts and hospital/court accompaniment. Now Kim is taking parts of the training here as a refresher, and to become familiar with the area agencies with whom we collaborate.

I want to express appreciation to all the members of the RRS Board of Directors for long hours spent in the hiring process. Under the leadership of Ann Hartman, President, Board members were dedicated to carrying out the transition plan that has been in place for about a year. Thank you, Board members! Welcome, Kim!

Hartman signed a letter to over 600 donors and friends of RRS on May 1st, informing them of the transition:

On behalf of the Board of Directors of RRS, I am writing to update you on the change in Executive Director at the agency. As many of you already know, Kathy Walker retires at the end of May after ten years of dedicated service.

Kathy has facilitated incredible growth and financial stability at RRS, and has helped to revitalize this agency as a respected resource throughout Penobscot and Piscataquis counties. She has built strong collaborations with diverse community partners, resulting in better services and supports for victims/survivors of sexual violence and their families. In her role as Executive Director, Kathy has brought expertise about sexual violence and trauma, passion for the agency's mission, and management, administrative, and supervisory skill. We have been so fortunate to have had Kathy with us, and we'll always remember her contributions. It is with love and admiration that we wish her all the best in her retirement.

We are very excited to welcome Kim Roberts, MSW as our new Executive Director. Kim comes to us after serving for four years as the Executive Director of the Maine Coalition to End Domestic Violence. Kim has worked in the non-profit field for the past eighteen years, gaining considerable experience and skill in advocacy, public policy, media and public relations, program development, and fundraising/grant writing. Her interest and dedication to the field of sexual violence began with her own volunteer work at a rape crisis center in the late 1980s, and her master's thesis focused on sexual violence. Kim brings a wealth of experience and accomplishments to her new position at RRS, and we feel very fortunate to have her join our agency. Kim plans to begin work on May 15th. I invite you to join us in warmly welcoming Kim to her new position. Thank you for your continued support of RRS and its mission throughout this transition process.

School-Based Programs

Starting early in the spring semester on the University of Maine campus, Carr-Slauenwhite co-taught with Tina Roberts from SR, a weekly course for which students could earn credits on interpersonal violence. Seven students were enrolled in the course. The curriculum had been developed the previous fall by Roberts and Walker, with input from Nason and Carr-Slauenwhite, but at that time, it was unclear as to whether the format would be a course or training. Some of the SCP grant funds to RRS paid Carr-Slauenwhite for an additional five hours per week. The RRS Board approved Walker's recommendation that Carr-Slauenwhite's hours remain at thirty per week after the SCP funding ended.

"Sexual violence a crime" was the title of a letter from Walker to the BDN, published on January 13th. This letter also mentioned the importance of the school-based programs at RRS:

A recent quote tells me how far we still have to go in our education efforts. At a sentencing for someone convicted of unlawful sexual behavior with a 13-year-old, a social worker pleaded for leniency because "the man does not fit the typical sexual offender profile."

If only there were such a profile! How convenient it would be if we could warn our children to stay away from certain people because they look or act like sex offenders. To further suggest that this particular offender "does not constitute a danger to anyone" is a slap in the face to the young woman who was his victim. She was threatened, and continues to live in fear because of the sexual abuse.

After presenting education/prevention programs to more than 10,000 K-12 students in Penobscot and Piscataquis counties in 2005, Rape Response Services is concerned when comments like these are made. Members of the public still do not want to believe that people commit crimes against children. Victim-blaming statements and ignorance of the impact of sexual violence on the victim are also widespread.

The sex offender registration process may even be experiencing a backlash, as juries and even judges ignore taped confessions, return not guilty verdicts, and accept plea bargains, thereby keeping people from being added to the registry. We have a sense of complacency about the registry, as if it is informing the public about all the sex offenders in our communities, instead of the relatively small number who have been caught and convicted of sex crimes against a minor.

A crime of sexual violence is the sole responsibility of the person who commits the crime. People make a choice to engage in this type of criminal behavior, and use power and control to carry it out. Making excuses for their criminal behavior only adds to the long-term impact of sexual violence on the victim.

Additional personnel news at RRS occurred in March when Moring left. Cindi Amato at SARS in Portland told Walker about a former employee there, Marcie Oechslie, who now lived in the Bangor area and might be interested in the vacant position. As soon as Moring gave her notice, Walker contacted Oechslie, and they came to an agreement that she would work temporarily during March, job shadowing Moring for a week and fulfilling the commitments that Moring had made for presentations in local schools. By the end of March, however, Oechslie had also left RRS. Student intern Hopkins filled some gaps in the schedule, and some school presentations were cancelled. The Board, acting on Walker's recommendation, decided that an educator would be hired by the new ED.

Despite the turnover within the position of School-Based Educator, over 2500 students in grades K-12 were reached by 135 RRS programs during the first three months of the year, with Carr-Slauenwhite, Moring, Hopkins, Oechslie, or Shaw as presenters. In April and May, Carr-

Slauenwhite alone provided school presentations, grades 5-12, for almost 1400 students in the two counties. Only the elementary programs were missing. Many staff members helped to make sure that drop-in hours continued at Penobscot Job Corps, Shaw House, Husson College, and EMCC.

Sexual Assault Awareness Month

The Stay-at-Home Ball on the first day of April was again hosted live on WEZQ 92.9, this time with Dorian Daniels and Walker from 7 to 9 P.M. Daniels had interviewed Walker on the radio several times in the past, and Walker wrote in her journal that the ball was "fun and relaxed." For the first time, two pledges totaling $125 were received on the air. Over 500 invitations to the Ball had been mailed in mid-March. One donor whom Walker knew by name only, not personally, had consistently contributed $1000 or more to the Ball, and this year gave $1250, a most welcome gift.

Perry and Walker met at Mr. Paperback in Dover-Foxcroft early in April to set up the window display for Sexual Assault Awareness Month. This year the focus was sunflowers with the RRS banner, a bouquet of silk sunflowers, and signed sunflowers collected at the Business Expo in Guilford the previous weekend. Fifty people had stopped by the RRS table at the Expo to sign the sunflowers, tie ribbons on the tree, or both.

Other community education events in April included tabling at the H.O.P.E. Festival, where Currie, Hopkins, and Walker distributed brochures and teal ribbons to 100 attendees, and at EMCC where Currie reached 44 students with ribbons and brochures. Requests for brochures and posters at both John Bapst High School (70) and Hermon High School (100) were received and filled despite the absence of a local educator to deliver them.

The last letter Walker wrote to the BDN as ED was published on April 21st, titled "Zero violence tolerance":

> *April is Sexual Assault Awareness Month. No one, however, wants the murder of sex offenders to be the reason why we're more aware of sexual violence in our communities. Sympathy is extended to the families of the two men who lost their lives on Easter Sunday.*

The sad truth is that violence in any form often leads to more violence.

The sex offender registry in each state was established to increase safety for our children. It began as a grass-roots effort in Washington state after a young girl was raped and murdered by a convicted sex offender who had moved into her neighborhood. Now parents and other interested citizens have the opportunity to go online and determine if any convicted sex offenders are living in their communities. Parents can then talk with their children about how to stay safe from sexual predators.

Sex offenders do not get on the registry unless they have been convicted of a sex crime and serve time in jail. This means that everyone on the registry has been found guilty by a jury or judge and sentenced by a judge. Some individuals may still claim they are innocent. It is difficult to get a jury in Maine to convict someone of a crime of sexual violence, so when a guilty verdict is handed down, there is compelling evidence to indicate that the individual is not as innocent as claimed.

The registry also does not include any information about sexual predators who have never been caught, convicted, or served time in jail. These individuals reside in many of our communities and are a potentially more dangerous threat to our children because of their anonymity. Keeping our children safe requires all of us, parents, legislators, educators, and the general public, to speak out against sexual abuse and victim-blaming. Zero tolerance for violence of any form is something to consider during April and every month of the year.

Hotline Volunteers

The March issue of *Our Monthly Advocate* contained an article by Walker titled "April: Sexual Assault Awareness Month and Volunteer Appreciation Month":

That both these events should fall during the same month seems just right because without you, our volunteers, RRS "could not do what we do" in April or in the other eleven months of the year. Thank you! Whether you are a hotline advocate, a Board member, or a volunteer in some other capacity, you are appreciated.

Each year in April, MECASA presents the Make a Difference
Award to an individual or group who has demonstrated a steadfast
commitment to the statewide mission of MECASA. This year you,
the volunteer hotline advocates at this and at each of the other nine
sexual assault crisis centers in Maine, will be honored with the Make
a Difference Award at the Blaine House Tea in Augusta on Thursday,
April 20 from 2 to 3:30 in the afternoon.

I have provided mailing labels to the MECASA office, and an
invitation to the tea will be mailed to your home. Recognizing that not
everyone can attend an event at this time of day, one representative
from each center will be present to pick up the certificates. Darlene
has agreed to represent RRS at the Tea. Any other volunteer hotline
advocate who receives the invitation is welcome to attend as well.
Please call the Bangor office to arrange for carpooling from here.

This statewide recognition of the work that you do, day in and
day out, is well-deserved. In the past fiscal year, the volunteer hotline
advocates at this agency alone provided almost $114,000 worth of
services. Long after I have retired and moved on, I hope you will
remember my words, "We could not do what we do without our
volunteers." It has been a privilege to know and to work with each of
you, in Dover-Foxcroft, Millinocket, and Bangor.

Bean, Smith, and Hopkins, along with Currie and Walker,
attended the event in Augusta. Personalized certificates were given to all
the advocates at their subsequent meetings in Bangor, Millinocket, and
Dover-Foxcroft.

The newsletter also included several tips for advocates that Currie
had pulled together as reminders and updates:

While at a hospital call, please remember to ask the victim/
survivor if she or he would like a follow-up call. If yes, ask for a
number to be called or an email address. For some, email is easier
and can be more private. If a call back is not wanted, remind her or
him to call the hotline.

If the nurse at the hospital is not familiar with the sexual
assault exam, let her know that there are step-by-step instructions in
the evidence collection box. These instructions are on the top inside

the cover of the box. While supporting a victim/survivor, if there are others waiting for her/him who also need support, call backup to be with these individuals. Your first obligation is to the victim/survivor, no matter what.

While on the hotline, if anyone inquires about support groups, remember to get a name, number, or email address, and what type of details to leave in the call back message. Let the caller know that you will give the information to the office, and someone will return the call. If someone calls the hotline from out of state, you can give our local hotline number (207/989-5678) because the toll-free number will not work outside Maine. Collect calls are accepted if the caller wishes to use the local number, or get the caller's number and call her or him back. Remember that RRS reimburses you for toll calls if you submit a copy of your phone bill.

Ardeana Hamlin from the BDN interviewed Bean and wrote an excellent article about volunteering for RRS, "Hotline volunteer relishes opportunity to help people." Appearing in the April 27th issue of *The Weekly*, Hamlin's article noted:

Darlene Bean's calm, quiet voice is one of her best assets as a hotline volunteer at RRS in Bangor. "Talking is the start of healing," she said. When her pager goes off and she returns the call, she never knows what she will hear. But chances are pretty good that it will be someone who is, or has been, the victim of sexual assault. Last year, 157 sexual assaults were reported in Penobscot and Piscataquis counties.

"My role is to get them through the crisis," said Bean, a 10-year volunteer at RRS. All information the caller shares with Bean is confidential and the caller is often anonymous, except for the sharing of a first name. The caller might be describing the crisis that ensues immediately after being raped, or maybe an emotional crisis that happens months, or even years, later. Bean's job is to listen and offer unconditional acceptance to the caller.

"We do a lot of support," she said. "We help callers [in emotional crisis] become calm and we help them brainstorm what they can do to get through the crisis. Sometimes it's as simple as suggesting they

make a cup of tea. Or we may ask if they need to call a counselor or therapist. We don't tell them what to do, we offer options. We let them know we are there for them." Sometimes a caller doesn't know what to call what has just happened to her. "They ask, 'Was I raped? What do I need to do? How do I get a referral to a counselor?'" Bean said. "I tell the caller I'm glad she called. I ask what she wants to do. Does she want to see a doctor? Does she want to go to the emergency room? Does she want to report the assault to the police? Does she want me to accompany her to the hospital? Does she want to see a counselor? I help her sort out the options. If she wants me to, I meet her at the hospital. We don't tell the caller what to do."

But it's not just women's voices Bean hears at the other end of the line. Sometimes it's a man who has been raped. "It's a myth that only women are raped," Bean said. "Men are raped, too—by women or other men. It's not about sex. It's about power and control."

One small down side of being a volunteer, Bean said, is that she doesn't always know the outcome of the situation the caller describes. "I have no way to know if the victim is safe or has resolved the issue." Bean is happy with her experience of volunteering at RRS. "It's a great agency. It's a very educational experience," she said. "I've learned a lot from being here. I feel that I am making a difference. Communication between staff and volunteers is very open. If we have taken calls that have been hard to listen to, clinical support from counselors is available to us." After ten years of volunteering, Bean has developed a philosophy about what she does. "If I've helped another, I've helped me. It's the kind of work where someone else needs you. We all want to be needed."

During the first five months of the year, RRS advocates had responded to 191 hotline calls, providing over 120 hours of volunteer service to the agency. In addition, the enhanced hotline, funded by DBDS, had taken calls from 24 individuals totaling 31 hours. Visits to the website during the period from January through March ranged from a low of 899 to a high of 1346, and included four inquiries that required an online response.

Bean and Currie completed part two of a TREM support group for four individuals, and co-facilitated training for six new advocates and

Roberts. Another support group began for new participants as soon as the previous one ended, meaning that a long-time RRS goal of providing ongoing groups had been realized. Perry and Shaw continued to carry out court watch programs in both counties, making sure the RRS presence was known in that venue.

A Community Presence

Trainings for community groups were facilitated by various RRS staff members. Carr-Slauenwhite and Perry gave a presentation on safety for a large group of life skills clients at CH&CS in Dover-Foxcroft. Best practices with people who had experienced rape were reviewed by Shaw in two-hour trainings at St. Joseph ER and for Region V law enforcement officers. Copies of the Best Practices Guidelines were mailed to police chiefs and sheriffs in the two counties.

The first of April found Walker at Hampden Public Safety to provide 2.5 hours of training about community notification of sex offenders to 54 police officers from around the state. She spoke primarily about the RRS experience of working with the local sheriffs' departments at community meetings. The following day, she provided a one-hour training session about responding to disclosures of sexual abuse for 18 adult crisis workers at CH&CS in Bangor.

Community sex offender notification meetings were held in Glenburn and in Greenbush in late April, attended by 11 and 15 people respectively. Walker wrote in her journal after the Glenburn meeting: "What I'll miss is that: speaking briefly in front of a group or on TV, to provide information. And writing editorials for the same reason."

Walker's last interview with Grover was aired in early May. She wrote in her journal: "It was bittersweet, ending a long-lasting collaboration. He did a good job as usual with segment, and pulled in an old clip of me without gray hair!" Grover had interviewed her at the WABI-TV Channel 5 studio earlier in the year, covering a wide range of topics that were aired during at least five segments of morning and evening newscasts, and precipitating a journal note that Grover "does such a good job of making me look better than expected."

A SCAN committee meeting, also Walker's last, was held early in May at EMMC with nine people present, including Hopkins who presented her findings from a child abuse needs assessment and research that she did during her RRS internship, looking at whether a Child Advocacy Center (CAC) would be supported in Bangor. Hopkins had traveled to Lewiston to view the CAC there, and shared photos from her visit. Walker noted in her journal that "I was pleased with Nikki's presentation." This was a follow-up to a presentation made at the SCAN meeting in February 2005 by Ann Lynn. Hopkins' written report described a CAC as:

> *...an agency that brings together law enforcement, child protective services, prosecutors, victim advocacy, child advocacy, and the mental health and medical communities to address the issue of child abuse. These members are referred to as a Multi Disciplinary Team (MDT). Each center is different and is built to address communities' specific needs. Some advocacy centers offer everything at the center. For instance, some centers offer interviews, medical examinations, family support groups, kids' groups, mental health services, and case tracking. Other centers offer a combination of their own services with referrals. An example of this would be a center doing interviews, family support groups, medical examinations, case tracking, and then referring their patients to other community agencies for the rest of the services they need. One thing that all CACs offer is a child appropriate, child friendly facility. All centers are comfortable, private, and physically and psychologically safe for clients. The whole philosophy behind a CAC is to do what is in the best interest of a child.*
>
> *A CAC is an agency that receives clients through referrals. These referrals come from either law enforcement or DHHS. A CAC won't accept referrals from any other agency. Once a child makes a disclosure of abuse, DHHS will go and do a safety assessment with the child. If the lead investigator feels a case is appropriate for referral to the CAC then the CAC Coordinator will contact all members of the MDT to form an investigative team for that particular case. Depending on safety and other circumstances, an interview with the child will be scheduled. Some CACs try to arrange this interview within 24 hours; other agencies arrange it within three to five days.*
>
> *One of the main purposes of a CAC is to reduce the number of interviews a child has to go through. Once an interview has been set*

up, the MDT comes together to discuss the case. When the child comes to the CAC, she or he is met by the victim advocate, and introduced to other team members. A child is then led into the interview room. The only person in the room with the child is the forensic interviewer who will typically be a member of law enforcement. All other members of the team will be in a different room watching the interview on a closed circuit television. A telephone will be in each room. At the end of the interview the MDT members can call into the room to ask new questions, or have some of the earlier questions clarified or elaborated. After the interview, and once the child leaves, the team will have a debriefing and decide on the appropriate steps to take.

During this interview process, if appropriate, the child's family will accompany her or him to the CAC. Parents will not be able to sit in on the interview with the child, or view the interview with the MDT. They will be talking with the victim advocate in a room separate from both the child and the MDT. If it isn't appropriate for a child to be accompanied to the CAC with a parent, the child will be accompanied by either a guardian or a caseworker. It's also usually appropriate only for a case to be referred to the CAC if the investigation is in its early stages. If a case already has a history of investigative interviews regarding the same incident, the case will not be accepted unless a recommendation is made by the prosecutor assigned to the case.

There are many different ways to get funding for a CAC. One of the major ways is through the National Children's Alliance (NCA). This program is a non-profit agency that oversees the CACs around the country. They oversee establishing new CACs and maintaining CACs that already exist. The NCA also provides funding for CACs through different grants. One of the grants they offer is a non-member development grant. This grant is for groups that don't have a CAC but would be interested in establishing one. The Androscoggin CAC received $50,000 in 2005 and $50,000 in 2006 through this grant. Other possible funding sources could be organizations like rotary clubs, the United Way, fundraising, and donations. It is also possible that Penobscot Pediatrics might be willing to help look for money in the Bangor area.

The NCA also provides grants for associate members and

full members. A CAC becomes either an associate member or a full member once they meet certain NCA criteria. To be an associate member you have to be well into the process of developing a CAC. To become a full member, your agency has to meet a certain set of standards. Some of these standards include having a child friendly facility, having an MDT, doing case review, and case tracking, just to name a few. The benefit of meeting these requirements is that both memberships have a grant that goes with them. Potential funding through the NCA doesn't end once you get a CAC up and running.

Hopkins went on to write in her report that she gathered her information through interviews with SCAN members including Lt. Paul Kenison, Bangor Police Department; Detective Jameson; Bobbi Johnson, DHHS; and Dr. Eric Brown, and Pat Philips, LCSW, both from EMMC. Other people interviewed were Jessica Pooler at the DA's office and Bridget O'Rourke, coordinator of the Androscoggin CAC. Written materials Hopkins consulted were from the Androscoggin CAC and from NCA. Her written report continued with a description of the pros and cons:

One of the best things about a CAC is the fact that it benefits children (under age 18 at time of abuse). Everything a CAC does has a child's best interest at heart. The CAC is a comfortable, interactive setting. It has games, movies, toys, and books that children can play with while they are there. Another great benefit that a CAC provides is information sharing. Through interviews I did with different community members, I learned that there is some information sharing between agencies going on, but more should be happening. The more communication there is between agency members the better and easier a child's experience is going to be. A child will find more helpful services in a more timely manner if everyone works together.

With all of these agencies working together there would be less of a chance of a child falling through the cracks of the system. It is also easier on a child and their family to be able to get as much support as they can from one agency rather than having to go from one agency to another for support. This process can be long and frustrating for a family, and there would be a better chance of a family giving up. CACs also do case tracking which would also help a child not get lost in the system. A center like this can help reduce long-term impact on families. A family who is dealing with abuse wants to get their lives "back to normal." So if a family doesn't have anyone who is there to help them deal with the abuse they will try and get things "back to normal," which won't be helping them. The final beneficial thing that CACs provide is fewer interviews. One of the biggest goals of a CAC is to put the child through the least amount of interviews possible.

However, there are some drawbacks to having a CAC in the Bangor area. One big issue that is going on right now at the Androscoggin CAC is the method of interviewing. The CAC does Corner House method interviewing, which is a completely different type of interviewing than what DHHS is mandated to use. So currently DHHS cannot refer to the Androscoggin CAC. Another issue is that there is no one who can do forensic examinations in the Bangor area; a positive side to this is that having a CAC in Bangor would allow for training of a forensic examiner so there could be one locally.

Another issue that the Androscoggin CAC is having right now is they aren't receiving any cases. As mentioned before, DHHS can't refer due to interviewing method conflicts. Another reason that they aren't getting any cases is people are just afraid to be the first ones to refer, even though all members of the MDT have signed on for the project. For a project like this to work in Bangor, not only would agencies have to sign on, but they also would have to really think a CAC was a good idea, and be ready to support the agency. The final issue with bringing a CAC to Bangor would be long term funding. Through my interviews I did find that some agencies might be willing to help look for funding sources; however, the fact is that the NCA grants won't last forever, and the grants aren't enough to support a CAC.

Hopkins concluded her report by noting: "A CAC in the Bangor area is something that should be seriously thought about and discussed among community members. It's a complex idea and it will take some time to figure out whether or not an agency like this would and could be supported by the community." The subsequent discussion at the SCAN meeting reached the conclusion that a CAC might not be appropriate for the area except in situations when a child comes through the ER and could be referred at that time directly to a CAC, which would do the intake process and report to DHHS. Police and DHHS could also together do the first interview. A suggestion was made that after Androscoggin does a couple of cases, a report to SCAN about the results could be made.

Carr-Slauenwhite was one of three presenters at an Internet safety and online predator informational forum in Guilford in mid-May. As usual, RRS was on the cutting edge of this issue, a few years before it became a major news item. The forum, which also included Lt. Robert Young from the Piscataquis CSD and Arnold Poland, computer technician in the Guilford school system, educated the 50 parents who attended about safe Internet use, parental controls, and what to do and how to report if a child is contacted online by a suspected perpetrator.

RRS Policies

At Walker's last Board meeting in May, she attempted to tighten up several existing RRS policies and also obtain the Board's approval for some new policies. New member Diane Tennies joined the Board at this meeting. All policies were developed and reviewed by staff members before presentation to the Board.

The Follow-Up Call Policy had first been adopted by the Board in September 1996, and as revised would read: "The hotline advocate may provide the caller with a choice regarding a follow-up call from an RRS staff member after a hospital visit or an immediate crisis (e.g. suicide threat, assault). If such a call is desired, the advocate will request a date and time that is convenient to the victim/survivor, what type of message can be left (if any) if victim/survivor is not there, and how many attempts to make. No follow-up call will be made without the caller's consent. During the initial follow-up call, the RRS staff member may provide the option of having continued follow-up calls from the SART Coordinator as part of SART services."

A new False Reports policy read:

RRS acknowledges that false reports do occur. We believe, however, that most reports of sexual violence are authentic, but the victim/survivor, for a number of reasons, changes her/his mind and recants the report. Eighty-five percent of sexually violent crimes are committed by someone known to the victim/survivor; the percentage is as high as ninety-nine percent for sexual crimes against children. Family members and friends, even the perpetrator, may encourage the victim/survivor to not report, or to change her/his story. The passage of time from the initial collection of evidence through investigation and repeated questioning is also a reason why a victim/survivor might give up and change her/his mind about proceeding through the criminal process. It is the policy of RRS to believe the victim/survivor, and to help create a safe environment, free of confrontation, during the evidence collection and preliminary interviews. A line of questioning that casts doubt on what the victim/survivor is saying, or accusations of a false report, may put the victim/survivor on the defensive and could cause that person to be reluctant to continue with the process.

Both the False Reports policy and a new third policy, Presence of an Advocate during Law Enforcement Interview, addressed issues raised by law enforcement officers at a SART meeting, prompting RRS to clarify positions on the issues. This latter policy stated:

> RRS promotes healing by helping a victim/survivor talk about her/his experiences in a supportive environment. The first interview with a law enforcement officer is a crucial time for the victim/survivor to develop rapport and trust with both the investigator and the criminal justice system. Providing the victim/survivor with the opportunity to request that an advocate be present during the first interview helps create a safe environment and develops rapport and trust. Knowing that there is one person who supports the victim/survivor and wants nothing from her/him, helps to lower anxiety about the process. A victim/survivor's anxiety can be detrimental to an investigation because it increases the inability to remember, to put information into the proper sequence, and to trust that others are not going to cause further harm. The ultimate goals of an advocate's presence during the first interview are to help begin the healing process, and to help produce a stronger witness for the prosecution.

A final short policy approved by the Board dealt with support group co-facilitators responding to hotline calls: "When current members of a support group call the hotline while one of the co-facilitators of the group is on call or backup, the caller will be referred to the reserve backup. Reserve backup will be the Executive Director or designee." As more support groups were held at RRS, co-facilitated by volunteers, this became an issue that needed to be addressed.

Annual Auction and Awards Night

Although she would not be involved in auction planning after May, Walker knew that the event was crucial to RRS for financial support and community outreach. The Board in January chose September 6th as the auction date, and agreed with Walker's suggestion that Sue McKay receive the Janet Badger Volunteer Award in recognition of her tenth year as auctioneer. Scott Arno was chosen by the board as the recipient of the Teal Ribbon Award at the recommendation of Perry and Shaw for his role in the Piscataquis SART.

An $850 contract with Jeff's Catering for the auction was signed by Walker the following month. Unknown at the time, this was to be the last RRS auction held at Jeff's, where Jeff Ashey and his staff had graciously hosted all the others. Underwriting support received early for the auction included Edwards Shop 'n Save in Dover-Foxcroft ($125), Machias Savings Bank ($250), Hollywood Slots ($250), and BSB ($125). A $200 donation was made by the Patawa Club in Bangor, and Monroe Salt Works provided a $75 gift certificate instead of items for the auction. The RRS contact at Monroe Salt Works, Tricia Largay, who had been so generous with donations of pottery, was no longer employed there. A surprise donation of $2000 had been received from Filene's in lieu of auction sponsorship.

Thanks to Greaney's initiative, Zonta International in Bangor was making a quilt for the auction, the first of many to be donated over the next few years. At Greaney's request, Walker had set up a "very attractive" table for the Zonta Fashion Show in late March, and had "made some good connections with about 45 women." The local Zonta organization had a long history with RRS, dating back to its earliest years.

The End of Walker's Tenure at RRS

In mid-May, Walker cleaned and cleared the ED's office of her belongings. Some were moved into the vacant educator's office which would be Walker's for the two-week overlap with Roberts. Her journal noted that she was "feeling a little sad at first as I tackled 'my' desk, and moved on to feeling good about my years there." Roberts was able to move into the ED's office on her first day, although the new computer and financial software would not be ready for a few days because of Falk's schedule.

On her last regular hotline shift that evening, Walker took what turned out to be her last hotline call. The last hospital call for Walker had occurred earlier in the year when she spent four hours beginning at 12:30 A.M. at St. Joseph, noting in her journal that the call "added an unexpected twist to my day. I was befuddled when the pager went off but very alert and okay at hospital."

Walker, according to her journal, was "totally blown away at the May advocates' meeting by an awesome wall hanging of twenty squares made by my RRS 'family.' And by the words each one said to me from the heart. They pulled off the surprise of the century right under my nose, and I feel much loved by all who made squares. More than 140 advocates have received training from me and/or have volunteered with me over the past twelve years. I am more privileged than they know to have been a part of their lives, to hear their stories for a brief period of time. I look good because of them. I feel so humble, loved, and appreciated." Earlier retirement parties had been held separately with the Millinocket advocates, the Dover-Foxcroft advocates, the Womancare staff members, and with MECASA, with SCAN, and with the greater Bangor community. Walker was not expecting anything more.

The last week in May, Walker entered all the financial data into QuickBooks and spent time tutoring Roberts on the system. Making the transition easier for Roberts, DHHS had ruled that a compilation or audit was no longer required for any contract of $500,000 or less. The final financial report from RRS would be sufficient. Mail no longer had to be picked up at the Bangor Post Office because the RRS Board had agreed with Walker's recommendation to have mail delivered to 157 Park Street, where there were separate locked mailboxes in the entryway. POB 2516 was cancelled after many years, saving ninety dollars annually.

The last accounts payable checks for which Walker was responsible were cut and mailed the day before she left RRS. Advanced Payroll at BSB had been working well all year, especially the direct deposit enjoyed by staff members. The balance sheet at the end of the day showed $27,356.89

in the checking account and $11,453.22 in the money market account, more total assets than had been available for several months, and with four months' worth of DHHS checks and proceeds from the auction still to come. Walker felt better about the financial picture at RRS than during the earlier months of the year. Community support was at an all-time high, evidenced by media requests, donations, and fundraisers. A solid infrastructure was also in place with three offices equipped with the latest technology. She knew she was leaving the center in the very capable hands of an awesome staff, many dedicated volunteers in Bangor, Dover-Foxcroft, and Millinocket, and committed Board members.

On Friday, May 26th, Walker left the RRS office for the last time, leaving her keys behind. No one else was there, and as written in her journal: "I wanted to be last one out so I could tour the rooms and say my farewells. I feel good about the impact I've had on people and places, and a bit sad to be leaving. I have learned so much from so many and have no regrets."

After more than a decade, Walker had finished writing on the pages of history at Rape Response Services.

GLOSSARY OF ABBREVIATIONS

AAUW: American Association of University Women
AG: Attorney General
BCFS: Bureau of Child and Family Services (Maine)
BDN: Bangor Daily News
BSB: Bangor Savings Bank
BSS: Bureau of Social Services (Maine)
BSW: Bachelor's of Social Work Degree
CAC: Child Advocacy Center
CAN: Child Abuse and Neglect
CAP: Community Action Program
CH&CS: Community Health and Community Counseling (Bangor)
CIT: Crisis Intervention Team
CPA: Certified Public Accountant
CPS: Child Protective Services (Maine)
CSD: County Sheriff's Department
CVAP: Crime Victims Assistance Program (Federal)
DA: District Attorney
DBDS: Department of Behavioral and Developmental Services (Maine)
DHS: Department of Human Services (Maine; precursor to DHHS)
DHHS: Department of Health and Human Services (Maine)
DMHMRSAS: Department of Mental Health, Mental Retardation and
  Substance Abuse Services (Maine; precursor to DBDS)
DOC: Department of Corrections (Maine)
DOE: Department of Education (Maine)
ED: Executive Director
EMCC: Eastern Maine Community College (Bangor)
EMMC: Eastern Maine Medical Center

EMTC: Eastern Maine Technical College (Bangor)
ER: Emergency Room
FBI: Federal Bureau of Investigation
FY: Fiscal Year
H.O.P.E. Festival: Help Organize Peace Earthwide Festival (Orono)
JAC: Justice Assistance Council (Maine)
KARE: Katahdin Area Response Effort for Non-Violence
KFI: Katahdin Friends Inc.
LCSW: Licensed Clinical Social Worker
LD: Legislative Document
LMSW: Licensed Master Social Worker
MCAR: Maine Coalition Against Rape (1993-1994)
MCEDV: Maine Coalition to End Domestic Violence
MCJA: Maine Criminal Justice Academy
MCR: Maine Coalition on Rape (prior to 1993)
MERT: Mary Ellen Rush Thibodeau (name of MERT founder)
MECASA: Maine Coalition Against Sexual Assault (1994 to present)
MOU: Memorandum of Understanding
MRSA: Maine Revised Statutes Annotated
MSW: Master's of Social Work Degree
NASW: National Association of Social Workers
NCA: National Children's Alliance
NOE: Northeast Occupational Exchange
NOW: National Organization for Women
PHHSBG: Preventative Health and Health Services Block Grant (Federal)
POB: Post Office Box
PSA: Public Service Announcement
PTO: Paid Time Off
QA: Quality Assurance
RAD: Rape Aggression Defense
RCAC: Rape Crisis Advisory Committee (1988)
RCC: Rape Crisis Center (first in Bangor, from 1976 to 1984)
RCCC: Rape Crisis Center Committee (1987-1988, precursor to RCAC)
RCS: Rape Crisis Services (first name of RRS, 1988)
RFP: Request for Proposals
RN: Registered Nurse
RPEG: Rape Prevention Education Grant (Federal)

RRS: Rape Response Services (1988 to present)
SACC: Sexual Assault Crisis Center (Lewiston)
SANE: Sexual Assault Nurse Examiner
SARS: Sexual Assault Response Services (Portland)
SART: Sexual Assault Response Team
SBI: State Bureau of Identification
SCAN: Suspected Child Abuse and Neglect
SCP: Safe Campus Project (Orono)
SFPSS: State Funds for Purchased Social Services (Maine; precursor to SPSS)
SPSS: State Purchased Social Services (Maine)
SR: Spruce Run
SSBG: Social Services Block Grant (Federal)
SSBG-PE: Social Services Block Grant-Prevention Education (Federal)
SWA: Student Women's Association (Orono)
TBN: Take Back the Night
TREM: Trauma Recovery and Empowerment Model
TTY: Teletypewriter
UC: University College (Bangor)
UMA: University of Maine at Augusta
UMC: United Methodist Church
UMO: University of Maine at Orono
UNE: University of New England (Biddeford)
UU: Unitarian Universalist
UWEM: United Way of Eastern Maine
VAWA: Violence Against Women Act (Federal)
VOCA: Victims of Crime Act (Federal)
VIP: Violence Intervention and Prevention Act (Maine)
WLAC: Women's Legislative Agenda Coalition (Maine)

ACKNOWLEDGEMENTS

One of my reasons for writing this book is to preserve a record that acknowledges the contributions to the growth and development of RRS made by many individuals through the years. First and foremost on this list of acknowledgements are Marilu, Kristan, Darlene, Janet, Alcinda, and all the other volunteer advocates in Bangor who went above and beyond to be sure every hotline shift was filled during my tenure at RRS. I was privileged to know more than 140 women and men throughout the two counties who participated in advocate training sessions, and signed up for one or many hotline shifts. Each person in Bangor, Millinocket, and Dover-Foxcroft made my job easier.

I also sincerely appreciate the work of Wendy, Ann, Norma, Sharon, Karen, Jen, Nicole, Lisa, Gail, Robin, Carey, Angel, Carrie, Sue, and Joyce, all staff members I hired. They put up with my idiosyncrasies and my red pen, and deserve credit for the positive impact of RRS during my years as ED.

From the original Board of Directors through the next 30 years, many women and men envisioned a viable rape crisis center in the Bangor area, and worked tirelessly to bring that vision to fruition, and to sustain it. No list of acknowledgements would be complete without recognizing each of those individuals, named in these pages, for their contributions. In addition, an anonymous group of people, the loyal financial donors to RRS, responded generously to every mailed appeal for funds. The names became familiar to me through the years, and although I did not personally know most of these supporters, their gifts often brightened my days.

Gratitude is expressed to the women of The Commons in Eastport, Maine, for providing inspirational space, and to Maine Authors Publishing in Rockland, Maine, for turning my dream of writing a book into reality.

Renate's willingness to allow the reproduction of her sunflower painting on the cover is sincerely appreciated.

My former "sister directors," Donna, Marty, and Sue, are still doing groundbreaking work at their respective rape crisis centers in Maine. I continue to be inspired by their perseverance, innovation, and integrity.

Many people helped with the writing of this book, including Barb, Beverly, Elizabeth, Jan, Janine, Jeff, Joanne, Laura, Marty, Ruth, Sandy, Sharon, Sue, and Tamar. Each of these people provided materials, answered endless questions, or edited the text. I am grateful for their assistance in helping me produce a more readable document. At the same time, I recognize that any mistakes are mine.

Last and certainly not least, the support and encouragement of my husband throughout all my endeavors, including the publication of this book, have meant far more than I can ever express in words.

ABOUT THE AUTHOR

KATHY WALKER received her undergraduate and graduate degrees from the University of Vermont and the University of Maine, respectively. Since the seventies, she has resided in Hampden, Maine, with her husband, and is the proud mother of a daughter, a son, and their spouses.